SEMIPERIPHERAL DEVELOPMENT
AND FOREIGN POLICY

To the memory of my mother and father

Semiperipheral Development and Foreign Policy
The Cases of Greece and Spain

M. FATİH TAYFUR
Middle East Technical University, Ankara

Taylor & Francis Group
LONDON AND NEW YORK

First published 2003 by Ashgate Publishing

Reissued 2018 by Routledge
2 Park Square, Milton Park, Abingdon, Oxon OX14 4RN
711 Third Avenue, New York, NY 10017, USA

Routledge is an imprint of the Taylor & Francis Group, an informa business

Copyright © M. Fatih Tayfur 2003

The author has asserted his moral right under the Copyright, Designs and Patents Act, 1988, to be identified as the author of this work.

All rights reserved. No part of this book may be reprinted or reproduced or utilised in any form or by any electronic, mechanical, or other means, now known or hereafter invented, including photocopying and recording, or in any information storage or retrieval system, without permission in writing from the publishers.

Notice:
Product or corporate names may be trademarks or registered trademarks, and are used only for identification and explanation without intent to infringe.

Publisher's Note
The publisher has gone to great lengths to ensure the quality of this reprint but points out that some imperfections in the original copies may be apparent.

Disclaimer
The publisher has made every effort to trace copyright holders and welcomes correspondence from those they have been unable to contact.

A Library of Congress record exists under LC control number: 2003105086

ISBN 13: 978-1-138-72234-7 (hbk)
ISBN 13: 978-1-138-72233-0 (pbk)
ISBN 13: 978-1-315-19356-4 (ebk)

Contents

Acknowledgements		vi
Preface		vii
1	World-System Analysis and the Concept of Semiperiphery	1
2	Greece: 1945-1974	39
3	Greece: 1974-2000s	73
4	Spain: 1945-1976	141
5	Spain: 1976-2000s	169
6	Conclusion	231
Bibliography		237
Index		255

Acknowledgements

This book is based on my doctoral dissertation written between 1990 and 1995 at the London School of Economics and Political Science (LSE). However, I updated and revised the original work for publication between September 2001 and September 2002.

I could not have completed my dissertation without the support of two marvellous people: Professor Margot Light and Professor Peter Loizos of the LSE. I am deeply indebted to Professor Margot Light by whom I had the privilege of being supervised, and whose friendship, help, encouragement, advice and tolerance at every stage of this work were invaluable. I owe special thanks also to Professor Peter Loizos without whose support I might not even have begun doctoral studies at the LSE.

I would also express my gratitude and love to my wife Meltem Dayıoğlu Tayfur for her continuous support, unselfish assistance and patience during the writing and printing stages of this book. I also thank Mark Ferrara who edited the language of the manuscript.

I was privileged to receive a London School of Economics Scholarship and a CVCP Overseas Research Students Award, a Montague Burton Award, and a Convocation Trust Award. This study would not have been possible without their financial assistance between 1990 and 1995.

I would also like to thank Professor Fikret Görün, Professor Oktar Türel, Professor Fikret Şenses, Professor Güzin Erlat and Professor Cem Çakmak of the Middle East Technical University for all the support, encouragement, and friendship they extended from Ankara which I enjoyed over several years while in London writing the doctoral dissertation.

Finally, I must emphasise my deepest respect and gratitude to two institutions: The Middle East Technical University and The London School of Economics and Political Science. The Middle East Technical University in Ankara have always kept the windows of the universe open to me, even in the darkest days of authoritarianism. At the LSE, I accumulated not only knowledge but also discovered the magic of academe.

Preface

Foreign policy can be analysed in different contexts and at different levels. Since it stands at the crossroads of different issues and academic disciplines, and also bridges the "internal environment" with the "international system", explanations of foreign policy depend on how the researcher perceives the foreign policy environment and formulates the explanatory/analytical framework. In other words, depending on the context different approaches and variables may elucidate the conduct of foreign policy. Indeed, there are several ways to explain the external behaviours of states. This being the case, the study of foreign policy as a sub-field of IR cannot be confined to any one approach. On the contrary, the study of foreign policy often requires inter- and/or multi-disciplinary investigations. This means that foreign policy can be examined at different levels and may be viewed from varying perspectives in the social sciences. Students of FPA are therefore confronted with a phenomenon whose boundaries are quite flexible and which allows various theoretical frameworks of study (see, Hill and Light, 1985 and Light, 1994). Thus, the explanation of foreign policy can range from the childhood experiences of an individual leader to the characteristics of the international system, depending on the research framework and the goal of analysis. What influences and what explains foreign policy depends both on the situation at hand and on how the researcher perceives and formulates his/her explanatory framework. In other words, different approaches and variables are best to explain the foreign policy phenomena in different contexts because what determines foreign policy behaviour is a complex set of variables, and only one or several of them will become dominant in any given situation.

In this study I analyse the foreign policies of Greece and Spain between 1945 and the early 2000s in the context of the modern world-system approach. However, world-system analysis does not directly and systematically deal with foreign policy, but it does provide a "social totality" - a modern world-system - in which foreign policy is integral to the interaction between "a single world-economy" and "multiple political structures" (nation-states). Thus in this study, I consider foreign policy a function of the complex interaction between "internal/societal" and "external/systemic" and "political" and "economic" factors. Accordingly, I investigate the relationship between the foreign policies of Greece and

Spain and the structure of the international system, the domestic economic and political structure of the states in question, and the external and internal economic and political elites.

Broadly speaking this is a study of the political economy of foreign policy. I analyse foreign policy in the context of both global and national levels of the organisation of power and production/wealth. I consider whether Greece and Spain belong to the debatable category of the "semiperiphery" in the world-system hierarchy of states, and whether they followed "semiperipheral foreign policies" during the period under investigation. In chapters devoted to each separate country, I illustrate how the foreign policies of the two countries are related to their developmental patterns. I divide the period from 1945 to 2000s into two sub-periods, the first from 1945 to the mid-1970s, and the second from the mid-1970s to the early 2000s. This division corresponds to the reorganisation of the world power and production/wealth structures in the mid-1970s. In world-system analysis, these periods are termed the "expansion" and "contraction" periods of the world-economy respectively. This provides the background for the examination of the changes in the power-production/wealth structures of Greece and Spain between the "expansion" and "contraction" periods of the world-economy. I demonstrate how these changes in world and national power-production/wealth structures led to changes in the foreign policies of these countries. One important point is that, although Wallerstein is not as certain as he was about the perpetuity of cyclical processes of the modern world-system since the mid-1990s, this study assumes that the contraction period of the world-economy is continuing at present.

Moreover, I argue that the concept of "semiperiphery" provides a productive framework for the study of the political economy of the foreign policies of "middle income" countries. In fact, the debates about the existence, shape, boundaries and so forth of the semiperipheral zone of the world-economy are still continuing. The last two edited works on the semiperiphery present various aspects of these debates and outline some basic shortcomings of the concept (see Arrighi, 1985 and Martin, 1990a). Thus the concept of semiperiphery has not yet been satisfactorily clarified. My study contends that there are a significant number of states that fall neither into the "developed" nor into "underdeveloped" categories of states. Among related concepts such as "developing countries", "newly industrialised states", "middle income countries" etc., the concept of "semiperiphery" as employed by the world-system approach provides a comprehensive framework, even in its present form, and is a good tool for studying and explaining various phenomena (here the focus is on foreign policy) in these "intermediate countries".

This work is originally based on my doctoral dissertation, which was completed between 1990 and 1995 at the LSE. However, since then much has changed in international affairs and much has been written both on Greece and Spain. Thus, this book in its present form is an updated and revised version of the original text. Between September 2001 and September 2002, I edited the whole manuscript and wrote new sections for Greece and Spain covering the developments between the mid-1990s and early 2000s.

In *Chapter 1*, first I examine "world-system analysis" and focus on its relevance in foreign policy analysis. The second part of the chapter focuses entirely on the concept of "semiperiphery". I discuss the nature and the characteristics of semiperipheral states and their mobility in the "world-economy" and the "interstate" system. I then examine various arguments on the operationalisation of the concept and emphasise the existence of different kinds of semiperipheral states in the semiperipheral zone of the world-economy. Next, I argue that semiperipheral states have common foreign policy orientations in the expansion and contraction periods of the world-economy. Finally I analyse the common elements in the political and economic development of semiperipheral Greece, Spain (and also Portugal) and their peculiar position in the interstate system in an historical context.

Chapters 2-5 are the case study chapters in which I apply theoretical and conceptual frameworks to Greece and Spain. Each chapter is divided into three sections dealing with the economic environment, the political environment, and foreign policy in the framework of semiperipheral development. In each chapter I show how developments in the economic environment go hand in hand with developments in the political and foreign policy environments.

In *Chapters 2 and 4*, I examine Greece and Spain respectively in the period between 1945 and the mid-1970s. In world-system analysis, 1945 to the mid-1970s is considered the period of "US hegemony" and an "expansion" period of the "world-economy". In this global context I discuss the nature of the national power-production/wealth structures in the two countries and the roles of the US, internal political institutions, and economic, political and military elites in the establishment and functioning of this structure. I show that the functioning of this structure fits the semiperipheral patterns described by world-system analysis. Finally, I illustrate that the foreign policies of Greece and Spain were an integral part of this power-production/wealth structure and were shaped according to the interests of the external and internal actors that formed it.

In *Chapters 3 and 5*, I examine Greece and Spain respectively from the mid-1970s-until the early 2000s. On the one hand, this period corresponds to the "contraction" period of the world-economy. On the other hand, it is the period in which there was a "relative decline of US hegemony" and that saw the emergence of Europe (especially the EEC/EC/EU) as a new economic and political seat of power. Accordingly, I consider changes in the national power-production/wealth structures in the context of these global level changes and emphasise the decreasing role of the US and the increasing influence of Europe/EU on the economic and political developments in Greece and Spain. I demonstrate how Greece and Spain benefited from these changes at both global and national levels; examine what changes took place in the position of the external and internal actors in the power-production/wealth structure; and consider to what extent the changes in the national power-production/wealth structure fit semiperipheral development patterns. Furthermore, I argue that the differences between Greek and Spanish semiperipheral developmental patterns occurred because of their different locations in the semiperipheral zone. Finally, I show that the foreign policies of both Greece and Spain were shaped in this period by their different semiperipheral developmental patterns and mobilisations in the world-system hierarchy of states, as well as by the interests of the external and internal actors that controlled the power-production/wealth structures.

As I show in the Greek and Spanish cases, despite its shortcomings, semiperiphery can be a very useful concept for analysing the links between the external/systemic and internal/societal economic and political sources of foreign policy, and also for explaining changes in foreign policy. More generally, the concept of semiperiphery enables us to understand the crucial links between foreign policy and political economy.

Chapter 1
World-System Analysis and the Concept of Semiperiphery

Despite their central location in IR studies, systemic-structural approaches have always occupied a marginal place in the sub-field of FPA. Perhaps this is because the subject matter of systemic-structural theories focuses and explains the structures, the processes and workings of the international system but do not specifically deal with external behaviour (foreign policy) of the individual states. However, the interaction between the system-structure and state actors is an important factor in understanding foreign policy phenomena. Thus this chapter deals with how the modern world-system analysis conceptualises and explains the international environment, as well as what kinds of framework it provides for studying foreign polices of states.

Modern World-System Approach: Economic Structure and the Conceptualisation of the World Context

Wallerstein's modern world-system analysis is the most advanced challenge to theories of modernisation that focus on the nation-state and its development. According to modernisation theory, the world consists of autonomous national societies each following a similar developmental pattern on the evolutionary ladder from tradition to modernity, although each started this process at different times and at different speeds. Modernisation theorists argue that every state must pass through the same stages that today's advanced (Western) societies once experienced in order to reach a position of relative well-being.

The first challenge to the developmentalist view of modernisation theory came from the dependency school. Dependency theorists argued that there is no such thing as a linear developmental pattern through which every society should pass in order to become an advanced society. On the contrary, they claimed that a capitalist world-economy exists, and that the present backward position of many countries is due to the disadvantageous relationship they have had with advanced countries within the capitalist world-economy, and not a question of internal structures or starting late. In other words, they focused on the theme of the development of underdevelopment, and they emphasised that the historical development of advanced societies and the underdevelopment of backward ones are two sides of the same coin. Accordingly, dependency theorists used this framework to analyse patterns of underdevelopment in Third World countries (especially in Latin America) where their primary interest lay.

Wallerstein's challenge came as a major step forward on the path opened by the dependency school. Wallerstein's modern world-system analysis is one of the most comprehensive approaches to social phenomena in the social sciences. It also establishes links between historical sociology, large-scale historical change and a complex web of international relations (Little, 1994: 12-14). In general terms, the central understanding of Wallerstein's approach is that any social phenomena can only be understood properly by examining a totality called the "social system", rather than by investigating arbitrarily constituted units of that totality. There are two kinds of totalities; "mini-systems" and "world-systems", but since the mini-systems no longer exist, the world-system is the only social system to be studied. For Wallerstein the phenomena that should be analysed in the world-system are the development and the functioning of the system itself, rather than the development of its major constituent units called nation-states (Wallerstein, 1974: 390). Accordingly, world-system analysis contends that there is something happening beyond the national societal level and hence there exists a collective reality at the world level of analysis. However, this does not include the study of international relations in the sense of multiple sovereign states interacting with each other. The world level collective reality is somewhat exogenous to nation-states; it has its own laws of motion which determine the social, economic and political phenomena in the national societies that it encompasses. The modern world-system has secular trends such as core-periphery relations, the division of labour, unequal exchange, etc., as well as the cyclical motions of expansion and stagnation and the rise and fall of hegemonic powers. While "the cycles" restore equilibrium in the system, the "secular trends" move far from equilibrium.

In a recent work, Hopkins and Wallerstein defined the structural properties of the modern world-system as "institutional domains" or "vectors" evolving since the 16th century within which the cycles and trends and social action has occurred (Hopkins and Wallerstein, 1996: 2). In the historical evolution of the world-system, Hopkins and Wallerstein identify six such distinguishable, but not separable, domains: the interstate system, the structure of the world production, the structure of the world labour force, the patterns of the human welfare, the social cohesion of states, and the structures of knowledge. These properties can be studied in their own right, or in terms of their effects on the development of national societies. However none of these properties has developed in isolation from the others, and thus any change in any one of them directly influences the others. Indeed, they form an imperfect organic whole.

Modern world-system analysis is basically synchronic; it investigates the structural relations among different societies within a given time period (Bergersen, 1980: 6). In this way, modern world-system analysis tries to understand the question of how nations are interrelated with each other in the world-economy. The concepts of core-periphery relations, the division of labour, unequal exchange, and so forth are the main concerns of modern world-system analysis in explaining the interconnections among nations and long-term social changes in the capitalist world-system. In Wallerstein's words, "if there is one thing which distinguishes a world-system perspective from any other, it is its insistence that the unit of analysis is a world-system defined in terms of economic processes and links, and not any units defined in terms of judicial, political, cultural, geological etc., criteria" (Hopkins, 1977 quoted in Bergersen, 1980: 8).

Nevertheless, the world-system perspective claims that economics and politics are not separate phenomena. A social system can only be understood by analysing how both power and production/wealth are organised. In this context, it looks at the political economy of the modern world-system, which focuses on the interaction and interdependence between economic and political activities. In other words, the world-system school investigates the "specific ways in which economic and political action are intertwined within the capitalist world-economy" (Chase-Dunn, 1989: 107). Accordingly, the world-system school argues that the interstate system, which is composed of unequally powerful and competing states, is the political body of the capitalist world-economy, and that the capitalist institutions of this system are central to the maintenance and reproduction of the interstate system, and vice versa (Chase-Dunn, 1989: 107). The interstate system is a creation and integral part of the modern world-system, and "above all [it] is a matrix of reciprocal recognitions of the (limited) sovereignty of each of the states, a framework that has been (more or less) enforced by the stronger on the weaker and by the strong on each other" (Hopkins and Wallerstein, 1996: 2).

One of the most important structural characteristics of world social systems is the existence of a division of labour within them. This means that different geographical areas in the system specialise in the production of different goods, and consequently each region becomes dependent upon economic exchange with others in order to supply the continuing needs of that region. However, there are two kinds of world-systems in which this economic exchange operates in different frameworks: world empires with a common political structure, and world economies without a common political structure. In the first case the economy is basically a redistributive one. This means that the whole economy is administered by a central political authority, and the economic benefits are redistributed from this centre to different regions. In other words, political structures dominate the functioning of the system. The second kind of world-system, which is known as the capitalist economic system or the modern world-system, is an historical system that came into existence in the 16th century in north-western Europe in a series of historical, geographical and ecological accidents culminating in a world-economy in the 19th and 20th centuries. In this world-economy the capitalist economic structure determines the operation of the system. The world-economy is defined without a common political structure, as there are multiple political structures. Since the primary structure of this world-system is the economy, politics takes place primarily within and through state structures whose boundaries are much smaller than the economy. In the modern world-system, it is not political-military competition but interaction between states and capitalist commodity production that occupies the central place (Chase-Dunn, 1989: 111). However, a world-economy does not mean an international economy. The theory of international economics assumes that separate national economies exist and that they trade with each other under certain circumstances. The sum of all these interstate economic contacts is called the international economy. By contrast, world-economy is defined as "an ongoing extensive and relatively complete social division of labour within an integrated set of production processes which relate to each other through a market which has been instituted or created in some complex way" (Wallerstein, 1984: 13). Today we call this the capitalist world-economy, and its boundaries are far larger than any political unit. There is no single authoritative political body in the world-economy but within it there are multiple political structures known as states. Within this system, there is a single division of labour between core and peripheral zones.

The division of labour within the world-system implies that different geographical areas in the system specialise in different productive tasks.

These productive specialisations may change over time, but it is always the case that different specialisations receive unequal economic rewards. Whatever the goods produced, the core zone is always specialised in relatively highly mechanised, high profit, high wage, and highly skilled labour activities, in contrast to the opposite specialisations in the periphery. In other words, in the world-capitalist economy, the division of labour and complementarity accompany inequality.

According to Wallerstein, the defining characteristic of the capitalist world-economy is production for maximum profit in the market. Production is based on the capitalist principle of maximising capital accumulation, which means reducing costs to the minimum and raising sales prices to the maximum feasible. The reduction of costs is maintained mainly by reducing the income of direct producers to a minimum and allowing the capitalist to appropriate the remaining value. In order to reduce costs, a legal system based on unequal contractual property rights becomes an essential element, and the state plays the most important role in the enforcement of these laws. On the other hand, the second principle of accumulation, the expansion of sale prices, is ensured through the creation of quasi-monopolies in the world market. In the absence of a common political structure, only quasi-monopolies can utilise state power in order to constrain potential competitors in the world market. This means the inevitable intervention of the state in the normal functioning of the market in order to create profitable conditions for some economic actors.

In the world-economy production is organised into cross-cutting networks of interlinked processes called commodity chains. This means that in the production process there are multiple product entry points. Wallerstein oversimplifies this process when he states, "there is a commodity chain that goes from cotton production to thread production, to textile production to clothing production ...[and] at each of these production points there is an input of other productive materials" (Wallerstein, 1984a: 4). On the other hand, almost all commodity chains cross national boundaries at some point. Most importantly, "at each point that there is a labourer, there is state pressure on the labourer's income...[and also] at each point that there is an exchange of product, there is state pressure on the price" (Wallerstein, 1984a: 4).

These two kinds of state pressure regulate the relationship between the bourgeoisie and proletariat, as well as the relationship between the different kinds of bourgeoisie. This means that while the state ensures the appropriation of value by the bourgeoisie, it might favour some bourgeoisie more than others in this process. The crucial role played by the state leads to two kinds of politics in the capitalist world-economy: a class struggle between the bourgeoisie and proletariat, and political struggles between different bourgeoisie. In the world-economy, various groups of bourgeoisie compete within a single world market in order to get the largest possible proportion of the world-economy's economic surplus. And since states are the most effective expression of power and political organisation of the world-economy, different bourgeoisie located in different states use their state's power in order to influence the market to their own benefit. In other words, the world bourgeoisie compete with each other and try to distort the normal functioning of the world market through state mechanisms. Accordingly the relative strength of the states becomes very important in this task.

In Wallerstein's modern world-system approach, states are classified according to two overlapping criteria. First, they are divided according to their relative strengths into strong or weak, and second, they are categorised according to their structural positions in the world-economy as core, periphery and semiperiphery. A state is defined as strong or weak in relation to its relative strength vis-à-vis other domestic centres of power, other states and external non-state forces (Wallerstein, 1984: 20). The power of a state can be measured by the amount of resources it is able to mobilise relative to the amount of resources that may be mobilised against it during a crisis period (Chase-Dunn, 1989: 113). Here, the crucial elements that determine the power of a state are two fold: the magnitude of resources, and the relative unity within and among classes (Chase-Dunn, 1989: 114). In order to gain the highest possible competitive advantage in the world market, the bourgeoisie want to increase the importance of the state's political structures, and hence its constraining power in the world market.

This drive to increase the power of states is greatest in states where core-like production is dominant. A strong state mechanism is the primary tool with which the bourgeoisie of core states can control the internal labour force and also manipulate and distort the world market in their own favour vis-à-vis the competing bourgeoisie of other states. Thus, strong states are greatly supported by an alliance of their economic elites with large resources, because the state supplies sufficient protection for successful capitalist accumulation (Chase-Dunn, 1989: 114). In a competitive world market, state protection becomes an important component for the profits of the economic elites. Consequently, while strong states fall into the core state category, the periphery contains the weak states. Thus the strength of states can be explained through the structural role that they play in the world-economy at any moment in time. However, the initial structural position of a state is often decided by historical accident or by the geography of a particular country. Yet once it is decided, the market forces operating in the world-economy emphasise structural differences and make them almost impossible to overcome in the short term.

Furthermore, there is a hierarchy in the structural positions of states in the world-economy, and at the top of this hierarchy are the core states. Core states are those in which production is most efficient and other economic activities are most complex. Politically, they have strong state machineries that provide them with the power to accumulate greater amounts of capital and to receive the lion's share of the surplus produced in the world-economy. At the bottom of the hierarchy are the peripheral states. In a sharp contrast to core states, production in the periphery is the least efficient, and it specialises in far less rewarded goods.

Since states play an important role in the process of capital accumulation (e.g., through providing external and internal protection and distorting the world market, etc.) economic elites wish to institutionalise their interests within state structures. However, the relative power of the states, and the nature of the demands that the capitalists make on the state are determined by the nature of the dominant economic elite within a country. Accordingly, the dominance of "industrial-commercial-financial bloc in core countries produces strong states, while export-oriented bloc in peripheral states produces weaker states" (Chase-Dunn, 1989: 240). In strong/core states where industrial-commercial interests are dominant, economic elites demand an aggressive foreign policy (commercial and military) in order to gain access to foreign markets both for raw materials and for the selling of both capital and consumption goods, and in turn they support increasing the strength of the state. On the other hand, in peripheral countries, where the dominant economic elite are producing and exporting primary products, there will be no such demands for an aggressive foreign policy because state action is not likely to increase the demand for primary goods. Thus, since there is less interest in an aggressive foreign policy, peripheral states are generally less strong than core states.

Production processes are also grouped according to geographical location into core-like and periphery-like production activities (Chase-Dunn, 1980: 191). These production processes are defined according to the degree to which they incorporate labour value, are mechanised, and are highly profitable. In other words, while core-like production employs capital-intensive techniques and utilises skilled and highly paid labour, periphery-like production employs labour intensive techniques and utilises coerced low wage labour. However, the defining characteristics of any core or peripheral products may change over time because of product cycles. For instance, while textile manufacturing was a core activity in the 19th century, it became a peripheral activity in the 20th century. Similarly, wheat production since the late 20th century is a core-like production in contrast to its peripheral position in the past. This means that it is not the product itself which is core-like or peripheral, but that the nature of the production process determines core-like or periphery-like characteristics.

According to the world-system approach, both core and peripheral structural positions are the result of a relationship based on unequal exchange. The appropriation by core states of the surplus produced in the periphery is called unequal exchange in the modern world-system approach. Without a periphery, it is impossible to talk about a core, and without either, there would not be capitalist development. Once we establish a difference in the strengths of states and the operation of unequal exchange between them, we come to the conclusion that capitalism involves not only the appropriation of surplus value by the owner from the direct producer, but also the appropriation of the surplus of the world-economy by the strong (core) states from the weak (peripheral) ones. This also explains the advantageous position of the bourgeoisie of the core zone, not only over its work force, but also over the bourgeoisie of the peripheral area. According to Wallerstein, the phenomenon of unequal exchange has been a constant feature of the world-economy since its beginning. In other words, core-periphery relations have always been characterised by the mechanism of unequal exchange. As a process, unequal exchange has operated through different historical arrangements and institutions such as colonial trade monopolies, multinational corporations, or bilateral or multilateral agreements among states. But whatever the form unequal exchange takes, the crucial point is that it has always reproduced the basic core-periphery division of labour and integration, despite the continual shifts in areas and processes constituting the core, periphery, and semiperiphery (Hopkins, 1982a: 21).

However, there is an intermediate category of states known as semiperiphery. The semiperiphery is a structural position in the world economy between core and periphery. Earlier, I defined the core as characterised by high profit, high technology and high wage production, and the periphery as characterised by low profit, low technology, and low wage production. In fact, these are categories defined in terms of economic activities. There is no *sui generis* semiperipheral economic activity as such, but there are semiperipheral states where economic activities reveal an even mix of core and peripheral types of production (Chase-Dunn, 1980: 191).

The production activity in these semiperipheral zones of the world-economy constitutes a mixture of core-like and periphery-like production. This intermediate category, being both exploited and exploiter plays an important political role in balancing and reducing the amount of opposition directed towards the core by the periphery. Unlike the core and periphery, it is much more of a political category than an economic one. The state is more important, and the struggle to control it, is more intense in the semiperiphery than in the core or periphery because of the roughly equal distribution and the contradictory interests of core-like and periphery-like producers. The relationship between economics and politics here is directly attributed to the relationship between state policies and the accumulation of capital. Hence, within the semiperiphery, to effect and transform state policies becomes the vital concern of various groups whose interests lie in the semiperiphery. On the other hand, since different types of economic elites tend to have opposing interests in the semiperiphery, it is often the case that the state becomes the dominant element in forming power blocks and shaping political coalitions among economic groups (Chase-Dunn, 1989: 241). Moreover, another important characteristic of semiperipheral states is that in those which have potential for upward mobility, state mobilisation of economic development is an important feature (Chase-Dunn, 1989: 241). I shall deal separately with this intermediate semiperipheral category later in this chapter.

It is also important to note that membership in these three categories is by no means constant. Mobility in structural position is possible since states in each category might become upwardly or downwardly mobile. In world-system analysis, national development is defined as upward mobility in the hierarchical divisions between core and periphery, and this upward mobility refers to a reorganisation in the relationship of the ascending state with the world-economy. Nevertheless, the world-system approach views upward mobility in the hierarchy as exceptional.

As an historical system, the capitalist world-economy has experienced cyclical movements. The growth and the development of the world-system have occurred in a process of ups and downs called expansion and stagnation (Wallerstein, 1984a: 6-8 and 1984b: 16-17). According to world-system analysts, there are recurring bottlenecks in the capitalist world-economy when the total amount of production exceeds the effective demand resulting from the existing distribution of world income. Periods of stagnation restructure the previous order in the world-economy. The volume of overall production decreases and an intensified class struggle leads to a redistribution of world income to the lower classes in the core zones and to the bourgeoisie in the semiperiphery and the periphery. This redistribution process revitalises effective demand and consequently expands the market. Yet, this is achieved through the incorporation of new peripheral zones in the world-economy where workers receive wages below the cost of production. Wallerstein points out that while the workers in the core countries strengthen their political positions and increase their standard of living, the incorporation of new lower strata in peripheralised countries keeps the real overall distribution of income in the world-economy nearly the same as in previous periods.

Moreover, the periods of stagnation and expansion also lead to other changes in the world-economy. For instance, the production costs of pre-stagnation core products are reduced either through advanced mechanisation or by shifting these activities to lower wage regions. Furthermore, at the end of stagnation periods, new core-like activities that create high rates of profits are invented. In this process of restructuring, inefficient producers are eliminated. Wallerstein argues that old enterprises, and the states in which they operate, are faced with steadily rising costs due to the cost of amortising older capital investment and rising labour costs resulting from the increasing political strength of the labour unions. As a result, newly emerging enterprises, and the states in which they operate, replace older ones in the competitive quasi-monopolistic world market. Wallerstein calls this process a game of musical chairs at the top. In other words, together with changes in the production process, the positions of the core states in the world-economy may change. But the game of musical chairs is not only played by core states, but also by semiperipheral and peripheral states. I shall return to this issue later in the discussion of semiperipheral states. However, the crucial point is that whether the game of musical chairs is played at the top or the middle of the hierarchy, the number of states in each category (core, semiperiphery and periphery) has remained proportionally constant throughout the history of the world-economy (Wallerstein, 1984a: 7).

Another most striking cycle in the interstate system of the world-economy is the rise and decline of hegemonic powers. This rise and decline is the most critical mobility that takes place within the core area. There exists a balance of power in the interstate system that primarily regulates the power relations among the core states. This means that no individual state ever acquires sufficient capacity to transform the world-economy into a world empire. However, states have repeatedly attempted to achieve a hegemonic position in the world state system. In three instances they managed to do so for relatively brief periods: United Provinces (The Netherlands), 1620-1650; United Kingdom, 1815-1873; and United States, 1945-1967 (Wallerstein, 1984d).

Hegemony differs from imperium in that its functioning is primarily based on the market, although there are always politico-military and cultural dimensions. Hegemony means that for a brief period of time one of the core states appears as the dominant state in the interstate system and can impose its rules in the economic, political, military, diplomatic and even cultural spheres. Hegemony over the system is established when a core state demonstrates its superiority in productive, commercial and financial spheres.

> Supremacy in the productive field means that the most advanced industrial production for a given period is preponderantly located in the state in question, and that it is capable of exporting such production competitively to other core states, as well as to the periphery and semiperiphery. Commercial supremacy means that the value of external and carrying trade is the highest in comparison with that of other core states, and that its services are used by other core states. Financial supremacy means that the value of capital being saved, lent or exported across state boundaries is the highest in comparison with others, and that it performs banking operations for other core states (Hopkins et al., 1982: 62).

Supremacy in those three fields constitutes hegemony and is reflected in political-military advantage in the interstate system. Hegemonic military power has primarily taken the form of sea and air power. According to Wallerstein, political hegemony refers to critical periods when allied core powers are client states and the opposing major powers are in a defensive position. However, fulfilling a hegemonic role is very costly and hegemonic states begin to lose their competitive advantages shortly after they acquire them. Hegemonic states lose their competitive advantage mainly for the reason that other core (and even semiperipheral states) improve their efficiency in production to the level of the hegemonic power by exploiting the advantage of latecomers in acquiring the latest technology (Hopkins et al., 1982: 62).

In all three historical cases of hegemony, hegemonic position was acquired by a very destructive thirty year land-based world war in which all the major military powers of the era participated: the Thirty Years War; the Napoleonic Wars; and the German Wars. Each of these world wars led to a major restructuring of the interstate system and the establishment of new alliances under the supervision of the new hegemonic power: Westphalia; Concert of Europe; and the UN and Bretton Woods. However as soon as hegemonic position or advantage in the production sphere begins to erode, the alliances established by the hegemonic power also begin to erode and reshuffle.

The ideology and the policy of the hegemonic powers have always promoted global liberalism. The free flow of goods and capital in the world-economy is the central concern of the hegemonic powers. The hegemonic powers advocate free trade and open door policies in the economic sphere. Furthermore, hegemonic powers extend this liberalism to the political sphere and become the defenders of liberal parliamentary institutions and civil liberties, while condemning political change through violent means. But Wallerstein also reminds us that the economic and political liberalism of hegemonic powers should not be exaggerated: they may make exceptions to their anti-restrictive principles, may interfere in the political processes in other states, and furthermore may become repressive at home when their interests so dictate (Wallerstein, 1984d: 41).

During the long period that follows hegemonic decline, two contending powers seem to emerge as the candidates for the next hegemonic cycle (Wallerstein, 1984d: 43). Historically, these two contending pairs were England and France after Dutch hegemony, the US and Germany after British, and Japan and Western Europe after US hegemony. Wallerstein also cites the historical tendency of newly emerged hegemonic powers to cooperate with the old hegemon as the principal partner in the new world order; for example Britain cooperated with the Dutch; the US cooperated with Great Britain; and perhaps, Western Europe or Japan will cooperate with the US in the future (see also, Wallerstein, 1996).

In world-system analysis, the creation of the state is considered to be an effect of the development of the capitalist world-economy (Wallerstein, 1984: Ch.3). The state is the political expression of this world economic structure. The relative power of the state is its most important property and, as is implied earlier, it more or less determines the structural position of the state in the system. Different groups exist within and outside of the state that try to increase or decrease the power of any given state or states. Their aim in seeking to change the power of the state is to create favourable conditions in the world market for their interests, since the state is considered to be the most convenient institution to distort the normal operation of the world market in favour of certain groups.

The key issues of state policy that occupy the attention of different groups are the rules that affect the allocation of surplus and the price structure of markets. This is because altering these two critical issues can change the relative competitivity of particular producers, and their profit levels. It is states that make rules in the world-economy and strong states intervene when relatively weaker states try to establish their own rules. In the capitalist world market, strong entrepreneurs do not need state aid to create quasi-monopolies, but they do need state aid to prevent others from creating monopoly privileges at the expense of their interests. Accordingly, in world-system analysis, states are defined as "created institutions reflecting the needs of class forces operating in the world-economy. They are not however created in a void but in the framework of an interstate system" (Wallerstein, 1984c: 33).

The proletariat and bourgeoisie may now be defined as classes in the world-economy, because they are formed in the world-economy and their interests are determined by their collective relationship to the world-economy (Wallerstein, 1984c: 34). However, when the bourgeoisie felt that their interests, vis-à-vis the working class and their competitors in the world market, were best served through creating and using state machineries, they began to define themselves as national bourgeoisies. Moreover, since class consciousness is a political rather than an economic phenomenon, and since the most effective political structure of the world-system is the state, in practical terms classes are considered national classes. In the capitalist world-economy, since the state is defined as the expression of power, it becomes the most appropriate instrument in the hands of the bourgeoisie for the appropriation of surplus from the working class of their country to the extent that the bourgeoisie are not restrained by the organised resistance of the proletariat. Furthermore, the power of the state also ensures the appropriation of surplus by one kind of bourgeoisie rather than another kind. If different kinds of bourgeoisie control different state structures, the fight for the appropriation of surplus may take the form of an interstate struggle. The working classes, through their organisations, may also attempt to influence the power of the state for their own ends. Since states are an integral part of the production relations in the world-economy, the nature and the degree of the relationship between various kinds of groups and the state are an important phenomenon.

On the other hand, world-system analysis argues that states may act both to control markets and to create them (Chase-Dunn, 1989: 120). Those states that successfully promote capitalist development not only supply social order, but also create necessary structures that promote profitable enterprises. Accordingly, state capitalism, instead of waiting for entrepreneurs, creates opportunities for them, and sometimes even takes the entrepreneurial role itself.

Although states came into existence to promote the needs of certain groups in the world market, they are by no means the mere puppets of their creators. Once created, any social organisation has a life of its own and acquires a certain autonomy, in the sense that various groups exploit it for various and contradictory ends. Moreover, all social organisations generate a permanent staff composed of bureaucracy/state managers whose interests lie in further strengthening the organisation independently of the varying interests of their creators (Wallerstein, 1974: 402 and 1984c: 30-31). In this sense states may promote the interests of different types of groups, and it is for this reason that different groups fight to influence state policies.

Although the end of the Cold War has made the structures and institutions of the post-1945 period somewhat archaic, world-system scholars indicate that the same institutional domains (vectors) will continue to organise the peoples' activities, although with increasing difficulty, over the next 25 to 50 years (Hopkins and Wallerstein, 1996: 2). Accordingly, this study develops its arguments for the post-Cold War period on the established assumptions of modern world-system theory.

One of the major criticisms directed against world-system analysis is that Wallerstein undervalues political structures and processes, and reduces state structures and politics to determination by economic conditions and dominant class interests. Consequently in world-system analysis states are treated as economic, rather than political, actors (Skocpol, 1977 and Zolberg, 1981). In this context what sort of external environment does world-system analysis present for the study of foreign policy? In general, Wallerstein's framework focuses on the impact of the external environment (modern world-system) on individual states as the determinant of their behaviours. In particular, Wallerstein offers an economics dominated external structure. This means that in conventional terms we can hardly study foreign policy using his model because his external environment for the study of foreign policy is the capitalist world-economy.

Does this mean that one cannot employ Wallerstein's approach in the study of foreign policy? According to Ray (1983), although the foreign policies of states are not central to Wallerstein's approach, one can pick out relevant points on foreign policy in his work and apply them to the study of foreign policy. As Ray argues, economic, rather than political interaction, is the driving force among states. However, foreign policy also comes to the fore when Wallerstein discusses the advantages enjoyed by the core states. What is relevant here for foreign policy is the concept of power, and more specifically, the use of power by core states in order to distort the normal operation of world market forces. According to Ray, this is the principal foreign policy goal of core states (Ray, 1983: 16). World-system analysis becomes relevant in this way to the foreign policy study of core states or great powers.

However, one may wonder whether it is proper to employ Wallerstein's framework for the study of foreign policy by simply picking the relevant parts of his framework. As Ray is aware, world-system analysis is an integrated whole and it cannot be studied by dividing it into various social science disciplines and then extracting the relevant points. If studied in this way, the world-system analysis' paradigm will suffer and research will probably end up with misleading conclusions. An alternative way to employ world-system analysis in foreign policy studies is to perceive the foreign policies of individual states as an integral part of that system, and to investigate to what extent in practice they are in conformity with, or diverge from, the premises of the framework proposed by Wallerstein. That is to say, one may study the foreign policies of individual states in a totality composed of economic and political history, political science, sociology, geography, etc. In other words, one may integrate those disciplines incorporated into world-system analysis, and investigate their impact on the phenomenon of foreign policy.

World-system analysis provides a very good starting point for foreign policy analysis. First, it divides states into three main categories of core (plus hegemonic power), semiperiphery, and periphery. States in each category have more or less the same characteristics, and consequently behave in a similar manner in the system. Second, world-system analysis provides us with cyclical rhythms of "the rise and decline of the hegemonic powers" and "expansion and contraction" periods in the world-economy. These processes reveal similar characteristics in each cycle. Furthermore, each category of state behaves in a similar manner during the different phases of these cycles in the modern world-system. Accordingly, it would not be unrealistic to employ world-system analysis in a study of foreign policy. The first task would be to determine the structural category of those states whose foreign policies are to be analysed. Then, the second task would be to determine the world-system time in the cyclical rhythm, for instance, is it an expansion or contraction period? Or is it an ascending or declining phase of the hegemonic power? These basic questions need to be clarified before examining the foreign policies of individual states in the framework of world-system analysis.

However, it might not be easy to provide clear answers to some of those questions, since Wallerstein is criticised for not giving clear cut definitions or accounts of the three structural categories of states (Snyder and Kick, 1979). Hence the main task for the researcher must be to include further clarification of concepts and their applicability to the states in question. In order to examine the foreign policies of Greece and Spain, therefore the next task will be the further clarification of the concept of the semiperiphery, and its relevance to those two states.

The Concept of Semiperiphery

Categorisation is one of the techniques used in science in order to make generalisations about a set whose membership is determined by defining characteristics. Accordingly, in Wallerstein's world-system analysis semiperiphery is the categorisation of a set of countries revealing similar structural, historical and behavioural characteristics. As noted earlier, semiperiphery is not an isolated concept; it is an intermediate category which is generally associated with the categories of core and periphery.

However, one might well be sceptical about a tri-modal categorisation (core-semiperiphery-periphery) of states and wonder why three rather than four, five or more categories of states? On the one hand, it is not an easy task to give satisfactory answers to such questions because it is almost impossible to create a few, mutually exhaustive, categories of states. In other words, unless one creates the same number of categories as the actual number of existing units (here states), one might not totally satisfy others. Furthermore, if you do this, the ability to generalise is lost. On the other hand, the aim of categorisation is to bring together those units whose general characteristics reveal significant similarities. Hence, generalisation, by nature, leads to the creation of as limited a number of categories as possible. The primary goal of categorisation being to reach generalisations, the number of categories must be limited. This is the underlying logic behind categorisation. Accordingly, in political science and international relations, depending on a criterion such as political, economic, military, etc., the tendency has always been to divide the states/countries into two or three set categories; e.g. developed-developing states, first-second-third world, developed-underdeveloped countries, super-powers or great powers-medium and small powers, North-South, democratic-authoritarian states, and so forth. This does not imply that the states within a particular category are copies of one another. On the contrary, states are considered similar in relation to a predetermined broader criterion (political, military, economic, etc.). Consequently, it follows that categorisation is, to a certain extent, an arbitrary but practical way of grouping states. Moreover, it is a plausible way to reach generalisations.

In fact, categorisation is not an easy task. Once you engage in categorisation, it is expected that all the units in your study should be located clearly in one of the categories defined in accordance with a predetermined criterion or criteria. However, as Wallerstein indicates (Wallerstein, 1985: 32), there are often borderline cases/units that cannot be located easily in any existing categories. Whenever the number of such cases is considerable, a general tendency has been to create an intermediate or an in-between category in which to locate the difficult cases. This explains also the formation of semiperiphery as an intermediate conceptual category between those of core and periphery in world-system analysis.

The concepts of core and periphery are relational concepts. The relation between the two is unequal in that the "coreness" of one region (or set of states) depends on the "peripherality" of another region (or another set of states). In other words, core-periphery division refers to the unequal distribution of the rewards of the world-economy resulting from the nature of core-like and periphery-like production processes dominant in the two regions. Semiperiphery, however, is not a relational concept since there are no semiperiphery-like production processes. On the contrary, production in the semiperiphery reveals an even mix of both core-like and periphery-like processes. That is to say, in world-system analysis semiperiphery refers to the balance between core-like and periphery-like activities within the boundaries of a given state. Being semiperipheral corresponds to a fairly even overall mix of the two types of activity (Wallerstein, 1985: 34). However, unless it is also an indicator of certain political processes, the above definition of semiperiphery might not be fruitful.

For Wallerstein, political, rather than economic, processes are important in analysing the concept of semiperiphery. In the semiperiphery, a roughly even mix of core-like and periphery-like activities and, accordingly, a roughly equal distribution of core-like and periphery-like producers (whose interests are conflicting) lead to intense competition over control of state structures. This is because state policies in the semiperiphery can immediately and directly affect the accumulation of capital by controlling the flows of goods and capital across frontiers, controlling the internal work force, taxation, redistributive expenditures and expenditures on social overheads, etc. Thus in the semiperiphery, the main internal and external economic actors (owner-producers, work force, state bureaucracy, multinational corporations) focus on state-oriented political activity in order to accumulate capital for their own interests. Accordingly,

> the closer the overall mix of core-peripheral activities is to an even one in a given state - that is the more semiperipheral the state - the more will the complex calculus tilt towards rewarding efforts to secure economic advantage via effecting (transforming) the state structure. This is because the nearer to

some median is the economic mix, the more immediately and directly can state policies affect the accumulation of capital (Wallerstein, 1985: 35).

Furthermore, since different kinds of economic elites tend to have opposing interests in the semiperiphery, the state usually becomes the dominant element in forming the power blocs and political coalitions among economic groups (Chase-Dunn, 1989: 41).

Another world-system scholar, Chase-Dunn, redefines core and peripheral activities as a continuum of relatively capital intensive/labour intensive forms of production (Chase-Dunn, 1989: 211). In other words, he focuses on relative levels of the capital intensity in commodity production. Chase-Dunn argues that semiperipheral areas have an intermediate level of production. For Chase-Dunn, there are two kinds of semiperipheries: first, states in which there is a balanced mix of core and peripheral activities, and second, states in which there is a predominance of activities that are intermediate in terms of the relative level of capital intensity/labour intensity (Chase-Dunn, 1989: 211-212). Thus, he emphasises that in the semiperiphery there is a preponderance of intermediate levels of capital intensive production (Chase-Dunn, 1990: 3).

In semiperipheral countries the state may attempt to change the mix of activities in favour of core-like or periphery-like production processes, and the state may easily affect the direction of internal redistribution of rewards. But this does not mean that core and peripheral states cannot do the same. Wallerstein believes that they can. However, there are two reasons that make the pay-off greater for semiperipheral states than for the core and periphery. First, it can be assumed that such state policies are more likely to succeed in semiperipheral than in peripheral states because in the periphery the opportunities for upward mobility are much more limited. Second, one can assume that there are alternative market mechanisms for core producers to achieve the same objectives without concentrating on state-oriented political activity (Wallerstein, 1985: 35). Hence, upwardly mobile semiperipheral countries have tended to employ more state-directed and state-mobilised development policies than have core countries (Chase-Dunn, 1989: 241).

An important defining characteristic of semiperipheral states is related to the possible improvement of their status in the world-economy during contraction periods. As mentioned previously, periods of expansion and contraction in the world-economy are one of the critical issues that concern world-system analysis. These cyclical shifts of the world-economy, in broader terms, are the function of the relationship between supply and effective demand in the world market. Contraction periods are periods of over-supply in the world-economy leading to changes in the production process and production relations in an attempt to reach a point of equilibrium. During expansion periods, on the other hand, world-wide effective demand is maintained by shifts in the production processes and relations. The direction of the surplus of the world-economy also changes during these periods. During expansion phases, the largest proportion of the surplus is extracted by core areas, while in contraction periods part of the surplus goes to semiperipheral states at the expense of the core states. According to Wallerstein, during contraction periods semiperipheral states can effectively control their internal markets and, furthermore, they can penetrate into peripheral markets at the expense of core producers (Wallerstein, 1976: 464). This is because intense intra-core competition takes place in world market shares of core products during these periods of oversupply. This gives semiperipheral countries the option of choosing among core producers when selling their goods, purchasing core products, and inviting core investments. In sum, during contraction periods semiperipheral states expand their national production, improve their terms of trade and may shift their position upwardly in the world-economy. Changes in the economic sphere are reflected in the politics of semiperipheral countries (Wallerstein, 1976: 464). Internally, political regimes may change, since the old structures can no longer cope with the changing nature of international politics. Externally, semiperipheral states may change the pattern of their international diplomatic alliances. And, as a result of economic and political changes, the degree of direct intervention in the internal affairs of semiperipheral states by the core powers decreases.

However, in world-system analysis the upward mobility of individual states is considered exceptional (Arrighi and Drangel, 1986: 42). First, semiperipheral states that take off into a core position are expected to experience extremely high rates of growth for a considerable period of time (Arrighi and Drangel, 1986: 52). Moreover, although all semiperipheral states can benefit from a contraction period in the capitalist world-economy, only a few succeed in shifting their positions in the world-system. The reason is straightforward. Among other things, the problem is intra-semiperiphery fighting. For "a semiperipheral country rising to core status does so, not merely at the expense of some or all core powers, but at the expense of other semiperipheral powers" (Wallerstein, 1976: 466). On the other hand, in times of expansion semiperipheral countries tend to become clients of core countries "seeking their aid to obtain a part of the world market against the other semiperipheral countries" (Wallerstein, 1979: 83). In this way they become agents of core states, and some play sub-imperial roles in relation to peripheral areas. Furthermore, semiperipheral states are often turned into ideological and political appendages of world powers.

Broadly speaking, in semiperipheral states the bourgeoisie is divided into two groups: the indigenous and the external bourgeoisie (Wallerstein, 1976: 469). The indigenous bourgeoisie is the national bourgeoisie whose activities are concentrated in certain sectors. They are small in number and weaker than the national bourgeoisie of core countries. However the indigenous bourgeoisie's striking feature is their strong structural links with corporations in core areas. For Wallerstein, this is one of the defining structural characteristics of semiperipheral countries. The external bourgeoisie, on the other hand, belongs to multinational corporations (MNCs). The critical point for MNCs is to remain profitable in the location in which they operate. Accordingly they are primarily interested in the policies of semiperipheral state.

Wallerstein argues that wage levels are an indicator of the position of a state in the world-economy (Wallerstein, 1979: 71 and 84-85). So, while low wage levels correspond to peripherality, high and medium wage levels indicate coreness and semiperipherality respectively. Accordingly, one should look at wage patterns and profit margins of particular products at particular moments in order to identify the positions of various states in the capitalist world-economy. In this system semiperipheral countries are defined by their medium wage level and profit margins in comparison to core and peripheral states.

The picture of semiperiphery that has been presented so far is a theoretical exposition of the concept, and it draws predominantly on the original views of its creator, Wallerstein. It is clear that Wallerstein's understanding of the concept of semiperiphery is rather complex. Moreover, it is difficult to operationalise. However, if semiperiphery, as a conceptual category, has some merits, there must be reasonable and manageable criteria (however arbitrary) to operationalise it.

How to Operationalise the Concept of Semiperiphery

In general, there are major criticisms directed towards Wallerstein's elaboration of the semiperiphery. First, Wallerstein is both vague and formal, according to Arrighi, in defining the concept (Arrighi, 1985: 243). He is vague in that he emphasises two aspects in his definition. He points to "a fairly even mix" of core-like and periphery-like economic activities in the semiperiphery, and he emphasises the intermediate semiperipheral position in the world-system. However, he does not indicate which of these criteria is more important in identifying semiperipheral countries. On the other hand, Wallerstein is formal because he does not substantiate his hypothesis, for how is one to identify core-like or periphery-like activities in the various commodity chains, and how do these two types of activities change over time?

Aymard also points to a dichotomy resulting from ambiguous usage of the concept (Aymard, 1985: 40). According to Aymard, Wallerstein defines semiperiphery on economic grounds, on the one hand, referring to those regions where the coming in and going out surpluses equal to zero. On the other hand, a semiperipheral state is defined on political grounds as a state pursuing a "catching up with the core" policy in order to improve its position in the interstate system. For Aymard these two definitions are hardly reconcilable.

Another major criticism directed at the concept of semiperiphery focuses on its empirical applicability. According to Arrighi, Aymard and Lange (Lange, 1985: 181), all three terms, semiperiphery, core and periphery, cannot easily be measured operationally in the writings of Wallerstein. For instance, Wallerstein does not tell us how to measure the overall "fairly even mix of activities", nor how to quantify them.

In fact, it is fairly clear in Wallerstein's writings that the international position of any country is a function of the dominant type of economic activity that falls within its boundaries, rather than vice versa. In other words, what makes a state core or peripheral is the type of economic activities (core-like or periphery-like) that dominate the production process. A state is core (or peripheral) primarily because its production processes are highly profitable (or less profitable) and dominated by capital intensive techniques, high-technology, skilled and highly paid labour (or low profit, labour intensive techniques and coerced low wage labour). Accordingly, a state is semiperipheral, first because a "fairly even mix" of core-like and periphery-like activities fall within its borders. Yet, in contrast to core and periphery, this is not enough to define a country as semiperipheral. Any definition of semiperiphery must be supported by certain political processes at the national political economy level. The relationship between state policies and the direction of capital accumulation is the second important criteria in identifying semiperipheral states.

In an economy dominated by a "fairly even mix" of economic activities, state policies can easily affect the direction of capital accumulation. This is because none of the economic actors significantly dominate state structures. Accordingly there is a precarious political balance of power between the economic actors of semiperipheral states. As a result, the state acquires and maintains a relative degree of independence from all economic groups. It follows that the different actors (fractions of the bourgeoisie, workers, external economic actors) engage in a political struggle to affect state structures and policies in favour of their respective economic interests. Hence, in order to label a country as semiperipheral, one must also consider the intensity of the state-oriented activities of national and external actors. Thus, Wallerstein proposes two criteria (economic and political) for the identification of semiperiphery. These two criteria together (not separately) determine the international position of a semiperipheral state. The economic criterion (a fairly even mix of economic activities) is the precondition of being semiperipheral. The political criterion, on the other hand, indicates to which international position a semiperipheral state is moving or is likely to move, and indeed whether it will move.

On the other hand, it must be admitted that Wallerstein does not provide sufficient means to operationalise the concept of semiperiphery. Indeed, it seems that he himself is not clear about what operational criteria are to be employed in identifying a semiperipherial state. Accordingly he classifies a vast number of states as semiperipheral:

> The semiperiphery includes a wide range of countries in terms of economic strength and political background. It includes the economically stronger countries of Latin America; Brazil, Mexico, Argentina, Venezuela, possibly Chile and Cuba. It includes the outer rim of Europe; the southern tier of Portugal, Spain, Italy and Greece; most of Eastern Europe; parts of the northern tier such as Norway and Finland. It includes a series of Arab states; Algeria, Egypt, Saudi Arabia; and also Israel. It includes in Africa at least Nigeria and Zaire and in Asia; Turkey, Iran, India, Indonesia, China, Korea, and Vietnam. And it includes the old white Commonwealth; Canada, Australia, South Africa, possibly New Zealand (Wallerstein, 1976: 465).

As Arrighi rightly points out, the concept semiperiphery, introduced to solve the problem of border cases, has itself become problematic. The difficulty of clearly operationalising this concept leads Wallerstein to include vastly different countries in the semiperipheral category.

Yet, there have been other attempts to clarify and operationalise the concept of semiperiphery. Lange, for example, in an article discussing Italy's special position in the world-system (Lange, 1985), proposes a sub-group of core states called the "perimeter of the core". A country located at the perimeter of the core is one that has recently shifted from periphery to core. In other words, Lange posits a sub-core-region where semiperipheral and core characteristics might coexist. One of his critical arguments is that domestic politics does play a role in changing the world-system position of countries. Indeed, one of the criticisms of world-system analysis is its neglect of internal politics. Wallerstein rarely refers to the importance of internal politics. For instance, in one article he maintains that semiperipheral countries' "internal politics and their social structures are distinctive, and it turns out that their ability to take advantage of the flexibility offered by the downturns of economic activity is in general greater than that of either core or peripheral countries" (Wallerstein, 1976: 463). Furthermore, as Lange himself points out, Wallerstein remarks on the importance of the relationship between the national political economy and the world-economy in moving from one position to another (Lange, 1985: 183). However, Lange argues that these remarks can only be useful at the macro level; they do not assist individual, or country level, studies. Lange believes that major domestic actors play a critical role in the process of shifting from semiperiphery to core. In other words, it is important to observe the struggles (if any) among the domestic actors over the distribution of economic shares and political power during the positional shift. According to Lange, in such instances domestic actors choose strategies in order to promote their own interests; thus they act intentionally. It is at this point that a state's position in the world-system enters the picture. Lange maintains that although this position strongly affects the opportunity structure for states, "it cannot determine the specific form of the opportunity structure for any individual country, much less the specific strategies that will be adopted by the relevant actors, nor can it explain which specific combination of strategies adopted will result in an alteration of that country's position in the world-system" (Lange, 1985: 184).

A second critical factor that Lange points out is the behaviour of a country whose position has recently shifted from semiperiphery to the core. For Lange, those states (in his case Italy) first arrive at the "perimeter of the core" and experience an adaptation period there, during which major domestic actors and the state try to formulate new strategies. Accordingly, their behaviour reveals a mixture of core and semiperipheral characteristics. An important point here is that the behaviours of the actors, and the adaptation period as a whole, are significantly influenced by the history and the national characteristics of individual states. Furthermore, there is always the possibility of falling back to a semiperipheral position.

In operationalising these and other points in the Italian case, Lange takes wage structure (wage levels and their rate of increase) as his main criterion. In fact, Wallerstein proposes six indicators by which the world-system position of individual countries can be assessed (Lange, 1985: 186): Gross

National Product per capita, the structure of national production, the structure of trade, the class structure, the wage structure, patterns of development and political response under conditions of economic crisis. In the postwar period, wage structure is an important indicator of a shift from semiperiphery to core for Lange because a change in wage levels are mainly a function of changes in terms and patterns of trade for a country within the world-system, and requires an upgrading of the average technological level of domestic production.

On the other hand, Arrighi and Drangel present a more comprehensive operationalisation not only of semiperiphery, but also of core and periphery (Arrighi, 1985 and Arrighi and Drangel, 1986). According to Arrighi and Drangel "there is no [direct] operational way of empirically distinguishing between periphery-like and core-like activities and therefore classifying states according to the mix of core-peripheral activities that fall under their jurisdiction". Furthermore "[in] order to classify activities as core-like and periphery-like one should minimally need a complete map of all commodity chains of the world-economy as well as an assessment of the relative competitive pressure at each of their nodes, and this is in itself an impossible task" (Arrighi and Drangel, 1986: 30). Arrighi, therefore, proposes an indirect measurement of the stratification of the world-economy. Referring to the ambiguous usage of the concept semiperiphery, he argues that there is a desperate need for a standard that could reflect a meaning of the concept as close as possible to its original purpose. Furthermore, the standard should also give the maximum possible clarity in categorising states into the three zones of the world-economy. He proposes GNP per capita as such a standard operational criterion that could satisfy these expectations.

According to Wallerstein, while core activities appropriate a large share of the total surplus produced in the world-economy, peripheral activities receive the remaining small amount. Arrighi believes that this disproportional distribution of the world-economy's surplus must be reflected in the GNP per capita differentials of the residents in the two types of states. In other words, since core activities command aggregate rewards that incorporate most of the overall benefits of the world division of labour, while peripheral activities command aggregate rewards that incorporate few of those benefits, the differences in command over the total benefits of the world division of labour must necessarily be reflected in commensurate differences in the GNP per capita of the states (Arrighi and Drangel, 1986: 31). Since semiperipheral states have a fairly even mix of core and peripheral activities, they receive a more or less average share of the world-economy's surplus, and accordingly their GNP per capita income reflects an intermediate position between core and periphery.

But what is an intermediate level of per capita GNP? At what level should we set the lower and upper boundaries of the semiperipheral zone? Arrighi again refers to Wallerstein for whom semiperiphery is neither a residual nor a transitional part, but a stable and permanent feature of the world-economy. It is easily differentiated both from core and periphery. Hence if the world-economy is composed of three permanent categories of states, "we should be able to set the boundaries of the semiperiphery simply by inspecting the distribution of states according to their per capita GNP" (Arrighi, 1985: 245). Here, one must look at the relative, rather than the absolute, differences between states, and at differences in command over world economic resources, rather than at differences in actual standards of living (Arrighi and Drangel, 1986: 31). Referring to 1983 World Bank data, Arrighi claims that Wallerstein's tri-modal distribution of states is consistent with the distribution of world GNP per capita. Leaving aside states with a population of less than one million, he reclassifies states into five categories of per capita GNP (Arrighi, 1985), arguing that this regrouping demonstrates the coincidence between tri-modal distribution of states and the distribution of GNP per capita levels in relation to population in each category (Arrighi and Drangel, 1986: 32-52). However, there appear to be two relatively depopulated, new categories (Arrighi, 1985: 246):

Class	GNP per capita, 1981 (in dollars)	Number of States	Percentage of world population
I	less than 800	50	58
I/II	800 – 1500	19	5
II	1500 – 4500	31	20
II/III	4500 – 9000	10	3
III	more than 9000	19	14

Class I Periphery. *Class II* Semiperiphery. *Class III* Core. *Class I/II* "Perimeter of Periphery". *Class II/III* "Perimeter of Core".

Arrighi points out that his "perimeter of the core" (Class II/III) and by analogy "perimeter of periphery" (Class I/II) have nothing to do with

Lange's understanding of "perimeter of the core". Arrighi's perimeters are intermediate zones, rather than lines demarcating two zones.

Now, let us consider if what Arrighi offers is new. His criterion (GNP per capita) for operationalising semiperiphery seems plausible and manageable. It would not be unrealistic to think first that the distribution of the world-economy's surplus among different countries is a function of a country's position in the production activities, and second that the distribution of GNP per capita income in a country is the function of the amount of (+) (-) surplus appropriated by that country. Hence, GNP per capita might indeed be a good indicator for identifying any country's position in the world-economy.

Arrighi's table is important because it provides us, roughly and in a modified way, with a representative picture of position in the world-economy in terms of GNP per capita. In other words, unless we develop a more sensitive and more reflective method of establishing groupings, Arrighi's table may be used by testing its reliability with other indicators of each category. In fact, it is not easy to locate every state in a clear-cut world-system position precisely. Thus if we need to identify state positions, we have to rely on some rough measures. Perhaps this is the main characteristic that one should take into consideration in the process of identifying, not only world-system positions, but also other comprehensive, macro classifications used frequently in the social sciences, for example First World/Third World, South/North, underdeveloped/developed countries, etc. In other words, there are no clear-cut indicators and measures for the demarcation lines between, say, South and North, other than rough and arbitrary ones.

On the other hand, when it comes to the modifications that Arrighi introduced as classes I/II and II/III, one can say that as a borderline case, semiperiphery is not an adequate category unless it is a broad one. As was pointed out earlier, in Wallerstein's categorisation semiperiphery includes a vast number of states, ranging from Zaire to Canada. This means that semiperiphery is not a homogenised category. Accordingly, there is enough reason for Arrighi to create two more categories for the further clarification of the semiperipheral zone. Arrighi and Drangel propose that (1986: 51) the semiperipheral zone of the world-economy, at any given time, includes not only its organic members, but also some states that have been more or less temporarily demoted from the core (or promoted from periphery) by one of the systematic shocks through which the world-economy operates. Thus Arrighi's table can be used with reservations, and through testing with other indicators, to operationalise the concept semiperiphery.

Arrighi and Drangel's classification of the position of states in the world-economy in terms of GNP per capita in the three periods 1938-1950, 1960-1970 and 1975-1983 (Arrighi and Drangel, 1986: 60-71), divides organic members of the three zones of the world-system as follows, *Organic Members of the Core zone* Australia, Canada, Denmark, New Zealand, Norway, Sweden, Switzerland, UK, USA, and Germany. *Organic Members of the Semiperipheral zone* Argentina, Chile, Costa Rica, GREECE, Hong Kong, Hungary, Ireland, Israel, Jamaica, Mexico, Panama, Portugal, Romania, South Africa, *SPAIN*, Turkey, Uruguay, USSR, Venezuela, and Yugoslavia. *Organic Members of the Peripheral zone* Afghanistan, Angola, Bangladesh, Benin, Bolivia, Burma, Burundi, Cameroon, Central African Republic, Chad, China, Egypt, El Salvador, Ethiopia, Guinea, Haiti, Honduras, India, Indonesia, Kenya, Liberia, Madagascar, Malawi, Mali, Mauritania, Mozambique, Nepal, Niger, Nigeria, Pakistan, Papua New Guinea, Philippines, Rwanda, Senegal, Somalia, Sri Lanka, Sudan, Tanzania, Thailand, Togo, Uganda, Upper Volta, Zambia, and Zimbabwe.

In the classification of states according to their GNP per capita, the cases of this study, namely of Greece and Spain, appear clearly as organic members of the semiperipheral zone. More specifically, in Arrighi and Drangel's study the world-system positions of Greece and Spain in the three periods appear as follows:

Period	Greece	Spain
1938-1950	Semiperiphery	Semiperiphery
1960-1970	Semiperiphery	Semiperiphery
1975-1983	Semiperiphery	Perimeter of Core

Here, another important point emerges related to the unique position of the world-system's semiperipheral zone. As Arrighi and Drangel rightly put it (1986: 59-60), neither of the two competing theories of modernisation and dependency establish an intermediate and persistent zone/group of states that is relatively large in number. The addition of an in-between zone, in turn, implies the inadequacy of classifying of states as developed/developing; developed/underdeveloped; or core/periphery, and emphasises the necessity to differentiate an intermediate group of states from other groupings.

Nemeth and Smith (1985) also attempted to determine empirically the structural positions of states in the world-system according to their patterns of commodity trade. Referring to a contention of world-system theory that states position in the world-economy is related to the types of commodities a state trades, Nemeth and Smith analyse the trade patterns of 86 non-centrally planned countries in terms of five types of commodities: heavy manufacturing/high-technology, intermediate manufactures, light manufactures, food products, and raw materials. They use data from UN Commodity Trade Statistics for the year 1970. On the basis of their findings, they group countries into blocks depending upon their structural similarities in relation to trade flows of various commodity types. In other words, they classify countries into discrete, mutually exclusive, and exhaustive categories based on their trade in all five commodity groups. The general decomposition patterns, and the direction and the magnitude of trade of each commodity type between blocks, resulted in an eight-group division of countries that can be characterised as representing four structural positions in the world economy: core, periphery, strong semiperiphery and weak semiperiphery. This regrouping is made according to commodity-trades and import and export destinations

Nemeth and Smith's analysis of these 86 countries' patterns of commodity trade support the world-system approach. They find that core countries trade with nations located in all the strata (blocks) of the world-economy and their strength is reflected in the type, diversity and quantity of their export. Peripheral countries trade mainly with core and some semiperipheral countries, and they specialise in the export of a few commodities. Finally, the semiperiphery forms a middle category in terms of commodity mixes and flows. On the basis of their findings, Nemeth and Smith argue that the international economic system is hierarchically ordered, and that the eight strata (blocks) derived from their model can be conceptualised to fulfil four distinct roles in the world-economy (core, strong semiperiphery, weak semiperiphery, periphery), roles which conform well to the world-system categorisation of states as core, periphery and semiperiphery. In other words, Nemeth and Smith emphasise that the structure of commodity exchange in the international system conforms to the expectations of the world-system approach. Another important point is that in Nemeth and Smith's study both *Greece* and *Spain* appear in the (strong) semiperipheral zone of the world-economy, although the criteria for determining their world-system position are different.

It seems clear that the semiperipheral zone of the world economy is a heterogeneous zone composed of rather different states. This is the major point that leads to problems for the semiperiphery. An alternative way to reduce these problems to some extent is perhaps to regroup and study the most similar semiperipheral states. This method, however, decreases the generalising power of the concept while increasing its practicality and operational ability. Yet if the concept of semiperiphery is to become a fruitful concept, it is necessary to study relatively more similar cases, rather than the whole range of semiperipherality. To do this, one needs to take into account a number of indicators of semiperipherality and to apply them to the states under consideration.

Having outlined the basic tenets of world-system analysis and the concept of semiperiphery, let me now explain how these shall be utilised in the framework of this study. First of all, it must be emphasised that although world-system analysis focuses on the study of the external environment and systemic-structural conditions and processes, this study investigates the effects of that environment and those conditions and processes on national development. This work also examines the consequences of occupying a given structural position in the world-economy. That is to say, the main concern here is to show the effects of the structures and the operation of the capitalist world-economy on the national development and foreign policies of two (semiperipheral) countries (Greece and Spain) between 1945-2000s. A common misunderstanding in relation to world-system analysis is that it can only investigate the systemic/structural or international levels; however, the study of other levels of analysis (such as zones, states, organisations, etc.) is also possible in world-system analysis (Chase-Dunn, 1989: 310). In fact, having a holistic structure, the world-system contains all those levels and the processes operating at the international and national levels. This study accordingly, attempts to analyse the foreign policies of two semiperipheral countries in relation to their economic position in the world-economy. In this context, this study shall look at how both power and production/wealth are organised, and investigate the interaction and interdependence between economic and political activities.

In this study, both Greece and Spain are considered semiperipheral states. They are provisionally considered semiperipheral, first, because neither country fits either the core or the peripheral end of the world-system hierarchy. Hence they are in the intermediate category of the semiperiphery. Moreover, using the operationalisation of Arrighi and Drangel and of Nemeth and Smith, these two states are clearly located in the semiperipheral category. The next chapters will investigate whether Greece and Spain are located in the semiperiphery and whether other economic and political indicators support this categorisation.

The starting point of this investigation is the economic and political histories of Greece and Spain, so as to analyse their semiperipheral characteristics in the periods between 1945 and the mid-1970s and between the mid-1970s and the 2000s, periods which roughly correspond both to the rise and decline of American hegemony and to expansion and contraction periods of the world-economy. In both periods, I shall consider the economic environment to investigate the production patterns, the role of the state in the economy, the nature of the dominant economic elite, the nature of the relationship between the state and the economic elites and among the economic elites themselves, and also the nature of the relationship between foreign capital and the Greek and Spanish states and the domestic economic elites. Furthermore, in the second period (mid-1970s to 2000s), I shall also investigate whether both Greece and Spain experienced upward mobility towards the core zone in the world-system hierarchy.

Second, this study will turn to the political environment to investigate the interactions between economic development and domestic politics and political structures, and to see whether these two states displayed semiperipheral characteristics. The world-system school proposes that, in expansion periods of the world-economy, semiperipheral states experience high degrees of intervention in their domestic affairs by the core/hegemonic powers. Furthermore, in these periods, semiperipheral states turn into satellites and become political and ideological agents of the hegemonic/core powers. Thus, in the expansion period (1945 to mid-1970s) this study considers whether either state was subjected to such experiences. Also, according to the world-system school, in contraction periods of the world-economy, semiperipheral states experience the collapse of old political structures, and the interventions of hegemonic/core powers come to an end. Accordingly, this work will investigate whether this holds true for Greece and Spain in the contraction period of the world-economy (after the mid-1970s).

The world-system approach implies that the foreign policies of semiperipheral states go hand in hand with developments in the economic and political spheres. It is argued that, during expansion periods, the foreign policies of semiperipheral states are directed towards the accomplishment of the global objectives of hegemonic/core powers. Furthermore, the policies to be followed may be dictated to semiperipheral states. In other words, semiperipheral states become satellites of the hegemonic/core powers, and their national interests and national sovereignty may be subordinated to the global/regional interests of the hegemonic/core powers. Thus, in the first period (1945 to mid-1970s) the following chapters will examine whether Greece and Spain displayed such foreign policy behaviours.

Similarly, in contraction periods, in parallel to the changes in the economic and political spheres, the foreign policies of semiperipheral states may change. According to world-system analysis, semiperipheral states change their international alliances in these periods. They give up their satellite-like foreign policies and pursue a relatively independent foreign policy. Moreover, some upwardly mobile semiperipheral countries compete with other semiperipheral states for further economic and political gains. Furthermore, I propose that, in their foreign policy orientations, these upwardly mobile semiperipheral states may also fulfil an intermediary/bridge role between the core zones and those areas that are geographically proximate and/or with which they have cultural and historical ties. They also seek to become involved in the management of international problems. Therefore this work examines whether Greek and Spanish foreign policies followed such a course in the period between the mid-1970s and the 2000s.

However, before examining their development patterns and individual foreign policies, it may be useful to understand why Greece and Spain (and, most of the time, Portugal) are considered a coherent group by a number of researchers.

Understanding Greece and Spain

The 1970s were one of the most eventful decades in the history of the modern world. The Bretton Woods system, that governed the international economic order since the end of the Second World War collapsed. In August 1971, the Americans abolished the fixed exchange rate system that had established the dollar as the international currency. In 1973 a war broke out in the Middle East and it led to the first oil-price shock and world-wide inflation and recession. In 1974 Greece and Turkey came very near to all out war over Cyprus. European Political Cooperation (EPC) came into being as a result of diverging European and American interests in the Middle East. Towards the end of the decade, a revolution occurred in Iran that ended with the establishment of a radical Islamic state. Soon thereafter another oil-price shock hit the world. Finally, the USSR invaded Afghanistan in 1979.

Among these major events, developments in three southern European countries, namely Greece, Spain and Portugal (GSP), were by no means of secondary importance. The 1970s witnessed the collapse of dictatorships and the establishment of democratic regimes in the GSP countries. The long standing authoritarian regimes of Salazar in Portugal (1926-1974), and of Franco in Spain (1936-1976) came to an end together with the seven year dictatorship of the Greek colonels (1967-1974). The successive overthrow of the dictatorships and the establishment of democratic structures in southern Europe aroused the interest of social scientists. In 1975, even before the death of Franco, the publication of Nicos Poulantzas' *La Crise des Dictatures*, which emphasised the similarity of the political and economic developments that led to social change in these countries, took the lead in regional studies on southern Europe and thus opened the way for comparative studies of GSP countries. Social scientists' interests in the issue increased when, in the 1980s, they (GSP) all become full-members of the European Community (EEC/EC/EU), and socialist governments came to power in all three countries. As the convergences in the political and economic histories of the trio proliferated, scholars, in order to explain the phenomenon, began to seek similarities in the underlying causes and patterns that govern social change in GSP countries (see Poulantzas, 1976; Giner, 1986; Pridham, 1984, 1991 and 1995, Wallerstein, 1985, Arrighi, 1985, Keyder, 1985).

Common Characteristics of GSP Countries

The geographical factor has played an important role in the political and economic developments of GSP countries. Their physical proximity to Western Europe, and the fact that they border strategically important points of the Mediterranean and the Atlantic Ocean, have had important consequences on both the shared and the unique national experiences of these countries. Moreover, historically, political and economic developments in Western Europe (see Malefakis, 1995) often created both constraints and opportunities for national developments in the south. To put it differently, their geographical locations have provided GSP with different paths to follow compared to the geographical locations of other semiperipheral states in Latin America and East Asia.

In this context, historically, the 19th century liberal-conservative (or modern-traditional) struggles in southern Europe reflect the political and social debates on liberalism, parliamentarism and constitutionalism then taking place in the West. Similarly, the destruction of both political and economic ideas, and institutions during the First World War and in its aftermath, led to the emergence of authoritarian and autarkic regimes in Western Europe, and the GSP countries followed the suit immediately. Finally, following the Second World War the establishment of a new international order under American hegemony, the advent of Cold War, the division of Europe into two hostile blocs and the reign of anti-Communist ideology played decisive roles in the continuation of authoritarian and restrictive parliamentary regimes in GSP. However, the emergence of Europe as an economic and political power in the late 1960s and early 1970s significantly contributed to the democratisation of political structures and further liberalisation of the economies of southern Europe. The existence of the EC, and the eventual incorporation of GSP into the organisation, indicate that the fortunes of these three countries are linked to developments in their Western neighbours.

Most studies of GSP have tended to identify these countries in a distinct category from both "developed" and "underdeveloped" countries. In each case the classification implies that they occupy a peculiar position in the international system. For instance, apart from the concept semiperiphery, the terms "underdeveloped Europe", "periphery of Europe" (Seers, 1979a), "European periphery" (Seddon, n.d. and Selwyn, 1979) have been used interchangeably to identify GSP countries. The terms "underdeveloped" and "periphery" imply that GSP countries have similar and shared characteristics with Third World countries. However, the terms "Europe/European" refer both to the significance of their geographical location, and to their core-like characteristics and distinct peripheral/underdeveloped positions (relatively better-off positions) in comparison to Third World countries. Accordingly, another common characteristic of most studies is their focus on the political economy of these three states. In other words, the relationship between the state, politics and economics, both at the national and international level, and the role of national and international actors in political and economic changes in relation to this interaction are all common themes (though to varying degrees and in different explanatory frameworks) of most comparative studies of GSP countries.

Indeed, there are some common points in the political economies of GSP. One of them is the dependent position of their economies in relation to the core, despite their relatively better-off positions compared to the periphery. The lack of technological capacity and capital goods industries, little control over the ownership of local manufacturing and over the use of resources (Seers, 1979b: 3), the inability to participate effectively in major economic decisions (for example, what to produce and where and how to produce) and lack of innovation (Selwyn, 1979: 37) are the main characteristics of the dependency of GSP economies on core countries, mainly the US and the EC/EU. Even the new international division of labour, which corresponds to the upward shift of GSP in the world-economy, has not altered the main characteristics of this dependency, for example the control of technology by the core and the location of management and research centres from the core to these countries (Williams, 1984: 15). Another common characteristic of the GSP is the flow of migrant workers to core countries and the flow of tourists from core to GSP countries. Especially in the 1960s and early 1970s, emigrant remittances and tourism revenues contributed significantly to the balance of payments accounts of GSP. A third similarity is the existence of few large, and a plethora of small firms side by side in the economies of the three countries. Thus, while the big companies owned by private, foreign or state capital are run on capitalist principles, uncompetitive small firms represent an inefficient part of GSP economies. Finally, a large parasitic service sector, mostly created through clientelistic networks, constitutes another common characteristic.

One of the most striking features of GSP countries in relation to this study is the existence of significant divisions among their social and political forces up to recent times, and their implications for political and economic development (Diamandouros, 1986a: 548-549). The introduction of liberalism and parliamentarism into these countries before industrialisation caused contradictions among existing social forces and led to long-lasting legitimacy crises in GSP. None of the forces was powerful enough to establish hegemony and this resulted in either restricted parliamentary or authoritarian regimes up to the mid-1970s. Hence, unlike in the developed West, in the absence of hegemonic bourgeoisies, the states began to play a crucial role in the economy through public enterprises, and in this way became the central actor in both economics and politics. It was only towards the middle of the 1970s that these cleavages between antagonistic forces began to dissolve for the first time through reconciliation, and the legitimacy of the internationalist capitalist system was established. In other words, old-style conservatives were either eliminated or incorporated by the pro-capitalist forces, and left wing forces were allowed to participate in the competitive politics through democratisation. Theoretically speaking, these are the characteristics of semiperipheral states: a roughly equal distribution of core-like and periphery-like producers; their struggle over state structures in order to control them and establish their primacy; and the central position of the state. Furthermore, the political and economic transformations that took place in the mid-1970s, namely the democratisation of the political regimes and the further interaction of the economies with international markets and their accession to the EC in the 1980s, implied the victory of the liberal-democratic and the pro-capitalist over the authoritarian-conservative and statist forces. This, in turn, indicated an attempt to shift the semiperipheral position of GSP towards the core in the world-economy at a time of the relative hegemonic decline of the US and the ascendancy of the EEC/EC/EU.

Postwar economic and political developments in GSP (see Sapelli, 1995) fall naturally into two main periods: the period from 1945 to the mid-1970s, and the period after the mid-1970s. In order to consolidate American hegemony, US policy makers concentrated on two things in the immediate postwar years: the establishment of a free market economy throughout the world, and the containment of the Soviet Union and communism. In these tasks the Americans were particularly sensitive about Western Europe. For this reason the immediate effect of the new hegemonic order in southern Europe was somewhat different from those in Western Europe. Since the economic structures of the south were not as developed as those in the north, the process of economic reconstruction in the south was directed towards the establishment of market integrated national economies by building roads and communication networks (infrastructure) and the development and modernisation of the agricultural sector in the 1950s (Seddon, n.d: 4-5).

On the other hand, in spite of the US rhetoric of democracy, the authoritarian regimes in GSP countries remained in power in exchange for their commitment to the market economy. In fact, in the immediate postwar years these authoritarian regimes briefly opted for autarkic economic policies: protective tariffs and quotas and import substitution were put into practice, and the state began to control the economy again. However, three factors contributed to the opening and internationalisation of these economies. The first was the structure and the rationale of the new international economic order established by the US that was hostile to autarkic tendencies. The second was that these autarkic policies themselves began to restrict economic growth at a certain point (Williams, 1984: 10). Finally there were pressures from newly established international institutions like the International Monetary Fund (IMF) and Organisation for Economic Co-operation and Development (OECD) for the opening up of GSP economies in order to ease their balance of payments deficits.

In the 1960s, however, the situation in GSP began to change. Between 1960 and 1973 they achieved growth rates of about 6 to 8 percent (Tovias, 1984: 159 and Williams, 1984: 8) and entered into the industrialisation processes. Massive labour shifts occurred from the agricultural to the industrial and service sectors (Williams, 1984: 8-9). The existence of low cost and surplus labour, together with the absence of labour unions, contributed significantly to the rapid industrialisation of these countries in this period. The internationalisation of their economies intensified and, accordingly, they signed association and special trade agreements with the

EEC: Greece in 1961 (an association agreement), Spain in 1970 and Portugal in 1972.

Three main factors played an important role in the process of internationalisation: foreign investment and technological transfer, emigration and tourism (Williams, 1984: 10). In relation to foreign investment, Hudson and Lewis (1984) enumerate four factors for the flow of private foreign investment capital into GSP: the availability of natural resources, the absence of environmental measures, access for domestic and third country markets, and the availability of low cost flexible labour. Of these four factors, market access was the most important because in addition to penetrating GSP's domestic markets, foreign capital gained better access to the markets of third countries. Between 1950 and the mid-1970s, the largest share of foreign investment capital in the GSP economies was American (Hudson and Lewis, 1984: 188). By investing in GSP, foreign industrial capital aimed at penetrating domestic markets and also at establishing platforms for export to North Africa and the Middle East (Williams, 1984: 15). Furthermore, US and Japan-dominated multinationals gained better access to EC markets (Hudson and Lewis, 1984: 188).

The second important element of the internationalisation of GSP economies was the emigration of southern European peasants to Western Europe where there was a demand for low-wage labour during the 1950s and 1960s. The remittances of these emigrant workers reached significant levels in the early 1970s, and although they spent on consumption rather than production, they made important positive contributions to the balance of payment deficits of these countries. Like workers' remittances, the third factor of internationalisation, namely tourism, contributed significantly to the balance of payments accounts. Increasing living standards in Western Europe, as a result of the postwar economic boom and the geographical proximity and climatic characteristics of GSP, led Western Europeans to spend their leisure time and money in their relatively poor southern neighbours.

Between the end of the Second World War and the mid-1970s, GSP dictatorships tried to adapt their economies to the requirements of new hegemonic structures and in this way they remained in power until the mid-1970s. However, the gradual liberalisation and expansion of their economies without concomitant political liberalisation paved the way for their eventual collapse in the mid-1970s. In fact, by the early 1970s, GSP dictatorships had almost totally lost their social bases. Hence even their attempts to liberalise the political system could not prevent their collapse. On the other hand, apart from being incorporated into new world economic structures, on the strategic front they had become faithful followers of American anti-Soviet, anti-Communist policies. Accordingly, while Greece and Portugal were incorporated into NATO, Spain was attached to the Western alliance through bilateral agreements with the US in the early 1950s.

Developments in the world-economy in the early 1970s slowed down economic growth in GSP countries. The abolition of the fixed exchange rate principle by the Americans and the collapse of the monetary system established at Bretton Woods, recession in the OECD economies and the two oil-price shocks, the first in 1973 and the second in 1979, led to economic difficulties in GSP. Moreover, the decline in tourism revenues and in the demand for emigrant workers, coupled with the sharp rise in energy costs, hit the energy dependent economies of the three countries. All these developments in the world and national economies contributed significantly to the collapse of GSP authoritarian regimes.

However, after the collapse of the dictatorships, the newly established democracies paid attention to political stability and the consolidation of democracy against a possible authoritarian counter-revolution, and they postponed dealing with economic difficulties caused by the dramatic developments in the world-economy (Diamandouros, 1986a: 551-556). On the strategic front, the oil crises increased the importance of the Mediterranean region and thus the necessity of pro-western stability in GSP countries, which in turn contributed to the democratisation processes and to increasing support from the West.

In order to strengthen their democratic structures and to neutralise any attempt to revitalise the old structures, the new or renewed political and economic elites of GSP undertook both domestic and external measures. Domestically, they focused on creating a consensus among social and political forces on the terms of the transition to democracy (see Agüero, 1995; Schmitter, 1995; and Morlino, 1995). Internationally, they sought economic, political and ideological support from international actors, especially from the EEC/EC (see, Pridham, 1995). I shall focus on this period later in the chapters on individual countries. Here, suffice it to say that in the domestic sphere dramatic shifts in the stances of both conservative and left-wing forces from extremist to moderate positions made consensus possible, not only on the terms of transition, but on the consolidation of democracy. The advent to power of democratic socialist parties in the three countries in the 1980s proved the success of the democratisation processes started in the mid-1970s. The measures taken in the international sphere for a peaceful transition to, and the consolidation of, democracy also proved fruitful. Accordingly, in the 1980s GSP became full members of the

EEC/EC. However, it should be emphasised that although at first primarily political and ideological support was sought in the external sphere, in the face of severe economic disturbances it did not take long before decisive international support was extended to GSP to neutralise the negative effects of world economic disturbances on the process of democratisation (Tovias, 1984: 169).

These are the major points that gave every GSP researcher the inspiration to employ a comparative perspective in studying the region. However, although the convergences provided their starting points, each individual researcher refined and redefined them in according with their respective frameworks. By taking these general issues into consideration in the context of world-system analysis, the following country chapters will specifically examine the impact of structural change in the postwar world-system on the economic and political structures of semiperipheral Greece and Spain. In doing so, I shall examine individual actions taken by Greek and Spanish economic and political elites vis-à-vis the observed changes and the impact of these changes on foreign policy developments.

Chapter 2

Greece: 1945-1974

This chapter analyses Greece's semiperipheral development and foreign policy between the end of the Second World War and the collapse of the military dictatorship in 1974. This period of Greek history overlaps the expansion period of the world-economy. In world-system analysis there is a close relationship between the world-economy, the state of the national economy, and the politics and foreign policy of a semiperipheral state. World-system analysis provides the global and national economic environments in which the main directions of the domestic politics and foreign policies of individual states are to be analysed. The world-system perspective examines system-wide dynamics, as well as national processes, and accordingly developments in these environments become the main sources for foreign policy behaviour of semiperipheral states. In world-system analysis, the general foreign policy orientations of semiperipheral states in expansion and contraction periods may take different forms. In expansion periods semiperipheral states tend to become satellites of a hegemonic power. In other words, the foreign policies of semiperipheral states are designed by the hegemonic power, and their national interests are mostly subordinated to the global and local interests of the hegemonic/core powers.

The Economic Environment

The state has a central place in the semiperipheral zone of the world-economy. In world-system analysis the study of a semiperipheral country essentially means the study of its state, because the political processes in relation to the economy, that is the relations between state policies and the accumulation of capital, are the key to observing developments in other spheres of activity in semiperipheral countries. The state is more important in the semiperiphery than in the core or periphery, since it is the main locus in which central economic actors can effectively promote their interests. Thus the struggle to control and/or transform state policies is the main activity of semiperipheral economic actors: owner-producers (both core-like and periphery-like), work force, and multinationals, and so forth.

Nevertheless the process of capital accumulation in the semiperiphery is not a one-way phenomenon. The direction of capital accumulation is not only determined through the state-oriented activities of different economic actors, but also through state policies as well. First of all, in the semiperiphery the state is not a passive recipient of the policies of different economic interests; it may favour the interests of different groups, which is why different groups fight for influence over state policies. Perhaps a more important point is that the semiperipheral state itself may take steps to create opportunities for entrepreneurs, and it sometimes takes on an entrepreneurial role itself (Chase-Dunn, 1989: 120). Thus, the state often becomes a pioneer of the development process in semiperipheral countries with potential upward mobility (Chase-Dunn, 1989: 241). In the semiperiphery, therefore capital accumulation is a process where both "state-oriented" and "state-originated" policies may play important roles.

A cursory glance at the Greek political economy in the 1950s and first half of the 1960s reveals that the Greek state intervened in the domestic market in favour of the interests of financial and industrial monopoly capital, which could be considered the periphery-like producers of the country. They were periphery-like in the sense that the capital equipment of even large scale industrial units was old or inferior in quality (Coutsoumaris, 1963: 309). This led to high cost and inefficient production, and hence, an unwillingness to compete with foreign and potential new domestic firms (Ellis, 1964: 180).

In this period, one of the main characteristics of Greek industry, which was composed of many small firms and few large ones, was its monopolistic and oligopolistic structure (Ellis, 1964: 175-179). Almost all monopolistic and oligopolistic sectors were protected against newcomers by the state regulation known as the "expediency licence law". State intervention was realised primarily through an extensive system of permits that were needed for establishing and locating business, and also for making changes, such as expanding, merging or moving, and so on (Ellis, 1964: 181). The stated aim of this policy was to prevent the entry of new firms into saturated fields, but under pressure from existing monopolistic firms to retain their privileged positions, it was misused (Ellis, 1964: 180). A striking characteristic of the "expediency licence law" was that it gave related ministers the right to issue the permits, which in turn led ministers to exercise subjective judgements and considerations based on political pressures and personal relations, rather than economic criteria.[1] Another type of state intervention that favoured "peripheral producers" was the tariff system and import policy that both provided a powerful shelter to inefficient Greek firms against competitive foreign products. The protectionist devices used by the Greek state were import licensing, import payment controls, preference for domestic producers in government purchases, tariffs, and quotas (Ellis, 1964: 333).

Although the Greek state provided both internal and external protection to domestic monopoly and oligopoly capital, this did not lead to increasing investment or to the introduction of new industrial technologies, which might be considered the logical consequence of such protectionist policies. On the contrary, it led to a decreasing propensity to invest and a further strengthening of the monopolistic structure. More seriously, it discouraged potential investors who could promote core-like production patterns by using advanced technology.

Another striking feature of the Greek economy in the 1950s and 1960s was the bilateral monopolistic relationship between industrial capital and powerful finance capital. Greek finance capital, which was dominated by two commercial banks (The National and Commercial Banks) controlling more than 90 percent of all assets and the insurance market in the country (Psilos, 1964: 186), was the most significant source of private finance for entrepreneurs. The relationship between these large financial groups (especially the two commercial banking groups) and large scale industrial monopolies and oligopolies was turned into a concentration of peripheral interests by way of participation of the commercial banks' capital in the share capital of many industrial firms (Ellis, 1964: 197 and Psilos, 1964: 189). This intimate relationship between finance and industrial capital was consolidated by the dependence of firms upon the banks' working capital, the direct or indirect participation of high level bank officers on the board of directors of these large firms, and also by the bank's preferential treatment in granting loans to these firms and refusing them to potential rival industrialists (Ellis, 1964: 197).

The relationship between the state and finance capital also revealed interesting features. Throughout this period, the state exercised considerable authority over the banking system by controlling the credit market and maintaining the rules for extending credits. The commercial banks for a long time depended on the state's central bank for the funds made available by American aid (Halikas, 1978: 3-10). Moreover, the governor of the National Bank, whose views on economic policies had decisive influence, was appointed by the government (Psilos, 1964: 193). It is also worth noting the influence of finance capital on state policies. Their continuous pressure on the state not to allow foreign banks to establish branches in the country, so that they retained their oligopolistic privileges in the finance market (Halikas, 1978: 15 and 30), and similarly their stubborn resistance to the establishment of long-term semi-state financing institutions via the governor of the National Bank, a state appointed official (Psilos, 1964: 192), demonstrated finance capital's powerful position in the Greek establishment. Accordingly, the state's long-term financial institutions, for example the Economic Development Financing Organisation (EDFO), were managed in a way that could not harm the interests of Greek financial capital. A significant part of their funds were allocated to inefficient undertakings out of political, rather than economic, considerations (Psilos, 1964: 226). Similarly, although EDFO was established to finance the industrial sector, a significant part of its credits went to the primary production and agricultural sector (Psilos, 1964: 226). The negative attitude of finance capital towards the state-owned EDFO became clear when the plan to turn EDFO into a semi-public, efficient investment organisation was cancelled because of their pressure on the Greek state (Psilos, 1964: 192-193).

It was obvious that the web of relations and interconnections between (periphery-like) industrial capital, finance capital and the Greek state was perpetuating the continuation of a stagnant, uncompetitive, labour intensive production structure with high cost production and outdated technology. Ellis argues that Greece lacked a dynamic economy because the small ruling elite in the political and economic spheres had close ties with one other:

> The ingrown quality of Greece's small ruling elite, closely interconnecting political, financial and industrial circles, is the major factor here. Thus, at both levels in Greece, no finance is desired from outside the group whether that be the family typically owning a small firm or the elite circle controlling the large firms and the banks. (Ellis, 1964: 63).

Consequently, state policies in Greece usually promoted the interests of periphery-like industrial producers, or the latter blocked the state's developmental economic policies.

A third section of capital that occupied a significant place in the political economy of Greece in this period came from shipping. Although the financing of Greek shipping was dependent on foreign, particularly American, sources (Serafetinidis, 1979: 59), the interaction between the Greek state and Greek shipowners has always been close. As Serafetinidis put it:

> The Greek state has been the *sine qua non* factor in the development of the Greek shipping industry. The dependence of Greece's shipping capital on the Greek state's support and protection is one more aspect of the latter's Greek nature... Whether or not some of these shipping firms have acquired a multinational character, in the crucial take off stage, as well as moment of crisis involving competition with shipping firms of other maritime nations, and in regard to more basic and daily questions of finance and taxation, it is to the Greek state that they have turned for help. (Serafetinidis, 1979: 61).

With American assistance, the Greek state contributed decisively to the revitalisation of the devastated Greek merchant fleet in the immediate postwar years. Moreover, in 1953 Greek shipping, like foreign investment, was granted extensive privileges and concessions through the foreign investment legislative decree of 2687/1953 (Serafetinidis et al, 1981: 249).

The relationship between shipping and finance capital is also worth mentioning. Although Greek finance capital did little to finance the shipping industry directly, it gave indirect support through letters of guarantee, assistance in the establishment of new companies and intervention in times of crisis (Serafetinidis, 1979: 61). Moreover, the fact that Andreadis, the owner of the Commercial Bank of Greece, was at the same time an important shipowner demonstrates the close relationship between shipping and finance capital. When it is added that Andreadis was the state's favourite banker (Psilos, 1964: 217), the web of Greek political economy becomes evident. Finally, the monopoly privileges given to Niarchos, another important shipowner, in the shipbuilding industry, and the unwillingness of the state to grant licences to competitors in this sector further underlines the close relationship between the Greek state and shipowners (Ellis, 1964: 185).

However, the most important actor in the Greek economy at that time was the US. The central global aim of US policy makers was the reestablishment of world-wide liberal economic transactions. Greece, strategically located at the crossroads of the sea and air routes of three continents and the oil-rich Middle East and with a long commitment to western liberal ideology, was crucial to the new liberal economic world order for the smooth recovery and the functioning of the system.

Yet the outlook for the Greek economy in the immediate postwar years was very grim: the economy was ruined by the Second World War and the civil war, and was without significant agricultural and industrial structure and production (see Kofas, 1989: 8-13). As the new hegemonic power of the world economy, it became clear to the Americans that massive aid would have to be poured into the Greek economy. Accordingly, US dollars were extended to Greece through the Truman Doctrine and Marshall Plan for the preservation of a liberal ideology and the reconstruction of the Greek economy. OEEC/OECD country reports between 1952 and 1963 show that this American aid continued until the early 1960s.

The terms and the conditions of American aid were set by US officials (Kofas, 1990: 54). The implementation of the aid plan was to be supervised and administered by an American team called the American Mission for Aid to Greece (AMAG), which was given limitless authority to control the organs of the Greek state and government. AMAG experts included military officers, economic advisers, agronomists, engineers, industrial technicians, and experts on finance, welfare, transportation and labour relations. They were installed in ministries and other state and governmental agencies to control the implementation of aid. Their powers were such that without the approval of the Americans, the Greek authorities were unable to take important decisions (Kofas, 1990: 55). The AMAG gave priority to economic and military affairs. In the economy, American officials influenced monetary, fiscal and commercial policies by dominating important committees such as the Currency Committee, the Foreign Trade Administration, and the Central Loan Committee.

The second American economic initiative in Greece came with the European Recovery Plan (ERP), also known as the Marshall Plan. It was put into effect when the Greek-American Co-operation Agreement was signed in 1948 and the AMAG was replaced by the Economic Co-operation Administration/Greece (ECA/G). The ECA/G, like the AMAG, controlled Greek credit and fiscal policies, and hence determined the direction of production, capital development, taxes, wages and salaries (Kofas, 1989: 110). Although credit policies were ultimately formulated by the state, the Americans controlled them through Legislative Decree 588. The second article of the law stated that "The Currency Committee shall determine from time to time by its decisions the details of the financing of each branch of production, the total amounts of credits to be granted and the terms and preliminary conditions under which they are to be made available by banks, other credit organisations, or any other kind of public law organisation whatsoever, either out of their own funds or out of funds made available to them by the Bank of Greece" (quoted in Kofas, 1990: 66). The ECA/G had the power of both advising and directing the Greek government in using aid, in planning, and disposing of domestic resources. Furthermore, the Greek government had to inform both the ECA Commission and the US government about any development or plan that could affect aid flows.

Nevertheless, the Greek state was given important roles for the distribution and implementation of the American aid program, which in turn contributed to the development of intimate relations with the Americans and the increase of US influence over the political economy of Greece. In this way, links were also established between the Americans and different factions of the Greek economic elite. First of all, links with finance capital were established by depositing American funds in the banking system (Halikas, 1978: 31). American aid funds, which were deposited mostly in the Central Bank of Greece, closely tied the Americans, state officials and finance capital to each other in the process of the management and use of these funds. In the absence of domestic savings,[2] commercial banks became dependent on the Central Bank whose loans were made up of US aid, and on the Currency Committee, which was also monitored by the Americans for their monetary and credit policies. Under these circumstances, it was not surprising that the interests of industrial capital were incorporated into the interests of other actors largely through the distribution of credits. Given the intermingled characteristics of Greek industrial and financial capital, it became easy to see the established interests between the Americans, the Greek state, and finance and industrial capital.

Long-term credits in industry, mostly from direct American aid, were granted under the auspices of American officials (Ellis, 1964: 272). Thus, it was apparent that the Americans were not against the way the Greek authorities distributed American funds among Greek industrial capitalists. However, the important point is that US funds were distributed to privileged large and old industrial interests, which were constituted of inefficient enterprises with antiquated machines and outmoded labour intensive production, and entrepreneurs invested in real estate and other speculative areas rather than in the modernisation and expansion of their industries - entrepreneurs that we may categorise as "periphery-like producers".

The relations between Americans and Greek shipping capital developed in parallel to these general practices (Serafetinidis et al., 1981: 292). During the Second World War almost 75 percent of the Greek merchant fleet had been destroyed. In order to reconstruct the shipping sector the Greek government, in collaboration with the AMAG, prepared a reconstruction program for which American funds were used (Serafetinidis, 1979: 62). Furthermore, a second decisive step was the purchase of 100 Liberty type ships from the US government under favourable conditions[3] guaranteed by the Greek state (Serafetinidis et al., 1981: 294).

US support to Greek shipping capital provided shipowners with the opportunity to realise large profits in the international market, which made

Greece one of the world's leading maritime powers. Accordingly, during the 1950s Greek shipowners became the major sea carriers of US imports and exports. Furthermore, a significant part of Middle Eastern oil was carried by Greek tankers (see Serafetinidis, 1979: 119-121 and Serafetinidis et al., 1981: 295-296) and Greek shipowners made immense profits through US protection and preferential treatment. Hence, Greek shipowners, whose prosperity depended on their American connections and effective American control of the sea routes, were also incorporated into the broad alliance between the interests of the Greek economic elites and American hegemony.

Economic relations between the USA and Greece took place primarily within the public sector until the early 1960s. American capital flow into Greece in this period took the form of public grants and loans. But the Americans also signed the US-Greek Agreement of 1948 that emphasised the global liberal principles of the new economic world order. It included provisions regarding private sector relations (Thomadakis, 1980: 76-77) that stressed the international free trade principle and the avoidance of protectionist and anti-trust policies.

The most significant step to liberalise the economy and to attract foreign investment capital was taken in April 1953 as a result of American pressure. The Greek government devalued the Drachma by a hundred percent and abolished quantitative restrictions on imports, special import taxes, and export subsidies. A special law, Law Decree 2687 of 1953, was introduced to attract foreign investment capital, and it became the basic Greek law for the protection of foreign capital. It was given constitutional protection in order to make foreign investment in Greece more attractive. It protected foreign investment against expropriation and made the terms of agreements irrevocable to protect against political change and unilateral alterations by governments. It also ensured capital mobility by allowing the free repatriation of imported capital and remittance earnings. The most important clause covered preferential tax treatment. It meant the reduction or waiver of import duties, fees and dues of various kinds, and freezing and forgiveness of income taxes on profits.

In this way, the formerly autarkic Greek economy was forced by US hegemony to reopen to core interests. From this perspective the 1948 US-Greek Economic Agreement and the liberalisation policies implemented in 1953, together with the accompanying foreign investment law, can be seen as deliberate attempts by the US, an external actor, to affect the policies of the Greek state in order to promote its own global interests.

In the semiperiphery, capitalists may have alliances with core powers based on their control of peripheral activities, or capitalists may follow independent policies that would expand core type activities. Furthermore, the state often plays a dominant role in the formation of political coalitions among economic groups (Chase-Dunn, 1989: 241). As far as Greece is concerned, the coalition between the US and finance, industrial, and to some extent, shipping capital served to consolidate peripheral activities in the economy, and the state played an important role in promoting the interests of these groups.

The Political Environment

In world-system analysis, during an expansion period semiperipheral countries are subject to high degrees of direct intervention in their internal affairs by hegemonic/core states. Semiperipheral countries tend to become satellites/client states of core powers and/or a political agent of a hegemonic power turning it ideologically and politically into a political appendage. In this context, it is illuminating to examine the political structure of Greece in this economic environment and to consider whether it revealed semiperipheral characteristics in the expansion period of the world-economy.

The politics of the postwar period in Greece was the politics of Greek-American relations. All the major Greek political actors and institutions came under US influence and policies were largely dictated by the Americans. The major preoccupation of US hegemony was the containment of communism and the Soviet Union, since communism was seen as the main threat to the legitimisation and consolidation of the new economic world order. Hence, anti-communism became the central political and ideological reference point around which almost all the personalities and issues in Greek politics converged. The Greek establishment was turned by its own political actors - the monarchy, the army and the parliament - into a faithful political agent for the implementation of anti-communist policies.

The American view of Greece at this time was that of a poor country devastated during the occupation and war, and a country fighting against a strong internal communist insurgency and surrounded by three communist neighbours, Albania, Yugoslavia and Bulgaria. If Greece fell into communist hands this would be a severe setback for the Americans and for the new economic world order. It would mean the loss of US control in the Middle East, Near East and North Africa, and it would also encourage other communist groups elsewhere in the world. Hence, the Americans concluded that Greece needed urgent and massive American political, economic and military aid for the salvation of its future and the survival of the new world order under US hegemony. Accordingly, the announcement of the Truman Doctrine in 1947 marked the beginning of heavy American penetration in Greece. Between May 1947 and June 1956, American aid had amounted to $2,565 million. This was the highest per capita aid received by any US aid recipient country in the early postwar years (Couloumbis, 1966: 28). Half of the aid provided by the Truman Doctrine went to the army and the other half was for reconstruction. American experts administered the relief program and helped to work out policies connected with finance, trade, exchange control, civil service, and price and wage regulation. These experts were assigned to the ministries in an advisory or supervisory capacity (Rousseas, 1968: 81). From this point onwards, a relationship was established which can be called "unconditional Atlanticism".

The monarchy was one of the three elements of the Greek establishment through which the Americans established control over Greek internal affairs. Government instability made it almost impossible to fight effectively against the Greek communist army. The Americans concluded that apart from military and economic aid, Greece urgently needed a stable political body around which anti-communist political forces could unite. Accordingly, in spite of their early criticisms and opposition, the Americans turned to the monarchy as a reliable anti-Communist rallying point.[4] The monarchy was re-established and the King began to be seen by the Americans as the "ultimate guarantor of political stability, military preparedness and loyalty to the western alliance" (Iatrides, 1980: 67).

The Americans also established control over Greek parliamentary forces. Although the main argument between the conservative and liberal parties before the war had concerned the legitimacy of the monarchy (Tsoukalas, 1969: 107 and Rousseas, 1968: 84), the new American attitude resolved this problem in favour of the King, and the liberals accepted the legitimacy of the Palace. The outbreak of the Civil War, and the American demand that the conservatives and liberals cooperate if they wished to receive aid, removed the differences between these two large political parties and hence united the Greek establishment. In fact, the Greek political elite welcomed American intervention. They believed that it was only through American aid and protection that the devastated economy could be reconstructed and the communist threat prevented. From then on, conservatives and liberals/centrists competed with each other for American favour. Their support to the Americans was so unconditional that the centrist Venizelos told the second secretary of the American embassy that both he and Kanellopoulos (a conservative) would abide by the advice given, twice repeating "We are desirous of following the instructions of the US government" (quoted in Roubatis, 1987: 35). The Americans frequently intervened in the formation and resignation of coalition governments. It became usual for high level American diplomats to control the resignations of Greek Prime Ministers. For example, Henderson, a senior State Department official in Near Eastern Affairs, simply told Prime Minister Tsaldaris that he would have to resign. Similarly, US ambassador Grady had sent Venizelos a letter saying that they did not want to work with his government (Roubatis, 1987: 40-42 and 83). In other words, governments rose and fell through American directives.

In 1952 the Americans, frustrated by the acute instability and repeated talk of "fresh" elections, announced significant reductions in American aid. The US ambassador, Peurifoy, intervened in order to convert the electoral system from a proportional to a majority system. At this time, the newly established conservative Greek Rally Party headed by the ex-chief of the Greek Military Staff, Marshal Papagos, appeared as the most suitable American ally. Indeed, he had shown his willingness to cooperate by stating that Greece exists because the Americans exist.[5] Accordingly, the majority electoral system "advised" by the US ambassador was adopted by the Greek parliament and Papagos's conservative Greek Rally came to power with an overwhelming majority. A twelve-year period (1952-1963) of uninterrupted conservative rule began with strong and stable governments.

The army was another important element of the Greek establishment through which the US exercised influence, becoming the main bastion of the Americans. It always maintained a high degree of autonomy in relation to parliament and the palace. The successes of the communists in the civil war, and the outbreak of the Cold War, had forced the Americans to give the Greek army a prominent role against the suppression of communism, and the army was turned into a die-hard anti-Communist institution.

Nothing could be changed in the Greek army without prior consultation and approval of the US authorities. Retirements and promotions were decided jointly by the Greek government, the Greek General Staff, the American ambassador to Greece, the chief of AMAG, and the American General in charge of the US Army Group in Greece (Roubatis, 1987: 44). Moreover, a Joint United States Military Advisory and Planning Group (JUSMAPG) was established to implement new US military plans in the civil war. The establishment of JUSMAPG envisaged the elimination of the Greek government's input on the question of changes to the Greek General Staff. In this way, "the Greek army was transformed into a military establishment made up of Greek soldiers and staffed by Greek officers but with foreigners having the final word on its make up and operations"

(Roubatis, 1987: 61). In other words, the army was freed from Greek civilian political control and answerable only to its foreign advisers. The Americans deemed it imperative for the Greek army to be isolated from society and freed from ideological quarrels, so that it could maintain unity and carry out its duties effectively against the communists (Veremis, 1988: 242). The position of the army was further strengthened by the outbreak of the Korean War and the subsequent incorporation of Greece into NATO. The Greek army, with its own secret service and intelligence agency, soon became the central actor fighting against the internal enemy - communism. Furthermore, in order to control left wing activities, the Greek intelligence agency KYP was founded under the direction of the CIA (Stern, 1977: 13). The personnel and functions of the CIA and KYP were closely intermingled: the KYP was equipped with American technology and its personnel were trained by the Americans (Iatrides, 1980: 67).

American intervention into Greek internal affairs was summarised in a document, which listed the duties to be carried out by the US ambassador to Athens. According to this document, the US ambassador had ultimate authority over:

a) Any action by United States representatives in connection with a change in the Greek cabinet.
b) Any action by United States representatives to bring about or prevent a change in the high command of the Greek armed forces.
c) Any major question involving the relations of Greece with the United Nations or any foreign nation other than the United States.
d) Any major question involving the policies of the Greek government toward Greek political parties, trade unions, subversive elements, rebelled armed forces, etc.
e) Any question involving the holding of elections in Greece (Iatrides, 1980: 65).

Thus in the 1950s a stable political environment and a strong coalition between the monarchy, army and the parliamentary right was established by the Americans. This authoritarian conservatism, which has been identified with the Americans and Atlanticism, ruled the country (except for a brief period between 1964-1965) until the summer of 1974. The establishment of political stability was a success for the global interests of the Americans. For the next eleven years, Greek governments would not oppose American interference in Greek internal and external policies, even when they were in conflict with "Greek national interests".

The main political preoccupation of the US in Greece was the suppression of communism. Communism was understood broadly as any kind of leftist or even democratic activity. The loss of Greece to communism or even to neutralism was unacceptable to the American designed new world order, since it would mean the loss of trade and oil routes and other strategic areas in the Eastern Mediterranean, Middle East, and North Africa. Hence, Greece became a politically stable pro-western and anti-Communist state after 1952 and was integrated into NATO. Once internal order and US control were established, Greek internal politics became less important to the Americans. Priority was now given to the country's external relations. Thus it is not surprising that important foreign policy decisions were taken in the eleven uninterrupted right-wing years of Greek political history.

Foreign Policy: Atlanticist Years

In world-system analysis foreign policy does not constitute a separate area of inquiry, because it is considered a function of internal and external economic and political environments. In expansion periods of the world-economy, the foreign policies of semiperipheral states are oriented towards the accomplishment of the global objectives of the hegemonic power, and most of the policies are dictated by the hegemonic power. In other words, in the sphere of foreign policy semiperipheral states tend to become satellites of hegemonic power in the expansion periods of the world-economy.

In parallel to the heavy American influence and intervention in other spheres, Greece (except for a brief period in the early 1960s) followed an American-oriented foreign policy almost unconditionally. Greek foreign policy was designed by the Americans to further the integration, consolidation and preservation of the new world order. Accordingly, Greece left the formulation and implementation of its defence policies to the Americans; sent troops to Korea; joined NATO; signed bilateral base agreements with the US; formed a Balkan Pact with Turkey and Yugoslavia; and signed an agreement with Turkey and Britain for the creation of an independent Cypriot state that was not in conformity with its "national interests". Finally, Greece became an associate member of the EEC. In the formulation and implementation of most of these decisions, Greeks were passive and did not raise any significant opposition to the subordination of Greek interests to the global and local interests of the US.

From the American perspective, Greece was vitally important for the new world order because of its strategic geographical location in the

Mediterranean and the Balkans. Hence, the territorial integrity and "political independence" of Greece became a major concern of US policy makers.

In the late 1940s and early 1950s, the relations between the two Cold War blocs deteriorated. NATO was established in 1949 as the major Western defensive institution against possible communist aggression. The first Soviet nuclear explosion, the loss of China to the communists, the Korean War, increasing Soviet pressure over Yugoslavia, and political deterioration in the Middle East caused the Americans to revise their global policies. They became much more suspicious of communism. This was soon reflected in American policy towards Greece. American support for civil rights was abandoned and Greek politicians were encouraged to take tougher measures against communists (Roubatis, 1987: 74).

A significant development was the admission of Greece into NATO in 1952 with the American initiative despite the opposition of some European members. Greek right wing and centrist parliamentary elites attached prime importance to NATO membership. During the parliamentary debates, their enthusiasm reached such a point that a leading conservative MP, Kanellopoulos, maintained that "Greece's membership in the NATO was a very good thing and hence prolonged debates on the subject were not required" arguing that "this would insult the western allies" (Couloumbis, 1966: 47). The treaty was passed by parliament quickly and without any serious discussion.

Hence, in 1952 Greece was integrated into the major military institution of the new world order by American initiative. However, NATO membership meant that defence and security policies and investments would be planned according to the needs of the Atlantic Alliance rather than Greece's specific interests. In other words, NATO membership would be beneficial only if Greek "national interests" coincided with the global interests of the Alliance. This situation came to the surface with the emergence of the Cyprus problem after the mid-1950s.

Another remarkable American initiative in this period was the 1953 Bases Agreement to establish US military bases in Greece. When the conservative Papagos came to power and political stability had been established, a bilateral agreement was signed on the use of Greek territory by the US armed forces. In fact, however the bases were established not in northern Greece, where the country faced its major threats, but on the islands and in the capital (Roubatis, 1987: 123). This suited the American strategic defence plan for Greece, which placed more importance on the islands than on the mainland.

The reactions of leading members of the conservative government to the Bases Agreement demonstrate that they were devoted to a policy of Atlanticism. Foreign minister Stephanopoulos argued that "those who were opposed to the agreement should also be opposed to Greece's continued membership in NATO since the two were closely interrelated...and that if Greece refuses to ratify the agreement she would be expelled from NATO".[6] Couloumbis points out that "Greek politicians considered entry into NATO a by-product of Greek-US cooperation which had commenced with the Truman Doctrine" (Couloumbis, 1966: 197).

The Balkan Pact in 1954 was another American project that consolidated Greece's satellite position. One reason for establishing this politico-military pact was the Soviet hostility towards Greece, Turkey and especially Tito's Yugoslavia. However, there was another important American consideration: through this pact Yugoslavia would be indirectly linked to NATO, and hence could serve as an example for other Balkan and Eastern European countries (Stavrou, 1980: 155). In other words, this was seen as the means by which the US could infiltrate the communist bloc.

Greece also had its own national external objectives. In the immediate postwar years, Greece had territorial claims on its neighbours: on southern Albania, the Dodecanese Islands (Italy), on Cyprus (Britain), and at the Greek-Bulgarian border. However, only the Dodecanase Islands in the Aegean Sea were ceded to Greece by Italy. The Americans were unsympathetic to Greek territorial ambitions in the Balkans and Cyprus, and these demands were frustrated immediately (Coufoudakis, 1987: 232).

In this context, Cyprus became a striking example of Greek "national interests" being subordinated to the interests of the Atlanticist world order. After the war, Greek claims for the unification of Cyprus with Greece were opposed by Britain, the colonial power. The US had supported the British position. The renewal of Greek claims on Cyprus stemmed from the acceleration of British decolonization in the second half of the 1950s. Greece was again rebuffed by the UK and the US, and attempts to raise the question in the UN were also frustrated by the Americans and other NATO partners. The conservative Greek government was accommodating, emphasising the primacy and importance of Atlantic relations over the Cyprus issue. The majority of the Greek political elite believed that although unification was desirable, it should not jeopardise Greece's relations with the US and NATO (Couloumbis, 1966: 201).

The strategic location of Cyprus in the Middle East and Eastern Mediterranean made control of the island vitally important to the Atlantic Alliance. The British did not want to lose its military stronghold on the island. Moreover, as long as the island was open to the use of US army and intelligence services, Americans preferred to see British domination of Cyprus, rather than its unification with a weak and vulnerable Greece. Furthermore, the increasing neutralist and leftist tendencies in Cyprus made the Americans cautious about control of the island.

However, a solution to the problem had to be found in order to reduce anti-colonial movements, and to decrease the nationalistic feelings of both Greeks and Turks on the island for the sake of the smooth functioning of the new world order. The US proposed a partnership between Greece, Turkey and Britain to administer Cyprus. This plan was an "embarrassment" for the Greeks because it made Turkey another legitimate party on the island. However, succumbing to US pressure, all the parties on the island agreed to the establishment of an independent Cypriot republic in 1959-1960. Although the agreement was not in conformity with the Greek objective of unification, it was ratified in the Greek parliament by a substantial majority.

This solution of the Cyprus problem was welcomed by the Americans because it maintained US global interests in the Eastern Mediterranean, which had been jeopardised by the dispute between Greece and Turkey, two NATO member countries. Not only did this agreement satisfy US strategic needs in the Eastern Mediterranean, but

> Britain was able to retain two large sovereign bases on the island that the US could use, and the listening monitoring stations of the Central Intelligence Agency were given permission to continue their operations there. Greece and Turkey did not go to war over Cyprus and the whole matter was kept away from international organisations where other states with interests in the area might have had a chance to exert influence that could have endangered American and NATO interests in the Eastern Mediterranean (Roubatis, 1987: 141-142).

Further evidence of Greece's pro-Atlanticist external policy is provided by Greek support for US Cold War policies in the UN, where it voted against or abstained on Chinese entry to the UN; US intervention in Cuba; and the creation of a zone free from nuclear missiles and bases in the Balkans and Central Europe (quoted in Couloumbis, 1966: 136).

An Early Challenge to Atlanticism

In the early 1960s there was a challenge to the established order in Greece from almost all directions that led to the collapse of the stability established among the economic elites, the political establishment, and the US in the postwar period. These changes were reflected in Greek foreign policy.

While close relations between the dominant economic elites were stable in the 1950s, there was increasing opposition to monopolistic and oligopolistic structures and state policies that favoured big business interests. As mentioned, the credit market conditions that favoured only the established firms had reduced the demand for long-term loans. In fact, it was very difficult for new enterprises to gain access to financial resources. The problem was not the lack of loans, but their allocation to speculative areas, and the excessive controls and formalities on free investment (OECD, 1963: 35-36).

In 1962, the Federation of Greek Industrialists (SEV) began to publicise factors that made it impossible to borrow money (Ellis, 1964: 62). The resentments and the demands of the Industrialists on the government began to appear in the Federation's fortnightly bulletin *Deltion*, (Lavdas, 1997: 124). It was obvious that the existing system was hindering industrial expansion and the inflow of new investment capital. These hindrances resulted in the strengthening of unfair competition and non-competitive industries, the dampening of entrepreneurial activity; the creation of monopolies, and production with antiquated equipment.

Two important developments in the early 1960s were the association of Greece with the EEC and the enactment of new incentive laws for the inflow of foreign investment capital. The Association Agreement with the EEC was considered a revolutionary step (Coutsoumaris, 1963: 326). Some thought that it would make the Greek economy more efficient and competitive through the modernisation of production techniques and equipment. Furthermore, private capital inflow from EEC countries would be increased. However, these developments challenged the vested interests of the American-oriented, periphery-like traditional economic elite.

The Federation of Greek Industrialists (SEV) immediately supported the Association Agreement and closer relations with the EEC (Lavdas, 1997: 123-125 and Serafetinidis, 1979: 230), and joined the Union of Industries of the European Community - UNICE (Lavdas, 1997: 274, endnote 45). Most of SEV's members were industrialists involved in light industry, and they were unhappy with the industrial practices established by the American-oriented traditional economic elite. They made their dislike of the system explicit and supported a more open system in which they could promote their interests more independently. In 1966, the president of the Federation called for the creation of a healthy capital market in Greece, arguing that "Greek industry could no longer be owned and run on a family basis; [and] consequently

Greek industrialists, like industrialists all over the world, would have to integrate their firms into efficient units and finance their enterprises through the capital market" (quoted in Serafetinidis, 1979: 230). They believed that closer relations with the EEC would remove barriers set by the periphery-like American-oriented economic elite.

Although substantial economic growth was achieved under the conditions of financial stability during the 1950s (OECD, 1966: 31), too little of it had gone to transformative sectors of the industry. The structural weakness of the economy continued, and chronic deficits in the balance of payments were covered by US economic aid until the early 1960s (OEEC/OECD, 1952 to 1963). Because of tight administrative controls and protectionist policies, foreign capital did not invest in Greece as expected (OECD, 1963: 29). The economic situation was not promising. Moreover, the Americans were increasingly unwilling to continue economic aid, and at the same time Greece had to adjust its economy to the economic policies of the EEC, as result of the Association Agreement. Thus there was no option other than renewing their efforts to attract foreign capital.

In fact, this renewed efforts to attract investment was partly due to covert pressure on the Greek state by the US government. The 1953 foreign investment law did not work properly because of Greek government intervention in the market. Hence, US aid cuts in 1962 were partly an attempt to force the government to open and internationalise the economy so that official, state-to-state, American capital could be replaced by private US and multinational capital. Accordingly, in addition to law 2687/1953, parliament passed foreign investment laws of 4171/1961 and 4256/1962, which further increased the favourable climate for foreign investment in Greece. From then on foreign, especially US, capital increasingly began to be invested in the Greek economy, and now this capital went to the transformative sectors where the traditional elite was not willing or able to invest. About $290 million out of a total of $347 million dollars of approved foreign investment, between 1953 and the end of the 1962, was realised between 1960 and 1962 (Ellis, 1964: 287). Two of these industrial projects (which amounted to $166 million of the total $200 million invested in this period) were the Esso-Pappas Oil Refinery Complex ($110 million) and the Pechiney-Niarchos Aluminium Plant ($56.8 million).

The conservative government's policy of granting extraordinary privileges to foreign investment capital was opposed by the European-oriented Federation of Greek Industrialists. One of the main concerns of the Federation was the loss of the domestic market, and accordingly they wanted the government to revise the open door policy so as not to discourage domestic initiative (Ellis, 1964: 299). The chairman of the Federation argued that "it is not in the spirit of the Treaty of Athens to attach undue importance to foreign investment capital which is, of course, welcome in Greece, but under equal terms and conditions with Greek capital, as an associate rather than as an intruder, as an equal partner rather than as a privileged master" (quoted in Ellis, 1964: 300). It was clear that the Federation was demanding a margin of independence from the Greek state vis-à-vis foreign capital.

The liberal Centre Union Party (CU) of Yorgos Papandreou, which promoted economic policies similar to those of the Federation of Greek Industrialists (see Lavdas, 1997: 273/endnote 44), came to power in 1964. The CU government was not against foreign capital, providing foreign investors were willing to invest in Greece under similar competitive conditions to Greek investors (Papandreou, 1967: 183). The new government opposed granting almost unconditional privileges to foreign capital investment and wanted to promote import substitution industrialisation. Moreover, Yorgos Papandreou emphasised the necessity of breaking up the domestic monopolies (periphery-like production units) that had dominated the economy and politics since the end of the Second World War.

As soon as it came to power, Yorgos Papandreou's government demanded a revision of the agreements signed with foreign investors by the conservative government. Disputes arose, first on the granting of a fifty-year monopoly to Pechiney-Niarchos over bauxite mining, and the manufacture and distribution of aluminium, and second with Esso-Pappas on privileges to explore for oil and the control of the distribution of its profits (Georgiou, 1988: 52-54).

The reactions of foreign interests to the CU policy clearly exemplified typical state-oriented policies of a group of (external) economic actors in semiperipheral states. It also illustrated the role of the state as an actor in interstate economic relations. Pechiney called on the French government for assistance, and France boycotted Greek borrowings from international banks (Georgiou, 1988: 53). The British, French and US governments requested Yorgos Papandreou to change his policy towards foreign capital. The American and French ambassadors encouraged rebel CU members to put pressure on the government in favour of foreign interests. Niarchos, a shareholder in Pechiney, demanded intervention by the King to settle the dispute. Andreas Papandreou, a government minister at the time, pointed to heavy American pressure on the government in relation to the Esso-Pappas dispute in an article (Papandreou, 1972: 16). Despite these pressures, Yorgos Papandreou did not change his position. Interestingly, immediately after his row with the King (seemingly over control of the Ministry of Defence, see below) and the subsequent resignation of his government, new agreements with increased incentives (which would be further enhanced by the military regime after 1967) were made with these foreign interests by the new government supported by the King.

Another striking aspect of the new government was its critical stand towards "US-oriented periphery-like capital". According to Andreas Papandreou, in order to increase economic efficiency, the elimination of these peripheral monopolies was imperative. First the credit system that favoured a few entrepreneurs and businessmen, who also had influence over politicians, had to be changed entirely (Papandreou, 1973: 22). Andreas Papandreou was also very critical of the poor technological and organisational standards of Greek industry, emphasising the need for modernisation and the establishment of rationality in all aspects of economic life (Papandreou, 1973: 121). This indicates that the economic policies of the CU government were directed towards promoting the interests of existing and potential (but weak) "Europe-oriented, core-like producers" who had found themselves a place in the Federation of Greek Industrialists. Andreas Papandreou stated that "the long run target of a democratically elected government should be the formulation of a new balance among the existing powers that will allow the government to promote the economic development of the country beyond the realm of vested interests, beyond the values of establishment (Papandreou, 1967a: 171-172) [in order to] lay the foundation for a free, democratic progressive, modern European nation" (Papandreou, 1968: 185).

The policy of the CU government was focused on the steady elimination of existing US-oriented peripheral capitalists, and of the excessive privileges of US dominated foreign investment capital, while supporting and cooperating with the Europe-oriented elements that aimed at modernising and rationalising the Greek economy. It was clear that the economic policies of the CU government threatened the basic pillars of the established system.

Perhaps the most striking development of the 1960s was the emergence of Europe (especially the EEC) as an important actor in Greek affairs. Once the Association Agreement with the Community was signed, it became an important source of financing for the debts and the development program of Greece (OECD, 1963: 34). Thus Greece received a loan of $125 million for a period of five years. The balance of payments deficits, which had been covered by American aid until the 1960s, now began to be offset mainly by the remittances of Greek emigrants working in the major industrial centres of Europe and the increasing inflow of European tourist receipts (OECD, 1964: 17; 1967: 33 and Maddison et al., 1966: 81). With regard to the geographical pattern of trade (import-export), there was a steady shift away from the US towards EEC countries (OECD, 1964: 25). Moreover, Greece was granted credits amounting to $90 million by the European Monetary Fund in 1966 (OECD, 1967: 33). Similarly, foreign capital investment approvals from EEC countries increased significantly after the Association Agreement (Serafetinidis, 1979: 231).

All these developments indicated the beginning of a change in the established economic mechanisms of Greece. The increasing involvement of Europe in the Greek economy coincided with the emergence of a new kind of economic actor (European-oriented elements in the Federation of Greek Industrialists) and economic policies (Yorgos Papandreou Government) critical of the actors (US-oriented periphery-like elements) and practices of the previous period (economic policies of the conservative government.

These developments were echoed in the political sphere. In fact, a part of the parliamentary elite (European-oriented parliamentary elements) challenged the political orientations of the Greek state, which had been practised since the end of the Second World War. The remaining part of the Greek establishment (the Palace, the Army and the rest of the Parliament), together with the US, strongly opposed this challenge. Consequently, this challenge was extinguished in a short period of time, but it was the first signal of a larger challenge that would occur in the contraction period of the world-economy in the mid-1970s.

In the early 1960s it became clear that the political stability of the 1950s, and the balance established between the King, Army and Parliament under the supervision of the US, was coming to an end. The central issue was a clash between the "developmentalist, progressive and European-oriented" political elite of both right wing and centre parliamentary groups and the "anti-developmentalist, authoritarian, and US-oriented" King, Army and the parliamentary elites of both right wing and centre. These divisions mirrored the respective positions of "Europe-oriented core-like capitalists" and "US-oriented periphery-like capitalists".

In the conservative camp, Prime Minister Karamanlis, despite his anti-Communist and pro-American credentials, began to resist US influence and manipulation and to act independently of the King (Couloumbis et al., 1976: 134). He was resentful of the army's independence from civilian authority and the prerogatives of the Monarchy (Clogg, 1986: 179 and Serafetinidis, 1979: 240). Moreover, he had signed the Association Agreement with the EEC. In 1963, however, his moderate challenge to the establishment forced him into self-exile in Paris until the collapse of the military regime in 1974. After Karamanlis, the developmentalist progressive right wing parliamentary elite converged around Kanellopoulos, who argued the need for modernisation in the Greek right (Katris, 1971: 295). It was probably because of the increasingly moderate and progressive attitudes developed within the conservative movement that the military regime, established in 1967, oppressed not only CU politicians, but also progressive elements of the conservatives as well. However, the main challenge came from the developmentalist progressive and Europe-oriented parliamentary elite of the Centre Union.

Yorgos Papandreou's Centre Union government remained in power from February 1964 to July 1965. The Centre Union was a major problem both for the Greek establishment and its authoritarian-repressive political system, and for global American interests in the eastern Mediterranean because of its anti-military, anti-royalist, anti-American and anti-NATO policies. After the rise of the Centre Union to power, it became clear to the establishment and the US that they could not easily maintain the political system established after Second World War. They were alarmed by attempts to purge the ultra-rightist IDEA group from the army, to remove rightist officers from key positions to the border points (Mouzelis, 1978: 126), and to bring the KYP under control through replacing its personnel (Roubatis, 1987: 197). The replacement of KYP personnel had annoyed the CIA chief in Athens. He began to complain that Russian agents had infiltrated the KYP, and the CIA stopped informing the KYP about its operations in Greece (Roubatis, 1987: 197).

However, the most important problem was not Yorgos Papandreou, but his son Andreas. From his first days as a minister in his father's government, Andreas became the main troublemaker. He began to investigate the relationship between the KYP and the CIA. When he was convinced that both his own and his father's telephones were tapped by the KYP/CIA, he established his own intelligence service and put the CIA officials in Athens under surveillance (Stern, 1977: 24). Furthermore, his uncompromising stand and unusual statements concerning the fragile Cyprus issue made him the major opponent of US policies in the eyes of the Americans. He was also very outspoken against the King and the army, calling for restrictions of the King's powers and the political neutralisation of the army. Within a short time, Andreas had become an obsession of US policy makers. When high level American officials were assigned to Greece, they were indoctrinated about Andreas beforehand. In a CIA-prepared file, he was described as a serious danger to United States' interests in Greece (Stern, 1977: 25).

The tension between the Papandreous, the establishment and the Americans turned into a crisis when Andreas was accused of leading a leftist conspiratorial group in the army known as Aspida. Yorgos Papandreou attempted to dismiss high ranking officers from the army and demanded the resignation of his defence minister, who had been secretly assigned by the King to investigate the Aspida affair. He hoped to put the defence ministry under his own portfolio in order to establish civilian control over the army. This was unacceptable to the establishment. The defence minister, Garofoulias, refused to resign and the King did not accept Yorgos Papandreou's assumption of the office of defence minister. Subsequently, when Yorgos Papandreou's bluff to resign was called by the King, and when 49 Centre Union deputies split from their party in favour of an conservative ERE government, the short but eventful period of Centre Union government came to an end.

The Aspida affair and the downfall of the Centre Union government was a Royal manoeuvre aiming at a return to the orthodox domestic policies of the pre-Papandreou period, and the return of a less adventurous, and a more US and NATO oriented, foreign policy (Couloumbis et al., 1976: 130). The Americans supported the King against Yorgos Papandreou and encouraged an atmosphere of political crisis. An American officer, who worked in Greece at the time, told the *New York Times* in 1974 that the CIA chief of station in Greece had helped King Konstantine bribe CU deputies so as to topple the Yorgos Papandreou government (Roubatis, 1987: 185 and 189).

Moreover, both Papandreous rejected American proposals for the solution of the Cyprus problem and firmly supported the Non-Aligned Greek Cypriot President, Archbishop Makarios. This annoyed American policymakers. Furthermore, Papandreous' and Makarios' flirtations with the Soviet Union, and Andreas' call for an anti-American, anti-NATO, and neutralist foreign policy, aggravated American mistrust of the Centre Union government. Consequently, when Papandreou attempted to establish civilian control over the army, the main US stronghold in Greece, thereby challenging the post-war pro-American royalist-conservative-authoritarian coalition, the Centre Union government could not be allowed to remain in power. Andreas Papandreou described the position of the Centre Union as follows:

> The party clashed with the Americans over the settlement of the Cyprus issue. It clashed with the King over his prerogatives, especially over those related to the leadership of the Armed Forces, for he was stubbornly committed...that the civilian government should have no substantive say over the Armed Forces. It clashed with "parallel government" of Greece including the Americans, over the control of the...[KYP]...It clashed with the economic oligarchy of the country

over a reformist and expansionist development policy, and with the large foreign investors who had obtained almost colonial terms (Papandreou, 1973: 22).

The downfall of the Centre Union government, however, paved the way for political instability. No strong government could be established while mass support for the Papandreous was growing. Demonstrations and strikes occurred, which implied that the Centre Union would come to power with an overwhelming majority in the coming elections. At the same time, the Papandreous were attacking the King, the army, conservatives and the Americans arguing that before the implementation of a reform oriented program, the distribution of power in the state had to be changed. To this end, according to the Papandreous:

> The king would have to learn to restrict himself to the constitutional limits of his authority; the army would have to learn to obey the order of the lawfully elected government; the Americans would have to learn that Greece belong to Greeks, that it was an ally but not a satellite; and the Greek oligarchy would have to adjust to the fact that the interests of the Greek people at large, and not only their own special interests, would be served by the government (Papandreou, 1973: 24).

The increasing popular support for the Papandreous alarmed the establishment and the Americans. The King feared that an overwhelming Centre Union victory would bring an end to the Greek Monarchy. The Americans thought that a Centre Union electoral victory would bring an end to the US presence in Greece, and hence would be a major setback to US global interests. Maury, the CIA Station Chief in Greece, enunciated the CIA's conclusion, "that a victory by the Papandreous would seriously damage the vital US interests in the Eastern Mediterranean area, weaken the southern flank of NATO and seriously destabilise the delicate Turkish-Greek relations then severely strained by the Cyprus situation" (Stern, 1977: 37). The election was set for 28th May 1967. However, it was pre-empted by the Colonels' Coup on 21st April.

The challenges in the economic and political spheres to US oriented policies were immediately reflected in Greece's external relations. From the semiperipheral policy perspective, this period was a brief exception in the broader period of 1945-1974 that we defined as the satellite, Atlanticist years of Greek foreign policy. One should bear in mind that these abortive challenges to US interests coincided with the increasing role of Europe in the Greek economy.

The brief challenge to Greece's Atlanticist foreign policy line focused on the Cyprus issue. Although an agreement had been reached in Cyprus, neither mainland nor Greek Cypriots were satisfied with its terms. Greeks believed that the agreement had been made in the interests of the Atlantic Alliance (that is the US) without taking Greek aspirations into consideration. Moreover, the Turks had become a principal party in any decision on the future of the island. The dissatisfaction of Makarios, the Greek Cypriot president, came to the surface as early as 1963 when he declared his unilateral revision of the constitution. However, this turned Cyprus into a major problem again in the Eastern Mediterranean, one which threatened US global interests: Suddenly, the status-quo on the island was abolished and Greece and Turkey, two NATO allies, came close to war. A war between Greece and Turkey would be a serious blow for the Atlantic Alliance, and it would provide opportunities for Soviet exploitation.

Although Yorgos Papandreou accepted Greece's existing alliances, he declared that Greece was no longer a satellite, but a sovereign nation free to develop its own foreign policy in accordance with its long-term interests. He gave full support to Makarios' policies. For him, Cyprus, the primary national issue of Greece, could not be sacrificed to the interests of the Atlantic alliance. He was very outspoken in his dealings with the Americans on the Cyprus issue, which angered them.[7]

Yorgos Papandreou argued that Cyprus had to be discussed in the UN, rather than in NATO, and refused all American efforts to arrange a meeting between Greece, Turkey and the US to resolve the problem. Furthermore, he sent 20,000 officers and men to Cyprus, well above the permitted legal number of 950 Greek soldiers on the island (Papandreou, 1973: 134). He remained silent when Makarios contracted with the Soviets for the delivery of substantial war material (Papandreou, 1973: 143), and he did not allow the Greek armed forces to participate in NATO exercises. He declared that his government would welcome Soviet assistance in preparation for a possible war against Turkey (Rousseas, 1968: 29). The Americans were worried that a Papandreou victory in the coming elections would lead to Greece's withdrawal from NATO, and the removal of US bases (Stern, 1977: 36).

The Restoration of US Influence: The Colonels Come to Power

The establishment of the military regime in 1967 opened a new phase in the political economy of Greece. Although almost all major economic interests supported the coup, the main winner was foreign capital. The minister of economic coordination of the Junta declared this from the outset, stating that "the state attributes particular importance to the influx of foreign capital. What interests us is the application of a development policy and not the conversion of the country into a testing ground for theories" (Shawb and Frangos, 1973: 28). It was true that if Greece were to follow a developmentalist policy, capital would have to be invested into key sectors of industry. Thus, if indigenous capital was unable or unwilling to invest in these sectors, foreign capital had to be given the necessary incentives. Accordingly, the Greek state became less selective about foreign capital and more willing to extend concessions (Pesmasoglou, 1972: 97). Under new legislation (89/1967, 378/1968, 916/1971), foreign capital was given reinforced constitutional guarantees for the servicing and export of investment profits. The extra privileges granted to the two giants, Esso-Pappas and Pechiney-Niarchos after their interests had been restored by the King, showed the eagerness of the military regime to cooperate with foreign capital.

In regard to the domestic economic elite, the military regime gave preferential treatment to shipowners. They were granted incentives, not only for their shipping interests, but also for their participation in industrial undertakings (Clogg and Yannopoulos, 1972: xiii). Accordingly, these shipping interests, which are sometimes called "comprador bourgeoisie" (see Poulantzas, 1976 and Georgiou, 1988), cooperated with foreign capital and became partners in the large industrial undertakings operating in key sectors of industry. Well-known families in this group were the shipowners Onassis, Niarchos, Andreadis, Karas, and Livanos (Georgiou, 1988: 75). However, the Federation of Greek Industrialists (SEV) was not happy with the policy of highly selective distribution of grants and subsidies and thus was in conflict with the military regime. The allocation of resources based on political criterion, and in favour of the shipping interests, led to an intra-business conflict in the Greek economic establishment. This special relationship between the state and the Union of Greek Shipowners (EEE) resulted in the imperial behaviour of the EEE over the SEV, which was considered an intervention into their own domain of representation by SEV industrialists (Lavdas, 1997: 131).

In fact, in the period between 1967-1974, SEV displayed an ambiguous behaviour in its relations with the military regime. SEV leadership always refrained from identifying the Federation with the Junta, but at the same time they sought to exploit opportunities in the military government's policies as much as possible (Lavdas, 1997:131). First of all, the SEV described the 1967 military takeover as "a government change". They pledged to cooperate with the new regime on the ground that industry is a national force and cooperates with all Greek governments, and hence they demanded close cooperation with the military administration in policy making (*Deltion*, May 18 and 31 1967, quoted in Lavdas, 1997: 131). However, they also portrayed the EEC "association agreement" as the "economic constitution" of the country and emphasised the promotion of its objectives (*Deltion*, 30 April 1967, quoted in Lavdas, 1997: 131). The SEV's vague approach towards the military government was based on mainly two motives (see, Lavdas, 1997: 131 and 275, endnote 51). First, frustrated by the labour unrest and the widespread strikes of the pre-Junta period, the Federation wanted stability in business and demanded "labour-free" state corporatism. Second, realising the possible negative consequences of the dictatorship on the Greece-EEC relations and the existence of a pro-parliamentary group within the Federation, SEV leadership emphasised the significance of eventual return to the parliamentary rule. This latter line was frequently and loudly pronounced by SEV industrialists as the conflicts with the military regime, the pro-Junta shipowners and the EEE over the business interests increased.

The Federation of Greek Industrialists (SEV) also assumed a mediating role between the military regime and the EEC after the suspension of association agreement by the EEC. Being a full member in the "Union of Industries of the European Community" (UNICE) since 1962, the SEV often called upon the UNICE to work together for the improvement of the Greek-EEC relations, and eventually in 1969 managed to hold a number of official UNICE activities in Athens (Lavdas, 1997: 132). The SEV's mediating efforts between the "Colonels' Greece" and the EEC meant two things to the military regime. On the one hand, such efforts seemed to help ameliorate the legitimacy problem of the Colonels. On the other hand, these efforts pressured the dictatorship to make reforms towards the constitutional normalcy. The military regime was not happy with this latter function of SEV's European policy, and eventually it caused into a strained relationship between the SEV and the Colonels. When these tense relations were worsened by the politically motivated selective subsidisation and grants policy of the government, the relations between the SEV and the Greek military government became further strained (Lavdas, 1997: 132). The tense relations between the Government and the Industrialists reached its apogee in 1970 when Prime Minister Papadapoulos asked SEV chairman Marinopoulos to resign, and then nominated a junta-friendly industrialist to his position (Lavdas, 1997: 275, endnote 53). Although Marinopoulos resigned after this incident, the SEV Council elected a new chairman with no links to the military regime, instead of the Junta's candidate.

On the other hand, while foreign capital invested in key industrial sectors that require high-technology and specialisation, areas of secondary importance were left to Greek enterprises. For instance, in the plastics sector the extraction of raw materials, a process of primary importance, was controlled by the two giant foreign enterprises of Esso-Pappas Chemical and Dow Chemical Hellas. Finishing the product, a process of secondary importance, was left to the Greek firms. Similarly, the Pechiney Company mined bauxite and produced aluminium and alumna, which was a process of secondary importance, but the phase of finishing the product, a process of primary importance, was completed outside Greece (Georgiou, 1988: 68). Furthermore, both Greek-controlled enterprises and joint ventures became dependent on foreigners in many respects: for technology, imported intermediate and raw materials, spare parts, the introduction of new products, and for the distribution of the company's products abroad through foreign partners' networks (Thomapoulos, 1975: 40).

Thus while Greek entrepreneurs were given secondary roles, US local and global economic interests consolidated their positions in Greece. Forty percent of the total foreign investment in Greece was American capital (Thomapoulos, 1975: 41) and this showed the degree of vested American interest in Greece. From the American perspective, the penetration of US capital in Greece was a requirement of the world order distinguished by the free flow of capital or direct investment. Hence consolidating and preserving US capital was vitally important to US foreign policy makers. The Greek Colonels were more than helpful in this task. Accordingly, the US supported the military regime. A significant indicator of this policy was the visit of US Secretary of Commerce, M. Stans, to Athens. During his visit, he declared, "We in the US government, particularly in American business, greatly appreciate Greece's attitude towards American investment, and we appreciate the welcome that is given here to American companies and the sense of security that the government of Greece is imparting to them" (quoted in Goldbloom, 1972: 251). Moreover, President Nixon wrote to the chief of the Junta, Papadopoulos, congratulating him on the economic progress of the military administration (Woodhouse, 1982: 195).

In world-system analysis, it is argued that semiperipheral countries become economic transmission belts in times of expansion. Greece became such a belt after the inflow of foreign capital, from the mid-1960s onwards. Foreign-controlled enterprises in Greece exported large quantities of their products, not only to traditional Greek markets, but also to their home or European markets: Phillips to Holland and Siemens to Germany; ITT to Germany, Belgium, Switzerland and France; Ethyl Corporation to Europe,

Africa and the Middle East; Republican Steel to Britain, the USA, Germany, Italy, Yugoslavia and Romania; Union Carbide to Italy, Belgium, Finland, Sweden and Austria; Westinghouse to the Middle East; and Pechiney to European and Middle Eastern countries (Georgiou, 1988: 67-68).

Although America was the leading actor in the Greek economy, Europe's role also increased in this period. The remittances of Greek workers in Europe and tourist receipts continued to offset the chronic balance of payments deficits (OECD, 1967 to 1975). Moreover, the amount of European investment capital also increased. Individual firms from European countries invested in different sectors of the economy (Negriponti-Delivanis, 1985: 289-300 and Georgiou, 1988: 67-68). The largest European investors were France (27 percent) and Switzerland (13 percent) (Thomapoulos, 1975: 41).

However, despite the increasing role of European private capital, the EEC as a whole, in sharp contrast to the US, downgraded its relations with the Colonel's Greece. The initial response of the EEC to the establishment of the military regime was to limit the Association Agreement to its current administration. Discussions on agricultural harmonisation were stopped, and the remaining $56 million out of $125 million in EEC loans frozen. Moreover, the EEC Mediterranean policy negotiated new agreements with other countries in the region with similar export structures, and downgraded the Greece's privileged position in the Community.

In the political sphere, the Greek state continued to be a political and ideological appendage of the US. After the Soviet invasion of Czechoslovakia and the increase of Soviet naval power in the Mediterranean, American foreign policy focused on the containment of the Soviet Union in Eastern Europe, the Balkans, and the Mediterranean. Moreover, Middle East events, which included wars and continuous tension between the Arabs and Israel and the Cyprus issue that putting the oil regions and trade routes into danger, made the control of Greece imperative for American interests.

In the period between 1967-1974, the Americans intervened in Greek politics and controlled the state through the Army. The Army was the stronghold of the Americans within the Greek establishment. Between 1950 and 1969, 1,129 Greek military personnel were trained in the US, and another 1,965 Greek students were trained in overseas US installations under the Military Assistance Program (Couloumbis, 1976: 126). Furthermore, the coup leaders were top KYP men (Stern, 1977: 45), an institution established, administered and financed by the CIA (Papandreou, 1972: 16).

The Colonels had small effective internal support from the economically powerful group of shipowners and internationally oriented financiers, as well as from some highly conservative sections among the peasantry (Ioakimidis, 1984: 36). The first two groups were mostly Greek-Americans, and they were very influential in US policy towards Greece. Onassis, Niarchos and Pappas were leading members, and they invested heavily in the Greek economy. Among them, Pappas was a close friend and the main financial backer of Spiro Agnew, President Nixon's vice-president. He had also been President Eisenhower's finance manager in 1956. Thus Pappas played a very useful liaison role between the Colonels and the Nixon administration (Woodhouse, 1985: 31), as he had very good contacts with various organs of the US establishment (see, US Congressional Hearings, 1971: 459-462). However, the Colonels could not consolidate themselves in the Greek society as a whole and hence they functioned in a political vacuum.

Although the Colonels did not succeed in establishing their domestic legitimacy, the Americans provided crucial external support for their survival (Clogg and Yannopoulos, 1972: xvi). They remained loyal to the US and NATO interests and cooperated closely with the Americans. The American administration, in turn, tolerated and defended the continuation of the military regime, despite strong opposition from the US Congress and Europe.[8] The Colonels proved so accommodating that the American administration was indifferent even to the King's failed counter-coup against the Colonels only eight months after the advent of the dictatorship. Furthermore, despite his close relations with the Americans in the past, Nixon refused to see the King during Eisenhower's funeral in 1966, but he did meet with Pattakos, one of the principal members of the Junta (Woodhouse, 1982: 191). The Americans no longer needed the King to ensure stability. On the contrary, they feared that the King might be the source of further instability, and they did not want to risk this in a period of increasing Soviet influence in the Mediterranean and Eastern Europe, and with the escalating Arab-Israeli conflict in the Middle East.

However, as in the economic sphere, there was a steady increase of European influence in Greek politics, especially among progressive elements of both right and centre. A significant development was the establishment of a common platform between progressive conservative and centre groups against the military regime. They converged around Kannelopoulos of the conservative ERE and Mavros and Zighidis of the liberal CU (Yannopoulos, 1972: 168). This rapprochement was encouraged by pressure from European conservative and social democratic circles who wanted the creation of an alternative centre of power (Yannopoulos, 1972: 168). Furthermore, Karamanlis the conservative former prime minister in self-exile in Paris since 1963, called for the overthrow of the Junta in a letter in which he accused the Junta of causing Greece's exclusion from the emerging European grouping - a situation that would be detrimental to the economy and Greek national security. He was supported wholeheartedly by leading pre-coup progressive conservative and centrist parliamentary elites (Schwab and Frangos, 1973: 116 and 119). Given these developments, it is not surprising that Colonels' oppression extended to liberal conservative elements. On the other hand, the Junta's rage against Europe had come to a head after Greece was forced to withdraw from the Council of Europe. The Junta controlled press, while praising the US as Greece's only trustworthy friend, strongly attacked the European nations (Katris, 1971: 309). It was apparent that a clash between Atlanticism and Europeanism was imminent.

The military regime further reconsolidated American interests in Greek foreign policy at a time of increasing tension in the Mediterranean, Central Europe and the Middle East. In other words, Greek foreign policy continued to play the semiperipheral satellite role, a role which had been interrupted briefly during the Papandreou period. Indeed, the Junta proved that they were the best option for US interests in Greece. Only two months after the Colonels' Coup, the Six-Day War between Egypt and Israel broke out, demonstrating the importance of US facilities in Greece for the defence of Israel. Furthermore, during the crisis the Junta fully cooperated in evacuation of 3000 American citizens from the troubled area. With the closure of the Suez Canal by the Arabs after the 1967 war, and the rapprochement between the Egyptian president, Nasser and Moscow, Soviet influence began to increase in the region at the expense of the US. Hence, Greece was an even more important military base and logistical asset for the Americans.[9]

Immediately after the Junta took power, the US Administration imposed an arms embargo on Greece in order to force the Colonels to return to the *status-quo ante* as soon as possible. However, although the delivery of heavy arms was halted, the supply of weapons suitable for internal security continued, and in 1968 the ban on heavy weapons began to be lifted progressively. In September 1969, the US National Security Council concluded that the Nixon Administration should restart full scale military assistance to Greece so that it could fulfil its NATO obligations (Stern, 1977: 58 and 67). This decision was not made public until September 1970.

The overthrow of the Libyan monarchy by Colonel Gaddafi in 1969 further increased the importance of Greece, because Gaddafi wanted the evacuation of the US air force base in Libya. Another crisis occurred in 1970 with the expulsion of Palestinian commandos from Jordan into Syria. The US 6th Fleet intervened in order to prevent another war, using the US bases in Greece and Greek territory and air space (Couloumbis et al., 1976: 138).

Moreover, tension and uncertainty increased with the death of President Nasser of Egypt and his successor Sadat's initial inclinations for an alliance with the Soviet Union. Furthermore, when the Labour Party of Malta came to power in 1971 under the leadership of Dom Mintoff, who declared that he would not allow NATO ships to use the Valetta harbour, the need to improve American military facilities in Greece became more urgent (Woodhouse, 1985: 96). Consequently, the Americans demanded home-port facilities in Athens for the US 6th Fleet in order to retain a full US presence in the region. US Assistant Secretary of State R. Davies maintained that this would promote stability in the Eastern Mediterranean and enable a peaceful settlement in the Arab-Israeli dispute (Woodhouse, 1985: 106). The agreement was signed in 1972 and the American military presence in Athens was more than doubled by 10,000 naval personnel and dependants (Stern, 1977: 72).

When the 1973 Yom-Kippur War broke out between Egypt and Israel, Greece declared its neutrality in the conflict. However, Greece continued cooperating with the US, allowing them to use communication facilities in Greece, and also airports in Athens and Souda Bay in Crete. No restrictions were placed on the movements or the resupply of the 6th Fleet. Thus it is clear that the US enjoyed close cooperation with the Greek Colonels in the Mediterranean throughout the dictatorship between 1967-1974.

These developments in the Eastern Mediterranean in the second half of the 1960s made Cyprus even more important for the security of the region and for US global interests. This necessitated an urgent solution to the island's problems. On this issue the Colonels also proved accommodating, and they clashed directly with Makarios. Whereas the Colonels were willing to give up a tiny part of the island to the Turks in return for the unification of the rest with Greece, Makarios was strongly opposed to any solution which would divide the island into two and bring it under US and NATO control. He firmly defended the "independence" of the island. In the eyes of the Colonels, Makarios was "a traitor to *enosis* (unification), a red priest who flirted with the local communist party, championed Non-Alignment, and consorted with such dubious Third World figures as Tito of Yugoslavia, and Nasser of Egypt, not to mention friendliness with Moscow" (Stern, 1977: 86).

Despite Makarios' objections, the Colonels agreed to negotiate with the Turks concerning Cyprus and they engaged in secret talks during NATO conferences to resolve the problem (Stern, 1977: 90-91). They withdrew the 20,000 Greek officers and troops that had been illegally stationed on the island since 1964. Meanwhile Makarios' firm stand against a US-NATO sponsored solution, and his pro-Soviet and pro-Arab policies, annoyed the Americans. President Nixon called him a "Mediterranean Castro" and Kissinger said that he was an enemy of Israel (Woodhouse, 1985: 155).

The Americans supported the military regime in Greece because the Colonels were extremely cooperative in promoting US global interests. For the Colonels, on the other hand, American support was their only source of survival and legitimacy, which they desperately needed both in the internal and external spheres.

At the same time, however, the European Community, the Council of Europe, and individual European states focused their reaction on the repressive nature of the military regime and the immediate return to democratic rule. The EC, for example, suspended the Association Agreement with Greece. The EC's negative stance towards the Colonels' regime led to the isolation of Greece in Europe. The Council of Europe, on the other hand, focused on the serious and systematic breaches of human rights under the Junta. The reports submitted to the Council concluded that the Colonels' regime was undemocratic, illiberal, authoritarian and oppressive (Woodhouse, 1986: 289). Hence the Parliamentary Assembly of the Council of Europe, as early as 1968, voted for the expulsion of Greece from membership, unless democracy was restored before spring 1969. Accordingly, after the negative report prepared under Dutch chairmanship in 1969, the Assembly called for Greece's resignation from the Council. US embassies in the European capitals began to lobby against Greece's expulsion, but without success (Woodhouse, 1985: 71). Since expulsion would be a humiliation, the Colonels withdrew Greece from the Council in 1969.

The Danish government was the first to officially condemn the establishment of the military regime and its repressive policies. Later, the Norwegian and German governments joined the Danish, and together they tried to raise the Greek question in NATO's Ministerial Council. However, their efforts were frustrated by US pressure aided by the Secretary General of NATO (Treholt, 1972: 216-218 and Woodhouse, 1985: 52). The Dutch government also attacked the Colonels at a NATO meeting, stressing the democratic and liberal foundations of the Alliance, but US pressure prevented any official action against Greece (Woodhouse, 1985: 118). Furthermore, Scandinavian, Italian, German and Dutch state authorities declared their support for the opposition in Greece (Woodhouse, 1985: 40). In general, most European governments allowed the organisation and activities of anti-Junta movements in their countries (Rousseas, 1968: 130).

In the period of the world-economy's expansion that started after the Second World War under the US hegemony, Greece exhibited the general characteristics of a semiperipheral state. This lasted for 30 years until the period of contraction in the world-economy set in. As discussed in this chapter, parallel to its semiperipheral economic development, Greece experienced direct intervention in its domestic affairs, and became a satellite and a political agent of a hegemonic power in its external relations.

Now, let us turn to the post dictatorship period and see whether Greece followed a semiperipheral foreign policy between 1974 and the 2000s, a period which overlapped with a contraction period in the world-economy.

Notes

1. Ellis gives typical examples on how the monopolistic and oligopolistic interests protected their privileged position in the market through political pressure, see Ellis, 1964, pp.185.
2. Ellis points out that in 1950, 80 percent of the total savings came from abroad, mostly in the form of US economic aid. This dropped to 12 percent in 1960.
3. In December 1946, the American and Greek governments agreed to the purchase of 100 Liberty type carrier ships, for $545,000 each, by Greek shipowners. Only a quarter of the total amount was paid and the Greek state was the guarantor of the remaining amount that was to be paid over 15 years, see Serafetinidis et al., 1981, pp.294-295.
4. At the beginning, the Americans were against the reactionary-conservative and far-right groups in Greece. The US State Department had opposed the British idea of restoring the monarchy. They were highly critical of the Greek monarchy, both as an institution and as personified by the King George II, see Iatrides, 1980, p.57 and Roubatis, 1987, p.15. The King was seen a man of limited vision and an arm of the Metaxas dictatorship. Yet official US policy had remained neutral on the issue, implying that the King should not seek American support for the restoration of monarchy, see Woodhouse, 1986, p.254.
5. Interview with Field Marshall Papagos, *Vema*, 27 April, 1952, quoted in Couloumbis, 1966, pp.58-59.
6. *Journal of Parliamentary Debates*, Athens, 25 November 1953, p.62, quoted in Couloumbis, 1966, p.85. Couloumbis also points out that there was no provision in the NATO agreement that envisaged Greece's expulsion in case of non-ratification.
7. For Yorgos Papandreou's bold conversations with the Americans, see Papandreou, 1973, pp.137-138 and also Roubatis, 1987, pp.176-177 and 180.
8. For a discussion on the American tolerance to, and European reactions against, the Colonels, see US Congressional Hearings, 1971 various sections and Treholt, 1972, pp.210-227.
9. For the official American assessment of Greece's importance to the global interests of the US and NATO in this period, see US Congressional Hearings, 1971.

Chapter 3
Greece: 1974-2000s

Greece's semiperipheral development and foreign policy in the contraction period of the world-economy is the focus of this chapter. In world-system analysis, the period that began in the early 1970s corresponds to the relative decline of American hegemony and the emergence of Europe (the EC/EU) as a new economic and political centre of power. Accordingly, this chapter investigates whether, in the changing world context, Greece's internal economic and political dynamics and processes responded semiperipherally.

In world-system analysis, it is argued that during the periods of contraction some of the strongest semiperipheral countries might be able to improve their position in the hierarchy of states by upgrading their production structures and trade patterns in the world-economy. In such cases core-like producers begin to become dominant in the production processes of the semiperipheral economy. Parallel developments are expected to occur in the internal and external politics of upwardly mobile semiperipheral states: political intervention by the hegemonic/core power(s) comes to an end; the old political structures collapse; and they change their international alliances, thus ceasing to act as satellites of hegemonic powers, and increasing their margin of independence to pursue their own national interests. They may also increase their influence in the management of international problems. Furthermore, upwardly mobile semiperipheral countries assert their intermediary (bridge/sub-imperial) role between geographically, historically or culturally contingent areas and the core regions. A main motive behind this orientation is create both privileged and stable markets for their export goods while reaping the (secondary) economic and commercial benefits of being a springboard for the core for those areas, and at the same time, to create their own political sphere of influence. Moreover, in contraction periods, intra-semiperiphery rivalries for favours from hegemonic and/or core powers will probably occur. When rivalries occur, the foreign policies of semiperipheral states are either directed towards curbing the inflow of benefits from hegemonic power or core states to rival state(s) or, conversely towards encouraging similar types of favours for themselves.

The Economic Environment: 1974-Early 1980s (Karamanlis Period)

Developments in the Greek economy after the collapse of the military regime and the establishment of democracy in 1974 created the impression that a significant shift from the old mechanisms was underway. The state, the most crucial actor in the semiperiphery was, again, at the centre of these developments.

During the post-junta period, the intervention of the Greek state in the economy acquired new dimensions (OECD, 1992: 57). In the 1945-1974 period, state intervention had occurred through subsidies, licences, protectionist policies, etc. The state had restricted its role to providing incentives (mostly financial) to the private sector, rather than directly contributing to the industrial development of the country (Giannitsis, 1991: 214). The state supported low-technology, labour-intensive uncompetitive traditional industries, and invited foreign capital to invest in non-traditional (mainly intermediate and capital goods industries) sectors. Accordingly, the state's overall participation in total industrial investment was only 0.7 percent between 1965-1974 (Giannitsis, 1991: 228). The state encouraged the accumulation of capital, either in the hands of periphery-like domestic producers or foreign investors who invested in relatively high-technology, non-traditional sectors of the economy. In the post-junta period, however, state intervention in the economy centred mainly around nationalisations and assuming the role of entrepreneurship. These policies indicated that the Greek state was attempting to become the engine of development.

Although the new Greek government had announced economic freedom as its principal policy (Karamanlis, 1974: 224 and 1979: 227), it undertook a number of nationalisations which enormously increased the economic sphere the state controlled. According to the Minister of Industry, the degree of state control in the economy had reached well over 60 percent in 1979 (Clogg, 1987: 157). Unlike postwar interventions, this new policy was aimed at achieving two main objectives. First, to balance economic and social inequalities, and hence replace private initiative whenever economic and social concerns required such a policy (Karamanlis, 1979: 226). Second, the new policy aimed to reduce the power of the economic elite (mainly the Union of Greek Shipowners - EEE who had collaborated with the military regime between 1967-1974) over the economy. Accordingly, the state established a great number of industries in the areas of sugar, fertilisers, petrochemicals, armaments, as well as others. They also nationalised Olympic Airways of Onassis, the Aspropyrogos refinery of Niarchos, the Commercial Bank Group and urban transport company of Andreadis

(Karamanlis, 1979: 228). The new government maintained development could be achieved through state control of the economy. In 1979 a cabinet minister stated that the state controlled 95 percent of the banks; 100 percent of the energy companies; 100 percent of the communications; 100 percent of the public utility companies; 100 percent of transport; 60 percent of the insurance companies; 50 percent of the refineries; 50 percent of shipyards; and 70 percent of the fertilisers (see, Loulis, 1981b: 23 and Kolmer, 1981: 300-303). Furthermore, following a government initiative, a consortium of four major domestic banks (ELEVME) was established to fill gaps in the industrial structure by creating new enterprises or financing investments by already existing private companies, especially to exploit the country's natural resources, such as mining and the chemical industry (OECD, 1976: 47). Hence in this period the Greek state gave the impression that it had taken on the entrepreneurial role itself and had become the pioneer of the development process

The political elite in power in the immediate post-junta years were developmentalist and progressive elements of both the right-wing and the centre in the 1960s and early 1970s. Their economic outlook was based upon the disintegration of the mechanisms and habits of the (periphery-like) postwar economic system. One of the most prominent technocrats of the new government, the governor of the Central Bank of Greece, X. Zolotas, expressed the principal expectations from Greek industrialists, emphasising the crucial necessity of a change in their habits:

> In industry the strongest effort must be made by the industrialists themselves...Greek businessmen must recognise, with boldness, realism and resourcefulness, that the strong financial incentives, excessive protectionism and low labour cost, which ensured the fast and comfortable growth of their firms, belongs to the past...[They] must also understand as early as possible that it is both a duty and an advantage for them to cooperate among themselves and with the state for the purpose of restructuring the economy, changing the attitudes shaped within the confines of a closely protected market, and at the same time strengthening the economy's export orientation and competitiveness...It is also necessary to change organisational, administrative, and marketing methods procedures at the level of business firm, with the ultimate objective of attaining optimum size. This is the only way in which Greek industry can cope with foreign and domestic competition, which will grow keener with the passage of time. Furthermore, business firms... should stop relying mainly on bank credit for financing their investments (Zolotas, 1976: 37-38).

One of the objectives of Karamanlis's interventionist economic policy was to reduce the economic bases of two groups: the monopolies, a point which was included in article 106 of the 1975 Constitution; and the economic elite, which had worked with the Junta by taking advantage of the enormous concessions it offered. Thus these nationalisations were politically motivated. This economic elite primarily constituted the "American-oriented comprador bourgeoisie" of Greece. In fact, in the summer of 1974, the Greek economic elite was in a very difficult political position because of their cooperation with the military regime. In an official meeting in 1974, Karamanlis told the Greek Shipowners Union (EEE) that they did not have good reputation among the people (quoted in Lavdas, 1997: 133). Indeed, Karamanlis used this opportunity to discipline the business community and to shift the power balance against the monopolies and the EEE. Accordingly, the Piraeus-based EEE leadership group under Andreadis was replaced by a rival leadership group with links to the diaspora shipping capital group, namely the London-based Shipping Cooperation Committee (Lavdas, 1997: 127 and 133). Andreadis, a shipping, a banking, and an industrial magnate, was put on trial for violating banking laws by channelling funds illegally to his business ventures and creating market obstacles to new entrepreneurs through credits and other mechanisms.

Initially the Federation of Greek Industrialists (SEV) was worried about the government's attacks on the EEE and its nationalisation policy fearing of the radicalisation of the political environment, and criticised these policies as "socialist attitudes" (Lavdas, 1997: 134). Furthermore, the SEV also criticised the government for not consulting the business community in the economic policy-making process. The new government's view however was that the political requirements of the transition to democracy necessitated political stability and social peace, which in turn required intensified investment, high employment, restraints on pricing and social dialogue. The business community, according to Karamanlis, had to understand these requirements and help the government attain its goals (*Deltion*, 31 October, 1975, quoted in Lavdas, 1997: 134).

Unlike in the Shipowners Union there were no drastic changes in the SEV leadership, but they were under the pressure of Andreadis' nationalised industrial, banking and shipping group to adopt a hard line against the Karamanlis government's economic policies (Lavdas, 1997: 127). However, despite the strong pressure coming from Andreadis group, the Federation preferred to keep good relations with the new democratic government. As a result of Karamanlis' reassuring message that "the main pillar of the economic development would be the private sector despite the state's necessary interventions in the production process for establishing economic democracy", the SEV followed a conciliatory line and thus declared industry's policy of cooperation with the state and the trade unions for a smooth industrial growth, political stability and social peace in the country (see Lavdas, 1997: 134-135). In 1976, the governor of the Central Bank of Greece, Mr. Zolotas, pointed out that the chairman of the Federation did not ask the government for any privileges but demanded the same treatment as that given by EC members to their own industrial sectors (Zolotas, 1976: 37-38). In this way, the Federation, taking into consideration the public perception of the notorious grants and business practices of the previous period, attempted to make a distinction between the SEV and the corrupt business community supported by the state during the Junta period (Lavdas, 1997: 136). The implication of this stand was also the SEV's consent to the punishment of its corrupt cousins, which was another venue for supporting the democratic government policies.

Thus, despite the heavy state interventionism and nationalisations in the economy, the Federation of Greek Industrialists[1] (European-oriented domestic bourgeoisie) was, in general terms, close to the Karamanlis government, and supported Karamanlis's primary aim of accession to the EC (Kohler, 1982: 119-120). The Federation took a very positive attitude towards the European integration and emphasised the need for quick EC accession. Accordingly, the SEV engaged in lobbying activities in the Union of Industries of the European Community (UNICE) in which it was a member since 1962 (Lavdas, 1997: 127). Indeed as early as December 1974 the UNICE issued a declaration that they enthusiastically supported Greek membership in the EC and emphasised their continuing support at the level of EC authorities until Greece become a full member (Lavdas, 1997: 140). SEV President Kyriazis declared the role of Federation in Greek-EC relations was twofold: First, to inform the Greek side about the EC, and second to lobby the European side (*Deltion*, 31 August, 1974, quoted in Lavdas, 1997: 126). To this end, SEV organised conferences, workshops and all kinds of meetings bringing together various business associations and public authorities to exchange information, views and debate on the EC issue. Furthermore, it established a research centre in 1975 to provide additional support to Greek industry in preparation for full membership in the EC. Indeed, although the Federation represented of all industrial interests, it was the big business faction that generally set the tone in the decisions, and particularly in relations with the EC (Kohler, 1982: 143). The Karamanlis government, in turn, supported the pro-European (core-like) economic elites in their preparations to join the EC through the Ministry of Economic

Coordination, the National Bank and the Development Bank, (Kohler, 1982: 119-120).

In the context of its European policy, SEV also developed a strategy for industrial relations and proposed an agreement between social partners (see Lavdas, 1997: 137-138). The plan was a national strategy in view of the EC membership in which all the partners (trade unions, government, employers unions) would benefit in the end, provided that everybody refrained from short-term benefits. This policy was presented as a struggle to make Greek industry more competitive within the European market, and the strategy was called "the commitment" for succeeding in Europe. In this framework a prominent member of SEV, Papalexopoulos, emphasised the need for the modernisation of industrialists, managers, trade unions and state bureaucracy in the new period. He suggested that employment policy should concentrate more on human capital, training and technical assistance for the better skilled staff than only in achieving certain employment levels.

The renewed Union of Greek Shipowners (EEE) also developed a favourable attitude towards Greece's membership in the EC (see Lavdas, 1997: 275-276, endnote 62). The shipowners' international orientation and their dominance in the Euro-Atlantic transport lines, EC's liberal policies in the shipping sector, and the possibility of influencing future developments in the EC shipping policy from inside encouraged the EEE to give its support to Karamanlis's accession policy. However, the EEE had reservations on the speed of the EC membership, as they did not want to lose their control over the domestic maritime lines, and also because of the problems with the manning of the vessels and harmonisation of maritime legislation.

From the point of view of semiperipheral Greece, the new interventionist policies of the state and the cooperation between pro-European (core-like) economic elites and the government gave the impression that in the absence of strong, core producers, the state took the economic initiative and cooperated with pro-EC, "core-like" economic actors in order to increase their strength in the economy, and hence to upgrade Greece in the world-system hierarchy of states. This policy was identified with catching-up with the EC economies, and with full membership in the Community. On the other hand, from the perspective of the Greek economic elite the choice for EC membership and siding with Karamanlis government's policies both at home and towards Europe meant probably two things. First of all, it was apparent that there was no other alternative for the post-junta Greek economic elite (SEV) other than to collaborate with the state, as they were not strong enough to resist state policies and/or promote their interests by themselves. Second, they wanted to control and minimise the power shifts associated with the regime change and establish the SEV as the most powerful representative of the Greek business world (see Lavdas, 1997: 128 and 137).

The relations between the state and foreign capital in the post-junta period was, however, no different from the traditional Greek approach. In keeping with the policy of attracting foreign capital, as specified under law 2687 of 1953, the government underlined the significance of enhancing the incentives and guarantees provided under that law by promoting them once more to the constitutional level (Democracy in Greece, n.d.: 91). Accordingly, article 107 of the 1975 constitution guaranteed the protection of foreign investment in Greece. The relatively advanced, core-like sectors of the Greek economy (chemicals, metallurgy, electrical material, transport means, plastics, etc.) have been under the control of foreign capital since the early 1960s (Giannitsis, 1991: 215 and 218). Indeed, the Federation of the Greek Industrialists was representing mostly the weak industries in the economy (Lavdas, 1997: 128). Accordingly, private foreign direct investment played a significant role in developing certain important industries, including some major export industries (OECD, 1976: 23). As a result, the economy depended significantly on the export of the industrial products of transnational corporations (Georgiou, 1988: 67). Under these circumstances in which domestic capital had shown little interest in the non-traditional advanced (core-like) industrial sectors, the Karamanlis government had no immediate alternative other than to support the inflow of foreign investment capital in order to encourage the process of catching-up with the EC economies. The policy of attracting foreign capital can be a semiperipheral means of upgrading the production structures as long as it leads to structural transformations in the economy. However this transformation did not occur in Greece in the post-1974 period. Foreign investment capital remained reluctant to invest in Greece and its inflow into new fields declined (OECD, 1979: 20 and 1986: 41; Georgiou, 1988: 65; Kleinman, 1988: 212).

The Karamanlis government considered full EC membership the most strategic target to restructure the Greek economy. From the semiperipheral development perspective, accession to the EC was pivotal in adjusting the economy to the core-like production structures. Zolotas, governor of the Central Bank of Greece, explained the Greek (developmentalist) expectations from the EC membership in this way (Zolotas, 1976: 22-24): first, the entry of a small country like Greece into a wider economic group would have the direct effect of expanding its market. Second, accession to the EC would give Greece the possibility of benefiting from the advanced and constantly improving technology of the member countries. Third, Greece would become familiar with new organisational and managerial techniques, and attract increased flows of venture capital. Fourth, it would relieve Greece's balance of payments problems. Fifth, membership would allow Greece to benefit from various EC funds that could help Greece to restructure and modernise its economy (Zolotas, 1976: 34-35). In June 1979, during the parliamentary debates on the Accession Treaty, Prime Minister Karamanlis echoed these expectations by emphasising: "social and industrial progress", "attraction of foreign capital" and "expertise, and stimulus of competition". According to Karamanlis, Europe should promote economic justice and help developing countries (Woodhouse, 1982: 275-277).

Greece's determined orientation towards full EC membership, coupled with its impressive macro-economic indicators in a period of world wide recession, had created an impression that it was moving from its semiperipheral position towards the core zone of the world-economy. This "upward mobilisation" was identified with Europeanisation. The Financial Protocol signed between the EC and Greece in 1977 provided for the Community's participation in measures to promote the rapid development of the Greek economy (Opinion, 1979: 65). Indeed, with the revitalisation of the Association Agreement in 1974, the Community accepted the necessity of reducing the disparity between the Greek economy and the economies of the member states (Opinion, 1979: 66). Given the Community's formal approval of Greek accession in 1979, it was not unrealistic to think that EC membership provided an important opportunity to upgrade Greece towards the core zone. Hence, it was expected that Greece (as an "upwardly mobile" semiperipheral state) would adjust its economy to the economies of the member countries by using the financial and technical opportunities of the Community. It was thought that the semiperipheral balance would shift in the Greek economy towards core-like production patterns.

After 1974, the Community focused on financial transfers to the Greek economy. In the pre-accession period (1974-1981) the EC's contribution was limited to the release of $56 million of the First Financial Protocol which had been blocked since 1967, and to the Second Financial Protocol that provided $336 million to Greece. There were also transfers from the European Investment Bank in 1975 and 1980 that amounted to $30 and $77 million respectively.

There was a further reason for the impression that the Greek economy had shifted towards the core-zone in the post-junta period: some economic indicators improved even in a period of increasing oil prices and world wide recession. For instance, Greece's average annual GDP growth rate between

1975-1980 was around 4.5 percent (OECD, 1982), and the GNP per capita increased from $2205 in 1974 to $4348 in 1980 (OECD, 1976 to 1981). According to OECD surveys, this relatively strong economic growth up to the 1980s was due to a rapid expansion in foreign transactions with the result that the share of total exports of goods and services in GDP rose from 12.5 percent in 1970 to 25.5 percent in 1980, and that of imports from 19 percent to 27 percent (OECD, 1983: 41).

Perhaps the most striking development was the rise in exports and, accordingly, a remarkable exploitation of new markets. In this period, Greek exports to the Middle East, North Africa and other oil producing countries rose particularly sharply (by 55 percent in drachma values) so that this group's share in total Greek exports rose to roughly 16 percent (OECD, 1976: 17). Greek exports to the Middle East continued to increase until the early 1980s; exports to the Middle East accounted for 23 percent of total Greek exports in 1980 (OECD, 1982: 26). Furthermore, another important export market for Greece in this period was the EC. Indeed, although foreign transactions between Greece and the EC had been increasing since the 1960s,[2] Greece's access to EC markets increased more than a hundred percent in value terms between 1974 and 1980 (however, this corresponded to an increase from 47.7 to 48.2 percent respectively in total Greek exports) (OECD, 1982: 27). Similarly, imports from the EC increased almost a hundred percent in value between 1974 and 1980 and constituted a large proportion of total Greek imports (more than 40 percent), but without a significant change in total percentage (OECD, 1982: 27). Another important development was the increasing share of semi-processed and manufactured goods in exports, mainly in value terms. They increased from 1.5 percent in 1977 to 11 percent in 1978, and to 19 percent growth in 1979 (OECD, 1978: 18 and 1980: 21). In sum the relatively quick rise in industrial exports until the early 1980s was due to increasing access to the EC market and, especially, to the rapid increase of exports to the Middle East (OECD, 1982: 26). When it is recalled that another indicator of positional shift in contraction periods is an improvement in the sphere of trade, these developments further strengthened the impression that Greece had shifted towards the core zone.

A final point which is significant from the perspective of world-system analysis is Greece's economic relations with the US. The 1982 OECD survey on Greece shows that trade between Greece and the US decreased significantly between 1974 and 1980 for while exports to the US decreased from 8.9 percent in 1974/1975 to 5.6 percent of total exports in 1979/1980, imports from the US fell from 7.7 percent to 4 percent of total imports in the same period (OECD, 1982: 27). Moreover, in the field of foreign investment there was a shift from American to European investment. In the post-junta period, the EC investment share became higher than that of the US: 7 and 6 percent of total assets respectively (Tsoukalis, 1981: 46 and Mitsos, 1980: 140). This pattern of increasing Euro-centricity in the post junta period was also apparent in the number of tourists visiting Greece. The number of European tourists reached 74 percent of the total in 1978, while those from North America remained around 14 percent (Couloumbis, 1983b: 98).

In fact, invisible items, mainly emigrant remittances, tourism and shipping have played a significant role in offsetting Greece's balance of payments deficits since the 1960s. The OECD surveys on Greece between 1975-1982 show that the role of invisibles in the economy increased in the post-junta period. For instance, in 1977 the substantial increase in the trade deficit (from $3.3 billion to $3.9 billion) was covered significantly by a sharp rise in invisible receipts with the result that the current external deficit widened by only $0.2 billion (OECD, 1978: 16). In 1978, the rise in net invisibles exceeded the rise in trade deficit by almost 18 percent (OECD, 1979: 17 and 19). In other words, the invisible surplus offset about four-fifths and two-thirds of the trade deficits in 1978 and 1979 respectively (OECD, 1980: 19), and the growth of net invisible receipts rose from an annual increase of about 17.5 percent in the few years prior to 1978 to 27 percent in 1979 (OECD, 1980: 24). Tourist receipts grew the fastest: the annual growth rate of tourism between 1975 and 1979 was 27 percent, while emigrant remittances grew by 5 percent and shipping receipts grew by 18 percent in the same period (OECD, 1982: 28). The important point is that both tourism and emigrant remittance receipts were heavily dependent on European tourists and Greek workers in Europe. This demonstrates that (together with the Euro-centric trade and investment patterns) the Greek economy was dominated by Europe in the period between 1974 and 1981.

It has been noted that developments up until the early 1980s created the impression that Greece had entered a process of upward mobilisation from its semiperipheral position in the world-economy towards the core region. In world-system analysis semiperipheral states are expected to improve their trade patterns in the contraction periods of the world-economy, and upwardly mobile states are expected to have high growth rates. In the case of Greece, therefore the (relative) improvement of trade patterns with the EC and especially with the Middle East (both qualitatively and quantitatively), coupled with high growth rates, indicated semiperipheral development in the second half of the 1970s. Furthermore the elimination of old financial, monopolistic and some shipping interests of the previous periods (mostly periphery-like producers) through state intervention, the increasing role of the state in the economy, the willingness to become a full member of the EC, and the state's support of the pro-European economic elite implied that the Greek state (as an agent of semiperipheral development) had taken on a developmentalist-entrepreneurial role and supported the strengthening of core-like producers in Greece.

The Political Environment: 1974-Early 1980s

Two main developments are expected in the domestic political spheres of semiperipheral states in the contraction periods of the world economy. First, the old political structures collapse, and second, the intervention of hegemonic/core powers in the domestic affairs of the state ceases. Politically, Greece experienced radical developments in the post-junta period. Three principal actors had previously dominated the Greek political establishment: the Monarchy, Army and Parliament, all of which collaborated closely with the Americans. In the immediate post-junta years these institutions were either abolished or had to abandon their old roles and habits as democratisation occurred.

First, the monarchy was abolished by referendum. Established as the agent of foreign powers, it had always been a powerful force against progressive change and a destabilising force in Greek politics by establishing and changing alliances with other conservative forces. In the 1974 referendum on the future of the monarchy, almost 70 percent of the electorate voted against it, and monarchy was abolished in December 1974. The Greek conservatives were forced to dissociate themselves from royalism.

The second issue was the question of the military. According to Karamanlis, the Greek military would have to disengage from politics and confine its activities to the defence of the country. Although the military had already been discredited by the junta experience, the mismanagement of the Cyprus issue and the subsequent defeat on the island, liberal-conservatives thought that the military should be transformed into a respectable organisation that would satisfy both its members and Greek civilians. Accordingly, the junta elements were purged from the army, and the so-called "Turkish threat" was used towards this end. In this way, the military was not excluded from the emerging national consensus, instead it was legitimised and integrated into the new political system as the country's protector against "external threat". The position and duties of the army were clearly prescribed by law without giving it any pretext for intervention in domestic affairs. Thus, after years of active intervention in Greek politics, the military was subordinated to civilian rule. This was the end of authoritarianism in Greece.

Perhaps the most critical transformation in the Greek political system in the post-junta period was the change in the outlook of the parliamentary political elite (especially the right wing). The main consensus among the Greek political elite in this period was upon the need to establish democracy with political freedoms and civil rights. The new conservative right, which widened its appeal towards the centre and even towards the left (Macridis, 1981: 11) took a liberal attitude and abandoned its old die-hard and simplistic anti-Communist stand. In this respect, an important event, which consolidated national reconciliation and the process of democratisation, was the legalisation of the Greek Communist Party. Under the impact of the Pax-Americana and in the context of the Cold War, a die-hard and passionate anti-communism had been the most important credential of the parliamentary elite (especially the conservatives) between 1949-1974. Thus, the new liberal-democratic outlook of the parliamentary elite was indeed a revolution in Greek political life. Couloumbis summarises the revolutionary change in the Greek right:

> The old traditional right known for its dynamic methods such as electoral manipulation, repressive techniques, royal and military intervention in politics, and monopoly control over the army and security services, is being pushed into a far and uncomfortable corner. The new right, mainly Karamanlis's creation...is a centre right coalition, committed to genuine parliamentary politics with a Western European orientation (Couloumbis, 1981b: 188).

Karamanlis's aim, however was to ensure bourgeois modernisation and rationalisation, which would be crowned by Greek accession to the EC. From the very beginning, he directed his main efforts to this endeavour (Mavragordatos, 1983: 75 and 76). When he formed the New Democracy party, he stated that:

> ND believes that Greece is not only entitled, but can assure the distinguished place and happiness of its people within the Europe to which she belongs, if it mobilises all its abilities and if it makes use of all the virtues of its people. A fundamental precondition, however for all this is the implanting in our country of a genuine and up-to-date democracy. Towards this end the great camp of ND is totally and unanimously dedicated (Karamanlis, 1974: 225).

Moreover, in the post-junta period constant American intervention into Greek politics came to an end. In the summer of 1974 the Junta collapsed as a result of Turkish intervention in Cyprus following a Greek coup that aimed at unification of the island with Greece. When the Junta collapsed, anti-Americanism was at the top of the Greek political agenda. There was a consensus among the political elite and the ordinary people that the US had helped the Colonels to seize power in 1967 and had supported them afterwards. The resentment against the US reached its peak during the Cyprus crisis, and Greeks began to accuse the Americans of being insensitive to the Turkish intervention and of siding with the Turkish arguments. In an environment in which their strongholds were either discredited and put under civilian control (the military), abolished (the monarchy), or had abandoned their unconditional Atlanticist orientation (parliamentary elite), it was almost impossible for the Americans, who had been experiencing a relative decline of their hegemony, to intervene and impose their policies any longer in Greek domestic affairs. The centre of the decision-making gravity in Greece moved to a pro-European cabinet and Prime Minister (Couloumbis, 1983b: 113). The Americans realised that "a return to the old bilateral relation of dependence was virtually impossible, and for many people also undesirable" (quoted in Tsoukalis, 1981: 157).

Foreign Policy: 1974-Early 1980s: "Europeanisation"

In the contraction period of the world economy, in parallel to economic and political changes, a number of developments are expected to occur in the external relations of an upwardly mobile semiperipheral state. It is expected to change its international alliances, abandon satellite-type foreign policies, and develop the ability to pursue foreign policy relatively independent of the hegemonic/core powers. Moreover, the upwardly mobile semiperipheral state competes with other semiperipheral states for economic and political gains, and tends to assert its intermediary and bridge (or sub-imperial) role between geographically, historically and culturally contiguous areas and the core regions. Furthermore, they attempt to become involved in the management of international problems. In the case of Greece, most of these characteristic semiperipheral foreign policy orientations can easily be observed. The foreign policy of Greece in the post-junta period was erected upon the following principles:

a) Greece still belonged to the West, but not simply as a loyal and unconditional ally. The Western alliance would have to accept that Greece had its own national interests that would no longer be sacrificed to the interests of Atlanticism.
b) In order to promote its economic and political interests and further diversify its foreign policy, and to also get rid of the "disillusionment" caused by the Atlantic Alliance (that is NATO and the US), Greece had to integrate into the European Community.
c) Greek foreign policy would not be unidimensional but would pursue a multidimensional orientation. To this end Greece would promote its relations with the USSR, Eastern Europe, China, the Middle East and Non-Aligned countries.

The most striking foreign policy change in the post-junta period was the extent to which Greece abandoned its postwar unconditional Atlanticism and followed a strong pro-European/EC line. This is what world-system scholars would call "a change in international alliances". The indicators of this shift were, first, Greece's withdrawal from the military wing of NATO in August 1974 ostensibly because of NATO's "inaction" against the Turkish intervention in Cyprus following the Greek coup on the Island. This demonstrated that Greek "national interests" would now come first, and would no longer be sacrificed to the interests of NATO or the US. Later, when Greek perceptions of NATO had changed somewhat, Karamanlis offered up a "special agreement": Greek forces would be integrated in NATO only in the event of East-West warfare. A second indication of breaking with Atlanticism and the US was the reduction in the number of US military bases in Greece from seven to four. These bases were brought under Greek control with the insistence that the operation of the bases would be permitted only when it was considered necessary for Greek national interests (Couloumbis, 1981a: 176). The status of the bases remained a problem between Greece and the US until 1983. Moreover, the home-porting agreement of the US 6th Fleet was also terminated. The changing nature of Greek-American relations was noted in a US Congressional Study Mission Report in 1975, which stated that "in January 1975, when the study mission arrived in Athens, the level of Greek-American co-operation had reached its lowest point in the entire postwar period. Even more important it seems likely that these relations will soon be redefined in a significantly different way" (quoted in Symeonides-Tsatsos, 1991: 19).

As Atlantic relations were put on a new track, Karamanlis proceeded with his policy of making Greece a full member of the EC as soon as possible. The Greek intention was first expressed to the French and German governments as early as September 1974, and they responded positively (Lavdas, 1997: 139-140). Karamanlis wanted to decrease Greece's security dependence on the US by making military procurement agreements with France, and by attracting French private investment capital. Thus, having secured the French and German support, Karamanlis emphasised, from the time of his first electoral campaign, that he would pursue a policy of accelerated entry of Greece into the Community (Clogg, 1987: 63). Karamanlis believed that Greece was a part of Europe, and that it should take its proper place in the realisation of a united Europe (Karamanlis, 1974: 225). His determined efforts to convince the nine EC leaders played a decisive role in the decision of the Community to accept Greece as the Tenth member (as of January 1981) in May 1979 (see Siotis, 1981: 99-110).

The signing of the Treaty of Accession in May 1979 marked Greece's formal shift from unconditional Atlanticism to Europeanism. EC membership was seen as an invaluable step in escaping from American influence and client status, and upgrading the position of Greece in the international sphere. A few months before signing the Accession Treaty, Karamanlis stated that "on joining the mighty European family as an equal member Greece will no longer be obliged to seek protection from one or another superpower" (quoted in Woodhouse, 1982: 274). "Europeanism" was not considered a new form of Atlanticism (dependence) because Greece would be an equal member in this new alignment, as opposed to the asymmetrical relationship of postwar Atlanticism. Karamanlis noted the "upgraded" position of his country in an address to the party congress: "within the Community...[Greece] will have a say not only in its own fortunes but in the future course of Europe, since it will influence Community resolutions through its vote" (Karamanlis, 1979: 226).

Another semiperipheral tendency of Greek foreign policy was to abandon its satellite-like policy and to emphasise its independent stance. Not surprisingly, this policy was explained as "independence-from-the-US". The Community was seen as an alternative alliance of Western states whose interests were not identical with those of the US. Furthermore, since Community decisions are taken by unanimous vote, a decision contrary to Greek national interests could not be imposed on the country, and this would strengthen Greece's independent foreign policy stance.[3] Greece also established independent relations with the Balkans, Eastern Europe, the Middle East, the USSR and China. Previously relations with the Soviet Bloc, Balkans, and China had been based on American established norms and policies. Even when western Europeans revised their policies vis-à-vis

Eastern Europe, Greece had refrained from taking an independent stance (Stavrou, 1980: 157-158). Thus Karamanlis's opening to the Soviet Bloc, the Balkans and China (on both political and economic grounds), and the setting up of bilateral and multilateral relations, were clear examples of Greece's new "non-satellite and independent" foreign policy line (see Woodhouse, 1982: 260-269).

Fighting against other semiperipheral countries like Turkey, Spain and Portugal for economic and political gains on the way to full membership in the EC was another semiperipheral characteristic of Greece's external policy (semiperipheral rivalry). The negative response of the EC Commission in 1976 to the Greek application for full membership, partly on the basis of the conflict between Turkey and Greece and its possible ramifications on the Community's future relations with Turkey, seemed an important obstacle to Greece's future membership in the organisation.[4] Turkey had enjoyed an associate status comparable to that of Greece until then. With the prospect of Greece's accession, Turkey could suffer discrimination both economically and politically in its relations with the EC (de la Serre, 1979: 41) and this would undermine the balance between the two vis-à-vis the Community. However, the reports linking Greek accession with the settlement of disputes with Turkey, and the emphasis on the identical status of the two countries were unacceptable to the Greek government. Karamanlis protested the Commission's decision on moral and political grounds (Verney, 1987: 261). He argued that Greece had no economic disputes with Turkey, and its accession would not affect the development of the Community's relations with Turkey (Siotis, 1981: 102). Karamanlis launched an intensive diplomatic campaign directed at the nine-EC member states. The problem was solved in favour of Greece thanks to his persistent and determined policy. A second problem emerged with the Spanish and Portuguese applications for full membership in 1977. Indeed, these developments changed the context of the Greek application in the minds of Community policy makers; concessions to Greece, once given, could be used as precedents by Spain and Portugal (Wallace, 1979: 23). Accordingly, they proposed the globalisation of the Community's Mediterranean policy. However, from the Greek perspective this would decrease the economic gains Greece expected from the EC. Once again, as a result of Karamanlis' swift and intensive diplomacy (see Verney, 1987: 262), which was based on the uniqueness of each application and Greece's special position in the Community because of the Association Agreement of 1959[5] as well as Karamanlis' policy of further acceleration of negotiations for accession

(Verney, 1987: 263), the problem of globalisation of the EC Mediterranean policy was also overcome.

A more striking example of Greece's semiperipheral foreign policy was the intermediary role it was willing to play between the EC and the Middle East and North Africa. In world-system analysis, this represents the sub-imperialist disposition taken by an upwardly mobile semiperipheral state. Karamanlis pursued a very active diplomacy in both of these regions between 1975 and 1980 (Woodhouse, 1982: 269-271). As noted above, Middle East markets had become a major outlet for Greek exports, and on this basis Greece was willing to play a sub-imperial or a bridge role in this region for the Community. This policy was justified by Greece's geographical proximity to the region and "historical ties" maintained over centuries (Zolotas, 1976: 20 and 1978: 50). According to the Governor of the Central Bank, X. Zolotas, one of the advantages the EC would gain from the accession of Greece was:

> the geographic position of Greece which lends itself to the establishment of industrial and other firms - involving the collaboration of Greek with foreign venture capital - that will be aimed at penetrating the markets of the Middle East and Africa (Zolotas, 1976: 20).

A further sound reason for the Community to use Greece as a bridge to these regions was the extensive activities undertaken by Greek architectural, planning and engineering firms in Iraq, Libya, Saudi Arabia, Iran, Syria, United Arab Emirates and Africa (Zolotas, 1976: 12-13 and 1978: 50-51). In 1978, there were about thirty Greek firms with a combined staff of over eight thousand Greek engineers and skilled workers, who undertook construction projects worth $5 billion in these countries. The activities of these Greek construction companies contributed heavily to the expansion of Greece's exports to the Middle East - from $66 million in 1973 to $533 million in 1977. These export items mainly consisted of cement, building materials, metal structures, transport equipment (see Zolotas, 1978: 51). This strong presence of Greek technical firms in the Arab countries, and the dynamic growth of Greek exports, would help to promote the EC's interests in the Arab markets:

> This could be achieved by setting up joint Greek-EEC ventures capable of developing their activities either in the construction sector or in the commercial penetration of the Arab countries...Greek technical experts and businessmen, who are fully aware of the special economic, political and cultural condition

prevailing in the Arab countries, would considerably facilitate the access of joint Greek-EEC companies to the area of the Middle East (Zolotas, 1978: 52).

Moreover, Greece was also seen as a springboard to African markets for joint Greek-EC ventures. Such joint enterprises could supply the developing countries of Africa with a wide variety of products, including building materials, chemicals, electrical and telecommunications equipment, clothing, foodstuff, etc. (Zolotas, 1978: 52). The intermediary and/or sub-imperialist tendencies that could turn Greece into a regional power were also evident in Greek efforts to make the country the financial and transit centre in the region (Woodhouse, 1982: 270-271 and Zolotas, 1978: 52-53).

The Federation of Greek Industrialists (SEV) also enthusiastically supported this bridge policy of the Greek state. The SEV continuously put its emphasis on the Federation's services for members in the Middle East and North Africa (Lavdas, 1997: 145). The Federation assumed the role of coordinating and assisting the Greek firms in order to reap the benefits of business opportunities in the Middle Eastern and North African markets, and emphasised that "Greece should take the full advantage of its Mediterranean position" (*Deltion*, 15 March 1975 quoted in Lavdas, 1997: 276, endnote 67).

With regard to the Balkans, Karamanlis's pledge to contribute to peace and order (that is, to European efforts at preserving detente and arms control) through its economic and cultural relations with the Balkans (Woodhouse, 1982: 274 and Veremis, 1983: 176) was an indication of Greece's aspiration to play a wider role in the region. The Balkan states conferences convened by Greece in 1976, 1979, 1981, 1984 and 1986 (Kofas, 1991: 115) that aimed at economic and technical cooperation were a step taken in this direction.

It was apparent that Greece attempted to present itself as a bridge between the geographically and historically contiguous areas of the Middle East, Africa and the Balkans and the EC core zone, and hence attempted to play a sub-imperial role in the Eastern Mediterranean. Woodhouse neatly summarises Karamanlis's policy: "He recognised that... he could enhance Greece's standing with her associates by providing them, through Athens, with a window to the East, looking out in particular on the Arab world and the Communist bloc." (Woodhouse, 1982: 287).

The Economic Environment: Early 1980s-1990 (Papandreou Period)

All the indications gave the impression that Greece was experiencing, in the terminology of the world-system analysis, a shift towards the core zone in the world-system hierarchy of states. There was indeed an improvement in the position of Greece. Yet the decisive point is that Greece's shift upwards in the hierarchy of states was not based on structural transformations in the production structures of the country. In world-system analysis, a shift from the semiperipheral position towards the core zone corresponds to a substantial shift in production patterns towards high profit, high-technology and high wage sectors of the world-economy. However, OECD surveys on Greece indicate that in the period between the mid-1970s and early 1980s, Greek industry expanded in the traditional branches such as textiles, food, beverages and construction materials (cement, steel and aluminium), but actually lacked investment in more sophisticated, technologically advanced new lines of production (that is core-like) and activities (OECD, 1977 to 1983). Almost all the traditional Greek industries were classified as regressive industries (that is periphery-like), and their relative importance in world demand stagnated or declined (Giannitsis, 1991: 218-219 and OECD, 1990: 74 and Table 25). Thus Greece continued to specialise in resource (raw material) intensive and labour intensive products, and it retained a comparative disadvantage in technologically advanced goods (OECD, 1990: 74). The sectors that typically use more advanced technology in both labour and capital intensive industries remained small (OECD, 1990: 75). Between 1975 and 1979 while the shares of resource and labour intensive industries in total Greek exports were 42.2 percent and 32.2 percent respectively, in technologically advanced sectors it was 18.2 percent for scale-intensive industries, 4.7 percent for differentiated goods, and 2.3 percent for science based industries (OECD, 1990: Table 24). The attempts made by the Greek business community and the state in the immediate post-junta period to transform the structure of the economy thus proved unsuccessful.

On the other hand, during this period wages increased considerably (see OECD, 1977 to 1983). The annual growth of unit labour cost in the private and non-agricultural sector was around 19 percent between 1974-1979, and it increased to 26 percent in 1980 (OECD, 1982: 23). In world-system analysis, substantial and successive increases in wages may also indicate an upgrade in the position of a state, because it is hypothesised that wage increases may correspond to an improvement in production structures. However, as OECD surveys show, this was not the case in Greece. On the contrary, the substantial increases in wages in this period contributed to the deterioration of the Greek economy in subsequent years, rather than indicating an upgrade in the status of the country.

Furthermore, despite the new developmentalist intentions of the government in the post-junta period, state ownership was limited to public utilities and was almost nil in the manufacturing sector (Tsoukalis, 1981: 36). The state's participation in total industrial investment accounted for 4.3 percent in the period between 1975-1980 (Giannitsis, 1991: 229).

In fact there were good reasons that could explain the unsuccessful performance of the semiperipheral Greek economy. First of all, the Federation of Greek Industrialist's (SEV) "commitment" strategy (see above) aiming to make Greek industry competitive in Europe was not put into practice successfully (see Lavdas, 1997: 138). The timing of the strategy coincided with both oil price shocks and political change that did not allow the government to follow accommodating policies. The state pursued expansionary policies and tried to reduce unemployment, but labour costs increased as a result of democratisation and the increasing power of trade unions, which in turn created a few incentives for labour to enter into a cooperative relationship with the other social partners. Furthermore, despite the SEV's efforts to differentiate themselves from the economic elite of the Junta period, the public image of the economic elite in the post-junta period remained poor and this also contributed to the failure of their "commitment" strategy that was based on cooperation between the private sector, the state and the labour unions. Second, starting from 1978, the SEV strongly and repeatedly emphasised the need for a reform in the public sector for "Europeanisation" and successful performance in the EC (Lavdas, 1997: 14). They also demanded strengthening of business confidence with a new incomes policy, and asked for new measures to curb public borrowing. Moreover, SEV also argued for the need of the retreat of the state from the economy and less state intervention in the market, and demanded a more responsive approach to the needs of the Greek industry. However, none of these proposals and demands was dealt with effectively. Yet, in view of the EC negotiations the SEV began to demand protection from the state (Lavdas, 1997: 145 and 276, endnote 65). For instance, the Industrialists lobbied for the preservation of the closure on public procurement as a policy line and thus pressed for preservation of national procurement contracts. Moreover and strikingly enough, they also demanded protection for the declining sectors of textiles, steel and shipbuilding, which were experiencing difficulties in the domestic and world markets.

In sum, although some economic indicators suggested an improvement in the Greek economy in the period between the mid-1970s and early 1980s, the improvement was not due to a structural transformation based on genuinely competitive, technologically advanced new lines of production. It was the result of the increasing share of invisibles and total exports (especially to the Middle East) in the GDP, and also due to the competitive advantage of Greek products despite the constant increase in labour costs (OECD, 1983: 41). To put it differently, periphery-like production patterns and producers continued to dominate the Greek economy in this period.

This situation in the Greek economy did not change throughout the 1980s. All the OECD surveys of this period indicate that the Greek economy could not adjust to changing production and worldwide trade patterns, and to technological progress (OECD, 1983 to early-1990s). Greek producers failed to adopt new productive structures in response to the new requirements of world demand (OECD, 1991: 27). The economy remained dependent on resource and labour intensive (periphery-like) industries for which demand in the world market was declining. Between 1980-1987 the share of ascending, technologically advanced (core-like) industries in total Greek exports remained between 2 to 13 percent, while the share of resource and labour intensive (periphery-like) industries was around 35 to 45 percent (OECD, 1990: 76).

Greek exports were concentrated in a few products. Textiles, clothing, footwear, cement, aluminium, iron and steel together presented about three-quarters of manufacturing exports and there had been no apparent tendency to change this since the mid-1970s (OECD, 1990: 75). Furthermore, the failure to develop new technologically advanced (core-like) lines of production, coupled with increasing labour costs and falling profits, caused further deterioration in the cost competitiveness of traditional (periphery-like) Greek products (see, OECD, 1982 to 1992). Additionally, essentially low average net profit rates turned negative after 1982 (OECD, 1982: 78).

Unlike Greece, most of the OECD countries adopted their production structures to new world demand, especially after the second oil shock in 1979. Moreover, new more cost efficient suppliers (in South East Asia) emerged for labour and resource intensive products in which Greek exports specialised. The level of wages for production workers was three times as high as that of production workers of Greece's Asian competitors (OECD, 1990: 78, footnote 32). In these fields South Korea and Hong Kong emerged as the most challenging competitors after the mid-1970s. Thus throughout the 1980s, periphery-like production patterns and producers remained dominant in the Greek economy.

In fact, the new PASOK socialist government's and Prime-Minister Andreas Papandreou's outlook on the economy and on the Greek economic elite was somewhat more radical than the conservatives (ND), especially in PASOK's early years in office. Soon after coming to power, Papandreou declared that the public sector (read state) would be the growth motor of Greece's economic development, while strongly criticising Greek big business (see Lavdas, 1997: 149-153). Papandreou declared Greek capitalism and the private sector as weak and unwilling and unable to become the motor of development, and accused them of being short sighted and speculative in their attitude. According to Papandreou, the weaknesses of Greek capitalism and big business was the result of their dependence on the generous and mismanaged state subsidies and the corrupt system of credit allocation. A second significant aspect of PASOK's new economic policy was a reform in the public sector, which was defined as the motor of economic modernisation. The reform aimed at restructuring industry through changing the role of the public sector, and redefining the goals, instruments and the institutions of the industrial policy, and resolving the problems of ailing private firms. Economic planning was perhaps the most striking part of PASOK's new policy, which included intervention in the economy by supporting the cooperatives, local authority enterprises and SMEs; engaging in public investment; and integrating private sector activities and investments into the goals of the plan. All these policies however caused strong resentment among the economic elite, and led to a confrontation between the socialist government and the big business.

The industrial restructuralisation policy of the PASOK government also aimed at extending incentives, subsidies and credits only to selected and target sectors of the economy in order to encourage the economic elite to invest in non-traditional lines of production (Lavdas, 1997: 152). Those dynamic sectors that would receive the state's generous investment support were electronics, information technology, biotechnology and precision instruments. On the other hand, the state support for investment in traditional industries such as construction, textiles, food and beverages etc., were considerably reduced, and so investment in these sectors discouraged. In other words, the semiperipheral Greek state attempted to support core-like industries and core-like investors while simultaneously punishing the periphery-like lines of production and economic elite. However, this new industrial policy did not work as planned, and once again the state support went to projects coming from the traditional sectors since some of those traditional industries still maintained a comparative advantage in the international markets, and also because of the resistance coming from the traditional (periphery-like) economic elite that dominated the Greek economy. The investments in new and dynamic lines of production continued to remain very limited. The Greek industrial world, and most big business, had concentrated their activities in traditional (periphery-like) production lines, and accordingly they saw the Papandreou's economic and industrial policy as a threat to their interests. Thus they strongly supported horizontal measures (expansion in the existing sectors and the usual investment policies), and resisted government intervention into the economy in favour of new and ascending lines of production (Lavdas, 1997: 152).

Thus state-economic elite relations during the PASOK's first term in power (1981-1985) were generally tense in nature (see Lavdas, 1997: 159-169). The structural adjustment policy and the state's role in its implementation; reform measures in industrial relations and the new labour law; and the expansionary policies of the government particularly disturbed the big business community. The Federation of Greek Industrialists (SEV) publicly attacked the government's economic policies, and the government responded publicly accusing businessmen of making use of semi-legal methods, manipulating public works contracts, defrauding public funds, and misusing investment loans. The SEV leadership, on the other hand, held that the state policies since the mid-1970s were responsible for the structural economic difficulties, without referring to the reorientation of the industrial elite to investments in declining traditional (periphery-like) sectors such as textiles, clothing, food and beverages. Consequently, private industrial investments declined to their lowest level in 1985, and the result was a significant loss in the competitiveness of Greek products in the international markets, not only because of rising labour costs in industry, but also as a consequence of a low level of diversification in high-technology products (Lavdas, 1997: 174-175).

The resistance of the economic elite to the economic policies of the PASOK government culminated in the establishment of the "National Council of Private Enterprise" (ESIP) for the coordination of all business interests, and the establishment of a common business policy vis-à-vis the government. This was followed by a series of middle class demonstrations organised in cooperation with the conservative New Democracy Party. In the end the strong resistance coming from the organised (periphery-like) business interests forced the PASOK government to reconcile with the economic elite. Papandreou declared the government's recognition of business demands for "satisfactory profits" and promised to extend necessary incentives for their investments in the Greek economy (Lavdas, 1997: 167). Accordingly, just before the 1985 elections and especially during the PASOK's second term in office, government-business relations were soothed and SEV's role was strengthened. This, in turn, marked once again the victory of the periphery-like traditional economic elite in Greece. Subsequently, a cooperation and partnership was developed between the government and the SEV during the preparation and implementation of the 1985 stabilisation plan (austerity program).[6] Immediately after the introduction of the plan, business investments and profitability increased, and this situation lasted until 1988 when the government abandoned the implementation of the plan and returned to expansionist policies in the face of approaching 1989 general elections.

State policies, and the relations between the state and capital, indicated that periphery-like interests continued to control the Greek state throughout the 1980s. In this sense, the post-junta "developmentalist image" of the Greek state diminished in this period. The Greek financial system (the two largest commercial banks, special credit institutions, and the biggest insurance companies) was under excessive (direct and indirect) state control[7] and hence four-fifths of the total credits extended to private business were controlled by state agencies (OECD, 1986: 55 and 1992: 72). The striking point was that credits were often given irrespective of banking and financial criteria, and they were extended especially to (periphery-like) large enterprises at the expense of better performing ones (OECD, 1986: 55). Furthermore, commercial banks sometimes refused to extend credit to efficient firms in order to protect enterprises with similar activities with which they had privileged relations (OECD, 1986: 71, footnote 56). Moreover, when the privileged but inefficient (periphery-like) firms faced difficulties paying back their credits, state controlled commercial banks participated in their management in order to protect their own interests. In this way, the banks either continued to supply credit to these firms, or acquired many of the loss making (periphery-like) enterprises, in this period (OECD, 1986: 56 and 1987: 34). Hence, far from becoming an engine of semiperipheral development, the Greek state itself turned into a periphery-like producer in the 1980s.

The state provided subsidies and grants to non-viable traditional (periphery-like) industries with problems of overmanning and heavy indebtedness.[8] This policy however diverted real and financial resources from the competitive economy and from more profitable uses (OECD, 1990: 61). The problematic firms absorbed about half of total state grants and subsidies, and a fifth of total bank credits. Even so, the financial situation of these enterprises improved very little (OECD, 1990: 61). Furthermore, problematic firms were comprised of some forty of the biggest companies in the country (OECD, 1991: 14). The financing of the large deficits of the inefficient, loss-making public enterprises by state grants and special bank loans further indicated that resources were allocated to the periphery-like production patterns (OECD, 1990: 61). In sum, it had become clear in the 1980s that the Greek state was unable to turn itself into a developmentalist state in order to accomplish a shift towards the core zone of the world-economy.

The PASOK governments, especially in the first half of the 1980s perceived the EC as an institutionally weak and organisationally loose framework, and they did not take its rules and regulations seriously (Lavdas, 1997: 155-158). Accordingly, Papandreou frequently violated the EC's institutional and legal framework, and such violations were rationalised as necessary de facto adjustment measures. At the same time, Papandreou strongly demanded (and managed) the renegotiation of Greece's EC entry conditions with the EC authorities on the basis of EC Treaty obligations, which allow for the adjustment of the economies of less developed member states to those of the developed ones. Accordingly, in a memorandum submitted to the EC in March 1982 (see Nicholson and East, 1987: 195-200), Papandreou demanded special agreements with the EC on the extension of Greece's transition period exemptions for a number of EC rules and regulations, and he also asked for increased EC financial transfers to overcome the difficulties in the Greek economy. Between 1982 and 1986, the memorandum became the basis for renegotiation of the Greece's entry terms. In the framework of the Integrated Mediterranean Programs (IMP), the overall response of the EC to Papandreou was basically positive (see Nicholson and East, 1987: 200-202).

In fact, a massive influx of EC transfers to the Greek economy materialised after Greece's accession in 1981. First, the Community extended 2.542 million ECU to Greece in response to the 1982 memorandum from the socialist government demanding recognition of Greece's special problems, and asking for special treatment and assistance to bring the Greek economy closer to those of its partners (Verney, 1987: 265). Net EC transfers increased substantially (77 percent) between 1981-1983 (OECD, 1983: 38), stabilising at around $700 million annually in 1985 (OECD, 1986: 15 and 35). The inflow of capital from the EC also played an important role in offsetting Greece's balance of payments deficits. In 1983-1984 EC capital financed an average of 35 percent of total Gross External Financing Requirements (Kefalas and Mantzaris, 1986: 70). Similarly, in 1985, in the face of a financial crisis when the current deficit stood at almost 10 percent of GDP, the EC provided 1.7 billion in ECU loans to support an austerity program (OECD, 1991: 24). Moreover, EC transfers to Greece continued to increase in the second half of the 1980s. Between 1980-1985 net transfers from the EC were equal to 1.5 percent of GDP, and they reached 4.9 percent of GDP in 1989 (OECD, 1990: 68). Furthermore, receipts from the EC amounted to $3 billion in 1990 (OECD, 1991: 24) and total outstanding EC loans represented 8 percent of GDP, or a quarter of Greece's foreign debt in 1991 (OECD, 1991: 24).

Although net EC inflows reached more than $20 billion (including special and EIB loans) between 1981-1991, the Greek economy was unable to match the growth and structural changes in other EC countries (Kapetanyannis, 1993: 80). EC transfers and loans either played a role in averting a balance of payment crisis, or limited the resort to foreign private credit throughout the 1980s (OECD, 1991: 22; Kleinman, 1988: 208 and Kefalas and Mantzaris, 1986: 78), or went into consumption rather than into investment, or were wasted (Tsoukalis, 1992: 155). In short, they did not contribute to the structural transformation of the Greek economy. As Verney puts it, "success in channelling more Community resources to Greece often seemed to become an end in itself. All too frequently, the Greek government appeared unable to absorb the financial support it was offered or to co-ordinate its use in a way that would help the country to adjust to the challenge of Community competition" (Verney, 1993: 150). Hence, despite the inflow of massive amounts of EC funds, and contrary to expectations, the Greek economy could not overcome its structural weaknesses, nor its low level of technology, poor infrastructure and its specialisation in regressive industries.

Furthermore, direct foreign investment in Greece was hardly influenced by EC membership, and Greece was little affected by the transnational mergers and acquisitions that restructured European industry (Tsoukalis, 1992: 155). Moreover, in the second half of the 1980s, it became apparent that foreign companies (especially European) were unwilling to use Greece as an intermediary in the Middle Eastern and North African markets (Tsoukalis, 1981: 45 and 47). While the share of the Middle Eastern and North African markets in total Greek exports amounted to 23.2 percent in 1981, this figure declined dramatically to 11.7 percent in 1987 (OECD, 1990: 104). However, trade relations between Greece and the Community increased significantly after accession. While the share of Greek exports to and imports from the EC were 46.3 and 47.7 percent respectively in 1981, they reached 60.3 and 54.3 percent in 1987 (OECD, 1990: 104). The increasing share of invisibles (especially European tourist receipts) in the Greek economy (OECD, 1987: 22), and their positive role in offsetting balance of payments constraints, were other significant developments in Greek-EC economic relations in the 1980s.

These developments in the 1980s show that the "Europeanisation" of Greece, which is identified with the concept of "semiperipheral development" or "mobilisation towards the core zone", can be explained in terms of the transfer of huge amounts of money from the EC, increasing Greek-EC trade relations, the inflow of EC tourists, and so forth, but not in terms of structural transformations in production patterns. In world-system analysis, an upgrade in the hierarchy of state refers first, to an upgrade in the sphere of production. This did not occur in Greece in the 1980s. On the contrary, the Greek economic elite invested in regressive industries rather than in technologically advanced sectors capable of inducing significant modernising and restructuring effects in industry (Giannitsis, 1991: 218 and Petras et al., 1993: 181). Greek industrialists were seeking easy profits (a periphery-like characteristic), rather than investing in productive spheres. An OECD survey shows that Greek industrial firms, which had privileged access to credit, borrowed more than they required in order to re-lend the money to domestic and import traders with which they had business relations (OECD, 1986: 57-59).[9] On the other hand, Lavdas argues that despite the agreements reached with the EC in 1982 over the Integrated Mediterranean Program, which brought the EC's substantial contribution to the Greece's "catching up" policy, the main aspects of the transitional regime remained in use. This, in turn, meant that the Greek state (as a defining characteristics of a semiperipheral state) remained the major target of the economic elite for lobbying for assistance, either in the form of subsidies, credit allocation and procurement in the domestic sphere, or as a lobbyist in the EC for achieving derogations or extensions (Lavdas, 1997: 159 and 184).

The state's continuous financial support of ailing and problematic firms, and the loss of competitiveness and foreign market shares, clearly indicated the dominance of "periphery-like" production patterns in the economy. An OECD survey on Greece points to the state oriented policies of these periphery-like producers, and to the way they articulated their interests at the state level. Moreover, it emphasises the central position of the state in the semiperiphery:

> [State intervention]...has had strong bearings on mentalities and behavioural attitudes as economic agents become accustomed to state interference and to petitioning the government for permanent assistance and protection whenever relative income positions are felt or perceived to be threatened by competitive forces and structural change (OECD, 1990: 58).

A point that seems to deviate from one of the semiperipheral hypotheses is related to the increases in the per capita GNP in this period. As we saw, per capita GNP can be accepted as an indicator of the world-system position of a state, and continuous and remarkable increases or decreases in GNP are a sign of upward or downward movement in the world-system hierarchy of states. The Greek GNP per capita income, which was $4348 in 1980, decreased to $3380 in 1984 and increased moderately to $3966 in 1986 (OECD Reports from 1980 to 1986). However, this trend came to an end when the GNP figures rose up to $5058 in 1988; to $5359 in 1989; and to $6629 in 1990. From the world-system perspective, it is strange for GNP per capita to increase in an economy that is dominated by periphery-like structures, and which performed badly for a decade (OECD, 1989 to 1992).

In sum, Greece did not experience an upgrade in its status in the world-economy in the 1980s. On the contrary, it fell to the bottom place in the OECD area at the beginning of the 1980s and remained there throughout the decade (OECD, 1992: 76). Greece's actual and potential output growth rate was 1.5 percent during the 1980s, one of the lowest in Europe (OECD, 1991: 18), and the growth of GDP fell to 0.1 percent in 1990 compared with 2.6 percent in the OECD area (OECD, 1991: 9). The poor performance of the Greek economy in the 1980s opened a development gap between Greece and the rest of the OECD area (OECD, 1991: 84) and the EC (Verney, 1993: 151). Subsequently, Greece fell behind Portugal in the EC to the twelfth and the worst economy (Kapetanyannis, 1993: 80 and Verney, 1993: 151). This in turn created a controversy about the economic and political status of Greece in the EC. On the one hand, Greece retained full membership in the prestigious Community of advanced (core-like) economies as an equal member. On the other hand, it created a "Greek problem", by becoming a discordant member and a constant drain on the EC budget (Verney, 1993: 151). From the perspective of semiperipheral development, all these facts once again indicated that although Greece was a member of the Community since 1981, membership did not lead to an upgrade in its status towards the core zone of the world-economy throughout the decade.

The Political Environment and Foreign Policy: Early 1980s-1990

Politically, Greece entered the 1980s with a socialist government, which indicated an important step forward for the consolidation of democracy. In the context of semiperipheral politics, this step is a continuation in the transformation process of the old political structures dating from post-junta period. Accordingly, despite the socialist government's unsuccessful performance in improving the structure of the Greek economy, democratic political structures remained intact during the 1980s. However, it should be borne in mind that the EC's massive transfer of resources into the Greek economy during this period played a decisive role in protecting Greek democratic structures.

In parallel with its poor economic performance, Greece did not exhibit the characteristic behaviour of an upwardly mobile semiperipheral state in the foreign policy sphere. What was expected from upwardly mobile semiperipheral Greece was a gradual increase in influence in the EC and in world politics; harmonious relations with its partners in the western alliance - especially in the EC; and the emergence of a Greek sphere of influence (though in a secondary sense) in geographically and historically contiguous areas. Greece did not attain these objectives in the 1980s.

In fact, in the 1980s Greek foreign policy was based upon the rhetoric of "independence",[10] a characteristic foreign policy orientation of upwardly mobile semiperipheral states. The main objective was to show that Greece was no longer a satellite state. However, now it was clear that the unconditional Atlanticist years were over, and Greece was an equal member of the highly prestigious EC. Furthermore, the re-entry of Greece into NATO in 1980, and the agreement reached with the Americans on the operation of US bases in 1983, were other indicators of Greece's non-satellite status in so far as the agreements (especially the bases agreement) observed Greek interests and established a balance in the relations between Greece and the US (Pranger, 1988: 256). Hence, the socialist governments' rhetoric of "independence" did not constitute a new phenomenon.

However, contrary to the expectations from an upwardly mobile semiperipheral country, Papandreou's "independent" Greek foreign policy disharmonised political cooperation both in NATO and in the EC. Moreover, Greece itself became a problem in the western alliances. In relation to the US and NATO, Papandreou declined to participate in NATO military exercises in the Aegean Sea because of Greece's disputes with Turkey. During the boycott of a NATO exercise in 1983, Papandreou permitted a Soviet fleet to visit the Greek port of Piraeus, which also coincided with an EC meeting on political cooperation in Athens. At a NATO Defence Ministers' meeting, he demanded a NATO guarantee of Greece's borders with Turkey. Furthermore, Papandreou responded negatively to the deployment of American Cruise and Pershing II missiles as part of NATO's Intermediate Nuclear Force Modernisation Program, while making no reference to the USSR's SS20s. He also defined the USSR as a factor that restricted the expansion of capitalism and its imperialistic aims (Loulis, 1985: 7), and he similarly described NATO as the first politico-military bloc that caused the inevitable emergence of the Warsaw Pact (McCaskill, 1988: 318). Papandreou promoted the Romanian idea of establishing a Balkan nuclear-free zone, which in turn led to significant rapprochement with the Soviet Union. He refused to condemn the shooting down of a South Korean Airliner by the Soviets on the grounds that it had been on a spying mission, and he established good relations with radical Arab states with which the US had problems.

In relations with the EC, Greece's disharmonising "independence" line was demonstrated in a number of ways. In 1981, the Papandreou government rejected the Community's plan to send peacekeeping troops to Sinai, and to be associated with Camp David. Papandreou also complained about an EC resolution that supported the withdrawal of Libyan forces from Chad. In 1982, he resisted Western sanctions following the introduction of martial law in Poland, and he also dismissed his deputy foreign minister for signing an EC communiqué condemning Soviet involvement in Polish affairs. Papandreou then vetoed an EC attempt to condemn the USSR for shooting down Korean Airlines Flight 007. Moreover, after the American bombing of Libya in 1986, Greece refused to apply measures against the Libyan regime unless there was tangible proof that Libya fostered terrorism. Finally, Greece refused to align itself with its EC partners in the condemnation of Syria for its role in blowing-up an Israeli airliner. Consequently, contrary to the expectations from an upwardly mobile semiperipheral state, in the foreign policy sphere Greece became a problem both in NATO and in the EC.

However, the socialist government's position towards the EC began to change in the second half of the 1980s due to the difficulties experienced by Greek economy (Christodoulides, 1988: 289-292 and Verney, 1993: 145-150). The financial transfers of the EC's Integrated Mediterranean Program and the Agricultural funds for the modernisation of the Greek agriculture, which increased the incomes in the rural areas, were the two important factors that led to a change in the socialist government's attitude towards the Community. Now it become clear that EC was the future framework and motor of economic development of Greece. As the Greek economy became more and more dependent on EC transfers, Greek foreign policy was modified. Moreover, PASOK clearly realised that the EC membership provided advantages in the international relations of Greece. One indication of this shift was the signing of the Single European Act in December 1985 and acceptance of the institutionalisation of the European Political Cooperation (see Verney, 1993: 146-147).

Relations with the US also began to improve because Papandreou realised that strained ties with Washington would be bad for Greece's defence policy. Greece's American friends also warned Papandreou that if he did not refrain from anti-American policies, Greece would lose the support of US Congress, which had been considerably influenced by the Greek-American lobby since 1974 (Haas, 1988: 63).

Another main indication that Greece had failed to achieve an upgrade towards the core zone was its inability to create a sphere of influence, and/or to participate in the management of international problems. In this context, Greece's relations with the Middle East represent the best example. As mentioned earlier, during the second half of the 1970s Greece asserted its intermediary role between the Middle East, North Africa and the EC hoping to become an economic and financial centre and a crossroads in the region. Although this policy proved unsuccessful in the early 1980s, the Papandreou governments continued the policy. In opposition years, Papandreou had already established close relations with the "progressive" and radical regimes of the Middle East such as Syria, Libya, PLO etc., (Elephantis, 1981: 113 and Clogg, 1984: 22). Once in power, Papandreou initiated a new opening to the Arab World. In contrast to Karamanlis, he based his Middle East policy on pro-PLO and pro-Arab policies. The PLO was granted recognition at the end of 1981; closer relations were cultivated with Libya and Algeria; Papandreou visited a number of Arab countries (Ioannides, 1991: 147-148); a direct line of communication was established between Greece and Syria (Kourvetaris and Dobratz, 1987: 115); and an agreement was signed with Syria against world imperialism and racist Zionism (Loulis, 1985: 28). Papandreou emphasised Greece's support for the Palestinian cause and denounced the Israeli occupation of Arab lands (Ioannides, 1991: 147). This new opening to the "progressive" and radical Arab states was largely based on an economic rationale; it was expected that this policy would bring an influx of Arab capital and investment into the Greek economy (Ioannides, 1991: 147 and McCaskill, 1988: 310). Various economic agreements (especially on oil and improved trade) were signed with Arab states during the 1980s (McCaskill, 1988: 316). However, the Arab contribution to the Greek economy (capital flows, investment, commercial and trade benefits, etc.) remained negligible; the Arabs were reluctant to embrace Greece (see McCaskill, 1988: 312 and 316; Ioannides, 1991: 147). Accordingly, although Greece attempted to contribute to the solution of the Middle East conflict as a member of the EC, pledged to work as a go-between (Kourvetaris and Dobratz, 1987: 115), and declared the need for an effective Greece-EC initiative to resolve the crisis (Constas, 1991: 52), all these attempts proved unsuccessful and did not bring any benefit to Greece. Furthermore, the pro-PLO and pro-Arab policies did not encourage the Arabs adopt a pro-Greek stands vis-à-vis Turkey on the Cyprus issue and Aegean problems. Finally, Greece did not participate and play a role in the international management of the Iran-Iraq War, or later in the Gulf War in 1990, other than sending a few warships for surveillance.

Similarly, Greece was no more successful in playing an active role in the Balkans (Kofas, 1991: 116). The Balkan conferences convened on Greek initiative in the 1970s and 1980s and the proposal to create a nuclear-free zone in the Balkans were important developments, because for the first time in the postwar period security problems began to be discussed in Balkan forums (Kofas, 1991: 116). However, the interests of the Balkan states soon waned and the Balkan conferences did not lead to a privileged status for Greece in the Balkans (Kofas, 1991: 115).

1990-2000s: Mitsotakis, Papandreou and Simitis Periods

During the latter phase of the contraction period of the world-economy, Greece revealed reluctance towards becoming an upwardly mobile semiperipheral state. Despite the modernising efforts of the new conservative government, the Greek economy did not experience a substantial transformation towards core-like production structures in the first half of the 1990s, and the periphery-like producers continued to dominate the economic and political domains. Thus semiperipheral Greece waited until Simitis' PASOK governments gave signs of a new phase of economic development and upward mobilisation in the world-system hierarchy of states towards the core zone. In the second half of the 1990s, together with the significant changes in the economic sphere, the influence of the core-like producers, and their representatives in the political domain (in the state structures), increased considerably. With the Simitis governments after 1996, the core-like interests gradually challenged the semiperipheral balance of power, which was in favour of periphery-like actors in both the economic and political spheres, and thus the fight over the state policies became intense in the second half of the 1990s. Clearly, these developments were reflected in the foreign policy of Greece.

The Economic Environment

In the early 1990s, the prospects for the Greek economy were not promising. Greece was burdened with heavy external debt, slow growth, high inflation, a large balance of payment deficit, poor state of infrastructures and inefficient public administration (OECD, 1991). Furthermore, state intervention in the economy increased rapidly in the form of state subsidies, financial assistance and transfers to the industrial, agricultural and service sectors (OECD, 1990: 50). The wide range of this state support was realised in an *ad hoc* manner, and the selection of branches and the instruments used in this policy were not carefully evaluated in that a considerable amount of capital was wasted and inefficient and low-technology (periphery-like) production patterns were protected.

Furthermore, the losses in Greece's market shares in world trade continued in the first half of the 1990s, and this was the direct result of the deterioration in the cost competitiveness, and the lack of adaptability of production structures to changing world trade patterns (see OECD, 1991: 24; 1993: 25 and 1995: 7). According to an OECD survey, Greece's economic performance sharply contrasted with the Spanish and Portuguese experiences. Spain and Portugal had similar market shares to Greece in the early 1980s but managed to make significant market gains in the medium and high-technology products thereafter (OECD, 1993: 25). In fact, in Greece the structure of the exports and the commodity composition changed very little after its accession to the EC, and Greece could not benefit from the trade creation effects of full membership as much as the other southern European countries did (OECD, 1990: 68 and 1993: 12). On the other hand, the competitive power of Greek products in the world markets was based not on product mix but on price and quality, which suffered from increasing labour cost and lack of investment respectively. Unlike Spain and Portugal, Greece's export output structure continued to concentrate on declining industries, medium to low technology and resource and labour intensive sectors of production (OECD, 1993: 29 and 1995: 9). Accordingly, the loss of Greek market shares reached 15 percent in the early 1990s in comparison to its world market shares in the late 1980s (OECD, 1991: 49 and 1995: 8).

The public sector, on the other hand, was strongly politicised in that the governing parties constantly appointed "political friends looking-for-jobs" to public sector managerial positions without taking into account any merit criteria (OECD, 1992: 57 and 1993: 33). In many branches of the economy, state controlled companies and institutions continued to represent a large portion of the firms especially in banking and manufacturing, and employment in the state controlled sectors reached more than 15 percent of the total employment (OECD, 1992: 65).

The level of foreign investment in the Greek economy also remained very low in this period. Again, compared with Spain and Portugal, the amount of foreign direct investments in Greece was very small (OECD, 1992: 41). In this regard, "lack of confidence" and "instability" appeared as particularly important factors for the low inflow of both entrepreneurial and financial capital in Greece (OECD, 1992: 53). The major reasons for the weak foreign investment in Greece (less than $2 billion in the 1980s, while it was $46 and $6.5 billion in Spain and Portugal respectively) were the external difficulties of the early 1990s (the Gulf War and especially the conflicts in Yugoslavia), but particularly the long standing domestic obstacles of "frequent policy changes (uncertainty)", "shortfalls of Greek bureaucracy", "lack of transparency and clear rules", and "infrastructural deficiencies", such as poor transport and communication lines and "the inability of Greek business elite to develop cross-border links with the foreign business" (OECD, 1993: 18-19 and 22).

The EC's contribution in the Greek economy was, again, profound in the early 1990s. The EC transfers that reached to 4 percent of the GDP largely offset the deficits in the trade balance, and total EC loans represented one-quarter of the Greek foreign debt (8 percent of the GDP). All together, total EC transfers and loans averted a balance of payment crisis in Greece, and given the reluctant attitudes of foreign creditors towards Greece, the 1990 EC loan of $3 billion was a well-timed relief for the Greek economy (OECD, 1991: 24 and 1992: 31). Thus despite the losses in the market shares and growing deficits in the trade balance, thanks to the EC transfers the overall Greek balance of payments deficits remained considerably lower and was in a downward trend after 1990 (OECD, 1993: 24 and 1995: 1). Moreover, the amounts of EC transfers increased towards the mid-1990s, reaching almost 5 percent of the GDP as investments in infrastructure increased and were financed by the EC structural funds (OECD, 1995: 9). In July 1993, the EC signed an agreement with Greece providing ECU 20 billion from the "Community Support Framework" for 1993-1998 period, and in July 1994 this agreement was replaced with a new one providing ECU 40 billion for the 1994-1999 period (OECD, 1995: 83 and 85).

In fact, the conservative New Democracy party that came to power in April 1990 came in with an all-encompassing reform policy for the economy in order to bring solutions to the long-lasting problems of the Greek economy. Thus the new government announced major institutional and structural reforms and prepared an adjustment program in fiscal retrenchment and public sector reorganisation, and it aimed at the ambitious target of preparing Greece for full participation in the economic and monetary union of the European Community (see OECD, 1991: 55-72). The adjustment plan was welcomed by international institutions, and the EC agreed to extent a loan of ECU 2.2 billion ($3 billion) to support it.

However, in 1992 the initial strategy and priorities of the Adjustment program changed. First of all, the key point and the short-term objective of the plan, fiscal adjustment, was abandoned (OECD, 1992: 15). Furthermore, although laws and regulations for the reorganisation of the public sector and the administration were passed by the parliament, they were not implemented properly. In fact, the opposition coming from the (periphery-like) vested interests within the administration, the strong lack of concern for a change in the system and the lack of badly needed political consensus for radical reforms were the major factors for the failure of the ND government plan for adjustment (OECD, 1992: 58). According to the 1992 OECD country survey, professional associations and labour unions effectively blocked the modernisation efforts of the Mitsotakis' ND government in order to provide high profits and incomes to their members (p.76).

Nonetheless, the New Democracy government managed to decrease the inflation rate from 23 to 18 percent in 1992 and to 12 percent in 1993, export subsidies and some regulatory import restrictions were abolished, and subsidies to ailing firms reduced. Perhaps more importantly, crucial reforms were introduced to deregulate financial markets in light of the plans for joining the European economic and monetary union (OECD, 1993: 36). Furthermore, competition laws were improved, controls on profit margins were abolished and almost all price controls were lifted, and monopolies over postal services, telecommunications and airways were also abolished (OECD, 1993: 41-42). On the other hand, the government had announced an extensive privatisation program in 1990, but it was put into practice properly only in 1992 (see OECD, 1992: 67). Initially, a number of small industrial firms were privatised. Only later in 1992 did the two largest state enterprises, AGET Heracles Cement Company and Elousis Shipyard follow suit. However, plans for privatising Olympic Airways and Athens Urban Public Transport Company were dropped due to a lack of domestic and foreign interest in these firms and the privatisation of Telecommunication Company (OTE) became a gradual process. In fact, the privatisation policy of the government was not satisfactory (OECD, 1993: 42) and moved slowly (OECD, 1995: 34). The economy was still in a difficult position with a public debt of 116 percent of GDP, Public Sector Borrowing Requirements remaining at over 10 percent of GDP, and the inflation rate at around 11-12 percent- meaning that Greece was very far from catching up with its EC partners and the Maastricht criteria (OECD, 1993: 79 and 1995: 1). Progress in structural reforms and in reducing the deficits were far below initial targets (OECD, 1995: 17).

On the other hand, by the mid-1990s the inflexible and the complicated framework of the Greek financial system was practically liberated. Foreign exchange controls were lifted in 1991/1992, controls on the movement of medium and long-term capital were lifted in 1993, and finally with the termination of the restrictions on the short-term capital movements in 1994, full liberalisation of the capital movements was ensured (OECD, 1995: 48-49). However, the restructuring of the banking system was far from being sufficient, because it continued to be dominated by the state owned banks with bad loans and public banks channelling resources to low value uses.

In order to overcome all of these difficulties in the economy and to participate in the European economic and monetary union, Mitsotakis's ND government prepared a convergence plan for the 1993-1998 period, and a Community Support Framework (CSF) agreement was signed with the EU providing Greece ECU 20 billion in the same period.

Yet the 1993-1998 Convergence Plan (structural reforms) was not implemented properly partly because of the 1993 general elections, and thus in July 1994 the new PASOK government drew up a new Convergence Plan for the 1994-1999 period which aimed at, among other things, fiscal consolidation and reduction of inflation to 3 percent and government deficit to 1 percent of the GDP by 1999 (OECD, 1995: 17). The previous CSF agreement was replaced by this new one, which provided Greece ECU 40 billion for the period 1994-1999 (OECD, 1995: 85). In fact, in the mid-1990s Greece was at a crossroads. The imperfect implementation of the restructuralisation program during the first half of the 1990s caused the persistence of the gaps between Greece and its EU partners. In this context, the OECD 1995 survey on Greece emphasised the strong need for an adjustment process through a credible strategy, and determination, in order to cope with the longstanding imbalances affecting the Greek economy: "there [was] not really any other solution if Greece [was] to continue along the path towards integration and play a full part in the construction of Europe" (OECD, 1995: 67). Thus the 1994-1999 Convergence Plan of Papandreou's PASOK government aimed at "a sustainable recovery of the Greek economy to a position where it is an equal partner in a common European market and competitive internationally". And, once again, the plans' key component was fiscal consolidation in order to attain the EU's Maastricht criteria (OECD, 1996: 22).

Indeed with the 1994-1999 Convergence Plan, the Greek economy began to perform considerably better in the second half of the 1990s (OECD, 1997: 37). The Community Support Framework II (CSF II) funds, which was extended for facilitating the Convergence Plan, aimed at upgrading the infrastructure of the economy in the transport, energy and telecommunication sectors (47 percent of the CSF II); stimulating private sector industrial productive investment (16 percent); and supporting health, education and training programs for improving the human capital (16 percent) (OECD, 1996: 50). From the outset the funds were timely and successfully used and considerable progress was achieved in the economic situation (OECD, 1997: 16-17). In fact, Greece began to show the signs of an upwardly mobile semiperipheral state in 1997. Perhaps one of the most striking indicators of the good performance of the economy was the decline in the rate of inflation from 9 percent in 1996 to 6.6 in May 1997. Furthermore, despite the remaining substantial fiscal deficits, the government was successful in reducing fiscal imbalances by almost halving the government deficit from 16 percent of GDP to 9 percent in 1996 (OECD, 1996: 1). Moreover, domestic business confidence and investment increased, the Athens Stock Market boomed (OECD, 1996: 3 and 8, and 1997: 33), and despite weak export performance in the EU and in the world markets, Greek exports made large inroads into the new Balkan and Central European markets (OECD, 1996: 13). The 1996 OECD survey underlined, the significance of central and eastern European markets for Greece, and also as a unique opportunity to undertake investments (p.106). Yet, overall losses in export market shares exceeded 10 percent in the period 1993-1996 (OECD, 1997: 27-30).

However, the major (peripheral) shortcomings of the Greek economy in this period continued to be the very low absorption of new and high-technology, inability to innovate, and a low level of educated workers (see OECD, 1996: 86-87). Medium and low-technology production structures and exports commodities continued to be a defining characteristic of the Greek economy. A tiny portion of the Greek GDP- only 0.5 percent- was spent on the R&D activities (the OECD average was 2 to 3 percent). Most of those funds came from the government, and the R&D projects were carried out by the universities that had weak links to the industry. Another significant shortcoming of the Greek economy was the long-lasting poor performance of the public administration and the privatisation program (see OECD, 1997: 51 and 63). The government remained reluctant to give up control of the state over the large public enterprises and state owned banks, and progress in the privatisation was disappointing.

In the latter part the 1990s the economic policies of the Greek government continued to register steady progress, especially in reducing the large fiscal imbalances and high inflation rates that existed at the beginning of the decade (OECD, 1998: 41). The strategic target of meeting the EU Maastricht criteria for economic and monetary union was relatively successfully implemented, especially after 1996. The general government deficit that was around 16 percent of GDP in the early 1990s was brought down to 3 percent at the end of 1998. Furthermore, inflation rate, which was around 23 percent in 1990, was reduced to 5.3 percent in November 1998. Moreover, in accordance with the monetary policy of the government that aimed at joining the European Monetary Union (EMU) at the beginning of 2001, the parliament approved the independence of the Central Bank in December 1997, and the Greek Drachma was devalued and entered the EU Exchange Rate Mechanism (ERM) in March 1998. These developments strengthened the credibility of the government's monetary policy and the Drachma joined ERM II (second stage) in January 1999 (OECD, 2001: 34). The structural reform program envisaged in the 1994-1999 Convergence Plan was thus largely attained at the end-1998 (see OECD, 1998: 68-73). In view of this favourable picture, the business sector continued strong investment in industry (OECD, 1998: 17).

The overall successful (core-like) performance of the Greek economy continued in and after 1998. In response to the Simitis government's tight fiscal and monetary policies, the inflation rate fell down to 3 percent in the first half of 2000- the satisfactory level set by the Maastricht criteria- and accordingly in June 2000 Greece's membership was accepted by the EMU as of January 1st 2001. Furthermore, the general government deficit dropped further to 1 percent in 2000 (see OECD, 2001: 33-36). Public enterprise reform, and the privatisation of public enterprises, that became a policy priority after 1996 progressed slowly but steadily despite significant obstacles and traditional (periphery-like) vested interests in front of it (see OECD, 2001: 73-85). In March 1998, with entry to the ERM, the Simitis government launched an extensive privatisation program as a part of the policy to join the European Economic and Monetary Union. In the private sector, business confidence and investment boosted (OECD, 2001: 21-22). Moreover, Greece signed the third Community Support Framework (CSF III) with the EU in November 2000 providing Greece $45 billion in the 2000-2006 period. Finally, at the end of 2000 the Greek government, together with EMU authorities, wrote a "stability and growth program" for the period 2001-2004 that foresees ambitious targets for economic growth, inflation, the fiscal balance and the public debt, and also outlines structural reforms to be carried out (EIU Country Report, April 2001: 19).

Catching up with the EU per capita income levels has been one of the primary objectives of upwardly mobile semiperipheral Greek governments especially after 1996, and in this regard significant steps have been taken since the early 1990s. Greek GDP growth exceeded the euro area average for the five consecutive years between 1996-2000, thus the sizeable gap in living standards have been reduced (OECD, 2001: 54). Accordingly, Greek per capita income levels have begun to show signs of convergence with those of its EU partners. Greece's GNP per capita income, which was $6825 in 1991, gradually increased to $8681 in 1993; $9610 in 1994; $11,181 in 1995; $11,514 in 1997, and to $12,159 in 1999 (OECD surveys 1993-2001). Thus Greek per capita GDP convergence with the EU average increased from less than 60 percent in 1990 to nearly 70 percent by the end of 1999 (Christodoulakis, 2000: 94). However, according to the 1998 OECD survey, compared with the faster growth experiences of Spain and Portugal after their incorporation into the EC in 1986 and in view of Greece's 1981 entry into the EC, Greece's efforts towards increasing its per capita income may not be considered a success story (OECD, 1998: 67). Furthermore, it is argued that even if the recent relatively high growth rates in the Greek economy are maintained, it would take almost half a century for Greece to catch up with the average living standards of the EU (Alogoskoufis, 2000: 150).

It is clear that after Kostas Simitis came to power in 1996, the Greek state took the initiative in overcoming the decades long Greek economic maladjustment problem in the face of the threat of missing, perhaps, the last chance of participating in the European Economic and Monetary Union, and thus being marginalisation in the EU. It was only after the March 1998 devaluation of the Drachma and entry into the ERM that the Simitis government seemed rather determined to effectively implement liberalisation reforms (see Pagoulatos, 2000: 237-238).

Despite all these favourable economic indicators and progress in the Greek economy, especially since 1998, a number of significant structural impediments have still been awaiting attention for a real convergence with the EU partners to be actualised. In other words Greece's semiperipheral characteristics still persist. The Greek GDP, irrespective of its recent high growth rates, is among the lowest in the EU area, just slightly ranking over Portugal. Greece's improved economic performance is largely due to the successful adjustment of fiscal imbalances, but important structural problems in the product and labour markets, public sector management and export markets, etc, are still challenging the Greek government (see, OECD, 1998 and 2001). The Simitis governments have accelerated the pace of structural transformation, but there still remains considerable scope for further improvement in many areas by international comparisons (OECD, 2001: 61). Even in the sphere of fiscal consolidation and financial markets where the Greek government took significant successful steps there remain important problems. Thus, the public debt ratio to GDP (debt/GDP ratio), though declining from 111 percent since 1996 to 103 percent in 2000, is still very high compared to the 60 percent limit of the EU Maastricht criteria for economic convergence. According to optimistic OECD estimates, reducing the very high debt/GDP ratio to the 60 percent limit would take Greece at least ten years, while the pessimistic estimates foresee not less than some forty more years (see OECD, 1998: 63 and OECD, 2001: 43-44). Moreover, despite liberalisation and the significant steps taken in the privatisation of state-owned banks, the Greek financial market structure is still very different from that of the EU financial markets (OECD, 2001: 44). The OECD 2001 survey emphasised the need for the privatisation of the remaining state-owned banks since two of the five biggest banks of Greece are still under the control of the state (OECD, 2001: 60 and 82). Although the direct holdings of the state in the National and Commercial Banks of Greece have been reduced or listed in the Athens Stock Exchange, the state has continued its control over these banks indirectly through state-owned pension funds (EIU Country Report 1st Quarter, 2000: 24 and April 2001: 24). The OECD 2001 survey also points out the necessity for strict supervision over reforms and further modernisation of capital market regulations (OECD, 2001: 60).

The Athens Stock Exchange Market (ASE), although highly volatile, began to play a significant role in the capital market for corporate financing since 1997 (see OECD, 2001: 85-88) with the result that the firms have applied less frequently to bank credits for their capital needs. In this way, perhaps, Greek firms have partly realised one of the dreams of the ex-chief of Central Bank X. Zolotas (see above). However, ASE is still a state-controlled institution. The Greek state controls the operation of the stock exchange market through the holdings of publicly owned banks and institutions, and the Ministry of National Economy has the ultimate authority over its operations (EIU Country Profile, 2000: 30 and 2001: 33).

In the product markets, Greece is traditionally known as a country providing a wide range of subsidies to industry often in combination with the EU structural funds (OECD, 2001: 68). State subsidies are still extended to declining, periphery-like, industrial sectors in the form of direct grants, tax incentives and soft loans, and furthermore there is a wide range of incentives to support investment in industry. It is only very recently that a law (2601/98) was passed that supports newly established enterprises investing in high-technology, alternative energy resources or protecting environmental resources. Despite these changes in the legal framework, public support programs can still distort competition and allocative efficiency, especially when granted in an *ad hoc* manner, and furthermore they have adverse budgetary consequences (OECD, 2001: 70). On the other hand, the effectiveness of the competition policy has been very small and the Competition Committee does not have the capacity and power to affect regulations and government decisions that impair competition through state subsidies (OECD, 2001: 76). Besides, the Committee is also unable both to deal with the competition problems arising from the policy of protecting the inefficient state-owned (periphery-like) enterprises and to investigate the sectors that show significant competition problems. Moreover, it is noted in the 2001 OECD survey that the rules and regulations governing the obtaining of licences and permits still presents a significant barrier to entrepreneurial activity (OECD, 2001: 52), which in turn implies the persistent traditional politicised nature of the state-business relationship in Greece. Inadequate state support to R&D and innovation is another significant problem in the product markets. Greece is lagging far behind the OECD average: as a percentage of the GDP, the total expenditure on the R&D in Greece is 0.49 percent compared to the OECD average of 2.23 percent[11] (OECD, 2001: 70, Table 11). On the other hand, agriculture is still important and the most heavily subsidised sector in the Greek product markets. It accounts for 7.2 percent of the GDP and 19 percent of civilian employment (OECD, 2001: 70-71). Furthermore, the Greek agricultural sector also suffers from (peripheral) structural weaknesses such as large number of small and inefficient farms, poor international competitiveness, weaknesses in promotion and distribution, a small percentage of processed goods (30 percent) and heavy use of fertilisers.

The public sector and its management are further problematic areas that need serious reform to affect convergence with the EU. In public sector, Greece is still known for its strongly centralised and bureaucratic structure with heavy favouritism and clientelism, and one that lacks a modern infrastructure (OECD, 1998: 73). The inefficient performance of the public enterprises, and the financial strain they put on the state budget, reached to 2 percent of the GDP annually in the late 1990s; and despite heavy investment expenditures, most of these enterprises remained unable to modernise their technological base or renew their infrastructure and equipment (OECD, 1998: 96 and 107). On the other hand, public sector management is still characterised by over-regulation and extensive administrative formalities, which in turn creates problems for private enterprises and causes corruption. Accordingly, in order to escape from these problems, private firms seek improper ways to speed up procedures or avoid regulations altogether (OECD, 2001: 52).

In the labour market, a Pact of Confidence was reached between the government and the social partners in 1997 on the necessity of structural reforms in the economy for job creation and improved competitiveness, but the practice fell short of the Pact's objectives (OECD, 1998: 69). Another round of talks between the government, employers, and the trade unions for labour market reform collapsed in late 2000. Yet, the government and parliament had passed a reform bill in early 2001 but without any real improvement in the labour market flexibility (EIU Country Report, April 2001: 8 and OECD, 2001: 62-65). Employment Protection Legislation in Greece is quite strict compared to EU standards. Another significant problem in the labour market is the considerable mismatch between private sector demands for new employees and their skills. The emphasis put on the training programs in the convergence plans have remained on paper, and most of the training programs have been delineated only for absorbing EU funds (Alogoskoufis, 2000: 153).

Another challenge comes from the sphere of export market shares and the export structure of Greece. Although the exports and imports have improved, and competitiveness increased since 1999, trade integration of Greece with the euro area remains lower than in any other European country, and Greece became an anomaly in the EU (OECD, 2001: 23 and 44). Greece has long been registering a large deficit on merchandise trade with exports covering only a quarter of imports (EIU Country Profile, 2000: 32), and Greece's current account deficit continued to widen in early 2000- from $3.3 billion at the end-1999 to $5.7 billion at the end-2000 (EIU Country Report April, 2001: 33). In fact until the late 1990s, Greece continuously lost its export shares in the international markets and that loss was concentrated in the Greece's main EU markets (OECD, 1998: 27). In the 1993-1997 period, Greeks exports experienced a 20 percent decline in the international market share for total goods, and loss of competitiveness (one-third) was observed in the traditional manufacturing sectors of footwear and clothing (OECD, 1998: 32). Its poor performance in the EU, however, was partly offset in the exports to Central and Eastern European markets, in that they accounted 20 percent of Greek total exports of goods in 1997 (up from 13 percent in 1994) (OECD, 1998: 35). Thus, better performance and market gains after the second half of 1999 reflect new business opportunities in, and increasing exports to, the neighbouring Balkan countries (OECD, 2001: 23).

Another problem is related with the export structure of semiperipheral Greece (see OECD, 1998: 32-35). First of all, agricultural products constitute more than one-quarter of total Greek exports, which is a high ratio by international standards. Second, it is emphasised that overall Greek manufactured exports have been concentrated in goods that compete on price rather than on quality basis, and Greece still continues to concentrate on traditional and declining (periphery-like) lines of production such as textiles, footwear, beverages, petroleum products, cement, raw materials and semifinished goods, minerals, cotton and tobacco. The declining power of Greek competitiveness in the export markets has also raised concerns for the domestic market shares. The government warned producers that there is a need for maintaining internal markets vis-à-vis foreign competition (EIU Country Report April, 2001: 35).

The lack of interest of the foreign direct investors in Greece has remained another persistent feature of the Greek economy. In the late 1990s, the amount of foreign direct investment (FDI) in Greece remained at $300 million on average (see EIU Country Reports and Profiles between 2000-2001). On the other hand, the level of portfolio investment, which was around $12.2 billion in 1998, decreased to 6.4 billion in 1999 before rising again to the level of $7.7 billion in 2000 (EIU Country Report, July 2000: 38 and Country Profile, 2001: 38). Moreover, foreign institutional investors are absent in the Greek market despite considerable efforts spent by the Athens Stock Exchange market (EIU Country Report April, 2001: 30). However, there has been increased investment activity by Greek investors abroad since the late 1990s, and thus Greece, in an upwardly mobile semiperipheral state manner, became a net direct investor in formerly communist neighbouring countries. In 2000, net outward investment of Greek firms reached $1.25 billion (EIU Country Profile, 2001: 39).

Despite the recent considerable investments financed mainly by the EU CSF funds, the relatively poor level and quality of the public infrastructure is another important obstacle facing the development and modernisation process of the Greek economy. Greece's very poor motorway and railway systems, inadequate capacity of airports, and telecom (communication) networks need to be upgraded to meet international standards in order to attract FDI, increase the competitiveness of the Greek economy, and become a business and transportation hub in the region (see Mamatzakis, 2000).

The EU on the other hand still plays the key role in the Greek economy without which the Greeks, by themselves, may not have been capable of carrying out a structural transformation program aimed at upward mobilisation in the world-economy. The Convergence Plans that have been implemented since the early 1990s have been made possible only with massive transfers from EU funds (see OECD surveys between 1990-2001). It is those large and ever increasing transfers from EU structural funds that have provided an opportunity for a structural change in Greece (OECD, 1998: 1 and 31). EU transfers financed the fiscal consolidation program in the second half of the 1990s. The large fiscal deficits and the public investment programs (equivalent to nearly 2 percent of GDP in 1997) were all financed by capital transfers from the EU (OECD, 1998: 41 and 49).

According to the 1998 OECD survey, between 1984-1997 the cumulative capital transfers to poorly performing public enterprises reached 30 percent of GDP, and to a large extent it was financed by EU structural funds (p.96). Since 1990, the EU funds, especially the CSF I and CSF II, have played a key role in narrowing large investment and technological gaps in the public sector (OECD, 1998: 107 and 2001: 22). It is estimated that the cumulative amount of the EU funds will reach to 20 percent of the current GDP in 2006 (OECD, 2001: 54). Annual GDP growth, averaging between 3.5 to 4 percent between 1996-2001, has been primarily investment led growth that is funded mainly by the EU (see EIU Country Profile 2001: 27 and Country Reports January and April 2001). Furthermore, in 1999 the current account deficit in the balance of payments exceeded 4 percent of the GDP, and again a sizeable amount of the deficit was offset by means of EU transfers (OECD, 2001: 23). Moreover, in the heavily subsidised agricultural sector, 75 percent of the total supports (2.8 percent of the GDP) comes from the EU's Common Agricultural Policy (CAP) transfer programs, and according to the EU's "Agenda 2000", Greek agriculture will receive the same level of budgetary transfers until 2006 (OECD, 2001: 71).

Another significant development since the mid-1990s has been the transformation of the Central and Eastern European Countries (CEECs), but especially the Balkans, into a Greek economic sphere of influence - a clear indication of upwardly mobile semiperipheral economic foreign policy. It is clear that Greece has been increasing its economic relations with the Balkans and aims to establish itself as a "trading centre" in the region (see EIU Country Profile, 2001: 10). In this respect, Greek tradesmen have taken advantage of the economic transformation in the Balkans and the Black Sea regions and quickly made inroads in the markets of the regional countries. The Greek state/governments have supported Greek entrepreneurs in these areas by providing commercial credits through state-controlled banks (EIU Country Profile, 2000: 33). Hence, Greece's share in Balkan trade has increased quickly, and Greece has begun to run trade surpluses by quadrupling its exports in the region in the decade after 1989 (Wallden, 2000: 433). According to reports, the Balkans and the Black Sea markets have absorbed at least 15 percent of the total value of Greek exports (EIU Country Profile, 2001: 37), which is reminiscent of Greek export performance in the Middle Eastern markets in the second half of the 1970s. The main Greek exports to the Balkans consist of food, industrial consumption goods, and intermediate industrial goods, while the main import items include intermediate industrial goods and raw materials (see Wallden, 2000: 435-436).

Greece also aims at becoming a "regional hub for telecommunication" in the Balkans, and to this end the state-controlled Telecommunications Organisation OTE has launched a policy of regional expansion. Accordingly, OTE acquired 90 percent of the Armenian telecommunication system, and subsequently controls 35 percent of the Romanian and 20 percent of Serbian telecommunications systems. OTE also became a part of the consortia operating a microwave network in the Ukraine and card phones in Georgia. Moreover, OTE acquired mobile services in Bulgaria and Albania through its subsidiary Cosmote (see EIU Country Profile, 2000: 15 and 2001: 17). In fact, it is partly because of the regional investment activities of OTE that the Greek state is willing to retain its control over OTE arguing that the organisation is instrumental to the Greek state's broader economic strategy in the region (EIU Country Report January, 2001: 21).

Another strategic aim of Greece is to establish itself as an "energy-exporting centre" in the Balkans (EIU Country Report April, 2001: 23, and see also Wallden, 2000: 438). To this end, in 1995, the Greeks signed a protocol with the Russians and Bulgarians for the construction of trans-Balkan oil pipeline to transport oil from the Caspian Sea to the Aegean Sea. A more concrete development in his field is that the state-controlled Hellenic Petroleum Company, El.Pet, has acquired a controlling interest in the oil refinery of FYR of Macedonia and is constructing an oil pipeline from the port of Thessaloniki to FYR of Macedonia (see EIU Country Profile, 2001: 19).

Greece also aims to play a "prominent role in the financial and the banking sectors" in the Balkans by providing finance and other services to the transition countries and to Greek firms operating in the region. Two state-controlled banks, National Bank and the Commercial Bank of Greece, and three private banks, Alpha, Piraeus, and EFG Eurobank, opened subsidiaries and branches in the Balkans and in Central and Eastern Europe (EIU Country Profile, 2001: 32). Accordingly, Greek commercial banks acquired a number of local banks in the Balkans: Post Bank of Bulgaria was acquired by EGF Eurobank in 1998, Kredinata Banka of Macedonia by Alpha Bank in 1999, Stopanska Bank of Macedonia by National Bank of Greece in 1999, Pater Bank of Romania by Piraeus Bank in 1999 and the Interlease of Bulgaria by National Bank of Greece in 1999 (OECD 2001: 85 and 137, endnote 80). Furthermore in the financial sector, an online satellite-trading floor was established to operate in Thessaloniki with the principal aim of providing services in the Balkans (see EIU Country Profile 2001: 33).

An important consequence of Greece's economic activities in the Balkans is increasing Greek foreign direct investment (FDI) in the region, which has reached nearly $1.5 billion in 2000 (EIU Country Profile, 2001: 28). Although they are not mature enough yet, Greek investments in the Balkans occur mostly in the fields of telecoms, banking, energy, food production, and distribution networks and are geographically concentrated in Bulgaria, Albania, Romania, FYR of Macedonia and Yugoslavia (see Wallden, 2000: 437 and EIU Country Profile, 2001: 28). The Greek investments in the region are indeed a remarkable achievement and can be considered a sign of upward mobilisation by semiperipheral Greece. The number of Greek foreign investor companies, which were almost non-existent in 1989 (just 3 companies all around the world), reached to 521 after the opening of the Balkans/CEECs markets (Labrianidis, 2000: 457). The majority of the Greek FDI projects are geographically concentrated in Bulgaria (41.7 percent), Albania (20.3 percent), and Romania (20.3 percent), and the distribution of these FDIs according to the sectors is 47.2 percent in trade, 36 percent in industry and 13.2 percent in service sectors (Labrianidis, 2000: 466-467). Furthermore, while industrial companies are mainly invested in clothing (47.8 percent) and food and beverages (25.5 percent), trading companies are active in the food (27.2 percent), general trading (22.1 percent), clothing (5.8 percent), oil products (5.1 percent), beverages (4.1 percent) and furniture (3.4 percent) sectors (Labrianidis, 2000: 467). A further development in relation to Greece's economic activities in the Balkans is the transfer of labour intensive lines of production to Balkan countries by some Greek firms operating in declining sectors, especially in the garment sector, by reorienting their production in Greece towards higher quality and higher value added goods (EIU Country Profile, 2000: 27 and 33).

A final indicator of Greece's attempt to play a prominent role in the Balkans, perhaps as an upwardly mobile semiperipheral state, is its active position in the reconstruction of the Balkans. In this regard, Greece unilaterally launched a 180 billion Greek Drachma ($500 million) worth "Balkan Reconstruction Program" for the 2001-2005 period. Through this program, Greece provides credits to the regional countries in infrastructural, industrial and social restructuring projects. However, Greek firms are given priority (51 percent) in the consortia that carry out these projects in the Balkan countries. Of the 180 billion Drachma, Dr 70 billion goes to Serbia; Dr 25.5 billion to FYR of Macedonia; Dr 25 billion to Kosovo; Dr 24 billion to Romania; Dr 18.5 billion to Bulgaria; and Dr 17 billion to Albania (EIU Country Report, April 2001: 17). In its new role in the Balkans, it seems that one strategic consideration of Greece is to upgrade the capacity and density of intra-Balkan transportation networks with assistance from the EU and the US-led initiatives towards southeast Europe (see Wallden, 2000: 437).

Greece's remarkable opening to the Balkans/CEECs as an upwardly mobile semiperipheral state, however, is not immune from drawbacks or negative effects (see Labrianidis, 2000 and Wallden, 2000: 440-442). First of all, by concentrating on the less demanding CEECs/Balkan markets, it seems that Greece is turning away from the highly competitive and demanding EU market thus risking a qualitative downgrading in Greece's production structures. Due to the limited income conditions and subsequently the demand for lesser quality products in the Balkan markets, Greek producers supply intermediate quality products with affordable prices, which in turn diverts Greece from upgrading its production structures towards high-technology, high quality and internationally competitive products (in short, core-like products and production structures). In other words, Greek products in the Balkan/CEECs markets compete on the basis of price, not on the quality/differentiation of the product (Wallden, 2000: 440 and Labrianidis, 2000: 458 and 472). Second, the present dominant position of the Greek investors in the region is basically due to the reluctant and "wait and see" policy of the leading Western economies towards the politically and economically volatile Balkans/CEECs region (Labrianidis, 2000: 458). Here, the threat to Greece is that when the Balkan economies are restored, and the domestic and western investors begin to establish themselves in these markets, Greece's comparative advantage will erode and Greek exporters and investors will face increasing competition from their both Balkan/CEECs and their EU counterparts (Wallden, 2000: 440 and Labrianidis, 2000: 476). Third, Greek investments in the Balkans/CEECs, despite a few notable exceptions, are basically labour intensive, small in size and operation, concentrated in commercial activities, present in industries with mature technologies, lack an established brand name, and have no experience in FDI (see Wallden, 2000: 436-437 and Labrianidis, 2000: 468-471 and 479). Furthermore, most Greek firms/investors in the Balkans/CEECs can be described as emigrant entrepreneurs who wants to try their fortune abroad using skills and capital, rather than real foreign direct investors (Labrianidis, 2000: 478). A fourth negative point is that Greek firms lack a clear-cut strategy in the Balkans/CEECs markets, and their basic drive for investing in these regions has been reducing labour cost. The result is that more than 95 percent of the total volume of world-wide Greek FDI takes place solely in the Balkans/CEECs region, and moreover only a negligible part of this amount has been invested in the relatively more mature markets of Hungary, Poland and the Czech Republic (Labrianidis, 2000: 472-473).

Not surprisingly, semiperipheral Greek state has remained an important and omnipresent actor in the economy in this period too. Accordingly, the other actors in the Greek economic establishment (mainly, financial, business and shipping elite) have continued to arrange their relationship with the state in such a way that protects and promotes their respective interests at the state level (see Tsoukalis, 2000: 35). In other words, fragmented powerful interests (periphery-like and core-like interests) have continued to compete for state favours and power in an institutional environment controlled by the public sector unions, party officials and bureaucrats (see Lavdas, 1997: 55). The economic environment of semiperipheral Greece has thus witnessed the effective hindering of the formation and implementation of state policies for liberalisation and privatisation by entrenched traditional, periphery-like, powerful interests, and the intervention of state in the settlement of conflicts over economic and social issues. In the 1990s, the economic reform policies of the semiperipheral Greek state for a real convergence with the EU were resisted by a number of actual and potential losers, some of whom are politically powerful (see Tsoukalis, 2000: 39-40). The losers include mainly the traditional sectors of Greek economic elite (periphery-like producers) who are protected from foreign and domestic competitors by the state, and whose survival is heavily dependent on public procurement contracts. Another group of losers resisting EU adjustment policies and processes are the public sector trade unions that represent organised labour in the overmanned and relatively high pay, but low productivity, state-controlled firms and utilities. Greek public sector unions have been based on clientelistic practices. They are in close contact with the state and party bureaucracy and in a privileged position in the system: "They [have] special status relating to service, low tax rate, extended subsidisation of a wide range of staff activities and indirect payments" (Liargovas, 2000: 215). Accordingly, they do not want their privileges abolished by reform programs (see also Pagoulatos, 2000: 232). A third major group of losers are the large traditional political class whose survival depends on the continuation of the patron-client relationship with the interest groups and with the society at large.

The financial system in Greece is still largely a credit-based and state-led system that gives the political authority important power in determining the direction and form of industrial adjustment (see Lavdas, 1997: 76). The traditional financial interests in the banking sector and state-owned/controlled banks have resisted privatisation and financial liberalisation since the early 1990s partly because of competition with the private and foreign banks in the domestic financial market. Industrial interests or the big business, mainly operating in the cement, chemicals, electrical equipment, and textile industries, are highly fragmented and dependent on state favours in credit allocation or public procurement contracts. This makes industrialists, financial elite, state, and party relations very important and highly politicise the economy (see Lavdas, 1997: 80-85). The shipping interests, on the other hand, seem to have a considerable degree of autonomy vis-à-vis the state compared to the others. However, the legacy of sectoral state corporatism, that favours reliable and necessary cooperation between the Greek state and shipowners, remains strong and still determines the shipping policy in Greece (see Lavdas, 1997: 72-79).

State-economic elite relations have entered into a new phase in the 1990s, although the Greek state remained the dominant actor in the economy. The 1989-1990 coalition governments followed the PASOK government's post-1985 policy line of increased consultation with business circles, and in turn, the Federation of Greek Industries (SEV) cooperated with the government. The advent of the New Democracy (ND) government in April 1990 however brought some changes to government-business relations in that the ND now considerably detached itself from traditionally friendly (periphery-like) business and commercial interests (Lavdas, 1997: 177-178). Accordingly, links with business interests were weakened and state support to ailing firms became indirect and less significant. The semiperipheral Greek state took a developmentalist role in the economy once again. The motive behind this policy was probably to accelerate economic modernisation (upward mobilisation in the world-economy) and restructure the uneasy integration process of Greece into the EC/EU. There was indeed a shift in the party platform of the ND from paternalism to neo-liberalism (Lavdas, 1997: 204), and the PASOK governments too increasingly followed this line after 1993.

One of the basic issues between the government and the business elite in the 1990s was the participation of the business interests in the administration and the allocation of the EU's (CSF) structural funds (see Lavdas, 1997: 232-239). The business world demanded more shares for industry related programs from the EU transfers, but the ND government paid more attention on infrastructural projects. It was only in the CSF II that more funds were allocated to industrial projects with the approval of the EU Commission. The business interests however were incorporated in the administration of the structural programs through ELANET, a development consultancy company established in May 1991 and controlled by the state, Federation of Greek

Industries (SEV), the Greek Shipowners Union (EEE), The Association of Greek Banks (EET) and the Federation of Hoteliers (POX). However, the established view among the business circles is that the main beneficiary of the EU structural funds has been the public sector and that this practice must be changed in favour of the private domain (Lavdas, 1997: 239).

The business elite in general supported the privatisation policy of the ND and PASOK governments because they have always demanded the abandonment of the state's role in business. However, in the privatisation process of some of the large state owned companies, e.g. Olympic Airways and Hellenic Telecommunication Organisation (OTE), the role of the business elite and organisations (e.g. SEV) have remained limited because of significant intra-business interest divisions (Lavdas, 1997: 248). In other words, in semiperipheral Greece privatisations come about against the interests of private capital in areas such as "public procurement", "the removal of constraints on competition and market entry", and "incentives for the restructuring other firms" (Lavdas, 1997: 202). Accordingly, in 1993 the PASOK government came up with a privatisation policy package that took in to account the interests of a number of policy-opposing groups (Lavdas, 1997: 209). For instance, the decision to keep OTE (State Telecommunication Group) in the hands of the state satisfied both the procurement beneficiaries in the private sector and the trade unions.

In fact, the underlying motivations of all the Greek governments behind the privatisations have been to improve public finances and reduce deficits, to receive EC funds and loans, to meet the convergence criteria with the EU economic and monetary union, and to attract international investors in the country (Lavdas, 1997: 204). However, in the face of both clashing intra-private sector interests and the priorities in state's agenda, not surprisingly, the (semiperipheral) Greek state has become the central actor in structuring the privatisation process (as is apparent in the OTE's privatisation) and in determining the use of privatisation receipts (in improving public finances and in infrastructural investments), which in turn considerably politicised the issue of privatisation in Greece (see Lavdas, 1997: 212). For instance, the state-privatising agency (OAE), under the influence of the governmental PASOK elements, local MPs, and the Greek Association for Textile Industries, obstructed the privatisation of a major Peloponnesian bankrupt textile manufacturing company, *Piraiki Patraiki*, for a long time (see Lavdas, 1997: 289).

On the other hand, PASOK governments have carefully avoided a clash with the trade unions in the process of privatisation, and accordingly followed a *sui generis* privatisation policy, called the "Greek model", whereby the state-owned companies are sold gradually and the government retains its control over the employment policy and appointments (EIU Country Report, July 2000: 23). It is argued that the PASOK government's policy of privatisation has been not to sell more than 49 percent of state companies in order not to provoke the trade unions (EIU Country Profile, 2000: 22).12

In fact, it is clear that there are major domestic obstacles to privatisation and economic liberalisation in Greece that make governments move slowly and cautiously. These obstacles have been the traditional entrenched political and economic interests in the system, labour unions, the ruling (PASOK) party members and the electorate (EIU Country Report, January 2001: 21-22 and April 200: 22). It is interesting that in the face of the significant domestic opposition for structural economic reform, the National Economy and Finance Minister of the reformist Simitis government, reminding one of the 1976 statement by the ex-governor of the Bank of Greece, X. Zolatas (see above), warning that "structural reforms would upset many individuals because they demanded a change in ingrained habits and practices" (EIU April, 2001: 19). In sum, in the second half of the 1990s and early 2000s, Greece attempted yet again to upgrade its position in the world-system hierarchy of states. However, in the face of effective resistance from the traditional economic and political elite and keeping in mind the previous unsuccessful post junta economic mobilisation, the success of these reformist policies still remains to be seen.

The Political Environment and Foreign Policy: Early 1990s-2000s

The Political Environment

The political environment, which was considerably instable in the late 1980s and early 1990, witnessed further consolidation of the democratic political system. During three successive electoral periods in less than a year, the old arc enemies the Conservatives and Communists, and later the Conservatives, Communists (Left Alliance) and Socialist parties, established coalition governments for the first time in Greek political history. Accordingly, the traditional divisions between the Greek right and the left were redefined and the political-ideological environment was normalised and further Europeanised. Thus, in the new domestic political environment of the early 1990s-2000s the political struggle has gradually moved to a new platform reflecting the ebb and flow in the economic environment towards a structural transformation. Freed from its traditional "leftist-rightist" division, the Greek political environment now shifted gradually towards the centre of the political spectrum and formulated its political question directly on the nature and degree of the state-market relationship. In general, the central political question directly and increasingly focused on the redefinition of the power positions of the state and market vis-à-vis each other, that is to say on the role, size, scope, function and morphology of the Greek state (Iokamidis, 1996: 40). The political concerns of the Greek political elite, regardless of their respective political identities in the right or left wing of the political spectrum, has now been primarily concentrated on the issue of either to what degree they should support the belated structural transformation policy (upward mobilisation), or to resist it. That is why it is not surprising to see that the major political conflict in Greece has for some time been dominated by less inter-party, but more of intra-party, conflicts (see Iokamidis, 1996: 34 and 44, and Keridis, 2001: 7-8). The Greek political elite thus clearly divided into "modernist" and "traditionalist" factions, whereby the former aims to reduce the controlling power of the state over the market and the latter aims to maintain traditional state control over the economy.

At another level, this division is illustrated as the division between the modernist pro-EU forces who want to achieve a real convergence with the EU in economic and monetary spheres, and the traditionalists who are resisting change and happy with the Greece's (and their own) peripheral, "free-rider" status in the EU" since 1981. In this regard, the central political question of the 1990s and early 2000s in Greece can be reformulated as either integration or marginalisation in the ever changing and deepening EU. In short, a politically dynamic sphere composed of a complex mix of pressure between continuity and change has dominated domestic politics in Greece since the early 1990s in which the forces of modernisation are trying to implant contemporary European values and ways of action into Greek political, economic and social structures while powerful traditional forces (political and economic elites and other actors) resist and reject this change (Featherstone, 1996: 15 and Iokamidis, 1996: 34). In the world-system analysis, this can be defined as the fight between the periphery-like and core-like producers of a semiperipheral state either to maintain or alter the ever-precarious balance of power in the political sphere so as to promote their respective interests. In this process, the state becomes the most important actor, since their interests are promoted most effectively by influencing state policies in the semiperiphery.

The Conservative New Democracy Party (ND) came to power in April 1990 with its liberal ideology redefined in the framework of European liberalism. Since the mid-1980s, the conservatives gradually began to shift from traditional state paternalism to European neo-liberal centre-right ideology, promoting less market regulation (Featherstone, 1996: 11 and Keridis, 2001: 6). Accordingly, Prime Minister Mitsotakis began privatisation and labour market liberalisation as soon as the ND came in to power, but his efforts for a structural reform ended with a little success. The Mitsotakis government was willing, but unable, to realise structural modernisation (Pagoulatos, 2000: 230). Mitsotakis' weak parliamentary majority and the resistance, mainly coming both from within the party and the state bureaucracy, were the main obstacles to the ND's modernisation policy (see Legg and Roberts, 1997: 185 and Pagoulatos, 2000: 228). The statist old guard faction in the ND, headed by Evert who later succeeded Mitsotakis as the head of the party after the 1993 electoral defeat, was in favour of the continuation of the traditional patronage and clientelistic practices and the expansion of public spending and investments. Since the 1993 electoral defeat, the ND has been suffering from internal divisions between euro-liberals (associated with Mitsotakis) and cautious and Gaullist reluctant reformers (associated with the new leader Kostas Karamanlis, Kostantine Karamanlis' nephew) and a traditional populist nationalist faction (Keridis, 2001: 15).

Although PASOK's political platform became less rhetorical and less radical after the mid-1980s, PASOK's political shift in the early 1990s was limited and confined to the policy of "less statism" (Featherstone, 1996: 12). After the PASOK's electoral victory in 1993, the Papandreou government reversed some privatisations initiated by the previous ND government such as the renationalisation of the Athens Bus Company and privatisation of the 49 percent of the management of OTE (Pagoulatos, 2000: 231). It was only after 1996, with the advent of Simitis' reformist PASOK governments to the power, that the socialists began to follow a relatively determined policy of structural reforms and market liberalisation. However, despite his remarkable economic success through economic reform programs especially in fiscal policy, bringing down inflation and making Greece a part of the European economic and monetary union, Prime Minister Simitis and his structural reform policies have not been immune to criticisms from within and outside the party. Prime Minister Simitis' reformist faction in the government and party has been resisted by the strong PASOK old guard (EIU Country Report, July 2000: 7). The divisions in PASOK along these lines deepened and prominent members of the party and even the government have openly criticised Simitis' reformist policies on the ground that his policies are against the PASOK's socialist ideas, the electorate, and against the trade union movement, a traditional voter base of PASOK (EIU Country Report, July, 2000: 7; January, 2001: 7-8 and 12-13; and April, 2001: 13). Faced with the criticisms of the party members, deputies and even the members of the cabinet such as the Minister of Defence Tsochatzopoulos and Minister of Culture Pangalos (later sacked), (see EIU Country Report, January 2001: 13 and April 2001: 13-14) and the resistance coming from the trade unions and the electorate against the reform policies (EIU, July, 2000: 15 and January, 2001: 7-8), the Simitis government has had difficulties in carrying out its policies of privatisation of the state enterprises, labour market reforms and the liberalisation of the utility markets, and it has begun to show signs of reform fatigue; and Simitis' willingness to shoulder the reform policies has weakened (EIU January, 2001: 7 and April, 2001: 7 and 13).

Indeed, both PASOK and ND have been experiencing political restructuralisation towards the European centre-left and centre-right parties respectively, both in party ideology and form. Charismatic leadership came to an end, and a younger pragmatic generation with pro-EU credentials (Simitis and his reformist team in PASOK and Kostas Karamanlis in ND) has been gradually replacing the old political class (EU Country Report, July 2000: 13). Yet, the above mentioned effective internal party opposition coming from the old political class in both PASOK and ND still seems to be an important obstacle in front of political renewal in Greece and explains the slow structural transformation process and incorporation of Greece in the EU.

In this environment, not surprisingly, the semiperipheral Greek state, once again, has become the central actor at the stage through which all the other actors have been trying to promote their respective interests. In Greek politics, the resolution of economic and social issues has taken place in a complex social environment whereby political parties, professions, unions, business interests and public sector officials compete with each other for state favours (Mossialos and Mitsos, 2000: 3-4). In this regard, in Greece the state has always been seen as the central mechanism for allocating favours and distributing state resources (Iokamidis, 1996: 45 and Legg and Roberts, 1997: 7). Accordingly, the state provides investment opportunities and distorts economic competition and entrepreneurship. The state favouritism of particular capitalists through subsidies, incentives and public procurement contracts etc., have made control of the state mechanism a very important issue for all the major actors in the Greek society (Legg and Roberts, 1997: 178). Hence, not surprisingly, in (semiperipheral) Greece, the competition for controlling the state has been strong because whoever controls the state has the power to promote the interests of certain groups and punish others. In this way politics has become a struggle for controlling the state apparatus in Greece (Legg and Roberts, 1997: 199). The political parties representing various interests, and the powerful trade unions, all have directed their activities towards affecting the Greek state and its policies (see Iokamidis, 1996 and Liargovas, 2000: 215). This is because for the Greek political parties the state has been the central mechanism to exercise control over everything from hospitals to universities and to sports (Tsoukalis, 2000: 41). The political have been reluctant to support reform policies, that is, to surrender the state's control over the society and economy (Pagoulatos, 2000: 233).

At first glance, it seems that this division in Greek politics and economics corresponds to the world-system division of core-like producers (representing the modernists) and periphery-like producers (representing the traditionalists), and their struggle to control the semiperipheral Greek state. In this struggle, the impressive fiscal and economic indicators registered since Simitis came to power in 1996, and furthermore his second electoral victory in April 2000, give the impression that core-like producers and social forces have gained an upper hand over their periphery-like counterparts, and thus that Greece has now become an upwardly mobile semiperipheral state moving gradually towards the core region of the world-economy. On the other hand, it is also argued that the recent remarkable economic performance of Greece is due to the Greek state's last minute mobilisation not to be marginalized in the ever-deepening EU (Tsoukalis, 2000: 40), rather than on the success of the core-like producers over the periphery-like producers and forces. In fact, the successful economic policies of the Simitis governments have come, not because of their inherent desirability, but because of their pragmatic necessity in the competitive EU environment (Pagoulatos, 2000: 239). Indeed, both the OECD surveys and EIU country reports show that in Greece the shift towards high-technology, high profit production structures remains low, something which is not expected from an upwardly mobile semiperipheral state. Accordingly, in the words of a senior Greek political economist,

> Within the large European market, Greece has the advantage of cheap labour, which reinforces specialisation in labour-intensive sectors and the

deindustrialisation of the rest. The industries reverting to labour-intensive sectors are certainly retrograde, but it is still a kind of specialisation within the context of European division of labour (Vergopoulos, 1995: 128).

It seems clear that the core-like producers and forces are not yet in true ascendance in the Greek political economy in the 1990-2000s period. On the other hand, the process of structural transformation, which was started in the early 1990s, and accelerated and successfully implemented after the advent of pro-European reformist Simitis governments to power, reveals that the Greek state, in the absence of powerful core-like producers but with the decisive assistance of the EU, has once again taken the leading role in the development and integration of the Greek economy in the EU environment. Although the state leadership in the economy of the upwardly mobile semiperipheral states is an alternative strategy for mobilisation towards the core region of the world-economy, in the absence of strong and powerful core-like interests in Greece in the 1990-2000s period, it remains to be seen whether recent successful policies and economic indicators will lead to a shift in the semiperipheral position of Greece towards the core region of the world-economy.

Foreign Policy

All these semiperipheral oscillations in the economic and political spheres are reflected in the foreign policy domain, and accordingly Greece has continued to follow the semiperipheral foreign policy line by going backwards and forwards through the thresholds of upwardly mobile semiperipheral state status of the world-system in the 1990-2000s period. Thus, from time to time Greek foreign policy has revealed the characteristics of an upwardly mobile semiperipheral state in foreign policy, but at other times not, depending on who is the winner in the game of musical chairs between the reformists and traditionalists in the domestic economic and political environments between 1990s and 2000s. Broadly speaking, again, it is only after the Simitis' PASOK governments came power in 1996 that the Greek state, gradually became willing to follow an upwardly mobile semiperipheral foreign policy.

In the latter stages of the contraction period of the world economy (between 1990-2000s), as a semiperipheral state Greece clearly continued to increase its margin of independence from the core states in pursuing its own "national interest" (e.g., Macedonian problem), continuing to assert itself as a bridge to Europe in its region (especially after 1996), aiming to create privileged and stable markets for (secondary) commercial and economic benefits (Balkans), and engaging in an intensive semiperipheral rivalry with Turkey over the broader region as a whole and on Cyprus in particular. However, it is only in the second half of the 1990s (with Simitis) that Greece began to follow an upwardly mobile semiperipheral foreign policy line based on relatively harmonious relations with its partners in the EU and NATO (to an extent, including Turkey). The new policy line, in turn, has increased Greece's weight and influence in the Western alliance as a whole and in its immediate region, which precipitated the formation of a Greek sphere of influence in the Balkans. Finally in the mid-1990s, Greece has been involved in the management of international/regional problems and issues as a junior partner.

In the first half of the 1990s, Greek foreign policy, in parallel to Greece's unsuccessful performance at upgrading its production structures and its economy, could not follow an upwardly mobile semiperipheral foreign policy line, contrary to the expectations from the "reformist" Mitsotakis's Conservative ND government.

In the sphere of foreign policy, Greece's failure to upgrade its position in the hierarchy of states was demonstrated in its policy vis-à-vis the Yugoslav crises in the 1990s. For instance, Greece openly supported Serbia in the Yugoslavian wars and split with its partners in the European Union over the name and recognition of Macedonia. The EU took Greece to the European Court of Justice during Greek presidency because of the unilateral Greek trade embargo on FYR of Macedonia. Thus, Greece became a part of the problem in the Balkans rather than an intermediary between the region and the EU, or an actor in the management of the Balkan crises.

In the Balkans, Greek foreign policy sharply diverged from the policies of the EU and US and caused further disharmony in the Western alliance in the early 1990s. First, despite its long established Western credentials, Greek foreign policy preferred to align with the policy lines of the "renewed" but outmoded communist (now socialist) parties in the former Yugoslavia and Bulgaria instead of the newly emerged non-communist contenders (Stearns, 1995: 59 and 62-63). In Bulgaria, Greece declared its preference for the ex-Communist Socialist Party over the Union of Democratic Forces, and in Yugoslavia, Greek governments approached the ethnic nationalism of the Milosevic regime in Bosnia with tolerance despite the fact that its EU partners viewed Milosevic as the most responsible actor in the dramatic ethnic conflicts and wars in the Balkans. In the first half of the 1990s, both the Mitsotakis (ND) and Andreas

Papandreou (PASOK) governments kept the lines open with Milosevic's regime (Glenny, 1997: 75) and Greece became an outspoken partisan for the Serbs. Thus Greece lost its chances of both playing a stabilising regional leadership role during the Balkan crises, and of strengthening its influence and prestige in NATO and the EU (Nicolaidis, 1997: 10). Second, after the disintegration of the Yugoslav Federation, the Greeks developed an argument on "Macedonian irredentism" built upon Greece's historical experiences during the Greek Civil War. They passionately insisted that the Yugoslav Republic of Macedonia must not be recognised internationally under the name of "Republic of Macedonia", and that Skopje must change its constitution because it contained "territorial designs" on Greek Macedonia and also must change its flag for it used the Vergina Star on it, the symbol of the ancient "Greek Kingdom of Macedonia" (see, Legg and Roberts, 1997: 67). However, Greece's messages and arguments over Macedonia were not understood and recognised by Greece's EU partners, and Greece in turn threatened to veto any move by the EU for the recognition of the new republic under this name, and even tried to isolate Skopje both politically and economically by imposing an unilateral economic and trade embargo on this country in 1994. However, both the support given to Serbia and the embargo imposed on FYR of Macedonia isolated Greece diplomatically and politically in the Western alliances; Greece was marginalized and became the odd man out in the EU. Third, Greece was involved in serious bilateral disputes with Albania on the "treatment" of the orthodox Greek minority in Southern Albania in the first half of the 1990s (see Legg and Roberts, 1997: 68 and Stephanopoulos, 1997: 136) claiming that these people were discriminated against and that the Greek Orthodoxy was persecuted in Albania. Moreover, Greece demanded the return of the property rights of the Greek citizens who were expelled from Albania in 1944, and also strongly raised the issue of some 300,000 Albanian illegal immigrants working and living in Greece. The relations between Greece and Albania were further strained in 1993 and 1994 by the deportation of a Greek orthodox clergyman, and the refusal of participation of an ethnic-religious Greek party in the elections by the Albanian government. The Greeks responded by expelling 22,000 illegal immigrant Albanians, and in turn the Albanians responded by reducing the number of diplomats in the Greek embassy in Tirana. Moreover, Greece vetoed EU financial assistance to Albania (Ioakimidis, 2000: 371, endnote 8). Consequently, Greece became a part of the Balkan problem and was isolated by its Western partners.

In the first half of the 1990s, the rivalry with Turkey in the Eastern Mediterranean and the Balkan region became another semiperipheral feature of Greek foreign policy. In fact, Turkey has always been the major rival of the Greeks, and Greek foreign policy has not taken any major initiative without intending to create a more favourable balance of power in the region with Turkey (Stearns, 1995: 60). Hence, Turkey has always provided a prism through which Greek foreign policy measures and evaluates the external environment (Constas, 1995: 72). However, the semiperipheral rivalry with Turkey has become more visible in the post-Cold War transformation period in Greek foreign policy with the dissolution of the Soviet Union and Yugoslavia, and with the emergence of new opportunities for both Greece and Turkey to exploit in the Eastern Mediterranean and Balkan region. Thus the Greeks evaluated the potential of the post-Cold War systemic opportunities through the prism of Greece's rivalry with Turkey, the state "with a superior displacement... that posed insurmountable obstacles to Greece's external balancing pursuits" (Constas, 1995: 79). In this context, Greece has often played the EU card against Turkey through either vetoing the EU decisions favouring Turkey or blocking EU financial assistance to Turkey, or mobilising the EU for condemning Turkey at every opportunity. (Constas, 1995: 78). In this regard, another semiperipheral foreign policy priority of the Greek Government in the post-Cold War period was to promote and realise the accession of Cyprus into the EU - a Turk-free western organisation in which Greece is a full member - and thus to change the strategic balance in favour of Greece in the Eastern Mediterranean. In this manner, the accession of Cyprus to the EU has become a vitally important issue for Greece's strategic calculations (Couloumbis, 1998: 16). In the context of this semiperipheral rivalry in the region, in order to strengthen its position vis-à-vis Turkey over Cyprus, Greece developed the idea that there was no difference between the Iraqi invasion of Kuwait and Turkish intervention on Cyprus in 1974 after a Greek sponsored coup for unification (*enosis*). Greece accused the US and the Western Alliance of applying double standards in Cyprus and Iraq- that is, not applying the same principles and same processes that were implemented in Iraq against the Turks in Cyprus (Constas, 1995: 82 and Coufudakis, 1996: 26). Furthermore, the Greeks signed a common defence agreement with the Greek Cypriots that extended Greece's defence perimeter over five hundred miles to the southeast from the mainland – from the Ionian Sea and Albania to Cyprus. The agreement with Greek Cypriots involved bilateral commitments over training, purchasing and production of military hardware, sharing of defence assets and coordination of military planning (Coufudakis, 1996: 36).

On the other hand, in the Balkans, post-Cold War Turkish-Bulgarian rapprochement worried Greece because it terminated the cordial Athens-Sofia Axis. Greeks developed the idea that Bulgaria should be careful not to alienate Greece because of the high potential for ethnic strife and the threat of Turkish intervention to protect Turkish minority in Bulgaria (Constas, 1995: 90). According to a senior former US ambassador to Greece, Greece's Bulgarian policy in the first half of the 1990s had probably less to do with Bulgaria than with Turkey (see Stearns, 1995: 62). Bulgaria's Turkish minority living in the region adjacent to Greece's Turkish minority was part of the answer why Greece supported the ex-communists in Bulgaria over the non-communist Union of Democratic Forces, the party that committed to granting all rights to the Turkish minority in Bulgaria. The Greeks believed that Turkish and Muslim minorities in the Balkans provided a pretext for Turkish expansionism in the region, and declared that in the post-Cold War period, Greece was encircled by an Islamic arc in the north (Constas, 1995: 91 and Coufudakis, 1996: 31).

In the context of the increasing importance of Turkey in the Eastern Mediterranean and broader Eurasian region, and in the American foreign policy considerations during the Gulf War and later with the emergence of new Turkic states in the Caucasus and Central Asia, the semiperipheral rivalry between Greece and Turkey intensified in the first half of the 1990s. The Greek response came often in the form of emphasising the negative aspects and the shortcomings of Turkey's international role in the region, and cultivated good relations with Armenia, Iran and Syria with which Turkey had problematic relations. According to the Greeks, for instance, Turkey could become involved in the Azerbaijani-Armenian hostility against Christian Armenia, the conditions in Iraq and Iran could lead to religious (Islamic) and/or ethnic (Kurdish) uprisings in Turkey, and so forth (see Constas, 1995: 85). Moreover, perhaps, again, because of this semiperipheral rivalry, Greece initially remained indifferent and/or reluctant towards the Turkish initiative to establish the Black Sea Economic Cooperation Region (BSEC), although Greece was invited to participate and became a member in the organisation from the very start (see Coufudakis, 1996: 38).

In general, in the first half of the 1990s, Greece's relations with the EU and the Western Alliance as a whole deteriorated further due to Greece's disharmonising foreign policy line, especially in the Balkans. Greece, in parallel with its unsuccessful economic and political performance, did not follow an upwardly mobile semiperipheral foreign policy line and was isolated from the West in this period. In fact, Greece presented itself as the representative of the EU in the Balkan Cooperation meetings in Belgrade (1988) and Tirana (1990) and later attempted to portray itself as the "godfather" of the Balkan diplomacy, while at the same time largely excluding its EU partners from playing a role in the region, a policy that developed into a serious problem between Greece and the EU (Glenny, 1997: 74). Furthermore, Greece's counterproductive policies during the Bosnian crisis and in the Macedonian issue increased the Greece's alienation in Europe and in NATO. It became a common view in EU corridors that Greece did not share European values and goals, and that it was a mistake to have admitted Greece in the EU (Larrabee, 1997: 109). In the eyes of the West, Greek nationalist hysteria in the Balkans (especially in Macedonia), and obsessive and constant preoccupation with Turkey as a "hostile threat", created an image of Greece as a Balkan country that was not fully European (Woodward, 1997: 117-118 and Prodromou, 1997: 130). The inefficient use of the EU structural funds and the long-lasting, unsuccessful adjustment of the Greek economy in the EU environment added further to this negative image of Greece in the West. Thus, in the first half of the 1990s, Greece appeared either unwilling or unable to follow an upwardly mobile semiperipheral foreign policy line, and it became an economic drain and a political nuisance in the EU. Greece was also the only EU member state with unsettled territorial and ethnic disputes with its neighbours, namely FYR of Macedonia, Albania and Turkey (Legg and Roberts, 1997: 64).

However, the second half of the 1990s and the early 2000s have witnessed remarkable improvements in the external relations of Greece. This, combined with the spectacular achievements in the economic (especially in the fiscal policy) and political spheres in the same period, has given the impression that Greece has now indeed entered the upwardly mobile semiperipheral threshold towards the core region of the world-economy. The Simitis governments, in other words, has brought significant changes in the foreign policy sphere too, and thus Greece has repaired its negative image both in the region and in the eyes of its EU and Western partners by quickly following a more accommodating and cooperative foreign policy line, improving its relations with all the neighbours, taking initiatives to solve its bilateral and multilateral problems and disputes, and making substantial efforts to play a stabilising role in the region.

First of all, in the Balkans, Greece has decided to become part of the solution. The solution of the problems with Macedonia began when Greece lifted the unilateral economic and trade embargo against this country, and also, with the American initiative and brokerage, signed an interim agreement with Skopje on the name of "Former Yugoslav Republic of Macedonia" in late 1995. In the second half of the 1990s, relations with Albania were also normalised. Albanian refugees were given work permits in Greece, and moreover political, economic and commercial relations with Albania, FYR Macedonia, Bulgaria and Romania and other new Balkan states improved remarkably (Couloumbis, 2000: 381). Simitis governments have promoted the policy of stabilisation and cooperation in the Balkans through interregional cooperation schemes, such as Inter-Balkan Co-operation and ultimately supported the idea of the incorporation of all Balkan countries into the EU (Ioakimidis, 2000: 364). Greece's Balkan policy has now been built upon the policy of strong interplay between the political and economic pillars and has promoted the idea that economic cooperation facilitates political cooperation and thus peace and stability in the region (Triantaphyllou, 2001: 61). Towards this end, Greece hosted a Balkan summit in Crete in 1997.

Secondly, since the second half of the 1990s, perhaps because of the pro-European Simitis government's advent to power, and in fear of being marginalisation in the Union, the EU has become more and more the foundation of the Greek foreign policy. Greece has increasingly become a compatible member and has defined its regional and international role and foreign policy through and in relation to the EU framework. The strategic aim of Greece is to find a place in the inner circle of the ever changing, enlarging and deepening European Union in the 21st century (see Kranidiotis, 2000). Thus becoming a part of the European Economic and Monetary Union and the Single Currency (EMU) was considered more of a political issue than it was an economic one. It is believed that participating in the EMU and single currency strengthens Greece's role in the wider European architecture, its institutional position in the EU decision making mechanisms and processes, and enhances its position as a stabiliser in the Balkans, Eastern Mediterranean and in the international system as a whole (Triantaphyllou, 2001: 60). It has been acknowledged that the Union is central in the Greek foreign and economic policy through which Greece has strengthened its diplomatic and bargaining power vis-à-vis its neighbours, and it is a vital source of finance whereby Greece draws € 4 billion annually (Kranidiotis, 2000: 33). Thus Greece has increasingly begun to take accommodating lines with the EU in foreign policy sphere, compared to its negative records in the first half of the 1990s, and has gradually began to internalise EU's interests and values into Greek foreign policy. Greece has begun to move from the politics of veto to the politics of interest in the EU (Nicolaidis, 2001: 253). The strong willingness and determination of Simitis governments for full integration with the EU in all spheres (which is the strategic objective identified with and illustrated in the slogan of "Strong Greece" in his last electoral campaign), Greece's changing role in the Balkans, and rapprochement with Turkey after 1999 have all indicated that Greece is no longer a divergent and discordant member in the Western alliances and in the EU in particular, and is following a upwardly mobile semiperipheral foreign policy.

Perhaps, improving relations with Turkey especially after 1999 is the most significant indicator of Greece's upwardly mobile semiperipheral foreign policy line. This new policy line vis-à-vis Turkey that has promoted dialogue and cooperation for the first time since the 1950s, was a decisive step forward in upgrading Greece's position in the world-system hierarchy of states. It has been a widely admitted fact that one of the major impediments in front of the modernisation of the Greek political system, democratic culture, and Greece's full integration into the EU, has always been the uneasy nature of the Turkish-Greek relations (see Lavdas, 1997: 253, Mitsos, 2000: 71, 76 and 77 and Keridis, 2001: 18), namely the unsettled major problems with Turkey over the Aegean Sea and Cyprus. It means that without settling those highly sensitive problems, which may easily lead to armed conflict between the two countries, Greece's full integration into the EU will always remain incomplete. In this context, realising the fact that the previous adversarial policy lines followed in relations with Turkey were harmful for Greece's interests in the EU, the Simitis Governments began a policy of dialogue and cooperation with Turkey. As a result of this rapprochement with Turkey that was started in the second half of the 1999, Greece lifted its veto over Turkey's bid for the official candidate status in the EU in December 1999, and bilateral agreements were signed with Turkey in the fields of tourism, trade, illicit drug trafficking, organised crime, environment, culture, education etc. Furthermore, a dialogue was begun between Turkey and Greece on the Aegean problems early in 2002.

Yet, the policy of improving relations with Turkey in late 1999 came, not only for making semiperipheral Greece a concordant member in the Western Alliance and in the EU in particular and thus for consolidating the upwardly mobile semiperipheral state standing, but also as a result of the intensified semiperipheral rivalry over the region between the two countries in the post-Cold War period (see Tayfur, 2002). The problem for Greece has been Turkey's "attractive and favoured ally status" among most of Greece's own allies (Triantaphyllou, 2001: 61). The increasing strategic importance of Turkey especially in the eyes of the Americans due to the vital US global interests in the Balkans, Middle East, Caucasus and Central Asia (see Larrabee, 2001: 226-231), and the possibility of the Turkish Mediterranean town of Ceyhan becoming the energy terminal for the Caspian oil, and furthermore the Turkish-Israeli rapprochement have all alerted the Greeks to the necessity of balancing Turkey in the region (see Triyantaphyllou, 2001: 63-67 and Theophanous, 2001: 184). In this context, Greece has been considering the "special" relations between Turkey and the US problematic for its vital national interests, and views the US with suspicion as a biased interlocutor between Greece and Turkey (Triantaphyllou, 2001: 73 and Theophanous, 2001: 196). Accordingly, contrary to the swift and positive changes in other problematic foreign policy fronts after the mid-1990, relations with Turkey have gone through a series of ups and downs during most of the 1990s, some of which were highly ominous. Despite the Greek approval of Turkish-EU Customs Union agreement in 1995 in return for the EU's commitment to the Greeks for starting the membership negotiations with Cyprus, relations with Turkey were increasingly soured until the second half of 1999. The conflict over the sovereignty of Kardak/Imia islets in the Aegean Sea in which the two countries came close to an armed conflict; the decision of the Greek Cypriot government to deploy Russian S-300 missiles on the island and the strong Turkish reaction; hampering the further development of Turkish-EU relations by vetoing Turkey's candidacy in the EU's next round of negotiations and making Turkey's candidacy conditional on the solution of Turkish-Greek differences in the EU's 1997 Luxembourg summit; retaining the Greek veto over the EU's financial commitments to Turkey emanating from the 1995 Customs Union Agreement (Mitsos, 2000: 76); and not to mention the acute "hegemonic rivalry" over the control of Cyprus (see Theophanous, 2000) were just some of the indications of the characteristic Turkish-Greek semiperipheral rivalry in the Eastern Mediterranean region after the mid-1990s and early 2000s. However, this semiperipheral rivalry with Turkey reached its zenith when Turkey's number one enemy separatist PKK leader Öcalan was given shelter in the Greek embassy in Kenya and captured by the Turks early in 1999. It was only after this fateful moment that the reformist Simitis government launched a policy of rapprochement with Turkey and had the opportunity to curb the power of the old style nationalist group in the state, government and the party (PASOK) and restrain their influence on the external relations, and moreover sack three members of the cabinet including the Minister of Foreign Affairs.

Another upwardly mobile semiperipheral foreign policy characteristic revealed by Greek foreign policy in the second half of the 1990s and the early 2000s has been Greece's bid to play a bridge role in the historically, geographically and culturally contiguous areas of the Balkans and Eastern Mediterranean (Keridis, 2001: 15). Emphasising Greece's comparative advantages as the more developed country in the region, and as a member of the EU, NATO and the other major Western institutions, the Greeks seek to become the region's link to Europe (Triantaphyllou, 2001: 59) and have declared their intention to play the leadership role in promoting the European values of stability and democracy in the Balkans and Eastern Mediterranean and for the progressive integration of Balkan countries into the European system (Kranidiotis, 2000: 35 and Tsoukalis, 2000: 45). Furthermore, Greek policy makers have extended Greece's bridging role into the economic sphere declaring their strategic aim of making Greece a business and transport centre linking southeast Europe with EU markets in the 21st century (Mamatzakis, 2000: 255). Moreover, like in the Balkans, Greece has declared its active bridging role between the Black Sea Economic Cooperation Region and the EU (Trianatphyllou, 2001: 62).

The economic opening in the Balkans (see the previous section on economy), in turn, has revealed another upwardly mobile semiperipheral state characteristic in Greece, because in this context a zone of major Greek economic sphere of influence has emerged in the neighbouring Bulgaria, FYR of Macedonia, Albania and Serbia, and Romania based on the factors basically of geographical proximity, historical an cultural affinities (Wallden, 2000: 439 and Labrianidis, 2000: 473). As a result, Greece, now freed from historical animosities, has asserted itself as the emerging economic powerhouse of the Southeastern Europe (Keridis, 2001: 11).

A final indicator of Greece's upwardly mobile semiperipheral foreign policy is Greece's increasing role in the management of regional/international conflicts after the mid-1990s. In this period, Greek foreign policy assumed a leading role in promoting peace, stability and good neighbourly relations and aimed at solving the problems in its immediate neighbourhood and beyond, namely in the Balkans and Eastern Mediterranean (Triantaphyllou, 2001: 59). Greece has contributed to the multinational peace keeping operations in Somalia in 1995 and in IFOR/SFOR in Bosnia since 1995; the Greek navy participated in the

NATO and WEU operations in the Adriatic Sea; and the Greek army participated in the international ALBA operation with a full regiment during and after the 1997 Albanian crisis (Corantis, 2001: 4). During the Kosovo crisis, though unenthusiastically, the Greeks opened their ports and roads to the Allied Forces and made its 34th Mechanised Brigade available to the Allied Armies. Greek forces have been serving in the KFOR since then. Furthermore, Greece has started to work with Turkey in the Balkan Co-operation initiative for enhancing the political stability in the region. Greece became one of the donor countries in Bosnia-Herzegovina in 1997 ($25 million) and extended $80 million. to the civilian population at the start of the crisis in Albania in 1997 (Corantis, 2001: 3). According to the Greek sources, as of mid-2001, in order to promote peace and stability in the region, Greece extended $1.1 billion in direct outlays to its Balkan neighbours over the last five years and $589 million is earmarked for the next three years to the region. Finally, Greeks also claim that the scope of Greek foreign policy has broadened, and now it is preoccupied with the problems of countries in Latin America, Asia and Africa as a result of Greece's participation in the European Political Cooperation and EU's Common Foreign and Defence Policy (Ioakimidis, 2000: 364).

Since the second half of the 1990s it seems that Greek foreign policy has considerably shifted towards the European track and is following an upwardly mobile semiperipheral foreign policy line which is overlapping with, and thus not independent from, Greece's successful performance in the economic sphere. It is a fact that the advent of the pro-European, reformist Simitis government to power in 1996 has opened a new era in Greece's semiperipheral development process and foreign policy, but it is still not clear that whether this is a true upward semiperipheral mobilisation or not in the world system hierarchy of states. Viewed from a pessimistic perspective, it seems that Greece's successful economic performance was realised basically in the fiscal sphere but not in the production sphere yet. In other words, Greece has not yet upgraded its technological level to core-like production patterns, and thus the core-like producers have not become dominant over the state policies. Also, the periphery-like producers and the traditional political class still seem to be powerful and still resist change. Accordingly, it is the policies of the Simitis's reformist governments, but not the changing power positions of the economic elite and the majority of the political class, that have brought the fiscal success and entry in the EMU. Similarly, although Greece has developed and is following a policy of accommodation with the EU and the West in the sphere of foreign policy, again, it is not clear whether the

Greeks will be able to continue this policy of "harmony" in the face of increasing Turkish-Greek semiperipheral rivalry over the Aegean and Cyprus, and in relation to the EU enlargement, in the years to come.

However, looking from the optimistic point of view it would also not be unrealistic to say that the successful economic performance might be a positive sign of a true upward semiperipheral mobilisation initiated and supported by the Greek state since 1996. Furthermore, the foreign policy shift towards accommodation with the EU, Balkan neighbours and Turkey; the initiatives to make Greece a bridge between EU and the region, creating a Greek sphere of influence in the Balkans; and taking part in the management of international problems can well be considered the building blocks of the upwardly mobile semiperipheral Greek foreign policy.

Taking into account all the negative and positive aspects in the economic, political and foreign policy spheres, and the ongoing power struggle between the "core-like" and "periphery like" producers and forces, and the central role of the state in Greek semiperipheral development and foreign policy, it still remains to be seen whether Greece will be successful in its struggle to move into the core region of the world-economy in the years to come.

Notes

1. The Federation changed its name from the "Federation of Greek Industrialist" to the "Federation of Greek Industries" in 1979 as a result of its changed basis of membership, and also to emphasise its institutional aspect (*Deltion*, 15 May, 1979, No.405, quoted in Lavdas, 1997: 274, endnote 45).
2. For instance while Greece's exports to the EC increased from 32.8 percent in 1960 to 47.7 percent in 1977, its imports from the Community increased from 33.6percent to 42.5 percent in the same period, see Tsoukalis, 1981, p.37 and Mitsos, 1980, p.129.
3. This point has recently been proved on the issue of the recognition of Macedonia under this name.
4. For information on the EC's considerations in the relations between Turkey, Greece and the Community see Siotis, 1981, pp.100-102; de la Serre, 1979, p.41; and Opinion, 1979, pp.50-51.
5. For an account of Greek arguments see Zolotas, 1978, pp.9-14 and Verney, 1987, p.262.
6. The stabilisation plan aimed at modification of the wage-price indexation, devaluation of drachma by 15 percent, the tightening of monetary policy and the reduction of public sector borrowing requirement.
7. For a detailed analysis of the Greek financial system see OECD, 1986, pp.52-64.

8   For detailed information on the ailing and problematic firms see OECD, 1987, pp. 34-36; OECD, 1992, pp.65-68, and various other OECD Country Reports on Greece from 1986 onwards.
9   For the rentier, anti-developmentalist character of Greek industrialists in the 1980s see also Petras, 1987 and Petras et al., 1993.
10 For Papandreou's tough foreign policy see Loulis, 1985; Pranger, 1988; and Christodoulides, 1988.
11 Greek government's share in the total GDP expenditure on R&D is 46.9 percent compared to the OECD average of 63.1 percent see OECD 2001, p.70, Table 11.
12 For major privatisations between 1990-1998, see Pagoulatos, 2000, p.223-234.

Chapter 4

Spain: 1945-1976

Similar to the chapters on Greece, in this chapter and the following one I shall analyse Spain's semiperipheral foreign policy in two main periods within the framework of world-system analysis. Chapter four will address the period between the end of the Second World War and the end of the Franco period in 1976. Chapter five will address the post-Franco period, 1976 to the early 2000s. As noted elsewhere, these two periods roughly overlap with the expansion and contraction periods of the world-economy. I shall begin by demonstrating various semiperipheral characteristics of Spain in the economic and political spheres in the period between 1945-1976.

The Economic Environment

A cursory glance at Spain's political economy in the period between the end of the Second World War and the late 1950s shows that the state intervened extensively in the economy. This intervention was realised in two ways: first, the state favoured the interests of finance capital, and indirectly the interests of the industrial capital, because of the intimate relationship between these two factions of the Spanish economic elite. Second, while creating opportunities for entrepreneurs, the state also took on an entrepreneurial role itself.

In this period, the Spanish state (or the Franco regime) relied on five main instruments of intervention in the economy (see Baklanoff, 1978: 13-37) all of which were adopted after the end of the Spanish Civil War in 1939. These policy instruments were a system of Syndical Organisation; the licensing of industrial investment; the establishment of a large public holding company called *Instituto Nacional de Industria* (INI); exchange controls and other means of direct supervision of external economic transactions; and limited foreign investment opportunity.

The Syndical Organisation, a vertical organisation in which employers and employees were obliged to co-operate, served mainly to regulate wages (Anderson, 1970: 48). It aimed to eliminate class conflict and anarchic competition. In practice, however, it operated as an effective means of controlling labour.

The practice of licensing industrial investment required all investment decisions to be approved by the government. It meant that the establishment of any industrial unit, or the expansion, modification, or relocation of an established firm, required an official permit (IBRD, 1963: 338). In this way established firms were protected against internal and external competitors. Furthermore, more efficient enterprises were prevented from improving their market shares at the expense of less efficient firms (IBRD, 1963: 339 and Baklanoff, 1978: 16). Additionally, the practice of industrial permits led to favouritism and arbitrary procedures being applied to some privileged entrepreneurs by officials in the Ministry of Industry (Baklanoff, 1978: 16). Thus good connections with state officials, rather than efficiency, cost or markets, were important in obtaining industrial permits (Donges, 1971: 44). Furthermore, a preferential category for industries of national interest was established by the state (IBRD, 1963: 338), and incentives were provided in the form of economic privileges to domestic "firms of national interest" by bureaucrats according to political rather than economic considerations (Liberman, 1982: 169-170).

On the other hand, INI meant state investment and entrepreneurship, especially in industry. It was assigned the goal of industrialising the country. One of its declared aims was to establish industries in which the private sector was incapable of investing, and its enterprises were considered in the category of "national interest". INI's activities were widespread and included almost all industrial sectors (IBRD, 1963: 346). It could even create new industries through state funding. Its primary investments were directed towards the strategic sectors of steel, hydroelectric power, chemicals, metal works, autos, shipbuilding, transportation and communication, etc. (Anderson, 1970: 40). However, INI was also active in areas where private industry was already well established, and it acquired interests in private firms (IBRD, 1963: 349).

The state also exercised direct control over Spain's external economic transactions, providing strong protection for domestic producers. Control was implemented through high tariff barriers, import quotas, import licensing, exchange controls, etc. (Baklanoff, 1978: 16). Moreover, discouraging laws and regulations limited the amount of foreign investment, and this in turn effectively prevented foreign competition and protected domestic producers.

Nevertheless, in spite of extensive state intervention in the economy, the financial elite had the political and economic power to influence state policies (Baklanoff, 1978: 18-19). Franco had relied heavily on the financial elite (i.e., the bankers) during and after the Civil War, allowing it to play a strong role in the reconstruction and development of the private sector (Anderson, 1970: 76). As a result, the private sector was to a great extent guided by banks in their investment decisions. Monetary and credit policies were supervised by a council consisting of representatives of the government, the commercial banks, and the Banco de Espana (Central Bank). Furthermore, the shares of the Banco de Espana were owned by commercial banks and private investors, as well as by the government (Whitaker, 1961: 230).[1]

Another striking feature of the Spanish economy was the intimate relationship between financial and industrial elites. In fact, economic power was concentrated in the hands of the five largest banks, which in 1957 held 64 percent of the nation's private deposits and 49 percent of total deposits (Baklanoff, 1978: 19). These five big banks were the Bank of Bilbao, Bank of Vizcaya, Bank of Hispano-Americano, Espanol de Credito and Banco Central. As a result of low levels of financing, and the lack of a developed capital market, almost all private firms were dependent on one of these banks (Baklanoff, 1978: 19 and Harrison, 1993: 69). On the other hand, the banks themselves invested heavily in industry, either by acquiring shares in enterprises or through lending operations (Wright, 1977: 102). In this way the seven largest Spanish banks controlled almost 600 of the major firms (Anderson, 1970: 76) and they increased their reserves and profits enormously throughout the 1950s (Harrison, 1993: 69). The dependence of large private firms on the banks was further consolidated through the membership of bank officials on the boards of directors of the largest firms. Hence they influenced the management and investment decisions for a great part of the Spanish private sector (Baklanoff, 1978: 19 and Anderson, 1970: 77). One study of the Spanish business and financial community reported that the larger Spanish entrepreneurs saw the banks as important components of their own decision process.[2] In this monopolistic environment, it was very difficult for newer firms to find long-term capital for their investment requirements without established banking connections (IBRD, 1963: 354).

The structural features of the Spanish economy revealed the dominance of periphery-like production patterns in this period. In 1963, a World Bank Mission described these characteristics (IBRD, 1963: 330-34) as follows[3]: first, Spanish firms were too small to operate efficiently, only a few relatively new industries were able to meet the necessary conditions for large-scale production. Second, the equipment used in most enterprises was obsolete, old or inefficient. For instance, while only 15 to 20 percent of the textile industry's equipment was modern, only one fourth of the equipment in the heavy machine industry was modern. Thus in a 1958 UNESCO Report, large segments of Spanish industry were characterised by low productivity, high cost and uncompetitiveness (quoted in Liberman, 1982:168). However, according to the same report, there were exceptions to this general pattern, which highlights the semiperipheral position of Spain. These exceptions reflected the intermediary status of Spanish industry; within a single branch of industry a mixture of old and new, large and small, efficient and inefficient could be found, and impressive modern plants existed side by side with the very outmoded ones (IBRD, 1963: 332).

Another principal actor in the Spanish economy in this period was the United States. In the postwar period when a new economic world order was being established under the leadership of the US, Spain was excluded from American-led international economic recovery programs, such as the Truman Doctrine or the Marshall Plan (European Recovery Plan). The primary reason for this trend was Franco's collaboration with Nazi Germany and Fascist Italy during the Second World War.

Yet, in many ways, Spain's exclusion was due to strong European opposition rather than to American decision. In 1946 the US administration concluded that only Franco could guarantee US interests in Spain (Dura, 1985: 136 and 160). Talks on including Spain in the Marshall Plan were started by the Americans as early as 1948, and the US House of Representatives voted in favour of Spain's inclusion by a large majority (149 against 52) (Gallo, 1973: 183-184). However, a joint committee of the US Senate and House of Representatives rejected the amendment in the face of European reactions (Dura, 1985: 200). Despite European opposition, US policy makers were determined to include Spain in the US-led economic aid program. Accordingly, in October 1949 US Secretary of State suggested to extend US help to Spain through the USIE program (Dura, 1985: 257). Furthermore, the American Administration made it clear that US had no objections to the extension of loans from private American banks to Spain.

America's policy of including Spain in the new world economic order was carried out in two main ways. First, until 1953 credits and loans to the Spanish economy were extended through private American banks, the US Export-Import Bank, and credits from the US Congress. In this way the Spanish government received loans from Chase Manhattan Bank and National City Bank of NY ($25 million and $30 million respectively); a $62.5 million Export-Import Bank credit authorised by the US Senate, and a further $100 million credit authorised by the US Congress (Rubottom and Murphy, 1984: 19). In order to obtain Export-Import Bank loans, the

Americans demanded that the Spaniards should prepare a recovery plan similar to those prepared by Marshall Aid recipient countries. Subsequently, an American team outside the Marshall Plan was appointed to administer the loans.

A second US initiative was realised in the Pact of Madrid (known also as Bases Agreement) of 1953. Under this agreement, the US administration extended $930 million economic aid and $374.236 million military assistance by the end of 1959 (Whitaker, 1961: 240-241). In addition, $392 million worth of surplus agricultural products, repayable in Spanish Pesetas, was supplied by the US. Additionally, more than $500 million was poured into the Spanish economy for the construction of US military bases (Dura, 1985: 347). American Catholic charity organisations collected a large amount of aid for Spain (Whitaker, 1961: 241). The Spanish government also accepted a US-authorised special economic legation called the US Operation Mission (USOM) to administer American aid (Rubottom and Murphy, 1984: 37). Another important characteristic of Spanish-American economic co-operation was the number of US agencies involved. Under a technical exchange program, several specialists from a variety of fields visited Spain, and more than 300 Spaniards were trained in the US each year after the agreement (Rubottom and Murphy, 1984: 38; Whitaker, 1961: 244).

However, this crucial and massive (by Spanish standards) US aid was extended on the condition that Spain liberalise and open its economy. The Americans demanded that the Franco administration devalue the Spanish currency, lift restrictive barriers to foreign investment, and reduce the power of government-controlled industries (Dura, 1985: 235 and 263). The Americans attached particular importance to the liberalisation of the foreign investment laws, and hence the flow of US private capital into the Spanish economy. Just before the 1953 agreement American pressure was intensified. S. Griffs, the US ambassador to Madrid at the time, made a revealing declaration to the American Chamber of Commerce in Spain:

> we are hopeful that many of the restrictions now applied to American business operations can be ameliorated or removed [..and] that American corporations may be encouraged to make investments in Spain through permission to obtain larger interests in Spanish companies than is now allowed (quoted in Dura,1985: 335).

From 1948 onwards there were also pressures on the US Administration from American businessmen for economic aid to Franco's Spain (Dura, 1985: 219). It was thought that US dollars would enable foreign exchange hungry Spain to purchase long desired and necessary American industrial and agricultural products. The economic potential of Spain attracted American businessmen. Travelling to Madrid in increasing numbers, they showed their willingness to do business in Spain (Dura, 1985: 220).

Simultaneously, the relations between the Americans and Spanish bankers/businessmen became closer. The Franco administration gave an important role to the Spanish banking/financial community in improving relations with and obtaining aid from the US. First, in 1948, a board member of a top industrial bank in Spain, was given the responsibility of creating a heterogeneous Spanish lobby in the US (Dura, 1985: 206-207), a mission which he successfully completed. Second, Franco appointed M. Arruba, the Minister of Commerce and an experienced banker, to head the Spanish team in negotiating the Pact of Madrid in 1953 (Rubottom and Murphy, 1984: 22). These appointments indicated the fusion of the Spanish state, Spanish financial circles and the Americans. For the Spanish bankers/industrialists and the American businessmen, the US-Spanish Agreement of 1953 signified decisive and determined US involvement in the Spanish economy and the stabilisation of the Franco administration. This reassured both domestic and foreign businessmen to invest capital in Spain (Ellwood, 1994: 163 and Gallo, 1973: 224).

From the point of view of the Spanish economic elite, the 1950s witnessed the consolidation of the power of bankers throughout the various sectors of the Spanish economy; by 1960 banking interests controlled more than 60 percent in the manufacturing, mining and utilities sectors (Dura, 1985: 334). Furthermore, the Americans were determined that Spanish private capital should also benefit from the 1953 agreement. Accordingly, American officials usually supported Spanish bankers and thus large Spanish private enterprises in their demands for funds for expansion and modernisation (Whitaker, 1961: 245-246; Rubottom and Murphy, 1984: 39).

US interests replaced the British and French through the acquisition of German holdings, and British and French shares in several Spanish firms (Dura, 1985: 340). In this manner, the Americans consolidated their participation in the electrical, chemical, pharmaceutical and rubber sectors, and also penetrated the mining, steel, food processing and insurance sectors in the 1950s. The increasing preponderance of US capital in Spain led to collaboration of the Spanish economic elite with American interests. In one such case, J.Luis de Anzar Zabala, an influential Spanish financier, bought two firms that represented 32 percent of the total production in the rubber sector. However, the real buyer was an American firm (General Tyre and Rubber Co.) for which Anzar played the role of an American agent in the deal (Dura, 1985: 340-41). Another important dimension of US involvement in the Spanish economy was realised through the participation of American private capital in major industrial concerns organised by INI. In the 1950s, for example, American firms participated with INI in the establishment of REPSA in the petroleum products sector and ENDIDESA in steel production (Liberman, 1982: 174).

Although Spain was excluded from the Marshall Plan, the Americans provided aid for the reconstruction of the Spanish economy. However, while US aid played a key role in importing desperately needed capital goods and also in offsetting the deficit in the current account balance (OEEC, 1958: 36-37), Spain was opened to US interests and at the same time was incorporated into the US-led new world economic order. Spain became the member of OEEC (later OECD), IMF, and the World Bank in 1958, and a member of GATT in 1963. As far as the Franco administration was concerned, the US connection meant accepting American prescriptions for the reorganisation of the Spanish economy. First, the US administration had some control over how American funds were to be spent. Second, American private capital decided where to invest and this did not necessarily coincide with Spanish priorities (Ellwood, 1994: 164).

The most decisive American intervention aiming at further integration of the Spanish economy into the new economic world order came with the Spanish Stabilisation Plan of 1959. The objective was to eliminate the body of controls, regulations and state intervention still affecting innumerable aspects of Spanish economic activity (OECD, 1960: 5). The main American concern was the liberalisation of external trade and the abolition of restrictions on foreign investment. Accordingly, the Spaniards devalued the Peseta and launched a program reviewing tariff laws, dismantling existing quantitative controls, globalising country specific quotas, and abolishing the public trading corporations responsible for importing and distributing raw materials. As for foreign capital, legislation (which would be strengthened in 1963) was introduced to encourage foreign investment, which offered substantial incentives and guarantees to foreign investors (see Harrison, 1985: 146-148). A decree defining the parity of Peseta within the gold-exchange monetary system brought Spain into the Bretton Woods Agreement (Liberman, 1982: 203). The plan was supported by $420 million in foreign aid, of which almost half was to come from US public and private sources and the other half from the IMF and OECD. American economic aid to Spain continued in the form of US Counterpart Funds for Public Finance and US Economic Assistance during the 1960s (OECD, 1960 to 1966). Total US economic aid reached $694.3 million during the 1960s, and it was roughly $130 million per annum in the 1970s (Cordata, 1980: 245).

In the early 1960s, the Spanish government invited the assistance of the World Bank in the preparation of a long-term development plan designed to expand and modernise the Spanish economy (IBRD, 1963: vii). Three such development plans were implemented between 1964 and 1975. Their main objectives were economic development, promotion of a market economy, greater integration into the international system and improvements in social welfare (Harrison, 1993: 25). In this process, while the public sector was urged to meet the targets of the plans, state officials directed private sector activities through a set of indirect policies such as the extension of credits, fiscal measures, special agreements and incentives. Broadly speaking, the introduction of development plan was another American initiative to place the Spanish economy into the new world capitalist economic order by assigning a new role for the semiperipheral Spanish state in the economy.

The laws promulgated in 1959 and 1962-1963 gradually lifted almost all restrictions on the amount of capital that foreigners could invest for the purpose of establishing new firms and expanding the capacity of existing firms (OEEC, 1960: 30; 1962: 24; and 1963: 8). Between 1960 to 1974, all forms of net private long-term foreign capital investment in Spain reached $7.6 million: 41 percent of the accumulated foreign direct investment ($2.016 million) came from the US, and a large proportion of the 17 percent Swiss share probably originated in the US (Baklanoff, 1978: 43-45). Of the 200 largest American industrial firms, 92 had subsidiaries in Spain of which 61 had majority participation (Baklanoff, 1978: 49-51 and Munoz et al., 1979: 169). Most of these firms were established either in relatively advanced technology or high growth sectors of industry (Liberman, 1982: 231). In fact, between 1960 and 1975 the American role in the Spanish economy changed from that of a supplier of official grants, loans, credits etc., to the major source of private investment capital.

In the period between 1953 and the late 1960s, the American presence was enormous in numerous sectors of the Spanish economy, including food, manufacturing, metals, agricultural products, building, banking, cinema and information technology, wholesale commerce, electronics and electricity, pharmaceuticals, finance, automobile, textile, engineering, shipping, marketing and public relations, paper, oil, petrochemicals, insurance, transport and communication and several other minor categories (Pollack, 1987: 30).

Despite liberalisation and further integration into the world-economy, the Spanish state remained a central actor in the economy during the 1960s and

1970s. In other words, in accordance with its semiperipheral position, the state controlled the economy by creating opportunities for entrepreneurs and taking on an entrepreneurial role itself. Three main forms of state intervention were put into practice (Wright, 1977: 38-45). First, the state intervened to bring about specific changes in a sector or a region using joint action programs in which private firms in a particular sector undertook to increase production, productivity, quality targets, in return for state credits and tax benefits. Other schemes encouraged firms to merge in order to increase production efficiency in return for tax rebates, and offered state investments in preferential industries. The second form of state intervention included low interest rates for private and official credits, and export incentives to stimulate industrial investment and exports. In this regard, the Banking Law in 1962 was enacted for the purpose of the speedy extension of private and official credits. The Institute for Official Credit played an important role in the extension of long-term credits for investments (OECD, 1966: 41 and Baklanoff, 1978: 37) that vigorously increased the trend towards private productive investment (OECD, 1966: 6). Furthermore, the state supported the private sector and encouraged domestic capital formation by keeping wages low. The Spanish state controlled labour relations through the Ministry of Labour and Syndicates, which were subservient to economic ministries, and when necessary, through direct and violent intervention (Wright, 1977: 80-81 and Anderson, 1970: 169). In this way the Spanish state, on the one hand, reallocated resources from the public to private sector in the 1960s and 1970s and hence contributed decisively to its dynamism (OECD, 1972: 40; 1974: 34).

The third way in which the state intervened in the economy was through ownership of industrial companies. In spite of Spain's commitment to the market economy after 1959, INI continued to play an important role in the economy. In 1976 its domestic activities represented 37 percent of the petroleum refined in Spain, 23 percent of the electric power generated in the country, 45 percent of national steel production, 50 percent of coal, 67 percent of aluminium production, 97 percent of national shipbuilding, and 46 percent of the domestic manufacturing of automobiles (Liberman, 1982: 171). Furthermore, the state owned hundred percent of Spain's major airlines, operated its national railways, postal and communications system and the distribution of tobacco products (Baklanoff, 1978: 35). INI also had effective control of 60 different firms that in turn, participated in almost 190 domestic and foreign subsidiaries and affiliates (Baklanoff, 1978: 35 and Wright, 1977: 45). Another important state economic activity was the allocation of funds for the building and improving of transport and electric power systems and the telecommunication infrastructure of the country (OECD, 1966: 40; 1974: 32).

As for relations between the state and other economic actors, after the 1959 Stabilisation plan the state continued to favour the accumulation of capital in the hands of the financial elite and their control over industry. First, although the Banking Law of 1962 de jure opened the way for newcomers in the banking sector, its conditions made the establishment of new banks very difficult. This in turn reinforced the dominant position of the big seven banks. In fact, the banking community was among the few interests that formulated the new economic policy with state officials in the early 1960s (Anderson, 1970: 202). Not surprisingly, during the implementation stage of the first development plan, the number of firms controlled by the six major banks increased considerably (Amodia, 1977: 215).

The relations between the state controlled savings banks and private banks are a good example of the intimate relations between the state and the big financial community. The deposits of the Savings Bank (which came mainly from less prosperous rural areas) were lent at rates well below the market rate to certain privileged industrial companies that were often owned by the big commercial banks (Wright, 1977: 110). Furthermore, throughout the 1960s and 1970s the big seven banks controlled some 70 percent of the total assets in the commercial banking sector, granted 60 percent of all loans, held 90 percent of all private assets and exercised direct control over a quarter of the country's 200 largest concerns (Wright, 1977: 106; Maravall and Santamaria, 1986: 75). In 1967 these seven banks figured among the 20 most profitable and important Spanish enterprises (Carr and Fusi, 1981: 163). Furthermore, in the 1970s the banking community made large profits from its linkages with the energy industry (Lopez, 1990: 27).

The close links between banks and industry continued in the 1960s and 1970s. Through majority and minority shares, the banks owned 40 to 50 percent of industrial concerns (Wright, 1977: 117), supplied boards of directors to large enterprises and guided their investment decisions (Anderson, 1970: 76). Another important dimension of the relations between the state and financial capital was the participation of private capital in state monopolies such as petroleum distribution (Campsa), telephones (Telefonica) and tobacco (Tabacaera) (Graham, 1984: 81). The state representatives on the board of directors of these firms were generally passive figures manipulated by private shareholders, who were dominated by the big banks. Similarly, half of the important board positions in INI were filled by members of the financial elite (Lopez, 1990: 27). Furthermore, private sector firms used INI as a partner in order to have access to cheap long-term credits (Graham, 1984: 81).

The connections between foreign capital, the Spanish state and banking-business community also reveal striking features. In the early 1960s both the state and the banking community welcomed American capital. For example, the state gave concessions to American firms to explore for petroleum in Spain's African colonies, and Franco appointed an Ambassador to Washington who had connections with American banks. Spanish bankers also welcomed US private capital investments as well as government-sponsored loans (Whitaker, 1961: 211 and 249). In the 1960s, foreign (especially US) investment capital was involved in joint ventures with the Spanish state and the Spanish banking/industrial sectors. INI, the state holding company, also became involved in joint ventures with US multinational companies, particularly in automobiles, heavy trucks, petroleum refining and iron and steel sectors (Baklanoff, 1978: 35 and 51). In 1972, foreign capital was present in 61 of the 300 largest industrial companies by sharing its interests with the Spanish banks and with INI (Munoz et al., 1979: 171). Of the largest 159 multinationals, 85 were American, 60 of which had interests in 351 Spanish companies (see Munoz et al., 1979: 168-171 and Baklanoff, 1978: 35 and 31).

As a consequence of the 1959 Stabilisation Plan and successive Development Plans in the 1960s and early 1970s, a relative change occurred in Spain's industrial structure. Previously the industry had been dominated by inefficient, high cost, low-technology production. In the mid-1960s, as a result of deliberate policies of liberalisation and rationalisation, Spanish industrialists obtained both the incentive and the practical possibility of importing modern equipment and advanced technology for the first time since 1930 (OECD, 1965: 15). These policies made possible the normal flow of raw materials and capital goods into industry, and opened the way for the rapid expansion of the Spanish economy during the 1960s and the first half of the 1970s. Chemicals, petroleum products, rubber products, basic metals, automotive industry, electrical machinery sectors grew rapidly, while the traditional sectors of textile, clothing, food and beverages lagged behind total industrial growth (Donges, 1971: 58-59). However, Spanish industry either remained dependent on foreign patents or on foreign capital, which was firmly established, especially in rapidly growing technologically advanced sectors (Wright, 1977: 47 and Munoz et al., 1979: 167). However, despite structural change and rapid economic growth (7.3 percent annual average) between 1960-1974, in most sectors a number of large firms continued to exist side by side with a multitude of small units (Wright, 1977: 46).

In the context of the semiperiphery argument, it is clear that core-like production patterns began to emerge in the Spanish economy at the expense of peripheral ones in the mid-1960s. Two economic actors played an important role in the process of modernisation: the Spanish state, and the Spanish financial/industrial elite that supported the liberalisation and development plans of the OECD and World Bank for Spain in the late 1950s and early 1960s (Whitaker, 1961: 200 and Anderson, 1970: 195). Spanish businessmen who had been unwilling to invest in new technology before the 1960s changed their attitudes when they realised that further industrialisation was impossible in the existing economic environment (Donges, 1971: 61). Hence, many entrepreneurs met the challenge of improving efficiency and adopting advanced technology in their respective branches through capital deepening investments.

The strong investment boom and the employment of relatively advanced technology in industrial production in the early 1960s led to the satisfactory growth of industrial exports and also to the diversification of Spanish exports. From approximately the middle of the 1960s, the growth of industrial exports accelerated markedly to 25 percent per year between 1963 and 1972 (OECD, 1973: 20). Moreover, Spanish exports underwent a fundamental structural change with regard to their commodity composition. Previously, Spanish exports had mainly consisted of food products, which accounted for 60 percent of the total. However, industrial exports (which had accounted for one-third in 1963) reached nearly three quarters of the total exports in 1972 (OECD, 1972: 31-32; 1973: 20). Furthermore, this spectacular growth in industrial exports was accompanied by important changes in their composition: while the share of cotton fabric, petroleum products, and pig iron decreased in total exports, commodities such as household electrical goods, electrical equipment, and machine tools and ships (capital goods) began to be exported in appreciable quantities from the middle of the 1960s (OECD, 1972: 32 and Baklanoff, 1978: 68). Another important result, from a semiperipheral perspective, is that Spanish industrial products successfully penetrated in the world markets. The Spanish share in world markets more than trebled between the mid-1960s and early 1970s (OECD, 1973: 20), rising by an average of 9 percent (OECD, 1975: 15).

Another significant development in the period between 1960 and the mid-1970s was the emergence of Europe as an important factor in Spanish economic development. American economic aid lasted until the mid-1960s, providing the necessary foreign exchange for imports and offsetting the balance of payments deficits (OECD, 1958: 36-37). However, while American involvement in the Spanish economy took the form of private direct investment in the mid-1960s, the role of official grants and loans decreased substantially (OECD, 1961: 30; 1962: 22; 1963: 25). Indeed, the tremendous expansion of capital goods imports that led to the breakthrough in industrial exports and structural changes in export commodity composition, and the subsequent trade deficits between the early-1960s and the mid-1970s, were not financed by official American economic aid but by new sources of foreign exchange: tourism receipts, emigrant workers remittances and foreign private capital inflow. OECD country surveys on Spain between 1961-1977 show the increasing importance of tourism receipts, emigrant workers remittances and capital inflows in offsetting the current trade balance deficit. The fact that 90 percent of tourism earnings came from European tourists (OECD, 1973: 11), and that almost all the workers remittances were sent by Spanish workers employed in major European industrial capitals, revealed Europe's increasing role in the Spanish economy in this period. Between 1962-1973, annual receipts from tourism increased from $500 million to $3,300 million, while emigrant remittances increased from $150 million to $900 million in the same period (OECD, 1977: 33).[4] Reconstruction of the European economies and rising economic activity and prosperity in Europe began to contribute to Spanish economic development indirectly in the form of tourist receipts and workers remittances.

Nor was Europe's increasing role in the Spanish economy between 1960 and the mid-1970s confined to providing foreign exchange through tourist receipts and workers remittances. Trade between Spain and the EEC increased remarkably between 1961 and 1977 (Tsoukalis, 1981: 85). In 1961, 26 percent of Spanish imports came from the EEC. The proportion of imports had grown to 43.2 percent in 1973 and 33.8 percent in 1977. Similarly, while 37.6 percent of Spanish exports went to the EEC in 1961, the proportion had increased to 46.3 percent in 1977. On the other hand, US-Spanish trade either diminished or remained stagnant in the same period (Tsoukalis, 1981: 85). Spanish imports of American goods fell from 25.2 percent in 1961 to 16.3 percent in 1973 and to 12.1 percent in 1977. In terms of exports, they rose from 9.9 percent in 1961 to 13.9 percent in 1973 and fell to 9.8 percent in 1977.

The EEC share of foreign investment also increased significantly from 1960 to mid-1970s period. EEC capital had represented only 20 percent of foreign investment in 1961-1962 (US 45 percent), but it reached 31 percent (US 32 percent) in 1969 (Rubottom and Murphy, 1984: 99) and 35 percent in 1975 (US 41 percent) (Baklanoff, 1978: 43). The signing of a Preferential Trade Agreement between Spain and the EEC in 1970 marked the institutionalisation of increasing European influence in the Spanish economy.

The majority of the Spanish business community had favoured some kind of association with the EEC since the early 1960s (Anderson, 1970: 191 and Gallo, 1973: 336). In fact, their enthusiasm for such an agreement was a clear indication of their orientation towards the modernisation and reorganisation (Europeanisation) of the Spanish economy. This is a characteristic behaviour of the economic elite of an upwardly mobile semiperipheral state. However, the support of the Spanish state towards, and its collaboration with, these modernising economic elite in this process was another important point which should be considered (Baklanoff, 1978: 25 and Gallo, 1973: 336).

The Political Environment

As is noted earlier, semiperipheral states are subjected to high degrees of intervention in their domestic affairs by hegemonic and/or core states during expansion periods of the world-economy. In this way, they become satellite/client states and ideological and political agents of hegemonic power/core states.

Spanish-US relations dominated the politics of the postwar period in Spain. The main preoccupations of the Americans were to dismantle the power of autarkic state policy-makers who opposed the new American liberal world economic order, and to integrate Spain into the US policy of containing communism politically, militarily and ideologically. Spain's geo-strategic assets were critical in the American decision to control developments in the country. Its geographical location between the Mediterranean and the Atlantic, and between Europe and Africa, made Spain a crossroads for shipping, sea-lanes and communication channels.

In the immediate postwar years, the US administration concluded that only Franco could provide the kind of order that would protect US global interests in Spain (Dura, 1985: 152). Accordingly, US policies were directed towards preventing any destabilisation of the Franco regime. While publicly condemning the fascist nature of the Franco regime, the Americans extended economic and military aid to, and signed economic and military agreements with, Franco's Spain. The Americans also tried to neutralise the diplomatic attacks on Spain that might endanger political stability in Spain. In one case, for example, the Americans urged France not to bring a proposal to the UN Security Council for the imposition of economic sanctions on Spain.

US policy was a severe blow to the hopes of the anti-Franco groups in and outside Spain, and it indeed enabled the Spanish dictator to survive. American support for Franco continued until his death in the mid-1970s. President Eisenhower emphasised even his support for stronger friendship and more active co-operation between the US and Spain during his visit to Madrid in 1959 (Whitaker, 1961: 81). Visits from top-level US statesmen continued until Franco's death in 1976, including those of Presidents Eisenhower, Nixon, Ford; Vice-Presidents Agnew and Ford; Secretaries of State Dulles, Rusk, Rogers, Kissinger; and several other ministers, congressmen, high ranking military officers, and directors of the CIA. An American admiral even participated in Franco's Civil War celebrations in June 1967 (US Hearings, 1971: 229-230), and US troops participated in joint manoeuvres to down a hypothetical rebellion against the Spanish government in 1969 (US Hearings, 1971: 296). US Secretary of State Rogers also refused to meet a prestigious group of opposition leaders during his visit to Madrid in 1970 (US Hearings, 1971: 297).

There were three main reasons for American involvement in Spanish affairs. First, Spain's economic and market potential had to be integrated into the new open-door world economic system. Second, Spain's strategic location was important for the world-economy and for the containment of communism. Third, the continuation of Spain's anti-Communist orientation had to be guaranteed.

As early as 1946, the State Department decided that since Spain did not threaten international peace, and since Franco served US economic and political interests satisfactorily, there was no justification for American intervention to topple Franco's administration (Dura, 1985: 160). American businessmen were also putting pressure on the Truman administration for an economic aid programme for Spain in order to provide the necessary foreign exchange to purchase American industrial and agricultural goods (Dura, 1985: 219). Despite administrative and financial difficulties, Spain's economic potential attracted American businessmen. For instance, major US oil companies such as Standard Oil, Texaco, Caltex and Aramco, had already invested in Spain (Dura, 1985: 220). In short, the potential of the Spanish market could not be ignored easily.

However, the condition for American aid was the elimination of autarkic policies, and hence the dismantlement of powerful autarkic political cadres and institutions in the policy making process. The Americans did not deal with a number of departments and/or personalities to bring about such changes in the Spanish establishment, rather they only had to convince Franco since the functions of Chief of State, Prime Minister, Commander-in-Chief of the armed forces, and Chief of the National Movement and its corporate representative Falange (the official party) were combined in the person of Franco. Furthermore, there was no separation of powers. Franco effectively controlled the Executive, Legislature and Judiciary in Spain (Gilmour, 1985: 23). In this system, factions in the establishment (Falange, Church, Army) were given neither monopoly power nor were totally excluded from office (Carr and Fusi, 1981: 35). Franco was the supreme political manipulator.

In accordance with the State Department's advice, the US administration used covert mechanisms to bring about changes in Spanish politics. Economic aid was the most important instrument in this process. First, the US Administration approval of loans to Spain from private US banks in the late 1940s was preceded by Franco's announcement that Spain was a monarchy. Second, the Pact of Madrid was signed after the Spanish cabinet was reshuffled in 1951 at the expense of pro-autarky ministers.

However, the decisive blow to the Falangist, pro-autarky ministers came before the 1959 Stabilisation Plan. After 1957 Franco sharply decreased the number of Falangists who supported import substitution, protection, exchange rate manipulation, and so on, in the economics ministries. Instead, a new group of technocrats with a strong commitment to liberal economic philosophy and who were closely associated with the Catholic secular lay organisation *Opus Dei*, were appointed to key economic ministries including Industry, Finance, Commerce, Public Works, and Agriculture. In sharp contrast to the Falangist technocrats, the *Opus* group supported a free market economy.

By 1962 *Opus Dei*, that represented big business and financial interests, became the most powerful group in the formulation of economic policy in Spain (Harrison, 1993: 24). *Opus* technocrats aimed to transform Spain into an efficient, dynamic and productive economy through rationalisation, planning, and elimination of inefficient and archaic structures (Gallo, 1973: 266). However, despite their liberal economic outlook, *Opus* ministers were authoritarian in the political sphere. Hence, the repressive nature of the Franco administration did not change.

The army was another element of the Spanish establishment on which the Americans exercised influence in the postwar period. The Americans saw the primary task of the Spanish army as the maintenance of domestic stability. The Bases Agreement of 1953 gave the Spanish armed forces a key role in the relationship between Spain and the US (Whitaker, 1961: 70). They were given the task of defending US bases against military attacks, but their fundamental duty was to maintain domestic stability (Whitaker, 1961: 71). For this purpose, the US extended money, military equipment, technical and professional training to the Spanish armed forces. Total US military assistance to Spain amounted to $849.3 million between 1951-1959, $679.3 million in the 1960s, and roughly $150 million during each year of the 1970s (Cordata, 1980: 245).[5]

After the Bases Agreement, joint military exercises with the US resulted in the integration of NATO concepts into Spanish military thinking and operational doctrines (US Hearings, 1971: 242). As a result of the close relations between the US and the Spanish armed forces, and in parallel to the increasing role of the *Opus* ministers, the numbers and the roles of military personnel in Spanish cabinets increased in the 1957 and 1969 cabinet reshuffles (Payne, 1968: 42 and Mackenzie, 1973: 73).

US influence probably strengthened Spain's die-hard anti-Communist stand. In fact, Franco had always been anti-Communist, but he was also strongly anti-liberal. As American influence increased, he gradually abandoned his anti-liberal stand and dismantled the power of corresponding political groups in the establishment. He also strengthened the anti-Communist nature of his regime. Yet, strikingly, there was no immediate internal or external communist threat to Spain. In the domestic sphere, the Spanish communists were crushed both during and after the Civil War. In the external sphere, the country's geographic location rendered communist aggression very unlikely. Nevertheless, anti-communism became a central policy of Franco's Spain. Throughout the 1950s, not a day passed without a declaration of Spain's determination to fight against communism (Gallo, 1973: 212).

The *Opus Dei* technocrats, who joined the cabinet between the late 1950s and early 1970s, were in favour of closer cooperation with the EEC. Indeed, they applied for an Association Agreement with the EEC in 1962 and were involved in the negotiations that resulted in a Preferential Trade Agreement in 1970. Although their basic aim was economic integration with the EEC, they emphasised the political aspect of their Europe-oriented position after signing the Preferential Trade Agreement. Foreign Minister L. Bravo (of *Opus Dei*), for example, stated that

> Spain ever attentive to three continents has now taken the decision to plant its roots in Europe: our destiny is worked out. This agreement indeed only represent a first step, but the practical irreversibility of the process is present in everybody's mind, as well as the certainty of the final objective (quoted in Baklanoff, 1978: 74-75).

However, the main obstacle to the Association Agreement was the nature of the Spanish political regime, which was incompatible with the democratic principles that governed the Community's member states.

In the late 1960s and early 1970s, it became apparent that the dynamism of the rapidly changing Spanish economy and society could no longer cope with the antiquated political structures of the Franco regime (see, Preston, 1986: 13-17, 57 and 68). The increase in the number and intensity of strikes, demonstrations and Basque terrorist attacks demonstrated the ineffectiveness of the control mechanisms (the various forms of repression and the official syndicates that controlled labour force) of Franco's regime.

The repercussions of the change were striking. On the one hand, with the establishment of a new form of capitalism in Spain in 1959, the nature of the working class threat had changed. The owners of many large and more competitive enterprises, who wanted to expand their operations in the EEC, emphasised the need to integrate labour into this new capitalism by reward-based productivity arrangements; in other words, the system of syndicates had become a major obstacle to the future growth their businesses (Preston, 1986: 17 and 1984: 33). In fact, from the outset Europeans had demanded the dismantlement of the syndicate system in Spain as a condition of full membership in the EEC. Accordingly, competitive big businesses entered into direct dialogue with both the Workers' Commissions and moderate opposition leaders. They had to risk liberalisation in order to avoid cataclysmic confrontation (Preston, 1986: 17 and 57). The dissatisfaction of the economic elite with the old institutional arrangements led to similar changes in the Francoist political structures (Preston, 1986: 17). First, the church began to withdraw the regime's moral legitimacy. Second, a group in the Francoist political elite (known as *Aparturistas*) began to defend the adjustment of political structures to the new form of capitalism (Preston, 1986: 16). Accordingly, in 1974 they launched a program that envisaged opening and wider participation in the system. The EEC's refusal to accept Spanish membership as long as its undemocratic political regime remained in power played a decisive role in changing the outlook of the business elite (who now wanted to expand into the EEC market) towards Francoist political structures.

Foreign Policy: Atlanticist Years

We now turn to Spain's semiperipheral foreign policy during the postwar expansion period of the world-economy. The foreign policies of semiperipheral states in expansion periods are directed towards the accomplishment of the global objectives of the hegemonic power. Accordingly, they tend to become satellites of hegemonic power and subordinate their national interests and national sovereignty to the global and/or regional (local) interests of the hegemonic power.

In the postwar period, Spain followed a pro-American foreign policy and assisted in the consolidation of the US-led world order. Hence, Spain signed agreements with the Americans, and allowed them to shape Spanish foreign and defence policies. Not surprisingly, Spain became a satellite state of the US, and Spanish national interests were subordinated to those of the US.

Located at the crossroads of the Mediterranean and the Atlantic, and of Africa and Europe, Spain was important to the Americans. Its control of oil routes and the shipping lanes, and its geographical proximity to the oil regions, made Spain important to the new world economic order. Spain was also important to the containment of communism in the Western Mediterranean and North Africa. Moreover, Spain's land mass down to the Pyrenees was seen as a reserve area in the case of a Soviet attack on Western Europe. Thus Spain was also important for the security of the new world order. This last point was emphasised in the US National Security Council (NSC) Report #68 in 1950, and in face of strong European opposition to Franco, the NSC Report #72/4 recommended a bilateral agreement for military co-operation with Spain (Dura, 1985: 269-270 and 291).

On the strategic front, the central aim of the US was to maintain the security of the new world capitalist system against the Soviet Union and world communism. In 1949, NATO was established as an important component of this global policy. The US administration wanted to bring Spain into NATO because of its geo-strategic location and to secure political stability in the country (which was also crucial for US economic interests). However, the Europeans strongly opposed Spanish entry into NATO both because of Franco's war time alliance with the Nazis and Fascists, and because of the undemocratic nature of the Franco regime. Under these circumstances, the Americans had to find another formula to incorporate Spain into the Western defence system. The formula came with the 1953 Bases Agreement (Pact of Madrid) between US and Spain. Under this agreement, the US was authorised to establish, maintain and use naval and air bases, military and transit facilities, and oil pipelines on Spanish soil. In this way the Americans indirectly linked Spain to NATO. The Spanish bases became part of US overseas bases, and hence a part of the US global defence system. The agreement clearly signified Spanish participation in the US policy of containment. H. Baldwin, a leading American expert on defence issues, described the Bases Agreement as follows:

the geographic and strategic importance of Spain, her mobilization potential of 2,000,000 men, her relative social, political and geographic security as a base, and her strategic raw materials of potash, iron core, zinc, lead and mercury are a major geopolitical asset... [on the other hand]... Spain's bases help to seal the Western gateway to the Mediterranean; her Atlantic islands aid in controlling and protecting trans-Atlantic shipping lanes and the Iberian peninsula provides additional disperse sites for light, medium and heavy bomber strips. And Spain behind the rampant of the Pyrenees provides a last line of defence if the rest of Western Europe should fall, and offers a springboard for offensive land, sea and air operations. Her bases are particularly important as an alternative to the great bomber strips in Morocco, surrounded by political and social unrest, and the great supply and air installations in France, which might be threatened by a Soviet advance across the Rhine or by a change in present French policies perhaps incident to German rearmament (quoted in Whitaker, 1961: 48-49).

The 1953 Agreement was renewed in 1963, 1969, 1970 and 1976. Each time its content was further enriched, and Spain was further integrated into US global designs. In the 1963 agreement, for example, US nuclear submarines were permitted to base on the US naval base Rota in southern Spain. Indeed, in 1963 Spain, with its naval and air bases, and its radar post and nuclear stock-piles, became an important country in the American overseas defence network (Gallo, 1973: 311). In 1964, the Americans decided to establish tracking stations in Spain for the US space program (Rubottom and Murphy, 1984:84). In the early 1970s, the Americans claimed the bases provided the infrastructure to support American forces deployed in Europe and the Mediterranean, contributed to world-wide strategic and tactical mobility, and also contributed to America's deterrent capacity, particularly by providing coverage for Polaris nuclear submarines (US Hearings, 1971: 218 and 248-249).

The increasing Soviet presence in the Mediterranean in the second half of the 1960s, and the loss of US base in Libya, had increased Spain's strategic importance. According to US Assistant Secretary of State, Spain could provide a springboard for the introduction of air and ground forces into the Eastern Mediterranean in times of tension. Since Spain was out of the range of the majority of Soviet high density short and medium range ballistic missiles, it would provide a rear area to the central Europe defence system (US Hearings, 1971: 258-259). Since Spain was also contiguous to North Africa, it would become even more significant if Soviet influence and penetration were to continue in the Western Mediterranean area. Moreover, Spain was also important for the defence of Israel, and to American oil interests in the Middle East (US Hearings, 1971: 294).

In the absence of formal defence relations between Spain and NATO, the Americans maintained informal contacts through briefings and consultations with Spanish officials on current developments in the early 1970s, and they informed them of the main points in the discussions after each session of the NATO Council and Defence Planning Committee (US Hearings, 1971: 272 and 293). To increase co-ordination between NATO and Spain, the 1970 Bases Agreement established a Joint US-Spanish Committee on defence matters, and the Commander-in-Chief of the US NATO forces in Europe was appointed its principal advisor. In sum, through these mechanisms, Spain was informally incorporated into the US-led Western defence system in the 1945-mid-1970s period.

Another semiperipheral characteristic of Spain's external policy was its client status vis-à-vis the US. In the early postwar period Spain was subjected to international political ostracism because of Franco's war time collaboration with Hitler and Mussolini, and the repressive nature of Franco's political system. It was not accepted in the UN, and UN member countries withdrew their ambassadors from Madrid. Furthermore, Spain was excluded from Marshall Plan and NATO. However, American diplomatic patronage played a decisive role in gaining Spain's admittance to a number of international organisations - chiefly the UN. First, the US played the leading role in revoking the 1946 UN ambassadorial ban on Spain by defeating a proposal in 1947 that demanded the reaffirmation of the resolution on the recall of ambassadors from Madrid (Whitaker, 1961: 30). In 1948, the US Secretary of State officially requested the annulment of the UN condemnation of Spain; and in 1950 the Americans invited UN member states to appoint ambassadors to Spain and demanded the admission of Spain into UN specialised organisations (Gallo, 1973: 188-189). As a result, Spain joined the WHO in 1951, UNESCO in 1952, ILO in 1953, and the UN in 1955.

The Americans also wanted to include Spain in the Marshall Plan and the US House of Representatives accepted such a resolution by a great majority in 1948, but the Europeans strongly opposed the idea. However, as mentioned, the Americans used other means to assist Spain. Similarly, the Americans were anxious to bring Spain into NATO and attempting to influence to their attitudes, they took every opportunity to remind other NATO members that Spain was important (US Hearings, 1971: 274; Rubottom and Murphy, 1984: 113). In this endeavour, however, the Americans were unsuccessful. Once again they resorted to bilateral links through the Bases Agreement in 1953.

American patronage and protection saved Spain from total international isolation, but it turned the country into a client and a satellite state and a political and ideological appendage of the US. Franco's emphasis all this time was on anti-communism, as well as stability and order in the country (Gallo, 1973: 184). Stability and order secured US official and private capital in Spain, while anti-communism indicated Spain's political and military commitment to US global objectives. Spanish foreign policy was largely based upon anti-communism in this period. In 1948 Franco emphasised "the necessity for building up an alliance against Soviet menace and the Spanish willingness to participate in this organisation" (Whitaker, 1961: 36). Similarly, in 1949 he declared, "as long as arms and economic aid come from the US there would be no need to spill American blood for the defence of Europe" (Dura, 1985: 254). A further Spanish commitment to the anti-communist crusade came in 1950 when the Spanish embassy in Washington declared that "Spain was willing to help the US to check communism by sending forces to Korea" (Gallo, 1973: 183). Franco was also anxious to sign a bilateral military agreement with the US, and to provide bases and other military facilities to the Americans on the Canary and Balearic Islands, and on the Spanish mainland (Whitaker, 1961: 35-36). At the time of the agreement, Franco called the 1953 Bases Agreement "a triumph and as the honour of fulfilment of Spanish foreign policy" in his message to the Spanish Parliament (Gallo, 1973: 223).

Indeed the nature of this agreement was proof of Spain's client and satellite status. The US Mutual Defence Assistance section stated that Spain agreed to cooperate with the US in controlling trade with nations that threaten world peace (Whitaker, 1961: 47). Not surprisingly, Franco issued a call for an international boycott of "communist goods" in 1954 (Shneidman, 1980: 162). The renewal of the Bases Agreement in 1963 and 1970 indicated the continuation of the Spanish commitment to US global interests. After the 1970 renewal, President Nixon and the Spanish foreign minister declared their determination to check Soviet expansionism, particularly in the Western Mediterranean and in North Africa (Cordata, 1980: 249). Spain's satellite characteristics were made apparent by the way the Americans utilised the bases, especially during the Middle East conflicts. The Spanish bases enabled the Americans to respond to the Lebanon crisis in 1958, the Congo crisis in 1954, and to the Middle Eastern crises in 1967 and 1973 (US Hearings, 1971: 218 and 220).

Spain's satellite status was evidenced on other fronts too. Spanish foreign policy towards Eastern Europe echoed Washington's, for example, in 1951 Franco proposed a Western "crusade of liberation" to free the "captive people" of Eastern Europe from Russian communism. Similarly, in 1952, the Spanish Foreign Minister announced "Spanish support for a Western strategy of roll-back against the Soviet menace" and stated that "such a policy was demanding all the military plans of the free world to be designed primarily for the rescue and liberation of East European sister nations who were subjected to the most appalling of oppressions" (quoted in Dura, 1985: 139).

Anti-communism was also an important aspect of the satellite Spanish foreign policy towards Latin America and the Arab World. In 1958, the Spanish Foreign Minister emphasised the danger of the communist penetration of Latin America, and he implied Spain's intention to assist the US in combating communism in the Southern Cone (Whitaker, 1961: 343). In fact, Franco abandoned Spain's *"Hispanidad* policy" in Latin America, which aimed at the restoration of Spanish hegemony in the Southern Cone (Rubottom and Murphy, 1984: 12).[6] Instead, the *"Hispanidad* policy" was converted into a cultural unity of Hispanic states (Whitaker, 1961: 30). Similarly, Spain no longer argued that the US had turned Latin America into a new kind of colony through investments and bases (Whitaker, 1961: 375).

Spanish foreign policy also followed a pro-American line towards the Arab World. During the 1956 Suez crisis, Franco altered his initial support for Nasser under American pressure and in consideration of the increasing Soviet penetration in Egypt (Whitaker, 1961: 330 and Flemming, 1980: 134). Franco sounded the tocsin against communist penetration of the Arab World (Whitaker, 1961: 343), and by the early 1960s, he had identified the radical and neutralist Arab states such as Egypt, Syria, Iraq and Algeria as potential dangers to the status quo and agents of the Soviet Union (Flemming, 1980: 141). On the other hand, although Spain refused to recognise Israel, Franco allowed the Americans to use US bases to assist Israel in 1967 and 1973.

Another characteristically semiperipheral foreign policy behaviour in periods of expansion is the subordination of sovereignty and national interests to the global interests of hegemonic power. A number of Spanish policies exhibited this characteristic. First, a secret clause of the 1953 Spanish-American Defence Agreement (which remained in force between 1953 and 1970 and was secret until 1981) gave the US the freedom to use the bases in times of emergency and actual war (Vinas, 1984: 41-42; 1988: 147). This clause allowed the Americans to take the initiative in acts of reprisal with no obligation to the Spanish administration, other than passing on information about their intentions (Pollack, 1987: 151-152). Similarly, a secret US NSC document in 1956 declared the American intention to use bases in Spain to attack the Soviet Union if it was deemed necessary (Pollack, 1987: 26). Other secret technical agreements, 22 confidential procedural agreements, and a non-public status-of-forces agreement for US personnel and dependants that further limited Spanish sovereignty were signed with the US between 1953 and 1960 (Vinas, 1988: 147).

In fact, the American bases were the only reason why there might be a communist attack on Spain. Thus, the deployment of the latest US B-47 aircrafts that capable of carrying nuclear bombs, and the construction of a sea-base for the US Polaris nuclear submarines, turned Spain into a principal target in case of an East-West conflict. Indeed, Spain was alarmed during the Cuban Missile Crisis, since it was a host country to US bases (Story and Pollack, 1991: 154). Another example of how Spanish interests were subordinated was the authorisation to build a nuclear submarine base in southern Spain. Permission was given without negotiations, and even without the knowledge of the Spanish foreign ministry (Vinas, 1984: 42-43).

During the 1950s and 1960s, Spanish defence policy was concerned, not about a possible communist attack, but about the growing Moroccan threat to Spain's North African possessions of Ceuta, Mellila, Ifni, the Spanish Sahara and Spanish Guinea (Whitaker, 1961: 322). Spanish perceptions of this threat did not change in the early 1970s. A strategic study prepared by the Spanish armed forces in 1971 defined North Africa as the most important security risk for Spain and also referred to the territorial claims of Morocco, emphasising the potential sources of conflict with this country (Vinas, 1988: 148). A retired American army officer who served in the American Embassy in Madrid pointed this out to the US House of Representatives Sub-Committee on Europe:

> The Spanish military see the principal external security threat to Spain posed for North Africa on the south rather than from over the Pyrenees in the north... They are concerned with the defence of Ceuta and Mellila which are considered parts of metropolitan Spain... (and) to a lesser degree, the protection of the Spanish Sahara (US Hearings, 1971: 243).

Despite their sensitivity over the North African possessions, the Spaniards lost almost all of them during the Franco period, except Ceuta and Mellila. In North Africa, the most striking example of the subordination of Spanish national interests to the US occurred in 1957 when Moroccan irregulars invaded Ifni. In this case, the Americans did not allow the Spanish army to use American weapons to put down the attack (Rubottom and Murphy, 1984: 61). Nowhere in the defence agreement was there a US obligation to assist Spain in case of an attack on Spanish colonies or protectorates (Pollack, 1987: 152). In fact, none of the military agreements signed between the US and Spain in the period between 1953 and mid-1970s included a commitment by the US to the defence of Spain (Payne, 1968: 38 and US Hearings, 1971: 226). Thus, while Spain might become a victim or become part of an East-West conflict, there was no US guarantee of support against threats or attacks on Spanish territory.

The erosion of Spanish sovereignty and the subordination of its national interests were also apparent in the way the US used its bases in Spain in the Middle East Crisis of 1967 and 1973. First, despite the traditional Spanish-Arab friendship and Spain's refusal to recognise Israel, the Americans provided logistical support to Israel from their Spanish bases in the 1967 Arab-Israeli war. The Spanish government was either kept in ignorance or unable to stop them (Pollack, 1987: 97). After this incident, although the Americans were told by the Spaniards that they would not be allowed to use the bases in any future conflict between the Arabs and Israel, USAF tanker planes in Spain refuelled American jets being flown non-stop from the US to Israel. This was done without prior notice to the Spanish government. The Spanish government protested, but they did so after the event rather than to interfering at the time of refuelling (Rubottom and Murphy, 1984: 107). An important consequence of these developments was that Spain's reliability diminished in the eyes of the Arabs, and its claim to be a bridge between Islam and Christianity was undermined.

Another semiperipheral characteristic of Spanish foreign policy in this period was to play a bridge role between the West and Latin America and the Middle East (see Whitaker, 1961: Chapter IX and Polack, 1987: Chapter 4). There was a constant interplay between Spain's "bridge policy" and its relations with the US (Whitaker, 1961: 320). The "bridge policy" in the Arab World was announced during the Spanish Foreign Minister's extended tour of six Middle Eastern countries in 1952 (Flemming, 1980: 134). Accordingly, Spain offered its good offices between Britain and Egypt, and the inclusion of Arab League into Western defensive system (Whitaker, 1961: 327). A similar attempt was made during the Suez crisis in 1956, but the "bridge" collapsed under the weight of the US bases in Spain (Whitaker, 1961: 330). In Latin America the "bridge policy" was put into effect mainly through the new *Hispanidad* program, which was redefined as "a system of norms destined to better defence of Christian civilisation and to the ordering of international life in the service of peace" (Whitaker, 1961: 343). In 1958 the Spanish Foreign Minister hinted that one of the aims of *Hispanidad* was to assist the US in combating communism in Latin America (Whitaker, 1961: 343). Thus the "bridge policy" indicated Spain's willingness to become a springboard for US interests in both the underdeveloped Arab

World and Latin America in return for economic and political benefits. However, the Spanish initiative was unsuccessful. The existence of US bases in Spain, and the strong neutralist tendencies among the Arabs, were the main causes of Spain's failure in the Arab World. On the other hand, Latin Americans were not willing to support Spain's "bridge policy" because the *Hispanidad* program reminded them of the close association between the US and dictatorships (Whitaker, 1961: 349-350).

As mentioned earlier, European-Spanish relations were mostly negative during the Franco period. However, the increasing power of the *Opus Dei* ministers in the Spanish governments during the 1960s gave the first sign of an Europeanist orientation in Spanish Foreign Policy. The *Opus Dei* ministers applied for an Association Agreement with the EEC in 1962. Nevertheless, despite their liberal economic philosophy, the new "Europeanist" team in the Spanish government did not aim to change the undemocratic, authoritarian nature of the Franco regime. As a result, the Community first shelved the Spanish application and only after two years started exploratory talks at the commercial level. Despite the Spanish desire for full integration (Gallo, 1973: 336-37), the EEC only granted Spain a Preferential Trade Agreement in 1970, one which provided a limited access in the economic sphere. In the 1970s there was increasing opposition in the EEC to the political developments in Spain (Harrison, 1985: 163). Member states increased their criticisms concerning the absence of fundamental political rights in Spain and attacked the attitude of the Franco regime against political dissidents. In 1975 they put strong pressure on Franco to convert the death sentences on five Basque terrorists to life imprisonment. Following the execution, they recalled their ambassadors from Madrid and postponed trade talks with Spain (in a sharp contrast to the US Secretary of State, Kissinger, who described the event basically an internal Spanish matter) (Rubottom and Murphy, 1985: 114). Another interesting point about Spanish-EEC relations was the strong American opposition to the tariff terms of the EEC-Spanish Preferential Trade Agreement (US Hearings, 1971: 228), which showed the contradictions between the US and Europe on the control of resources in the Mediterranean in the 1970s. The American reaction to the Preferential Trade Agreement was putting an article into the US-Spanish Friendship and Cooperation Agreement (the Bases Agreement) during its renewal in 1970 stating that, "the government of the US declares its sympathetic understanding of Spain's objective of full integration [into the EEC]. The two governments [the US and Spain] agree to consult with each other to keep in close contact in seeking to arrive at mutually satisfactory solutions for any problems of principle or procedure as may arise for either of them in this connection" (US Hearings, 1971: 264).

In sum, in the period of expansion of the world-economy under US hegemony, Spain, though not to the same extent as Greece, exhibited the general characteristics of a semiperipheral state. Various economic actors directed their activities to affect state policies. Spain experienced covert US intervention in its domestic affairs. Moreover, the Spanish state, which was also a central actor in the economy, was gradually transformed from an autarkic structure into a liberal one, as a result of continuous American pressure for a change in terms of political cadres and institutions. Furthermore, in the foreign policy sphere Spain became a satellite/client state and a political and ideological agent of the hegemonic US. Now, let us consider the contraction period in the world-economy in order to assess whether Spain also demonstrated semiperipheral characteristics in this period.

Notes

1   Nevertheless, Banco de Espana was closely controlled by the government through the appointment of its governor and four of the twenty-four members of the board of directors who had the right to veto any decision.
2   A. Miguel and J. Linz "Los empresarios espanolas y la banca" *Moneda y Credito 84*, March 1963, pp.3-12, quoted in Anderson, 1970, p.77. For more information on the role of the banking sector in the economy in this period see Anderson, 1970, pp.76-77.
3   For peripheral characteristics of the Spanish economy, see also Donges, 1971 p.45.
4   For further information on the relationship between exports, imports, trade deficits, tourism, workers remittances, foreign private capital and European contribution see, Roman, 1971, p.44-45; Baklanoff, 1976, pp.193-196 and 1978, p.56; Keyder, 1985; and OECD Country Reports, 1969 and 1973.
5   After the Bases Agreement, Spanish pilots were trained in American planes, and many soldiers received American training in other spheres of military operations, both in Spain and the US. 4800 members of the armed forces received American military training in Spain between 1954 and 1958. In 1959, almost 700 military personnel were trained in the US, in third countries, or in US bases overseas (Whitaker, 1961: 71-72). The number of US trained Spanish soldiers reached 6061 in the early 1970s (US Hearings, 1971: 259), and the Spanish armed forces became largely reliant on the US for modern equipment (Wright, 1977: 43).
6   The *Hispanidad* programme was based on Spain's cultural ties with the Spanish American nations and represented a perversion of the relatively innocuous Pan Hispanism of the pre-Franco generation. The *Hispanidad* programme was launched during the Civil War with Axis aid. It was countered the economic influence of the US in Latin America, see Whitaker, 1961, p.6.

Chapter 5

Spain: 1976-2000s

In this chapter Spain's semiperipheral foreign policy, in connection to the economic and political developments in the period between the mid-1970s and the early 2000s, will be considered. As we have seen, this period corresponds to both a "contraction period" and the "relative decline" of American hegemony, as well as the emergence of Europe (EC/EU) as an economic and political power in the world-economy. Whether Spain's economic and political structures, and its foreign policy, responded to these changes in a semiperipheral way will be the focus of this investigation.

The Economic Environment

An overall examination of Spain between the mid-1970s and early 2000s shows that it was in the process of upgrading its position towards the core area. The establishment of democracy after Franco's death in 1975 and the transformations in the economy, especially during the 1980s revealed that a shift from the old mechanisms was underway. Not surprisingly, the Spanish state was at the centre of these developments.

In spite of the rapid economic growth of the 1960s, Spanish industry was dominated by traditional heavy sectors of iron, steel, non-ferrous metals, shipbuilding, etc., while the traditional sectors of textile, clothing, footwear, leather, etc., predominated light industry in the 1970s (OECD, 1986: 50; 1994: 59). The world economic crisis of the mid-1970s and early 1980s, which stemmed mainly from the two oil-price shocks, hit the traditional industries in which Spain specialised in the 1960s and early 1970s. Moreover, large investments were encouraged in these declining and technologically backward sectors until the late 1970s (OECD, 1986: 32). Hence, the Spanish production structures did not adjust to the changing patterns of world demand; manufacturing was still concentrated in those sectors in which world supply exceeded demand. Spain's comparative advantage in these sectors eroded as a result of increasing competition with the low cost, newly industrialised countries (NICs) of South East Asia, Latin America, and Eastern Europe (OECD, 1981: 10-11) and of rising energy and real wage costs in Spain (OECD, 1982: 26). Furthermore, economic difficulties were aggravated by insufficient product differentiation and lack of high-technology sectors like consumer electronics, data processing equipment, electronic components, optical and photographic equipment, aircraft, telecommunications, and so forth, in which world demand was briskly increasing (OECD, 1981: 11).

Moreover, in spite of the transformations in the 1950s and 1960s, the economic system was still rigid and under state protection. Excessive protection in the domestic market, the proliferation of subsidies and transfers to enterprises, and difficulties in the credit and financial markets hindered the normal operation of market forces and effective resource allocation, and therefore also the structural transformation of industry (OECD, 1984: 18). In general, small firms, which were overdependent on bank credits, survived because of protection (OECD, 1981: 11). Thus, extensive state intervention, regulatory framework, corporatist attitudes, and inefficiency and protection from foreign competition remained the main characteristics of the Spanish economy until the early 1980s (OECD, 1986: 50; 1992: 63).

In the 1970s the state played an important role in the economic development of Spain. At the end of 1978, INI, the public holding institution, participated directly in seventy different firms and indirectly in over two hundred firms. It was involved in 15 percent of the electricity generated; 35 percent of automobile and 30 percent of industrial vehicle manufacturing; 65 percent of the petroleum refined; 60 percent of steel production; 50 percent of the coal mined; and 95 percent of shipbuilding. INI also had large holdings in the fields of air transport, tourism, regional development, banking, and foreign trade (Gobbo, 1981: 64). It was responsible for one-third of all industrial investment and a significant source of employment in the country (Gobbo, 1981: 73). The situation hardly changed in the early 1980s (Moxon-Browne, 1989: 6). Furthermore, through INI, the Spanish state entered into joint ventures with foreign governments in oil prospecting in Kuwait, Iran and Libya, and iron and bauxite mining in Brazil and uranium mining in Niger (Baklanoff, 1978: 35). It also invested in the electronic computer industry with a Japanese company, Fijutsu, and held shares in the Arab-Spanish Bank (Liberman, 1982: 308).

One of the consequences of the world economic crisis in the 1970s and early 1980s was the nationalisation of loss making private enterprises, and a concomitant overmanning in the large public enterprises of iron, steel and shipbuilding. In addition, heavy subsidies and wage increases led to chronic losses in public enterprises (OECD, 1984: 9; 1986: 35). Thus, during the economic recession of the second half of the 1970s and early 1980s, the public sector became a huge dustbin for inefficient private industries, and for the excess capacity developed in these sectors (Salmon, 1991: 33 and Harrison, 1993: 48). Consequently, in this period, Spain pursued a defensive strategy that aimed to shelter the existing structure of economic activity and employment from the deep changes affecting the world-economy (OECD, 1984: 51). The two main weaknesses of the Spanish economy during the mid-1970s and early-1980s were its reliance on excessively labour-intensive technology, and excess productive capacity supported by subsidies and privileged tax treatment (Liberman, 1982: 355).

Nevertheless, the Spanish state was aware of its economic shortcomings and after the 1977 elections took steps to restructure the industrial sector, improve competitiveness, reform economic institutions and increase the flexibility of factor markets (Salmon, 1991: 9). The first step was the 1978 Moncloa Pact that established price and wage guidelines and envisaged a program of basic economic and institutional reforms. It set up a norm for wage increases, intended to dismantle the complex system of government intervention, eased institutional rigidities and government controls on distribution of credits, and allowed foreign banks to operate in Spain (OECD, 1978: 33-34). Second, a medium-term economic program adopted in 1979 was based on three points: increasing reliance on competitive market forces, efficient resource allocation, and the transformation of the production system against higher energy prices and competition from the NICs (OECD, 1980: 26). Spanish policy makers concentrated their efforts on providing competitive stimuli to the domestic market through import liberalisation, attracting foreign direct investment, creating more flexible capital and financial markets, and improving the pattern of resource allocation both through market mechanisms and government incentives (OECD, 1980: 26).

At first, however, state industrial policy was mainly focused on restructuring the crisis-stricken sectors of steel, shipbuilding and consumer goods (refrigerators, television, radios, etc.) (OECD, 1980: 39). The major role of the state in this process was to provide the necessary legal, fiscal and financial support, and to monitor the fulfilment of the objectives set by the private sector (OECD, 1981: 29). Accordingly, a legal base was prepared in 1980, and the Law on Industrial Reconversion was promulgated in 1981 to solve the underlying problems (OECD, 1982: 37 and Harrison, 1993: 49). In the same vein, capital transfers, subsidies, and tax benefits were offered to both public and private sectors in order to accelerate industrial restructuring (OECD, 1981: 40 and Harrison, 1993: 49).

This new industrial policy also aimed at adapting Spanish industry to new patterns of world demand and increasing its competitive advantage. Funds were earmarked in the budget for the advancement of Research and Development (R&D) (OECD, 1981: 29). Rationalisation was promoted by abandoning the policy of nationalising private companies in crisis (OECD, 1979: 30 and Salmon, 1991: 33). Moreover, investments in the energy sectors (mainly in the electric power industry) increased substantially from 7 percent in 1979 to over 40 percent in 1981, and a new state energy holding (INH) was established in 1981 (OECD, 1982: 35). Between 1978 and 1981 the Spanish state also tried to establish a more flexible labour market through a series of agreements (Aguliar, 1984: 128) that liberalised the dismissal of workers and recognised the right to strike (OECD, 1979: 34; 1980: 21). Further liberalisation of tariffs, quotas and licenses also occurred in this period.

Yet, in spite of various attempts to raise the efficiency of state enterprises, industrial restructuring lagged behind the targets in the early 1980s. Although state transfers for industrial restructuring reached 171 billion Pesetas between 1979 and 1982 they usually went to absorb losses rather than to deal with structural problems (OECD, 1986: 33). Indeed, emphasis was placed upon cushioning the effects of restructuring on traditional industries (Salmon, 1991: 9). According to one OECD survey, Spain had to reduce the funds being transferred to uncompetitive enterprises, which benefited from subsidies, tax exemptions and official credits, and hence cease passing this burden on to more dynamic and efficient firms (OECD, 1982: 43).

The process of fundamentally transforming the Spanish economy began only in the beginning of 1983 when the new Socialist government decided to re-examine the method of implementing industrial restructuring. A white paper on reconversion and reindustrialisation was prepared, and it was supported by a law. This new law complemented the 1981 Law on Industrial Reconversion and was based on a tripartite collaboration between the authorities, employers and employees (OECD, 1984: 46-47). The socialist government seemed to revolutionise the economy.

The new policy was based upon two key elements: first, to improve productivity and restore a healthy profit position by cutting excess capacity and overmanning, and by restructuring the financial liabilities of excessively indebted enterprises; and second, to promote investment and technological innovation in those activities with good future profit potential (OECD, 1986: 33 and 35).

OECD surveys on Spain after 1986 point out that the industrial restructuring program was going well. Excessive labour costs and plant capacity in ailing industries were reduced, the modernisation of economically viable industries was supported through investment credits and subsidies, and flexible contracts were introduced in the labour market. Emphasis had been given to technological development in industry. Operational losses of public enterprises were first stabilised and then reduced, and subsequently a number of them became profitable companies.

Substantial public sector expenditure and private sector investment contributed to the implementation of the reconversion plan (Salmon, 1991: 118). Eighty percent of the investment targets in the plan were realised (OECD, 1989: 40). The role of the state in the successful implementation of the reconversion plan was apparent, since the subsidies and credits of the Industrial Credit Bank were equivalent to some 85 percent of the total investments undertaken by reconversion firms (OECD, 1989: 40). As a result, the latest plants were installed, and Spanish industry was reorganised (Salmon, 1991: 118).

Indeed, from the mid-1980s, Spanish industrial policy stopped supporting traditional industries and promoted investment in new sectors. As a result of replacement investments and additions to the capital stock embodying new technologies, efficiency gains and rationalisation became possible in production structures (OECD, 1990: 71). Seventy percent of Spanish firms introduced new technologies in this period (OECD, 1990: 73). The composition of industrial output changed as output began to grow faster in high-technology sectors (OECD, 1990: 71). In other words, Spanish companies achieved diversification by increasing the technological element in the product's added value (Aledo, 1993a: 26). The establishment of larger and more competitive enterprises through successful mergers (as in the fertiliser industry) was another significant development in this period.

Public sector activity was also reoriented. This was important because public holding companies were not only concentrated in the utilities and strategic sectors but also existed across the whole spectrum of economic activity. In the early 1990s, the public sector was one of the largest industrial groups and Spain's leading exporter (Salmon, 1991: 28-30 and OECD, 1989: 48; 1990: 40). As a result of the restructuring plan, INI abandoned its dustbin approach to unprofitable and inefficient private firms. Indeed, except in some rapidly declining industries (such as shipbuilding), INI achieved a spectacular growth of productivity in many sectors towards the end of the 1980s, and its financial situation improved appreciably (OECD, 1988: 37). In

1987 its overall losses were reduced to a fifth, and by 1989 it had turned into a profitable organisation (OECD, 1989: 38; 1990: 40).

A striking indicator of the upwardly mobile nature of the Spanish economy was the significant change in the state's view of R&D activities (see Aledo, 1993b). In accordance with Spain's policy of "catching-up with the EC economies", a law for the Promotion and General Co-ordination of Scientific and Technological Research was passed in 1986. Co-ordination between public research centres and private companies was improved, and co-ordination with and participation in international R&D programs were promoted. In 1988, R&D projects began to be subsidised by the Ministry of Industry and priority was given to high-technology sectors. Thus, while computer and space technologies received 15.9 percent and 11.4 percent of the subsidies respectively, traditional sectors received only about 1 percent of the total (Aledo, 1993b: 33). In the early 1990s, Spanish research activities focused on the ascending sectors of new materials, computer and telecommunications technology (Aledo, 1993b: 32).[1] Furthermore, the government encouraged private and public research institutions to participate in European and international R&D programs in order to absorb and generate technology in the domestic production system. Henceforth, Spanish enterprises took part in various EC and international projects such as BRITE, ESPRIT, RACE, EURAKA, Airbus, European Nuclear Research Organisation, European Molecular Biology Laboratory, and so forth. (Aledo, 1993b: 34).

From the world-system school perspective, it was apparent that the Spanish state supported the consolidation of core-like (efficient, high-technology, high profit) production patterns, while gradually dismantling inefficient, declining, periphery-like industries. Nevertheless, the state was not alone in this process. The Spanish economic elite also influenced state policies. The seven biggest banks (the financial elite) were the most important and dominant group in the economy and industry, controlling 80 percent of total assets and investments in all sectors (OECD, 1984: 44 and 50 and Moxon-Browne, 1989: 10). They exerted decisive influence on economic and political spheres (Moxon-Browne, 1989: 9). Indeed, Suarez's centre-right *Union de Centro Democratico* (UCD) party represented the progressive wing of the Spanish financial and industrial elite (Preston and Smyth, 1984: 36). The government was linked in various ways to the more progressive sectors of Spanish capitalism; the vice-president of the National Confederation of Spanish Business Organisations (CEOE), the mouthpiece of big modern enterprises (Kohler, 1982: 59), was appointed Minister of Industry, for example, while the Minister of Labour was a member of the inner group of the UCD. Several ministers had close personal ties with the powerful Spanish banks (Preston, 1986: 93; Menges, 1978: 34 and Coverdale, 1977: 626). Accordingly, the promulgation of laws and preparation of plans for the restructuralisation of the economy was not a mere coincidence; there were intimate relations between the political and economic decision making bodies. The removal of numerous government regulations and controls, tax benefits, subsidies, etc., changed the protected and secure business environment and upset the traditional business sectors (OECD, 1981: 40).

Nevertheless, concurrently with the relative failure of the Suarez government to implement the new economic measures, the business elite began to express dissatisfaction with the government in the early 1980s (Martinez, 1993: 136-138). According to Martinez's research, although a number of businessmen still preferred old paternalistic and statist policies, many others favoured a free market and a competitive economic environment (Martinez, 1993: 137). The Spanish business elite wanted to be a part of Europe, and it sought a more assertive political voice in economic and efficiency terms (Martinez, 1993: 136-138). The Spanish Socialist Party (PSOE) managed to reassure many important bankers and businessmen of their determination to remove economic obstacles (Preston and Smyth, 1984: 64). F. Gonzalez, the Socialist Prime Minister, declared that the party would "undertake serious and profound reforms which in principle [were] difficult to approach from a socialist perspective" (quoted in Gunther, 1986: 34). The re-examination and later the successful implementation of reconversion and restructuralisation plans were clear indications of the success of the "core-like" producers' policies at the state level. The Socialist government's decision to allocate resources to high- technology and competitive industries promoted the interests of the "core-like" fraction of the Spanish economic elite (Lopez III, 1990: 66).

In the context of semiperipheral development, another state policy that played a decisive role in the process of upgrading the Spanish economy towards the core zone was to attract foreign investment. OECD surveys between 1977 and 1985 indicate that the net inflow of foreign direct investments in Spain increased considerably. The incentives given by the Spanish state, the relatively large domestic market, and the prospect of Spain's membership of the EC were the main reasons for the increase in foreign investment (OECD, 1984: 12 and 1986: 14). A substantial inflow of foreign investment (both direct and portfolio) was realised between 1983 and 1985.

Net foreign direct business investment in Spain in the first half of the 1980s averaged around $900 million, and the total amount of gross foreign investment reached $2.5 billion in 1985 (OECD, 1986: 14). However, a particularly spectacular rise in foreign investment was registered between 1985 and 1990 (OECD, 1988 to 1994). In 1986 foreign investment increased by 75 percent (Salmon, 1991: 19), and it reached $14 billion in 1990 (OECD, 1994: 21). According to Harrison, the amount was $16.6 billion in 1989, which was roughly equivalent to 3 percent of Spanish GDP (Harrison, 1993: 63). Between 1985 and 1990, foreign direct investment contributed to 40 to 50 percent in the growth of total business investment (OECD, 1990: 9). In this period, many multinational firms shifted production to Spain, and foreign companies acquired controlling interests in Spanish companies (OECD, 1988: 22 and 25).

The greater buoyancy in the inflow of foreign investment after 1986 was due to a number of factors. First, 1986 legislation enabled foreign entrepreneurs to transfer unlimited amounts of capital, profit and dividends abroad (Salmon, 1991: 19). Second, full EC membership reduced the political risk of investing in Spain. Third, labour market rigidities were abolished. Fourth, a good social climate; regional, financial and fiscal incentives; links with EC and Latin American markets; the strong Peseta; and the decision by European countries to establish an integrated market by 1992 all contributed to the inflow of foreign investment in Spain (OECD, 1990: 65 and Salmon, 1991: 20). Furthermore, the Spanish privatisation policy actively encouraged foreign penetration (Salmon, 1991: 39). Although the upswing in the foreign investment was shared by all sectors, investment largely went into technologically advanced (machinery and equipment) and scale intensive (car production, food, paper, chemicals) industries (OECD, 1990: 65).

Full membership in the EC was one of the priorities of the Suarez government. In fact, the political and economic elite thought that EC membership was the precondition of Spain's long-term healthy economic development (Medhurst, 1984: 32). A 1979 opinion poll showed that 67 percent of the Spaniards, and all major interest groups (industrialists, the business community, both big and small and medium-sized business organisations, the chamber of commerce, trade unionists, farmers), were in favour of membership in the EC (Tsoukalis, 1981: 122 and 127). In fact, the Spanish business community had been in close contact with the Community since the Franco years (Tsoukalis, 1981: 127). Immediately after the first democratic elections in 1977, the Suarez government prepared a plan called *Programo Economico del Gobierno* that set out the government's liberalisation plans as a prelude to Spain's eventual membership of the EC (Harrison, 1985: 181).

From the semiperipheral development perspective, EC membership constituted the most important developmentalist goal and an opportunity to adjust the Spanish economy to core-like production structures. Spain's expectations from the EC were that it would force Spanish entrepreneurs both to modernise and to compete in international markets. They also thought that they could benefit in the medium and long-term from its ability to sell in a market comprised of more than 250 million people. Moreover, membership would expand the volume of foreign (European) capital in Spain, and expand Spanish exports to the EC (Liberman, 1982: 297).

The Socialist government, which came to power in 1982 also emphasised the importance of the EC for the economic development of Spain. In 1983, the Spanish Secretary of State stated that "[The Community] will represent for us as the definitive modernisation of our productive apparatus and of the country in general" (quoted in Preston and Smyth, 1984: 14). Indeed, Socialist's policy ensured the rapid entry of Spain into the EC and the adjustment of the Spanish economy to EC norms and regulations as early as possible.

When Spain became a full member of the Community in 1986, the role of the EC in its transformation process increased significantly. A striking indicator of this development was the massive inflow of foreign (European) investment in Spain, which played a decisive role in the upward mobilisation of the economy. Indeed, long-term European private capital inflow was one of the principal forces behind the sharp upturn in investment activity after 1985 (OECD, 1988: 74 and 1990: 62). While the main source of foreign investment was the US during the 1960s and most of the 1970s, after Franco's death, the balance in foreign investment tilted towards the EC. In 1975, the figures for US and EC investments in Spain were 40.6 percent and 35.6 percent of the total respectively, but they decreased to 11 percent for the US and increased to 51 percent for the EC by 1983 (Salmon, 1991: 21 and Pollack, 1987: 140). Furthermore, the EC's share of direct investment increased from 48 percent on average in the three years prior to 1985, to 65 percent in 1986 (OECD, 1988: 25). Similarly, while the foreign direct investment shares of the EC and the USA were 38.4 percent and 18.4 percent respectively in 1984/5, between 1986 and 1989 the EC share increased to 52 percent while the US' share decreased to 4.9 percent (OECD, 1990: 64). In fact, a large part of the foreign investment, especially in the second half of the 1980s, aimed to extend Spanish export capacity to the rest of the EC (OECD, 1989: 27).

Spain's trade relations were another indicator of its orientation towards Europe. In the immediate post-Franco period, Spain signed an agreement with the European Free Trade Association (EFTA). Meanwhile, Spanish-EC trade relations had been increasing since the 1970 agreement, particularly with regard to imports and exports: 43.2 percent of imports and 48.5 percent of exports were from and to the EC in 1973. By 1985 these figures were 36.8 percent and 52.2 percent respectively (Harrison, 1993: 63). After Spain joined the EC in 1986, the Community's share of Spanish exports and imports continued to increase (OECD, 1988: 22; 1990: 70). In 1990, for example, the EC's share in total Spanish imports reached 59.2 percent, and the exports to the Community were 68.9 percent (Harrison, 1993: 63).

The EC's contribution to the Spanish economy through traditional invisibles receipts continued in the post-Franco period. According to the OECD reports, until the 1990s, higher invisible earnings from EC countries virtually offset Spain's trade deficit. Most of the invisible receipts came from growing tourist receipts, while emigrant remittances declined in importance as many Spanish workers began to returned home from the mid-1970s onwards.

EC transfers to the Spanish economy after 1986 provide further evidence of EC's increasing role in Spain's economic transformation. Between 1986 and 1988, Spain obtained more than 3.5 billion ECUs from various EC funds; most of the money was used to develop public infrastructure and for training programs (OECD, 1990: 61). According to the OECD reports between 1989 and 1992, net EC transfers to Spain continued to rise rapidly (thereafter they declined). After 1989, EC structural funds were directed to serve infrastructural development, regional development, industrial reconversion, youth training, reduction of long-term unemployment and agricultural support (OECD, 1990: 61 and 1994: 34).

Another important development after the early 1980s was Spanish willingness to adapt and harmonise its economy to EC practices, indicating the determination to upgrade Spain in the hierarchy of states. The first step was the successful implementation of industrial reconversion and restructuralisation, which led to the reorganisation and installation of modern plants in almost all industrial sectors and to the promotion of research and development (Salmon, 1991: 117-118). The aim was to transform production structures in order to cope with the competitive economies of the EC. Secondly, Spain paid particular attention to product differentiation strategies and to improving the country's international competitiveness by increasing the technological element in the added value of products, and by improving their quality and design (Aledo, 1993b: 34). Similarly, science policies and technology systems were reformed to enable Spain to participate in European and EC research programs (Aledo, 1993b: 34). After 1986, the interventionist policies of the state decreased in favour of market oriented reforms in order to align Spain with the EC economies. In this context, a new law in defence of competition was passed, and a Competition Court was established in 1989 (OECD, 1990: 39). Foreign investment legislation was brought into line with EC laws (Salmon, 1991: 19), administrative impediments to competition between banks were lifted and financial institutions were restructured to improve efficiency (OECD, 1990: 37). The banking sector was rationalised and transformed, and restrictions on foreign banks were gradually lifted (OECD, 1990: 38). Furthermore, a draft law was prepared giving the Bank of Spain complete independence and forbidding monetary financing of public sector deficits (OECD, 1993: 49). The Peseta entered the Exchange Rate Mechanism (ERM) of the European Monetary System (EMS) in June 1989. All remaining trade barriers (quotas, tariffs, taxes, etc.) were dismantled, trade flows were completely liberalised (OECD, 1988: 7; 1990: 53-55) and restrictions on the movement of capital were removed (OECD, 1989: 41). Moreover, all foreign exchange controls were lifted in February 1992, and in March the government designed a convergence program for 1992-1996 to prepare for Spain's full participation in the next phase of European integration and to meet the strict Maastricht criteria (OECD, 1993: 48-49; 1994: 9). By the early 1990s, Spain had successfully integrated into the EC.

There were also other indications of Spain's upward mobilisation. Since 1964, Spain had gradually increased its international market share of industrial products; by 1975 finished industrial products (consumer and capital goods) constituted the most important item in total exports (various OECD surveys from 1967 to 1975). The rapid expansion of Spanish industry was largely the result of the technological renovation of antiquated capital equipment (OECD, 1976: 38). In the immediate post-Franco period, Spain lost part of its previous market gains due to the international competition of the NICs. However, by 1978, Spain had regained its competitiveness and had gained substantial market shares (OECD, 1979: 15-16). Spain continued to increase its competitiveness, and expand its industrial exports and market shares, in the period between the late 1970s and the mid-1980s (OECD surveys from 1979 to 1984), thus building up new outlets in EC and Latin American markets (Minet, 1981: 49 and OECD, 1980: 19), in the Middle East and OPEC countries (OECD, 1978: 16; 1981: 35) and in COMECON and Japan (OECD, 1982: 15). Spain's export performance was strongly influenced by the foreign investment wave of the mid-1970s (OECD, 1984:

12), and it performed especially well in intermediate technology sectors such as vehicles, machine tools, avionics, etc. (Harrison, 1993: 47). Furthermore, the Spanish capital goods industry competed in major international bids.[2]

After 1986, Spanish exports to Latin America, OPEC and COMECON countries declined as a result of EC membership, while EC markets became more attractive to Spanish exporters (OECD, 1988: 20-22; 1989: 27-28). Nevertheless, export performance improved and export markets continued to grow (OECD, 1990: 22 and 44). Spanish entrepreneurs increased their share by nearly a fifth, and market share gains were concentrated in the EC countries. In the early 1990s, sizeable gains in EC markets were obtained (OECD, 1992: 23 and 71). In 1990/91, market share gains by industrial goods were 7 percent on average, buoyed by the coming on-stream of a large number of new industrial plants (OECD, 1993: 26).

Another significant development from the world-system perspective was the shift in the product composition of Spanish exports towards goods with higher unit values. This shift resulted in big terms-of-trade gains (OECD, 1990: 71). For example, in 1993, export-import coverage rose to 76 percent from 64 percent on average the previous five years (OECD, 1994: 21). The Spanish share in total OECD exports for medium and high-technology products also increased by two-thirds and four-fifths respectively between the mid-1980s and early 1990s (OECD, 1994: 21).

Another significant development has been the export of Spanish investment capital, particularly to Latin America and southern France initially (OECD, 1973: 25 and Tsoukalis, 1981: 94) and later to the EC and the US (OECD, 1981: 36; 1986: 14 and Salmon, 1991: 21). Furthermore, this growth persisted in the early 1990s (OECD, 1992: 25; 1994: 23), indicating that Spain's upward mobilisation towards the core region of the world-economy continued.

The final index of Spain's upward mobilisation was the dramatic increase in the GDP per capita. As we have seen, according to world-system scholars, successive and remarkable increases or decreases in the GNP (and GDP) per capita are a sign of upward or downward mobilisation in the world-system hierarchy of states. In parallel to the transformation in Spain's production structures since the mid-1970s, Spanish GDP per capita, which was $2,890 in 1976, increased to $3,960 in 1978, $5,648 in 1980, falling back to $4,778 in 1982 and $4,192 in 1984, but increasing steeply again to $5,927 in 1986. GDP per capita continued to increase to $7,449 in 1987, $9,658 in 1989, $12,770 in 1990, $13,520 in 1991, reaching $14,704 in 1993 (OECD surveys from 1976 to 1994). From the world-system perspective, these successive and steep increases, together with the establishment of core-like production structures clearly demonstrated Spain's upward mobilisation. Therefore, all the economic developments in Spain between mid-1970s and early 1990s show that the process of upgrading Spain from its semiperipheral position to the core region of the world-economy continued successfully.

The Political Environment

One may wonder if, in the political sphere, Spain's economic development coincided with semiperipheral political developments in the post-Franco period. There are two basic contentions of the world-system school about the political developments of upwardly mobile semiperipheral states in the contraction period of the world-economy: first, the old political structures collapse, second, the intervention of hegemonic/core powers into their domestic affairs come to an end.

Spain experienced radical developments in its political establishment in this period; the principal institutions of the Francoist establishment were either abolished or made to abandon their old roles and habits as a result of democratisation. First, the system of Francoist "representation" was abolished through the democratisation of the Cortes (Parliament). In the old system the Cortes, (its members were selected arbitrarily by Franco) was no more than a sounding board for Francoist speeches. The other chamber, the Council of Realm, was an "advisory" unit composed of dignitaries and economically powerful families of the Francoist regime (Ben-Ami, 1984: 2). When the Law for Political Reform of 1976 introduced the principle of popular sovereignty and universal suffrage, the Francoist Cortes was manoeuvred into voting itself out of existence, and the Council of Realm was also abolished. Spaniards overwhelmingly (nearly 95 percent) approved of these reforms in a referendum in December 1976. In 1977, the 30-year old National Movement, the state party, was also dismantled by a royal decree. A new Law of Political Association opened the way for the establishment of political parties. Furthermore, the outlawed Communist Party was legalised.

A second step was military reform, which aimed to prevent the intervention of the armed forces in politics. Under Franco, the military was a highly privileged body (Vinas, 1988: 153). Its basic duty was to prevent possible internal revolts and defend the institutional order against the enemy from within (separatism and communism) (Ben-Ami, 1984: 18). The first democratic government aimed to subordinate the military to civilian power. At the organisational level, the Military High Command was dismantled, and the armed forces were brought under the authority of the Defence Ministry in

1977 (Graham, 1984: 200). In 1978, the first civilian Defence Minister was appointed, the scope of Military Justice was reduced, and promotion and retirement systems were overhauled. Article 97 of the 1978 Spanish constitution established the supremacy of civilian authority over the armed forces, stating directly that the armed forces must obey the civil authority of the government (Giner and Sevilla, 1984: 126). The National Defence Law of 1984 further reinforced civilian supremacy over the military (Payne, 1986: 185-186), thereby giving real power in decision making regarding military issues, such as defence policy, command and co-ordination of the armed forces, the approval of defence and strategic plans, economic and financial programs for equipping the armed forces, to the Prime Minister, Defence Minister, and government (Vinas, 1988: 175).

The active participation of the military in politics was restricted. The armed forces were ordered to respect all political options, to refrain from publicly expressing any political preferences, and to avoid participation in politics (Jordan, 1979: 8 and Gilmour, 1985: 235). After an attempted coup in 1981, new legislation was passed to eliminate pretexts for future coups (Diaz-Ambrona, 1984: 33).

A third reform provided a framework of new objectives to soldiers to shift their attention from domestic to external issues. The new constitution defined the military's mission as one guaranteeing the sovereignty and independence of Spain, and defending its territorial integrity and constitutional order (Graham, 1984: 202).

State-Church relations were also transformed. The Spanish Church had been dominated by Franco, and had in fact identified itself with the Franco regime by functioning as the dictatorship's principal legitimiser (Szulc, 1976: 67 and Graham, 1984: 215). In return the Church was supported by grants and incorporated into state structures through representation in the government, the Cortes and the Council of Realm (Szulc, 1967: 67; Graham, 1984: 215; and Bardaji, 1976: 201). In the immediate post-Franco period, the Church was separated from the state by the constitution (Graham, 1984: 219). In fact this transition was greatly facilitated by the Church. Beginning in the early 1970s, some Church groups (especially those of the younger generation) had progressively dissociated themselves from the Francoist system, and by the mid-1970s the Church had abandoned its strong anti-democratic characteristics (Carr and Fusi, 1981: 155). In the post-Franco period, upper Church echelons distanced themselves from Francoism and supported the transition to democracy. Further, they refused to be identified with any political party, and for the first time in its history, the Spanish

Church deliberately disengaged from the political realm (Graham, 1984: 212 and Brassloff, 1984: 61).

Labour relations were another important indicator of structural transformation. Throughout the forty years of Franco rule, trade unions were banned, and the employers and employees were organised in a Syndicate system in which the corporatist state acted as final arbiter between labour and management. One of the priorities of the new government was a complete break with the old corporatist practices. Accordingly, in 1976/77, a series of laws were enacted allowing independent unions to organise and engage freely in collective bargaining. The right to strike and to dismiss employees was regulated (Rubottom and Murphy, 1984: 123; Liberman, 1982: 328).

A further step in political restructuring was the official recognition of regional autonomies. The autonomy of Basque and Catalonia were approved by the parliament in 1977, and later ten other regions were granted pre-autonomous status. The 1978 Constitution recognised and guaranteed the right to autonomy of the nationalities and regions that constituted the country (Gilmour, 1985: 199).

Perhaps the most important indicator of Spain's upwardly mobile semiperipheral status was the extremely favourable attitude of the economic elite towards political reorganisation/democratisation. Important sectors of Spanish capitalism informed the King that they were anxious to abandon Francoist political mechanisms (Preston, 1986: 77). Furthermore, the governing party between 1977-1982, the UCD, was a coalition of financial and industrial elites (Preston, 1986: 23). The positive attitude of the economic elite towards democratisation was confirmed by data revealing strong support on the part of Spanish capitalists for a democratic system (Martinez, 1993: 118). At first, they did not support the conservative Popular Alliance Party but voted for Suarez's moderate-centrist UCD between 1977 and 1982 (Martinez, 1993: 124). Indeed, AP was the representative of the old-fashioned, subsidised (periphery-like) businessmen (Menges, 1978: 52). Second, Spanish capitalists strongly supported the institutionalisation of the democratic system by voting "yes" in the 1978 Constitutional referendum (Martinez, 1993: 121). Moreover, their public actions and statements, after the abortive military coup in 1981, showed their firm support for democracy (Martinez, 1993: 126). Although they withdrew support from the UCD government in the 1982 elections, Spanish capitalists voted not for the old-fashioned conservative AP, but for the Socialists Party. In accordance with their aspirations to become part of the EC (core area), they recognised that the country required coherence between its increasing economic well-being and its political system. As Martinez argued, Spanish business wanted a political voice that reflected its economic and market confidence (Martinez, 1993: 136).

American intervention in Spanish domestic politics came to an end after Franco. For example, when US Secretary of State H. Kissinger suggested a slow and essentially Francoist transition and encouraged the Suarez government not to legalise the Spanish communist party (Ben-Ami, 1984: 6 and Gilmour, 1985: 174), his proposals were ruled out by both the King and the Suarez government.

In fact, there was a consensus among Spaniards across the political spectrum that the US had given credibility to the Franco regime by its economic and military support, and hence had sustained him in power (Pollack, 1987: 153 and Treverton, 1986: 6). The leader of the Spanish Socialist party, F. Gonzalez, stated in 1981 that "America helped Europe to free itself from fascism and it not only did not help Spain but condemned it to dictatorship for many more years...We have little for which to thank the United States"(quoted in Treverton, 1986: 6). According to survey data, only 24 percent of Spaniards favoured friendship with the US in 1979 (Leon, 1986: 202), and in 1985 a public opinion poll showed that 74 percent of Spaniards disagreed that the US and its president were loyal and sincere friends of Spain (Maxwell, 1991: 8). S. Eaton, the US Deputy Chief of Mission in Spain between 1974-1978, describes the American position in Spain as follows:

> the relationship...was a delicate one and for the sake of sound long-term relations we had to be careful how we managed our side of it. We had to be sure we did not appear to be intervening when we merely wanted to be helpful. We had to be sure we did not appear to play favourites among the democratic parties...Of the all democratic parties [Socialists] distrusted us most because of our past intimacy with Franco (Eaton, 1979: 118).

In contrast to their anti-Americanism, Spanish political parties revealed pro-European attitudes, and increased their co-operation with European political parties. There was a consensus about Spanish accession to the EC (Medhurst, 1984: 45). The support of leading conservative, liberal, and Christian Democrat parties of Western Europe was appreciated at the first congress of the UCD (Kohler, 1982: 33). The Socialists, on the other hand, were supported by Socialist International, the Confederation of European Socialist, and Social Democrats, and by the German Socialists (Kohler, 1982: 42 and Coverdale, 1977: 621). European support to both parties included extensive financial and organisational assistance (Kohler, 1982: 43).

A final point worth mentioning is the advent of the Socialists, who were persecuted throughout the Franco years, to power in the early 1980s. This was a significant indication of the success of transition and the consolidation of democratic practices.

Foreign Policy: Europeanisation

World-system analysis proposes that following main developments are expected in the external relations of an upwardly mobile semiperipheral state in contraction periods of the world-economy: they change their international alliances, give up satellite-type foreign policies, and pursue relatively independent foreign policies, compete with other semiperipheral states for economic and political gains, and tend to assert their intermediary and bridge (or sub-imperial) role between core zones and areas (or countries) with which they have geographical proximity and/or cultural and historical ties. Furthermore, they seek to become involved in the management of international problems. Spanish foreign policy in the post-Franco period conformed to these expectations.

An important indicator of Spain's "semiperipheral foreign policy" was its break with postwar Atlanticism, and its shift to Europeanism. This also signified a change in Spain's international alliances. The evidence was clear. First, the Spaniards redefined the status of US bases and installations. The 1976 bases agreement established Spanish sovereignty over US bases (Vinas, 1988: 157). The Americans agreed to reduce the number of US air-refuelling K-135 tankers to a maximum level of five, to withdraw the US nuclear submarine squadron by 1979, and not to store nuclear devices or their components on Spanish soil. Furthermore, the use of bases in emergency cases was subjected to urgent consultations between the two governments, and a joint council was set up for this purpose (Rubottom and Murphy, 1984: 117 and Klepak, n.d: 87). S. Eaton emphasises that the Spaniards were attempting "to establish a lower profile for Spain's relations with the US as part of the better balance in Spain's total foreign policy". This, he says, was apparent from the attitudes of the Spanish government. For example, while official foreign policy speeches on Europe, Latin America, Arab countries and the Third World tended to be long, only short references were made to relations with the US. Furthermore, the government was careful to interpret the terms of the 1976 Treaty strictly so as to avoid charges of weakness towards the Americans (Eaton, 1981: 114-115). On the other hand, Spanish Chiefs of Staff bitterly criticised the US, even arguing for a break in the relationship and in favour of closing the bases (Eaton, 1981: 114).

A new bases agreement signed in 1982 was more balanced and precise than were previous agreements (Vinas, 1988: 163). First, it clearly defined the notions of "operational and support installations" and "authorisations of use", terms which the previous agreement left vague. In this way, possible misinterpretations of the agreement in critical moments were eliminated. Second, the status of US forces in Spain was brought in line with their status in other West European countries. Third, the notion of "geographic area of common interests", which existed in the previous agreement, was eliminated. Nor did the new agreement limit Spain's freedom to develop a security policy out of NATO.

A second sign of a shift from Atlanticism was the first democratic government's lukewarm attitude towards Spain's integration into NATO. Although the first democratic government advocated Spain's eventual integration into NATO, it clearly stated that NATO membership was not a priority (Pollack, 1987: 154). According to Suarez, a national debate was required on the issue, which could not take place at short notice. The matter, he felt, was neither urgent nor immediate (Minet, 1981: 14). According to Suarez, Spain needed a special arrangement for NATO membership. Spaniards felt that NATO served the interests of the US more than anyone else. On the other hand, the widespread view in the army was that NATO needed Spain much more than Spain needed NATO (Preston and Smyth, 1984: 54).

The anti-NATO, anti-American opposition argued that NATO membership would not provide additional security for Spain's two small African possessions of Ceuta and Mellila, since they were outside the NATO area. The opposition also pointed out that NATO did not promise support for Spain in the dispute over British sovereignty, or Spanish claims over Gibraltar. In any case, NATO membership would raise the tension in East-West relations and place Spain directly against the Soviet Union in a possible East-West conflict. Nor would NATO membership protect the nascent Spanish democracy against military coups, as exemplified in the Greek and Turkish cases.

All these changes and attitudes were clear indications of a policy aimed at getting rid of the old American shadow over Spanish foreign and defence policy, while emphasising the primacy of Spanish national interests and independence. According to Eaton, the Americans had begun to worry about

US vital interests in Spain in the face of such anti-Americanism (Eaton, 1981: 26).

The policy of breaking with Atlanticism went hand in hand with a European oriented foreign policy. The Spaniards were anxious to be a part of the political and economic map of Europe. Indeed, only two days after the Franco's death, J. Carlos, the King, expressed the Spanish orientation towards Europe to the Cortes (parliament): "The idea of Europe would be incomplete without a reference to the presence of the Spaniards and without a consideration of the activity of many of my predecessors. Europe should reckon with Spain and we Spaniards are Europeans" (quoted in Preston and Smyth, 1984: 24). Accordingly, the Spanish Foreign Minister started a series of visits to European capitals in order to establish closer relations between Spain and Europe. During his meetings with the Europeans, the Foreign Minister emphasised the democratic intentions of the King, and Spain's wish for full membership in the EC (Eaton, 1981: 110). Another important development was Spanish accession to the Council of Europe in November 1977.

The Suarez government gave priority to EC membership (Pollack, 1987: 154), and in July 1977 Spain applied for membership. A cabinet level position was created for relations with Europe, and Suarez travelled to each EC state to explain Spain's candidacy (Salisbury, 1980: 104 and 116). Negotiations opened in 1979, and Spanish officials announced the government's intention to approximate Spanish foreign policy to European Political Co-operation (EPC). In this context, the EC Council of Ministers began to inform Spain about discussions in the EPC Committee (Minet, 1981: 67). It was not only the centre-right UCD, but the Communists and Socialists also strongly supported Spain's membership in the Community (Vinas, 1988: 152 and Klepak, n.d: 138 and 190). In sum, for Spain, Europe was both a model and an aspiration. The process of Europeanisation was further accelerated when the Socialist government came to power in the 1980s.

In this context, Spain became a member of NATO but remained outside its Integrated Military Structure. Second, Spaniards separated NATO interests from those of the US, and underlined Spain's sovereign rights. However, the Spaniards were careful not to become a troublemaker in the Western Alliance. By 1980 the policy of keeping EC and NATO membership apart was abandoned. The Suarez government believed that integration into NATO was a necessity for Spanish integration into European politics (Minet, 1981: 29). This did not mean a U-turn in policy, but rather indicated that foreign policy was being framed to accord with the core states of Europe. The remarks made by the Spanish Defence Minister about the advantages of NATO membership in 1981 were revealing:

> In the first place, the advantage of being in the same system of defence as the majority of democracies. In the second place, it is not a question of what NATO is offering, rather it is that Spain...has a right, on account of its own essence as a European country, to be a power within the group of European democracies...In this sense I believe that it is necessary to take Spain's European dimension to those heights which it must attain (quoted in Preston and Smyth, 1984: 22-23).

It was thought that NATO membership would be a means to influence decision making in one of the principal organisations of the Western World (Minet, 1981: 28). Spain became the 16th member of NATO in June 1982, just before the Socialists came to power.

Once in office (October, 1982), the Socialists announced a freeze on the integration of Spanish armed forces into NATO's Integrated Military Command, and repeated their commitment to a referendum on remaining in NATO. At the Atlantic Council in December 1982, the foreign minister explained that his government's policy was "to act as a loyal, co-operative and solid member but to detain the process of integration into the military structure with the objective of studying rigorously Spanish national interests" (Marquina, 1991: 36). The Socialists' policy, vis-à-vis the Atlantic Alliance in 1984, was to remain a member without becoming part of its military structure. Although the Socialists recognised that Spain's membership in NATO secured an important link with Europe, they defined Spain's position in NATO in their own terms.

A second Socialist challenge to postwar Atlanticism came in the form of further limitations on the use of the American bases. The American material and human presence in Spain was substantially reduced, and US interests were strictly separated from those of NATO in the bilateral Spanish-American Defence and Co-operation Agreement, which was renegotiated in 1983. It contained important clauses in favour of Spain, including the provision that no clause or circumstance should presuppose Spain's integration into NATO's Integrated Military Structure. Moreover, each government reserved the right to initiate the procedure for the revision or modification of the Agreement, and, if in the future the Spanish government were to decide to modify its attitude with respect to the Atlantic Alliance, the relevant texts could be re-examined (Marquina, 1989: 60-61). The Agreement also provided stricter Spanish control over the US use of bases (Rubottom and Murphy, 1984: 144). As the Spanish Minister of Defence put it, "there are no US bases in Spain, rather there are Spanish bases which are loaned to the US under certain conditions for certain uses and in return for certain benefits" (quoted in Rubottom and Murphy, 1984: 144).

In 1986, the Socialist government decided to make substantial reductions in the number of US troops on the Zaragoza base, and to replace US forces at the Torrejon air base with Spanish military personnel and aircraft (Pollack, 1987: 172). The aim was to replace Americans where Spanish personnel of equivalent competence were available (Gooch, 1986: 312). In 1986, the Americans agreed to reduce military personnel in Spain by approximately 50 percent, and in 1988 they unwillingly accepted the complete withdrawal of American fighter planes from Torrejon air base, and the replacement of American by Spanish personnel at the 16th Air Force General Headquarters. This was important because the activities of Torrejon wing included out-of-area missions (Marquina, 1991: 59).

Any formal link between the American use of bases and Spain's precise relationship to NATO was removed (Treverton, 1986: 3). In the 1988 Spanish-US Defence and Co-operation Agreement, a regulation for the use of the bases and facilities for out-of-area activities was introduced thereby limiting the area of agreement to the one covered by NATO and establishing a mechanism for consultation and authorisation for out-of-area activities (Marquina, 1991: 59).

On the other hand, the Socialist government followed a pro-European (EC) policy by announcing that "Spain belongs to Europe" (Klepak, n.d: 138). The socialists declared themselves the only party that could unlock the European door (Leon, 1986: 209), and made accession to the EC the first priority of their foreign policy. An intensive diplomatic campaign was conducted in EC capitals for rapid and favourable accession, and the Europeans were impressed by their determination and seriousness (Preston and Smyth, 1984: 78).

Spain became a full member of the EC in January 1986 and it became one of the strongest supporters of an integrated Europe in terms of monetary issues, in concerted action on social legislation, and especially in matters of foreign policy and security. In 1987, Prime Minister Gonzalez declared that "the moment has come to make a reality of the idea of reinforcing the European pillar of the Atlantic Alliance...both in the field of harmonisation of their policies and in the production of defence means" (quoted in George and Stenhouse, 1991: 94). Indeed, the Spaniards wished to enter the WEU as soon as possible in order to participate in the construction of a European Defence System. It became a member of the organisation in 1990. Spain also participated in various arms co-production programs and agreements to homologise its weapon systems with other European countries (Marquina, 1991: 59; Story and Pollack, 1991: 137).

The European dimension of Western security turned into a more important issue after Spain's accession to the WEU. At a special NATO summit in July 1990, Prime Minister Gonzalez argued that:

> The reduction of US and Canadian troops in Europe and our own European vocation make it imperative that the Europeans fortify the pillar of a renovated Alliance on this side of the Atlantic. In this scenario the EC has a decisive role to play in building up a common foreign and security policy and becoming a privileged interlocutor of its North American allies (quoted in Rodrigo, 1992: 105).

Similarly, in an Atlantic Council session in the early days of the Gulf Crisis, Spain proposed that the WEU should co-ordinate any military action that would be undertaken by European NATO members (Rodrigo, 1992: 101-102). In the early 1990s, Spain became an ardent supporter of European Political Co-operation and advocated the incorporation of all aspects of security into the EPC.

Another semiperipheral aspect of Spanish foreign policy was its abandonment of the country's postwar satellite position and emphasise on its independent stance. An important aspect of Spain's relatively independent foreign policy can be seen in the caution about being identified with the US in world politics (Treverton, 1986: 17). In this connection, Spain banned the US from refuelling a squadron of F-15 fighter planes en route to Saudi Arabia during the Iranian Crisis in 1979. The Spanish government also gave full recognition to the PLO, then considered a "terrorist organisation" by the Americans, while refusing to establish full diplomatic relations with Israel. Furthermore, the Spaniards participated in the Non-Aligned summit in Cuba as an observer in 1979. Moreover, Spain called for the creation of a regional co-operation system in the Mediterranean in order to reduce the level of extra-Mediterranean forces. Similarly, Suarez implied that NATO entry might jeopardise Spain's special relations with the Arab and Latin American countries (Preston and Smyth, 1974: 71). These actions were clear manifestations of the fact that Spanish interests did not necessarily coincide with those of US. Spain's broader options and wider interests were pursued through multilateralism and the principle of universality in foreign relations. In 1979, the Spanish Foreign Minister stated, "the Western world is a free world rather than a monolithic one in which each individual state may follow its own policy to protect its own interests" (Minet, 1981: 4). As a result, closer relations were cultivated with Latin American and Arab countries, and contacts and connections were expanded with the neutralist and Third World blocs.

After a forty-year gap, diplomatic relations were resumed with the Soviet Union and East European states. The King's visits to Soviet Union and China emphasised this new opening to the Communist world. Spanish and Soviet views on Middle East issues, Mediterranean co-operation, and aspects of disarmament converged in this period (Minet, 1981: 22), and bilateral relations with Eastern European countries improved. Thus, Spanish foreign policy was no longer under the tutelage of the US, and Spain pursued a relatively independent course with a special emphasis on Spanish national interests.

The Socialists also followed an independent foreign policy line, although they were careful not to create major discord in the Western (especially the European) alliance. They increasingly considered themselves a partner in the Western alliance, not a client and satellite state (Gooch, 1986: 313). In 1983, Gonzalez described Spain as "a part of the Western defensive system but with a margin of its own" (Preston and Smyth, 1984: 84). Accordingly, the Socialists did not allow the use of air bases and Spanish air space for the US attack on Libya in 1986. In this manner, Gonzalez replied to the American request that "Spanish bases that have American forces stationed on them...be used by those forces for the defence of the West but never in any bilateral conflict between the US and another country" (quoted in Gooch, 1986: 313). Similarly, throughout the 1980s, the Socialists were sharply critical of American support of the Contras in Nicaragua and of the US invasion of Panama in 1989 (Marquina, 1991: 13). They saw the roots of the Central American conflict in domestic economic and political factors, rather than in the East-West conflict, as presented by the US. Further proof of Socialists Spain's independent stance was the refusal to accept economic counter loans from the Americans in 1988 for the use of the bases any longer.

A significant PSOE initiative was to support the Spanish arms industry in order to reduce Spain's dependency, especially on the US. Instead, Spain became involved in a series of agreements with its European partners for the co-production of defence equipment (Heywood, 1987: 394). In the new national defence plan of the PSOE, priority was given to strengthening southern Spain militarily in order to face any possible conflict with Morocco (and/or any other Northern African state) over the Spanish enclaves of Ceuta and Mellila, or against threats on the Canary islands that might come from the Saharan Corridor in Africa (Vinas, 1988: 179-181).

Spain also intended to play a bridge (intermediary) role between the EC and regions with which Spain had historical ties and/or geographical proximity - namely Latin America and the Arab world, and to strengthen Spanish sphere of influence in these regions. In this context, Latin America became a central concern. Mexico supported Spanish claims to act as a link between Europe and Latin America, and stated that this initiative would enable developing countries in the region to diversify their economic contacts abroad, in particular with the EC countries (Minet, 1981: 50). Moreover, the 1979 EC Commission's report (Opinion) on Spain stated that "because of the historical ties between Spain and the countries of Latin America, the enlarged Community may be able to forge new political and economic links with this part of the world" (Opinion, 1979: 55). Accordingly, at a meeting of the Andean Council in Madrid in 1980, negotiations were opened between the Andean Pact and the EC, and a month later, a declaration in Brussels was made for closer links between Latin America and the EC (Minet, 1981: 52-53).

The Socialist governments emphasised Spain's function as a bridge between the EC and Latin America. During the EC accession negotiations, the Spanish delegation tried, without success, to obtain a preferential position for the Latin American countries similar to that given to all former colonies of member states (Treverton, 1986: 18 and Grugel, 1987: 606). The Socialist government was more successful in lobbying for the passage of a motion supporting the Contadora process at the European Parliament.[3] Due to Spanish efforts, the Contadora Group, composed of twelve EC, five Central American and four Latin American ministers, met in Costa Rica in 1984 to promote the Contadora process (Leon, 1986: 235). Furthermore, Spain became a meeting place for European and Latin American social democrats to discuss Latin American issues. The aim of the Socialists was to increase European sensitivity towards the region with the belief that, in the long term, it would eventually bring increased private investment, increased aid and softer credits to Latin Americans, as well as international support for political sovereignty (Grugel, 1987: 605). During the Spanish presidency of the Community in 1989, special emphasis was put on promoting relations between Latin American and European states. However, the EC has remained reluctant to implement radical programs in Latin America. Nevertheless, in the early 1990s, the Spaniards still considered Spain "the natural spokesman for Europe in Latin America and for Latin America in Europe" (Gooch, 1992b: 133-134).

Spain also wished to play a "bridge role" between the West and the Arab world. Compared to Latin America, however, its activities remained weak in this region. Nevertheless, in 1980 Spain actively attempted to explain the Arab position in the Middle East to the Americans and Europeans, and the Jordanians, Syrians and Saudi Arabians expressed their gratitude to Spain for its efforts to make the Western world understand the Arab posture (Minet, 1981: 37). Subsequent Socialist governments continued to present Spain as a bridge that linked the Arab world to Europe and vice versa (Moxon-Browne, 1989: 100 and Gooch, 1992a: 5).

Spain also hoped to create a sphere of influence (or what world-system scholars call a form of sub-imperialism) in Latin America and the Arab World. In this way, the Spanish government aimed to increase Spain's influence and bargaining power in external relations. The Spanish policy towards Latin America was based upon interdependence and multifaceted co-operation. The new constitution endowed the King with a special responsibility in relations with Latin Americans (Minet, 1981: 51). In this context, an Ibero-American Centre for Co-operation was established (later the Ibero-American Institute for Co-operation) (Pike, 1980: 205), and co-operation agreements were concluded concerning Spanish participation in Latin American industrial, civil engineering, and fishing projects. Agreements were signed with Mexico and Venezuela for the transfer of technology and capital, for example, and a series of joint ventures were agreed upon, notably with Argentina, Brazil and Mexico (Minet, 1981: 50).

The Spanish quest to increase its presence in Latin America led to other developments. Spain was admitted to the UN Economic Commission for Latin America in 1979, and it transferred its membership in the IMF Executive Committee from Southern Europe to the Northern Latin America group. Furthermore, Spain joined the Inter-American Development Bank in 1976 and became an observer in the Council of Foreign Affairs Ministers of the Andean Pact in 1979. Spanish-Latin America trade volume increased steadily in the second half of the 1970s, and over half of Spanish foreign investments went to Latin America in this period (Minet, 1981: 49).

Socialist governments continued to build a sphere of influence in Latin America, arguing that Spain's influence in Europe and the US would depend on establishing a stronger "special relationship" outside Europe and North America, even against the US wishes (Grugel, 1987: 604). The main emphasis was given to development programs in Latin America under the umbrella of the "Plan for Integrated Co-operation" which included projects in the scientific, technological, agricultural, educational, transport, health, shipping and engineering areas (Grugel, 1987: 610-611 and Pollack, 1987: 72). The most important part of this general scheme was implemented in Nicaragua, Cost Rica and Honduras in conjunction with the Ibero-American

Institute for Co-operation. By 1987, the program's budget had more than quadrupled (Grugel, 1987: 611). Furthermore, Spain extended financial aid to Southern Cone countries like Argentina and Chile (Leon, 1986: 235) and gave import credits to Nicaragua during the US economic blockade of that country (Grugel, 1987: 614). Finally, in order to deepen its influence in Latin America, Spain brought Latin American leaders together in series of conferences in Mexico, Madrid and Bahia (Maxwell and Spiegel, 1994: 84).

These initiatives created a new image of Spain in Latin America. Not surprisingly, Latin American countries hoped to see Spain or the EC as a counter-balance to US influence and to US support for oligarchic and military dictatorships in the region (Grugel, 1987: 603 and Pollack, 1987: 71). Moreover, Latin Americans saw Spain as a model for their own future development (Grugel, 1987: 603). The PSOE governments emphasised Spain's support for the strengthening of democracy and extended financial support for a number of projects in order to foster democratic development, participation and human rights in Latin America (Pollack, 1987: 92). However, in both the economic and political spheres, Spanish attempts to create a sphere of influence had modest outcomes, mainly because of financial constraints and the little concern paid by the EC to Latin America. Nevertheless, some scholars have concluded that these attempts provided Spain with a role in the region, and underlined its intentions to build up a sphere of influence and act as a bridge between the Western and the Latin worlds (Pollack, 1987: 92 and Gooch, 1992b: 133-134).

As we have seen, upwardly mobile semiperipheral states also attempt to strengthen their country's position in the international system and seek out a wider role in the management of international or local problems. After 1980, Spanish foreign policy revealed these characteristics.

After establishing a margin of autonomy in NATO and clearly separating NATO and American interests, the Socialists gave their full support to Western/European unity and cohesion. In 1983, for example, Gonzalez expressed sympathy with the NATO decision to deploy Pershing II and Crusie missiles in Europe. In 1985, Gonzalez declared Spanish support for the Strategic Defence Initiative (SDI) (Pollack, 1987: 171). Moreover, the Spaniards adopted a very narrow definition of Spanish non-involvement in NATO's military structure and tried to maximise Spain's importance in NATO. Indeed, Spanish Foreign and Defence ministers participated in the Atlantic Council and NATO Defence Policy Committee, Spanish representatives attended meetings of the Nuclear Planning Group (despite Spain's anti-nuclear policy), Spain's air defence and radar network was coordinated with that of the Alliance, Spanish forces participated in NATO exercises, and Spain participated in NATO's Military Committee (Leon, 1986: 225 and Gooch, 1992c: 243).

While harmonising its policies with the Western world (especially with Europe), Spain also improved its relations with its neighbours by signing defence and co-operation agreements with Tunisia (1987), Morocco (1989 and 1991), Mauritania (1989) and establishing much more cordial relations with Portugal (Gooch, 1992d: 61).

Spain further strengthened its international position by increasing its capabilities and influence in the field of defence. By the early 1980s, Spain was capable of producing much more sophisticated weaponry (Payne, 1986: 190). However, the central aim of the Socialist governments was to bring Spanish defence structure into line with the West European countries, and to make it more independent from foreign suppliers - especially the US (Vinas, 1988: 175 and Moxon-Browne, 1989: 19). This is why Spain participated in the Independent European Program Groups for the co-production and development of weapons systems; co-operated in the production of the European Fighter Aircraft project with Germany, and co-operated with the UK and Italy on the acquisition of new technologies in aeronautical research.[4] As a result of the rapid modernisation of the defence industry during the 1980s, Spain became technologically competitive with its European partners and became the eighth leading arms exporter in the world (Maxwell and Spiegel, 1994: 56).[5]

Spain has also aspired to a wider role in the world, and to increase its weight internationally by becoming involved in the management of international and local problems. As we have seen, Spain gave full support to the Contadora group of Central American States, which came into existence to stop the conflict in the region without the interference of outside powers. On the other hand, Spain supported a peaceful solution to the problems in Nicaragua and in 1986 offered to mediate between the Sandinistas and the opposition. However, while the Nicaraguan government showed its sympathy to this offer, the civilian opposition that was supported by the US refused it. Moreover, Spain's policy to strengthen democracy in Latin America was supported by a number of projects for democratic development, participation, and human rights in the region (Pollack, 1987: 92). In El Salvador, Spain contributed 120 observers to the UN mission and provided technical and financial support. The Spaniards also announced that they were willing to increase their financial contributions for peace-keeping operations in Latin America (Maxwell and Spiegel, 1994: 54 and 83-84). In Cuba, however, Spain criticised human rights abuses, while keeping the channel of communication open in order to contribute to a democratic transformation.

Spain also became involved in the Middle East peace processes. Based on Spain's historical ties, good relations and special contacts with the Arab world, the UCD government intended to play a role in the Middle East in the early 1980s and they received encouragement from the Germans and the Americans, as well as from the Arabs (Minet, 1981: 37). Accordingly, Prime Minister Suarez undertook diplomatic initiatives in Iraq, Jordan, Syria and Saudi Arabia where there was a warm reception to Spain's potential mediatory role. In the second half of the 1980s, after the Socialist government had recognised Israel, Spain presented itself as an "honest-broker" for a pragmatic solution to the problems in the region. The selection of Madrid for the opening of the Middle East peace talks in 1991 was a clear indication of Spain's favourable position vis-à-vis the Arabs and Israel, and an acknowledgement of its increasing international status (Gooch, 1992a: 7; Maxwell and Spiegel, 1994: 55).

During the Gulf Conflict, Spain supported the UN embargo imposed on Iraq in accord with the Western alliance by allowing the US to use bases in Spain before and during the hostilities. Furthermore, the Spanish government sent one frigate and two corvettes to the Gulf region to participate in the blockade, and committed itself to defend Turkey in the event of an Iraqi attack on this country. Prime Minister Gonzalez stated that Spain was:

> not going to follow the traditional policy of not participating in the destiny of Europe or not sharing the international unanimity about the conflict. I am not for an isolated Spain. We are going to remain firm in our new role (quoted in Rodrigo, 1992: 102).

Spain's call for the creation of a regional security and co-operation system in the Mediterranean was another manifestation of its aspiration to a wider role in world politics. In 1990, Spain and Italy proposed an International Conference on Security and Co-operation in Mediterranean (CSCM), which was similar to the Conference on Security and Co-operation in Europe (CSCE). The Spanish Foreign Minister introduced this idea first in a CSEC meeting in 1990, pointing out that the basic problem in the Mediterranean was the increasing economic, demographic and value differences between the Northern and Southern shores, which could lead to future instability. Hence, an overall approach (rather than a bilateral one) was needed to face up those problems and to prevent a possible confrontation between "Islam and the West" (Rodrigo, 1992: 112). This initiative was not supported by the US or other European states, but Spain did participate in the 5-plus-5 talks between Northern shore countries (Spain, France, Italy,

Portugal and Malta) and the Arab Union of the Maghreb (Mauritania, Morocco, Algeria, Tunisia and Libya) in an attempt to improve communication in the region. However, these talks were adversely affected by the intensification of the Bosnian war.

Another example of Spanish involvement in the management of international problems was the deployment of Spanish soldiers in Bosnia under the command of UN peace-keeping forces, and the Spain's contribution to the cost of the UN mission in Bosnia ($25 million) (Maxwell and Spiegel, 1994: 57). Spain was made one of the vice-presidents in the UN Peacekeeping Commission for former Yugoslavia at the Hague. Spain's participation in the peacekeeping forces in Namibia, Angola and Central America, as well as in Bosnia, has further marked its active participation in international problem solving mechanisms. Thus, Spanish armed forces have become a crucial element of Spain's international activism.

At this point, it would not be unrealistic to say, from the world-system point of view that the further integration of the Spanish economy into the international (especially the European) economy requires a military capable of fulfilling Spain's new role as a [junior] partner in policing European interests (see also Petras, 1993: 117). Moreover, Spain became the ninth largest contributor to the UN budget (Maxwell and Spiegel, 1994: 83) and participated in humanitarian and technical assistance programs in the former Soviet republics (Mojon, 1993: 101).

In the contraction period of the world-economy, semiperiphery Spain showed a certain ability to adapt its production structure to core-like production patterns. The transformations in production system went hand in hand with radical developments in Spanish politics and foreign policy. Accordingly, while democratisation occurred in the domestic sphere, Spain, an upwardly mobile semiperipheral state, gave up its satellite type foreign policy, asserted its intermediary role between core zones and periphery, and increasingly became involved in the management of international problems. In short, in this period, unlike Greece, Spain clearly mobilised from semiperiphery towards core region in the world-system hierarchy of states.

Mid-1990s-2000s: From Socialist to Conservative Period

The Economic Environment

In the mid-1990s-2000s period, the economic policy followed by the Spanish state has generally continued to reflect the characteristics of an upwardly mobile semiperipheral country. The Spanish economy achieved a strong performance and thus attained successful macro-economic indicators during the second half of the 1990s and early 2000s (see OECD Surveys from 1996 to 2001). Thus economic activity has been buoyant for the four consecutive years between 1997-2001 with the average growth rate reaching about 4 percent annually, and Spain has become one of the fastest growing economies in the OECD area. The strong economy created new jobs, and the unemployment rate fell from 23 percent in 1995 to 15 percent in 1999 and further to 13.4 percent in early 2001. Monetary policy was highly successful in combating inflation and it decreased from 7.25 percent in 1996 to 4 percent in 2001. As a result of sound macro economic performance, combined with fiscal consolidation Spain became a member in the European Monetary and Economic Union from the outset (EMU) in 1999. In fact, the wide-ranging economic restructuralisation reforms of the Spanish conservative government were successfully implemented after 1996 and these reforms reactivated the economy. In other words, in this period, Spain has continued its economic development process by adjusting the structure of Spanish economy to the core EU economies. In accordance with Spain's upwardly mobile semiperipheral orientation towards the core area, the major institutional and structural reform programs have aimed at establishing further efficiency in the production structures of the country.

The semiperipheral Spanish state has continued to be the central actor in the restructuralisation, the management, and the development process of the economy during and after the second half of the 1990s. In line with its upwardly mobile semiperipheral status, the Spanish state, which took a strong entrepreneurship role in the economy until the mid-1990s has shifted its policy recently towards an alternative semiperipheral development policy: being the pioneer of the development process, the Spanish state has taken decisive steps to create necessary structures that promote profitable enterprises and also create opportunities for especially to the banking capital/financial elite in the mid-1990s.

The Spanish state aimed at the formation of large Spanish companies in the domestic sphere that are able to compete in the international economic environment (Salmon, 2000: 23). Under the umbrella of "neo-liberal" ideology, the Spanish state (first, under socialist Gonzalez and after 1996, under conservative Aznar governments with a much more strong ideological footing) intervened in the market and delegated greater role and power to the private sector, especially to the financial elite in the economy (see Salmon, 2000: 35). Thus the state first encouraged and supported mergers among private financial groups and then sold the largest public companies in the profitable sectors to these newly emerged, state favourite, domestic financial giants, and then provide protection and assistance for their international expansion in Latin America. In this way, Spanish state created new poles of economic and political power.

In this process, both the socialists and conservative governments established political influence and control over business through state regulatory authorities, and made political appointments to key public holding companies, enterprises and business institutions among their supporters (Salmon, 2000: 38-39). After their electoral victory in 1996, particularly the conservatives brought state and business closer together through appointing personalities from employers' organisations to key political posts, and political figures to business organisations (quoted in Salmon, 2000: 39). Thus the decision making process of restructuralisation and especially the privatisation, which focused on the issues of "which companies should be allowed to participate in or acquire companies to be privatised" was manipulated and politicised by the governments.

Starting from the mid-1990s, the Spanish government announced its plans for wide-ranging structural reforms in the economy. The structural reform programs has envisaged liberalisation of the critical sectors under public control by first privatising large public companies such as the financial holding company Argentaria, the telephone monopoly Telefonica and the state petroleum and oil company Repsol, and second, containing public expenditure through reduction of subsidies to especially loss-making public enterprises in the declining industries (OECD, 1996: 45). Starting from 1995, and mainly with the change in government in 1996 (from socialists to conservatives), an ambitious and accelerated liberalisation and privatisation program was implemented. One of the main objectives of this program was breaking the public monopolies and improving the economy's competitiveness in the product markets (OECD, 1998: 12). Accordingly the old National Institute for Industry (INI) and National Petrol and Gas Institute (INH) were liquidated in July 1995, and two new public entities were created to deal with the restructuralisation of the public companies.

Accordingly, between 1996 and 2000 the government implemented structural reforms for public enterprise modernisation, which accelerated restructuring and privatising public enterprises in electricity, gas, oil, telecommunications, steel and non-ferrous metal sectors. In a short period of time, the Spanish liberalisation process achieved significant progress by reducing the size of the public sector and surpassed many of its European partners in certain areas (OECD, 1998: 86). Thus, the Spanish state sold its remaining shares in the telephone company Telefonica and its international call subsidiary Tisa, the oil company Repsol, the gas company Gas Natural, the steel company CSI, the aluminium company Inepsol, trenches of shares in the electricity company Endesa, the second telephone operator Retevision, and, in 1998, financial company Argentaria.[6] The liberalisation and privatisation program was so rapid that in 2001 ownership of most of formerly largest state-owned companies was transferred into private hands (EIU, Spain Country Report, August 2001: 7). Only a few large companies in declining sectors (those large chronic loss-makers) remained in state hands, namely coal mining, shipbuilding industries, and the public service enterprises in the railways, postal services, seaports and national and regional public television channels (OECD, 2001: 58).

With this strategy of the modernisation of the public enterprises, the Spanish state redefined the business environment and the role of the state in the economy (Salmon, 2000: 38). Indeed, this program aimed to shift public enterprises to private hands (OECD, 1998: 96). Both the socialist and, since 1996, the conservative governments have made an effort to establish big, Spanish-controlled companies that are able to compete internationally (Salmon, 2000: 23). Accordingly, the governments have encouraged mergers among the Spanish companies, reorganised those companies to be privatised prior to their sale, followed both a selective approach among the companies in trade sales and specific privatisation strategies, and furthermore made legal arrangements for the formation of stable shareholder groups (Salmon, 2000: 23 and 39). Some of the successful outcomes of these policies are the large companies of *Banco Bilbao Vizcaya Argenteria* (BBVA) and *Banco Santander Central Hispano* (BSCH) in the financial sphere, *Telefonica* in the communication sector, *Endesa* in the electricity sector, *Repsol YPF* in the oil and gas sector, and the Hotel group *Sol Melila* in the sercive/tourism sector. Indeed, the Spanish state, especially after 1996 (with the Aznar's conservative governments) has created new centres of economic power by launching major private sector enterprises and fostered the internationalisation of the Spanish companies (Salmon, 2000: 39).

In this process of restructuralisation, the semiperipheral Spanish state has paid a special attention, and created a favourable environment for, the financial elite and promoted their interests both at home and abroad. Indeed, it has been the apparent desire of the Spanish governments to create new "national champions" by concentrating economic power in the hands of a small number of companies by providing covert protection at home and supporting their expansion abroad (EIU Country Reports, January 2001: 20 and August 2001: 20). In this context, first of all, the process of banking consolidation was achieved through an active policy of mergers and acquisitions among the Spanish banks. The number of the big players in the banking system reduced from six to two as a result of these mergers and acquisitions, and the process of banking consolidation was completed in 1999 (OECD, 2001: 87). One of the two giant banks, BBVA, was created after *Banco de Bilbao* merged with *Banco de Vizcaya* (*Banco Bilbao Vizcaya*/BBV) in 1998, and BBV merged with the state-owned *Argenteria* in October 1999 giving rise to *Banco Bilbao Vizcaya Argenteria* (BBVA). The other giant financial grouping (BSCH) was formed gradually beginning with the merger of *Banco Central* and *Banco Hispano* (*Banco Central Hispano*/BCH) in 1992. This was followed by the acquisition of *Banesto* by *Banco de Santander* in 1994. Finally in April 1999, a sizable merger occurred between BCH and *Banco Santander* creating *Banco Santander Central Hispano* (BSCH) (see OECD, 2000: 74 and 150, endnote 49). Secondly, these giant financial groupings acquired significant shares in the ownership structure of those formerly state controlled, newly privatised large enterprises (OECD, 1998: 100). Accordingly, both BBVA and BSCH have obtained important shares in these new big companies in the oil refining and gas, electricity, and telecommunications sectors. According to an observation made by the OECD, "in this relationship banks' monitoring functions are associated with their double capacities as lender and significant shareholders" (OECD, 1998: 100), which in turn, reflects the traditional intimate and strong ties between the Spanish financial and industrial capital/elite. The role of the Spanish state in the establishment of these big firms and the formation of intimate ties in the financial and industrial spheres were decisive. On the other hand, the measures taken by the state to "prevent" an increasing concentration of economic power in the product markets has not dealt with the inherited market structures and, thus, has not changed market power of the existing firms significantly (OECD, 2001: 72-73).

From the semiperipheral state perspective, another significant aspect of the restructuralisation policy is the Spanish state's insistence on retaining its regulatory control over the economy, which, in turn, creates a favourable environment to the financial interests. First of all, despite those structural reforms in the economy and the overall business environment and the existing web of regulations, the legal and institutional frameworks have generated significant impediments to entrepreneurial activity (see OECD, 1998: 136-139). The entry restrictions in those critical industries, including the telecommunication, electricity, gas and petroleum sectors in which the financial capital have acquired significant shares during the restructuralisation process, have provided the existing firms in these sectors a safe and "protected" business environment and high profits (OECD, 1998: 88). Furthermore, obtaining finance for business in Spain has been difficult and costly because the banks have preferred to extend credits mainly to those better established and larger enterprises (OECD, 1998: 138) in which the Spanish giant banking groups, in a number of cases, are among the main shareholders. Finally, the Spanish state retains "golden shares" in a number of privatised large industries that enable it to exercise substantial control over key strategic decisions of those firms, such as large share transactions (OECD, 1998: 102). The state's golden share thus deters the entry of new investors/competitors in those sectors, and the state controls the ownership structures in those industries. (OECD, 1998: 102). It is in this business environment that the major Spanish financial groups have grown in size and extended their influence into energy, communication, media, urban and environmental services, construction, real estate and transport, and they have become new poles of economic and political power (Salmon, 2000: 23). The favourable domestic environment and covert protection provided by the Spanish state to banking groups and to a small number companies in close relations with the financial capital has resulted in the concentration of the economic power in the hands of the banks BBVA and BSCH, and the energy groups Endesa and Repsol YPF, and telecoms giant Telefonica (EUI Country Report, January 2001: 20), in other words those companies in which BBVA and BSCH are the important shareholders.

Moreover, being seen as the "national champions" of Spain these companies were also been supported in order to become capable of competing internationally by the Spanish state. Indeed, the Spanish state has strongly supported many of those investments in Latin America through various means such as tax incentives and credit facilities (Youngs, 2000a: 108). Moreover, high-level Spanish politicians and statesmen have played important political roles in the arrangement of large-scale Spanish investments in Latin America. For instance, the take over of the Argentinean Airlines by Spanish Iberia was realised after a deal between Spanish Prime Minister Gonzalez and Argentinean President Menem. The Spanish King Juan Carlos, on the other hand, lobbied hard for the purchase of Argentinean petroleum company YPF by the Spanish giant oil company Repsol (Youngs, 2000a: 112).

Accordingly, another striking development since the second half of the 1990s has been the rapidly increasing concentration of Spanish economic activity in Latin America – an obvious sign of Spain's upwardly mobile semiperipheral orientation. Since the mid-1990s, in many cases those highly profitable firms operating in the financial, energy and telecommunication sectors used their profits for substantial international expansion, especially in Latin America where Spanish companies became key players in their respective sectors (OECD, 1998: 88 and 2000: 16). For instance, particularly after investing heavily in technology in 1997, the Spanish banks acquired strategic control of major banking institutions especially in Argentina, Bolivia, Chile, Columbia, and Venezuela (OECD, 2000: 76 and 2001: 88). Since the late 1990s, the geographical distribution of the major shareholdings in Latin American Banks by BSCH and BBVA has developed as follows: BSCH, in Argentina, Bolivia, Brazil, Colombia, Chile, Mexico, Paraguay, Peru, Puerto Rica, Venezuela; and BBVA, in Argentina, Brazil, Colombia, Chile, Mexico, Peru, Puerto Rico, Venezuela (OECD, 2000: 168). Accordingly, in 2001 Spanish Banks have controlled almost 20 percent of the Latin American banking sector (OECD, 2001: 88). However, the geographical expansion of the Spanish banks has concentrated in Latin America and remained weak in the European financial markets -limited only to collaboration agreements and equity exchanges with foreign institutions (OECD, 2001: 88). The other "national champions" have also heavily invested in the Latin American markets largely in the sectors of communication (Telefonica), energy (oil group Repsol YPF, and electricity utilities Endesa and Iberdola), and construction and hotel companies (Sol Melila) (Salmon, 2000: 34 and EIU Country Report, August 2001: 28). Furthermore, in the stock market a special market for Latin American companies, *Latibex*, created in 1999 (OECD, 2001: 91). Not surprisingly Latin American region has been transformed into a Spanish economic sphere of influence.

Further Europeanisation and establishing Spain one of the hardcore EU countries is another upwardly mobile semiperipheral orientation of the Spanish governments in this period. In fact this objective was set and followed enthusiastically by every individual Spanish government in the post-Franco period. In line with this policy, Spain followed a successful integration policy within the EU. Both the socialists and later the conservative governments, always favoured all the initiatives enhancing European integration. Spain has not asked for opt-outs and has always been in the first wave of key EU developments and initiatives, and moreover Spain has promoted its basic national interests within a strongly pro-European tendency and never employed a nationalistic approach (Granell, 2000: 66-67).

During the 1990s and early 2000s, the process of Spain's integration with the EU was focused on meeting the Maastricht Treaty convergence criteria that Spain signed in 1991, and, especially, on joining the European

Economic and Monetary Union (EMU) on time (see OECD surveys between 1996-2001). The Spanish EU Convergence Programs implemented between 1994-1997, 1998-2000, and 2000-2004 aimed at successful integration of Spain with the EMU. In fact Spain's wide-ranging restructuralisation and modernisation programs in the economy, implemented since the mid-1990s, have been a part of those EU Convergence plans. Thus, in Spain, during this process of restructuralisation and integration with the EU, enormous volume of legislation has been passed and reforms have been implemented by the governments for harmonising product, labour and financial market conditions with the Maastricht criteria, as well as promoting competition, thereby radically changing the business environment in Spain by the turn of the century (Salmon, 2000: 35). In accordance with the Spanish commitments under the Maastricht Treaty, the Bank of Spain became independent in 1995 and, furthermore, fiscal adjustments were carried out with determination and strong fiscal consolidation was achieved as early as 1998 by bringing inflation, budget deficits and debt ratios to GDP to Maastricht criteria levels. Accordingly, Spain joined the EMU form the outset in 1999 and became a member of the euro area, thus Spain moved one step further towards the hardcore of Europe.

It is clear that there are a number of benefits for Spain in becoming a part of the EMU (see Salmon, 2000: 40 and Granell, 1980: 68), such as moving into Europeanised economic governance, thus creating a stable environment for business (eurozone), while being protected against financial and economic turbulences. However, it seems that there are other important motivations in Spain's commitment to the EMU from the outset, which indicates the upward mobilisation of Spain in the world-system hierarchy of states. In the EMU the Spaniards now have had a voice in the determination of the European economic monetary policy, and thereby showed the EU partners that Spain is a credible economic partner to be considered in the heart of the European core. The Spanish conservative Premier Aznar's reportedly self-confident and increasingly pro-active style in shaping the economic policy of the EU and his criticisms of the some of the EU partner's economic policies as being "driven too much by outmoded and inappropriate interventionist economic management" (Granell, 2000: 74) can be considered as a reflection of Spain's upward mobilisation towards the Europe's hardcore.

Yet, the role of the EU transfers and structural funds have already continued to play a significant role in Spain's economic development process, and the country's integration into the EU (OECD, 1998: 33 and Salmon, 2000: 28). This, in turn, indicates the still decisive role played by the

EU in the semiperipheral development of Spain. From the mid-1990s onwards the net EU transfers to Spain, together with structural and cohesion funds altogether amounted to around to 2 percent of the GDP annually, and in terms of structural and cohesion funds received per capita, Spain ranked third after Portugal and Greece (OECD, 1998: 33). These EU transfers and structural funds were primarily directed to the agriculture, infrastructural investment, regional development, and economic and social cohesion. The amount of structural fund transfers to Spain reached to €7.7billion per year (1.6 percent of GDP) between 1994 and 1999 (see Salmon, 2000: 28-29).

The successful performance of the Spanish economy in the mid-1990s and early 2000s can also be observed in Spain's international trade. The contribution of net exports to economic growth reflected the strong competitiveness of the Spanish exports. In 1996 and 1997, Spanish merchandise exports increased strongly at an annual average rate of more than 10 percent in volume terms, increasing its export market shares by 10 percent (OECD, 1998: 23 and 30-31). In the late 1990s and early 2000s, the Spanish volume of exports has continued to rise (over 10 percent annually), and Spain retained its competitiveness and continued to increase its share of the world markets (OECD, 2001: 11 and EIU Country Reports, January, 2001: 27 and May 2001: 30). As a percentage of GDP, the growth of Spanish international trade (exports and imports of goods and services) has also been remarkable, rising from 48 percent in 1995 to 55 percent at the end of the 1990s, and growing faster than the world average (Salmon, 2000: 30).

The sectors that heavily contributed to the impressive export performance of Spain in this period have been the agriculture, intermediate manufacturing, consumer, and capital goods sectors (OECD, 1998: 30-31 and EIU, Country Report. May, 2001: 30). However, Spain's high level of competitiveness and gains in world market shares have broadly based on the strong and highly competitive automotive/motor-vehicle sector (owned by a small number of foreign multinationals), which besides enjoying relatively cheap labour cost, heavily invested in human and physical resources and infrastructure in the 1990s (OECD, 2000: 36). As a result, it is mainly through the automotive sector that Spain diversified its production and export base towards higher quality products (OECD, 2000: 36).

In terms of the geographical destination, the EU comprises about the 70 percent of the Spanish export market (OECD, 1996: 5 and EIU, Country Report, January, 2001: 27). Other than the key EU market, Latin America, Asia and North America are the other important markets wherein the Spaniards have been making important inroads and increasing their world market shares since the mid-1990s (EIU Country Report, August, 2001: 30).

The share of Spain's exports to Latin America, Asia and the US were 6 percent, 5.2 percent, and 4.2 percent in 1996 and grew by 25 percent, 29 percent and 27 percent respectively in 1997 (OECD, 1998: 155, endnote 12) and is still growing in the early 2000s (EIU Country Reports, January 2001: 27 and May 2001: 30).

Tourism has continued to be a highly competitive sector contributing heavily to the economic development by improving the balance of payments deficits of Spain. Spain's tourism receipts reached to almost 4 percent of the GDP in 1996 making Spain the second most important tourism centre in the world in terms of revenues and number of tourist (OECD, 1998: 31 and Salmon, 2000: 30). Indeed, analogous to the export sector, Spain has gained significant market shares during the 1990s (OECD, 2000: 36). Thus, the number of visitors to Spain increased from 55 million in 1992 to 74 million in 1999, and strikingly enough, over 90 percent of this amount came from the EU countries (Salmon, 2000: 30).

The form and amount of inward and outward flows of foreign investment to and from Spain may be considered another indication of semiperipheral Spain's upwardly mobile status in the world-system hierarchy of states. According to Salmon, Spain's integration with the world capital market during the mid-1990s was far reaching in terms of capital transactions (Salmon, 2000: 31). In terms of portfolio investments, Spain has initially experienced a flow of investment in the mid-1990s, but the outward flow exceeded the inward flow portfolio investments in the late 1990s. The majority of the both inward and outward investment flow was with the EU reaching up to 80 percent in 1998 (Salmon, 2000: 32).

As regard to foreign direct investment (FDI), Spain has been one of the targets of international, especially the European, investors. During the 1990 Spain has continued to be an important place for both inward and outward FDI flows occupying the 6th place in terms of inflows and 12th for outflows in the OECD area in the period between 1990-1998 (Salmon, 2000: 32). In the mid-1990s, the increase in FDI into Spain reached about 2 percent of GDP, and it dominantly went into the share increases of existing manufacturing firms and real estate property investments (OECD, 1996: 21). The tendency of inward FDI to go into the existing investments continued in the late 1990s indicating the maturing of the earlier investments. Meanwhile Spain also attracted inward investment in other more modern industries, especially in motor vehicles in this period (Salmon 2000: 22).

Nevertheless, regarding FDI, the most striking feature of the late 1990s and early 2000s was the expansion of the Spanish outward direct investments in Latin America (see EIU Country Reports, 1997-2002). The size of the

Spanish FDI has grown at such a pace that in 1999 and 2000 Spanish investments, mainly in Latin America, represented on average more than 8.25 percent of GDP a year compared with 2.75 percent in 1997-1998 (OECD, 2001: 32). Thus, although ranked 12th between 1990-1998, Spain ranked fifth in terms of FDI outflows in the OECD area in 1999 as a result of this increase. Accordingly, giant Spanish banks, and recently privatised companies, became leading foreign investors in Latin America in the late 1990s and have invested in the banking, telecom, energy, tourism and construction sectors (Salmon, 2000: 33-34). It is striking from the semiperipheral state perspective that in the process of expansion of Spanish economic interests in the region, the Spaniards, in line with their upwardly mobile orientation, have emphasised that their comparative advantage in the region lay in the shared cultural heritage with the regional states, and more importantly, they also reveal a core-like aggressive foreign economic policy motivation that may consider using Mexico as a bridge to penetrate the US market through the North American Free Trade Area (NAFTA) (see, Salmon, 2000: 34).

Although smaller in proportion compared to Latin America, the EU has been the other area of interest for the Spanish FDI. The Spanish FDI in the EU area, which slowed down in the mid-1990s, increased towards the end of the decade through mergers and acquisitions fostered by the EU Economic and Monetary Union (Salmon, 2000: 33). The two giant financial groups BBVA and BSCH, which have been trying to strengthen their position in the European financial sphere, are the major actors in Spain's FDI activities in Europe (Salmon, 2000: 33-34). In Europe, the main area of interest for Spanish companies is Portugal where they have already invested significantly in banking and financial services, telecommunication and energy sectors. There are various incentives for Spanish investors to invest in Portugal (see Salmon, 2000: 34), such as creating a more integrated market in the Iberian Peninsula for goods and services and access to cheap labour. However, similar to the aggressive Spanish foreign economic policy in Latin America, there is one more defining incentive that gives upwardly mobile semiperipheral Spain a core-like image: the incentive of establishing bridges to Brazilian markets, the largest in Latin America, by investing in Portugal.

In terms of GDP per capita, Spanish incomes, which increased remarkably up to $14.704 in 1993, have remained almost the same thereafter. Therefore, the GDP per capita figures of Spain from the mid-1990s to 2000, which amounted to $12.331 in 1994, $14.788 in 1996, $14.676 in 1998, and $14.187 in 2000, (OECD, 1996-2001) do not reflect the remarkable achievements in the Spanish economy. This is probably because the positive effects of the significant economic developments of the late 1990s have not yet become visible in the per capita figures. In fact, the ability to preserve the $14.000 level until 2000 can also be considered a success in terms of the upward mobilisation process of semiperipheral Spain in the world-system hierarchy of states. Indeed, as of the late 1990s, Spanish GDP per capita has come closer to the EU average (OECD, 2000: 53). At the end of the 1990s, the gap between the Spanish GDP per capita and the EU average was narrowed to 18 percentage points in terms of purchasing power parities (Salmon, 2000: 19). But in terms of living standards and productivity, Spain has remained still below the core EU area average (OECD, 2000: 53).

In fact, although Spain has displayed a strong macro-economic performance and experienced a striking public sector restructuralisation and modernisation, and also successfully internationalised a part of its business sector since the mid-1990s, a number of weaknesses or peripheral characteristics still persist in the Spanish economy, indicating its continuing semiperipheral (though upwardly mobile) position in the world-economy.

Traditional heavy industrial actives in the declining sectors of coal, iron, steel and shipbuilding have continued their existence and received assistance from the state. However, the subsidies extended to these sectors are below the EU average and have decreased substantially since the mid-1990s (see OECD, 2001: 73). These loss-making industries have continued to be affected by technological developments and by the emergence of new cost efficient competitors in other parts of the world (OECD, 1998: 89 and 121). Thus, they need severe restructuring but there have been political considerations: many of these industries are located in northern Spain and in Andalucia where unemployment rates are high. Closure of these industries would lead local problems because about three-quarters of the total labour force in these industries (about 35.000) are geographically concentrated in these regions (OECD, 1998: 121 and 2000: 63). Furthermore, other small scale and family owned traditional industries in the light industrial sectors of textiles, clothing, food and beverages, leather, footwear, ceramics and toys and wood product have remained in business in Spain and continued to employ substantial portion of the labour force (Salmon, 2000: 21). Nevertheless, these declining industries in both traditional heavy and light industrial sectors have continued their path of long-term decline throughout the mid-1990s and thereafter (Salmon, 2000: 21 and EIU Country Report, May 2001: 25).

Despite the labour market reforms since the mid-1990s, notably the reform of 1997 that reduced the high-level employment protection, and the government initiative of March 2001, labour markets have remained relatively inflexible in Spain (OECD, 1998: 143, 2000: 13, and EIU Country Report, May 2001: 8). As a result of the failure of the negotiations between the business confederations and trade unions for further reforms, the Spanish government, which distanced itself from the labour markets for some time to facilitate the labour market reforms (Salmon, 2000: 39), intervened again in conformity with its semiperipheral character, and imposed its own soft reforms in March 2001, but without significant effect on Spain's traditionally rigid market. Given the divided trade union movement in Spain, a major industrial confrontation appears unlikely (EIU, Country Report, May, 2001: 8).

In the field of R&D, Spain has lagged far behind the many of its core EU partners despite the special attention to R&D activities and innovation by Spanish governments and the substantial progress achieved in developing research and technological capacity in industry since the early 1980s. The share of R&D in GDP was doubled from 0.4 percent in 1981 to almost 1 percent in 1992, but total spending on R&D remained well below the OECD average of 2.2 percent and EU average of 1.8 percent in the mid-1990s (OECD, 1996: 74 and 1998: 146 and 2000: 147, endnote 12). It has been the public sector that has promoted the R&D activities and use of Information Technologies (IT) in industry in Spain. In the mid-1990s, over 50 percent of the R&D activity was realised by the government sector and the government offered credits, and they provided tax deductions to private sector R&D activities (see, OECD, 1996: 74 and 2000: 42). The Spanish private sector, because of its specialisation in the consumer goods, has generally performed low levels of R&D. Only 11 percent of firms in manufacturing introduced or developed innovations in products or processes between 1992-1994, and around 80 percent of manufacturing small and medium size enterprises (SMEs) have no R&D activities (OECD, 1998: 146). The number of researchers who work for the business sector has also been traditionally very small, which in turn limited the scope for technical innovation in Spain. It is argued that a significant proportion of Spanish production has been in sectors, such as tourism, where formal R&D is less significant (OECD, 1998: 14 and 146). Accordingly, labour intensive sectors have still represented a significant driving force of economic growth in Spain (OECD, 2000: 27).

However, in the mid-1990s and early 2000s, Spanish governments have taken initiatives to support and improve the R&D, innovation and technological development projects (OECD, 1998: 152 and 2001: 48). Furthermore, Spanish state significantly increased its support to R&D (more than 50 percent) between 1993-1997, and high-technology sectors of aeronautics and microelectronics have been given the lion's share of R&D

support (OECD, 2000: 63 and 2001: 73). The government has also taken measures to boost the scientific and technological development including the creation of a new Ministry for Science and Technology (OECD, 2001: 73).

Another semiperipheral characteristic of Spanish economy has been the significant barriers in front of the entrepreneurial activity. Several aspects of the institutional arrangements, rules and regulations of the Spanish state have made opening a new business a lengthy and complicated process. For instance, opening a business takes between 19 to 28 weeks in Spain. Furthermore, excess to finance is not easy for a new entrepreneur because of high interest rates, and often bank credits are available to established and larger enterprises. This in turn undermines the development of more innovative and flexible business (OECD, 1998: 136-138). Moreover, in Spain the venture capital market has remained relatively underdeveloped and dominated by the state, and investments in the market has been low in international comparison. The banks and the government are the main providers of new venture capital (37 and 20 percent respectively) (OECD, 1998: 139 and 2001: 91-92). Since the end of the 1990s, the stock market has registered a rapid growth, but the stock market turnover is concentrated in a few sectors (telecommunication, banking and energy) and in some large firms. Therefore it has been rather difficult for private business to access to non-bank credits too (OECD, 2000: 79 and 2001: 91).

The Political Environment

In the period between the mid-1990s to the early 2000s, the domestic political environment of Spain experienced a change in political power that paralleled the restructuring in the economy. Towards the end of the 1995, all the political parties in Spain, including the ruling PSOE's coalition partner Catalan Convergence and Union party (CiU), the business representatives, trade unions and media demanded the immediate dissolution of parliament and general elections (EIU, Country Report, 4th Quarter: 4). The main reason for this was the Spanish state, under the 13–year socialist administration, was no longer powerful enough to shoulder the existing and potential dynamism of the Spanish economy and aggressiveness of the Spanish economic elite. Thus, like in the early 1980s, there was a strong demand for a fresh and dynamic administration in Spain. Accordingly, in the 1996 March elections, the conservative Popular Party (PP) came to power with the support of three regional parties.

The characteristics of an upwardly mobile semiperipheral state in the economic domain were reflected in the Spanish domestic politics during the conservative administration. First of all, the advent of conservative Popular Party of Jose Maria Aznar to power in March 1996, after 13 years of PSOE socialist rule, was a reflection of further consolidation of the democratic practices and institutions in Spain. This was the first electoral victory for the ex-Francoist conservative party (former Popular Alliance/AP) since the establishment of democracy. Mr. Aznar convinced the Spanish electorate that PP is now a European centre-right party with no resemblance to the Francoist right. In fact, in the general elections the centre-right PP gained 156 seats with 38.9 percent of the votes, but remained 20 seats sort of an absolute majority in the parliament. However, Mr. Aznar, who spoke of an historic opportunity for a new era of consensus politics (EIU Country Report 1996, 2nd Quarter: 9), sought for a coalition with the regional Catalan (CiU) and Basque Nationalist (PNV) parties as well as the Canary Islands Coalition (CC). After gaining their support, the PP created a minority government in May 1996. The new cabinet was formed by a new generation of conservative politicians with no links to the Franco era (EIU Country Report, 3rd Quarter 1996: 9).

Besides indicating a further consolidation of democracy in Spanish politics, a consensus appeared between the PP and other regional parties for a minority PP government, which also provided a strong political background and a decisive support to the wide-ranging economic restructuralisation program implemented by the PP government between 1996-2000. Despite their distinct regional characteristics, the common centre-right political outlook, the common economic ideology, and the similar economic policies of all the four coalition parties were more than instrumental in the successful implementation of the economic restructuralisation in the Spanish economy in the second half of the 1990s. The strong political personalities appointed by Prime Minister Aznar to the head of the economy ministries increased the authority of these departments, and indicated the priorities of the conservative PP government and restored the confidence of the financiers and the foreign investors (EIU, Country Report, 3rd Quarter 1996: 9-10). In fact, Aznar's PP government pursued a liberal economic policy similar to the PSOE governments', but with strong ideological enthusiasm and rigour. There was a clear commitment to create favourable conditions for private business by all the coalition parties (EIU Country Report, 3rd Quarter 1996: 10). As mentioned before, the PP government appointed new presidents for large public companies that were to be privatised and those who were the close friends of either the Prime Minister Aznar or Minister of Economy, Mr. Rato (EIU, Country Report, 4th Quarter 1996: 10) in order to facilitate new mergers and acquisitions among the Spanish businessmen. One can say that almost the entire Spanish political elite strongly supported the upward economic mobilisation process of Spain in this period.

Another clear indication of the Spanish political elite's enthusiasm for Spain's upward mobilisation was their decisive support for government efforts to meet the Maastricht criteria and make Spain a founding member of the European Economic and Monetary Union - an objective which Spain achieved successfully in 1999. For the Spanish political elite, Europeanisation and further integration with the EU meant further modernisation and prosperity (EIU, Country Report, 4th Quarter, 1996: 11).

The conservative PP leadership, whom portrayed a reformist and "forward looking" political elite picture, won the approval of the Spanish electorate in its first term in office (EIU Country Report, 2nd Quarter 1999: 11). Accordingly, in the general elections of March 2000, the PP received the 44.5 percent of the votes and won 183 of the 350 seats in parliament and established a majority government. According to the EIU analysis, the PP's electoral victory was mainly the "reward for four years of sound economic management and political stability which has enabled Spain to re-establish a sense of national well being and enjoy a period of economic prosperity and renewed international standing" (EIU, Country Report, 2nd Quarter 2000: 15). In fact, there was a broader consensus between the conservative and the socialist political elite over major political issues such as liberalisation of the economy, further integration with Europe (mainly the EMU participation) and regional autonomy (EIU Country Report, 1st Quarter 2000: 9), all of which in turn contributed heavily to the upward mobilisation process of Spain in this period.

With a clear mandate in the parliament, the new PP conservative administration ensconced a new generation of business-friendly technocrats into the cabinet at the expense of the old style political elite (EIU Country Report, July 2000: 7), which fostered economic restructuralisation in the process of upgrading Spain in the hierarchy of states (see EIU Country Reports, 2000-2002). It is clear that upwardly mobile Spanish state has sided with a group of economic elite that may be labelled as core-like, and that Spanish governments, and the majority of the political elite in the mid-1990s-2000s period, have deliberately afforded opportunities to the domestically and internationally aggressive core-like Spanish economic elite by providing protection and supporting their expansion both at home and abroad.

Another important dimension of the Spanish domestic political environment in this period has been the changing nature of the relations between the central Spanish state and some of the strongest autonomous regions. The degrees of autonomous status and the democratic rights granted by the 1978 Constitution to these regions have increasingly begun to be questioned by regional centres of power. One of the significant challenges has come from the historic Catalan autonomous region that demands further rights and more autonomy. However the major challenge to the Spanish state, and its constitutionally defined unitary character, has come from the autonomous historic Basque region in the form of self-determination or independence. Indeed, the strength of the upwardly mobile semiperipheral Spanish state has essentially been put to the test by the ethnically defined demand of self-determination and/or independence of the Basque autonomous region. It is most likely that the solution to be found for the regional issue will affect the semiperipheral upward mobilisation process of Spain because the relative strength of national coalitions plays an important role in determining the position of the states in the world-system hierarchy of states.

There are significant differences over the conceptualisations of the Spanish state between the Catalans and the Spaniards. For instance, while the Spaniards and the national parties of PP and PSOE accept Spain as a multi-cultural single nation, the Catalans (and the regional Catalan Nationalist Party, CiU) envision Spain as a pluri-national state where different nations co-exist (EIU, 2nd Quarter 1996: 11). In fact, the demands coming from the Catalans basically aim at greater autonomy for Catalonia, such as more fiscal autonomy and more powers for the regional police. Catalan nationalism is basically moderate and generally respect the limits established by the Spanish constitution (EIU, 2nd Quarter 1996: 11). The performance of the Catalan nationalist party, Convergence and Unity (CiU), in the coalition governments in which it participated (first, in the PSOE and later in the PP governments between 1993-2000) revealed the pragmatic and moderate nationalist outlook of the Catalan party (see EIU Country Reports, 1996-2000). Catalan nationalism has been inclusive meaning that "they want home rule while remaining a part of Spain" (Hargreaves, 2000: 23). In fact, the Catalan leaders denied any concern with independence and defend the Catalan interests within unity of Spanish state (Heywood, 1995: 161).

It is clear that the main regional issue lying in front of the Spanish state is the Basque problem. The Basque is the most privileged region among all other autonomous regions in terms of rights and powers delegated by the Spanish state after democratisation. The Basque autonomous region enjoys a high degree of autonomy including having its own regional parliament and government, running its own police force, education system, TV stations, and collects and spends its own taxes (EIU Country Report, 4th Quarter

1998: 12). But at the same time, Basque is the only region where the people pursue the objective of self-determination and/or independence through a number of ways, including the armed struggle against the Spanish state. In fact, the Basque demand and struggle for independence is not a new phenomena. Since the 1960s, ETA, the Basque separatist organisation has been carrying out terrorist activities (murders, assassinations, street vandalism) in Spain and threatening to destabilise the political environment. ETA's political wing *Batasuna* (formerly *Herri Batasuna* or *Eskual Herritarok*) has operated as a legal political party, and participated in the regional elections until very recently.

The participation of the moderate Basque Nationalist Party (PNV) in the PP coalition government from March 1996 to March 2000 raised hopes, but did not bring the long desired political reconciliation between the Spanish state and the Basque local powers despite the PNV's attempts to play an intermediary role between the Spanish state and ETA in order to bring a peaceful solution to the conflict (see EIU Country Reports, 1996-2000). The moderate nationalist PNV is against the ETA terrorism, but together with *Batasuna*, the political wing of ETA, and the other smaller moderate regional party *Eusko Alkartasuna* (EA) it has supported the idea of self-determination for the Basque region. The PNV thinks that further integration with the EU will sooner or later overcome the Spanish state's resistance against Basque independence. As a result, either a confederal political system with Spain will be established or Basque could become a fully independent member of the EU (EIU Country Report, 4th Quarter 1998: 12 and 1st Quarter 1999: 13).

The relations with the Basque region were strained further in the late 1990s and early 2000s mainly because of the increasing challenge coming from local political parties and institutions against the authority and the sovereignty of the Spanish state. For instance, the moderate PNV signed a pro-sovereignty pact with *Batasuna* in September 1998 (Pact of Lizarre). The PNV and *Eusko Alkartasuna* (EA) coalition, which was running the regional government with the parliamentary support of *Batasuna*, followed a policy of tolerance to the ETA organised street violence and threats against the members of the national Spanish parties in the region. Furthermore, the Basque regional parliament issued a resolution calling for UN observers to supervise the next regional elections (EIU, 2nd Quarter 1999: 13). In September 1999, the local Basque parties established a forum among the municipalities of the region aiming to promote national identity and political structures in the Greater Basque Country (EIU, 4th Quarter 1999: 13). Furthermore, the PNV and EA abandoned their moderate line, and their traditional alliances with the Spanish political parties, and tilted towards *Batasuna*'s more radical posture for full independence (EIU, 1st Quarter 2000: 7). Finally, the PNV's refusal to end the pro-sovereignty Pact of Lizarre has led to increasing polarisation between the nationalist and non-nationalist opinion in the region, and brought the relations between nationalist Basque and Spanish political parties (mainly, PP and PSOE) to the point of complete breakdown (EIU Country Reports, October 2000: 7 and January 2001: 13). In 2001, the parties have become as far a part as ever on the key political issue of holding a referendum on Basque's independence from Spain, which has been the ultimate aim of the PNV (EIU Country Report, August 2001: 3). At the end of the year, the political situation has deteriorated further as the Basque regional government demanded a direct representation in the EU in exchange for the extension of the region's economic charter (EIU, Country Report, 2002: 17).

The conventional approach of the Spanish state, and the two major Spanish parties of PP and PSOE, towards the regions and their regional demands have, in general, been sympathetic and responsive with regard to granting more rights and delegation of powers, but cold and closed to the demands for federal or confederal political resettlements. The conventional attitude is to give emphasis to the constitutional state of affairs that recognises the existence of autonomous communities or regions, but within the indissoluble unity of the Spanish nation. The position of the governing PP is identified with the concept of a great and unified Spanish nation in a pluri-cultural formation (EIU Country Report 2nd Quarter 1996: 11). The PSOE is also an enthusiastic defender of Spanish unity (EIU, Country Report 4th Quarter 1998: 13). Thus neither the PP nor the PSOE is willing to amend the Spanish constitution, which emphasises the indissoluble unity of the Spanish state. In the late 1990s, all the openings made by the governing PP for negotiating the status of Basque autonomous region (including secretly meeting with the ETA leaders in March 1999) have always emphasised that any negotiated settlement must respect the Spanish constitution (EIU Country Report, 4th Quarter 1998: 12 and 3rd Quarter 1999: 15), which appears to be the main obstacle in front of a political solution. Thus, the demands for questioning the constitutional structure of Spain in order to reach a political settlement in Basque region have alarmed the Spanish establishment concerning the consequences of such a development and its spill over effects on the other regions (EIU, Country Report, 4th Quarter 1998: 12-13). Accordingly, as a result of the ETA's rigid policies (e.g., a fully independent state and not to hand in weapons, etc.) that threaten the territorial integrity of Spain, and the resumption of ETA terrorism after a brief ceasefire in early 2000, the bloc that sees the Basque question as more of a security issue than a political question in the Spanish government has strengthened (EIU Country Report, 1st Quarter 2000: 8). The PP majority government, especially after their electoral victory in March 2000, has increasingly viewed the Basque question as a terrorist problem (EIU Country Report, July 2000: 15). In the face of increasing ETA terrorism, the tough stance taken by the Spanish establishment vis-à-vis the Basque issue has led to an alliance and the signing of an anti-terrorist pact between the governing PP and main opposition PSOE. The pact identified the moderate nationalist PNV's Basque policy as one of the major causes of the escalation of the problems in the region, and demonstrated that the Spanish parties are firmly united for the territorial integrity of the country as well as against terrorism (EIU Country Report, January 2001: 12-13). The suspension of the activities of the ETA's political wing *Batasuna* for three months by the Spanish parliament in late August 2002 is a clear sign of this determination, as is the continuing tough stance of the Spanish state in defending its constitutional unitary character.

In the early 2000s, the main domestic political challenge facing the Spanish state continues to be the regional problem, especially the issue of independence of the Basque region. According to the observers, in what has traditionally been a cohesive society, polarisation between the regions and the centre (e.g., nationalists and non-nationalists) is a dangerous development (EIU Country Report, October 2000: 7) that, in turn, could easily derail Spain from its upwardly mobile semiperipheral trajectory. The future status of especially the Basque and Catalan autonomous regions has been one of the most important political questions that need to be answered by the Spanish political elite in order to maintain Spain's semiperipheral upward mobilisation and desire to eventually find a place in the core region of the world-economy.

Foreign Policy

In the external sphere too, Spain has continued to reveal the characteristics of an upwardly mobile semiperipheral state in a number of cases during the mid-1990s-early 2000s period. Accordingly, Spain has increasingly asserted its intermediary or bridge (or in the terminology of the world-system analysis, sub-imperial) role between the geographically, historically and culturally contingent areas and the core regions with the motive of creating its own economic and political spheres of influence. Also, Spain has participated in the management of the international problems in this period and maintained harmonious relations with its partners in the Western alliances. Consequently, Spain's influence and weight in the EU and world politics gradually increased. In this context, Spain has increasingly reasserted its primacy and intermediary role between Europe and both the Southern Mediterranean and Latin America, and at the same time Spain has attempted to become an actor in the political and economic development of both regions. Besides, Spain has increasingly become involved in the management of the international security issues in various parts of the world, notably in the Balkans. Moreover, while pursuing an active but harmonious foreign policy within the EU, Spain has upgraded its relations with the US and the NATO as well.

First of all, Spain's constant efforts for the establishment of a security and cooperation scheme in the Mediterranean region since the early 1990s (Mediterranean CSCM, Five plus Five, etc.) came to fruition with the establishment of Euro-Mediterranean Partnership (EMP) in November 1995. In fact, after the end of the Cold War, Spain was anxious about a shift in the EU's geo-strategic priorities towards Central and Eastern Europe and became the most ardent advocate of promoting the importance of the Mediterranean basin for European security in the EU. The Spaniards, who emphasised the political, economic, demographic, religious and development problems in the southern Mediterranean, tried to link European security with Mediterranean stability (Barbe, 1998: 158). In the first half of the 1990s, Spanish lobbying had already played an important role in establishing closer relations between the EU and the Maghreb countries. Spanish governments believed that historical ties with the region would enable Spain to play a leading role in the development of a Mediterranean policy for the EU, and that Spanish activism in the Mediterranean would increase the weight of Spain within the EU (Gillespie, 1994: 27-28). Mediterranean policy was seen as an integral part of Spain's European policy and one of the basic instruments to establish the Spanish influence in EU decision and policy-making (Gillespie, 1996: 193-194). Thus after those relatively unsuccessful earlier attempts to carry the Mediterranean to the top of the EU agenda, Spain, during its presidency of the EU, successfully took the initiative to convene a Euro-Mediterranean summit between the EU and southern Mediterranean countries, and managed to make the Mediterranean a priority area for EU in Barcelona in 1995. The Barcelona Declaration aimed to establish a permanent multilateral framework for cooperation in the economic, financial, political, security, and social fields among the Mediterranean basin countries. Furthermore, in the Declaration the Spanish objective of creating a free trade area in the Mediterranean region by 2010 was also included. The Spanish government's efforts (though not exclusively) were decisive in convincing the northern Europeans to build up a Mediterranean outlook for the EU, and also divert a EU financial package of ECU 7 billion (compared with ECU 6.7 billion to Eastern Europe) to the southern Mediterranean countries. Indeed, Spain became the main protagonist of the EU's Mediterranean policy and the main EU documents on the Euro-Mediterranean initiative were drafted by the Spaniards (Gillespie, 1996: 207). Moreover, the negotiating performance and the mediation of the Spaniards (especially the Spanish Foreign Minister) were largely responsible for the final form of the Barcelona Declaration (EIU, Country Report, 4th Quarter 1995: 12 and 1st Quarter 1996: 8). On the other hand, in the Mediterranean region but especially in the Mahgreb, Spain has portrayed itself as a useful bridge between Maghreb and Europe seeking solutions to the region's problems by relying on its expertise stemming from geographical, historical, and cultural associations and traditional relations. Accordingly, Spain declared itself as the corridor between Brussels and the Maghreb and the guardian of the Maghreb's interests there (Villaverde, 2000: 129 and 136).[7]

In fact, geographical proximity, as well as historical, cultural and traditional associations and relations facilitated Spain's increasing interests in the Mediterranean. Spain, an upwardly mobilised state in the world-system hierarchy of states, has increasingly realised the economic and commercial potentials, as well as the threats in the geographically, historically and culturally contiguous area of the Mediterranean and took the leadership in the EU for diverting attention to the Mediterranean. The Euro-Mediterranean Partnership has provided Spain potential economic benefits and greater political influence in the region in the medium and long term. Moreover, in a core-like manner, Spain has also developed a somewhat pragmatic policy towards the Mediterranean that involves avoiding from taking partisan positions and working with the diverse regimes in the region by respecting conflicting national interests (see Barbe, 1996: 198 and 201-202). This attitude, which based on supporting democratic and liberal openings rather than criticising the authoritarian policies, is apparent in the Spanish policy vis-à-vis the authoritarian regimes of Algeria, Morocco, Tunisia, Libya in North Africa. The Spaniards do not let authoritarian philosophy and practices of the North African governments to prevent bi-lateral and multilateral cooperation in the region.

Another region where Spain has continued to assert its bridge (or sub-imperial) role has been Latin America, a traditional area of potential influence and a continent with which Spain shares deep historical and cultural ties. During its EU presidency in 1995, the Spanish government unsuccessfully initiated a policy of increasing and strengthening the links between the EU and Latin America. In this context, the Spaniards attempted to sign an associate trade agreement between the EU and Mercosur countries (Brazil, Argentina, Uruguay and Paraguay) and to begin parallel trade negotiations with Mexico and Chile. The Spaniards also attempted to sign an economic aid agreement for Cuba in return for political reforms (EIU Country Report, 4th Quarter 1995: 13). Despite the Spanish governments efforts since the mid-1980s, the main difficulty in bringing Latin America to the priority agenda of the EU has been that there is no vital interest or strategic factor in Latin America for the EU (Barbe, 2000: 54-55).

However, indirectly, Spain has managed to become the main intermediary between the EU and Latin America. First of all, the vast majority of the EU investment funds allocated for Latin America have always been used by Spanish businessmen for their investments in Latin America (Youngs, 2000a: 110). The indifferent attitude of European investors towards Latin America played an important role in transferring EU investment funds to the region by the Spanish investors. Furthermore, Spain played a decisive role in correlating a significant amount of the EU funds to the democratisation process in Latin America at the expense of other developing regions (Youngs, 2000a: 113). Spain's intermediary role has become more apparent when the Socialist government agreed to the principle of EU's enlargement towards the East after obtaining an agreement with the EU that envisaged similar increases in the new aid transfers to both Eastern Europe and Latin America. Furthermore, it has always been the Spanish pressure that secured a generous amount of EU development funds for Latin America than would otherwise have been allocated (Youngs, 2000a: 123). During the EU's 1999-2003 budgetary process, the Spanish government thwarted other EU members attempt to divert development funds from Latin America to poorer regions (Youngs, 2000a: 121). In the face of these observations, it is generally argued that although Spain has always been pressing for a region to region dialogue and a formal multilateral EU aid and development framework for Latin America, Spanish governments, until now, have already obtained generous commitments from EU members states over the region than a possible modest EU frame would have offered (Grugel, 1995: 154 and Youngs, 2000a: 126).

On the other hand, in the diplomatic sphere, although Spain has been systematically promoting the democratisation in Latin America, Spanish governments have always protected Latin American countries from harsh criticisms by the EU, generally insisting on less coercive and less critical EU positions and initiatives towards the region (see Youngs, 2000a: 113-114). The EU, on the other hand, acknowledges Spain's privileged position and its special role in the region as a representative of the EU transmitting the European policy goals in the region (Youngs, 2000a: 126).

An upwardly mobile semiperipheral state characteristic of Spain has been apparent in the Spanish objective of building up sphere of its own influence in Latin America. Indeed, Spain, in parallel with its increasing economic power and influence, has been gradually increasing its profile and political weight in the region, which in turn contributes to the increasing Spanish influence in world politics. Since the mid-1990s, in a core-like manner, Spain's main political concern is to implant democratic values and support democratisation processes in Latin America (see Youngs, 2000a: 112-116). The active Spanish involvement in political modernisation, institutionalisation and democratisation in Latin America has aimed to cooperate with regional states and help them in dealing with the issues such as human rights, corruption, electoral transparency, political party reforms, etc. The Spaniards have spent a higher proportion of their aid in Latin America on this project.

The increasing authority and weight of Spain in Latin American politics, (probably in the EU and the world politics as well) is also apparent in the core-like Spanish attitude towards the regional countries of Cuba, Chile and Argentina. First of all, after 1996, in protest of the "anti-democratic" nature of the Castro's political regime in Cuba, Spanish Prime Minister Aznar undertook an anti-Castro line that put an end all official Spanish aid to, and ruled out further cooperation with, Cuba at a time when the Spanish private sector heavily invested in this country (EIU Country Reports, between 3rd Quarter 1996 and 1st Quarter 1997). Later in April 1998, when the tension seemed to have come to an end, the Spanish government hardened its policy again by not allowing the Spanish King's official visit to Cuba, and moreover during the Ibero-American Summit in Havana in November 1999, the Spanish Premier met with the Cuban dissidents, expressed his opposition to forty-year communist "dictatorship" in Cuba, and pledged to press for democracy. At end of the Summit, Mr. Aznar also secured the establishment of a Human Rights Commission within the Ibero-American Secretariat, and in the final communiqué, all the participants signed and expressed their commitment to democracy, political pluralism, human rights and basic freedoms (see EIU Country Report, 2nd Quarter 1998: 13; 1st Quarter 2000: 16 and Youngs, 2000a: 114). Second, in October 1998, the former Chilean dictator Pinochet was arrested in the United Kingdom after an international detention order issued by a Spanish investigating judge. And, in November

1998, the Spanish government demanded the extradition of Pinochet from the United Kingdom for trial on charges of genocide and crimes committed against humanity while rejecting the Chilean government's call for international arbitration (see EIU Country Reports, 1st Quarter 1999: 13 and 4th Quarter 1999: 13). Finally, in November 1999, the same Spanish investigating judge issued new international detention order warrants this time for 98 Argentinean military officers on charges of genocide, terrorism and torture during the Argentinean dictatorship from 1976-1983 (EIU Country Report, 1st Quarter 2000: 14).

The foundation of the Ibero-American Community in this period is another indication of Spain's upwardly mobile semiperipheral foreign policy line that aimed to increase Spanish influence and prestige both in Latin America and in international affairs. The Ibero-American Community was established by the Spaniards to develop a common Hispanic identity in international relations, and to coordinate policies between Spain and Latin American countries (Barbe, 2000: 55 and Youngs, 2000a: 117-119). The Aznar governments' Latin American policy has been to transform the Hispanic world from a cultural community into a community of nations with a separate and distinctive identity cooperating on the world stage. In 1997 Prime Minister Aznar declared the Ibero-American Community as an instrument to enhance Spain's own profile in international affairs and thus as "an essential strategic option" (quoted in Youngs, 2000b: 118). Accordingly, Spain proposed the creation of an Ibero-American Peacekeeping Force in 1998, and the permanent Ibero-American Community Secretariat was established in Madrid in 1999.

Another upwardly mobile aspect of semiperipheral Spanish foreign policy has been the Spanish governments' willingness to upgrade relations with the US and NATO (Atlantic Alliance) and to play an important role in the redefinition process of the Euro-Atlantic relations. The Spaniards tried to increase their profile both in the Atlantic Alliance and in the US. Accordingly, during their EU presidency in 1995, Spanish diplomacy took the initiative and worked hard to start negotiations with the US concerning a new Transatlantic Agreement and an agreement for a free trade area between the EU and the US (EIU Country Reports, 3rd Quarter 1995: 5 and 4th Quarter 1995: 13). In these two initiatives, Spaniards were successful in negotiating and signing up an agreement on a new Transatlantic Declaration between the EU and the USA (between Bill Clinton, Jaques Santer and Felipe Gonzalez) in December 1995, while plans for a formal free trade area was abandoned (EIU Country Report, 1st Quarter 1996: 8).

After 1996, conservative governments have been particularly careful about upgrading the relations with the US and portraying a reliable ally image in the US (Barbe, 1998: 157). As soon as he came to power, Aznar, in a joint press conference with the US vice-president Al Gore in Madrid, declared Spain's policy of ending all cooperation with the Castro's "undemocratic" regime in Cuba, a country where not only the Spanish business stakes were high but also one threatened by US trade embargoes (EIU Country Reports 3rd Quarter 1996: 13). During the NATO's summit in Madrid 1997, the Spanish-US relations seemed to be further improved by US President Clinton's presence; he stayed almost a week in Spain and held extended meetings with the King Juan Carlos and Premier Aznar (EIU Country report, 3rd Quarter 1997: 14). It is strikingly enough that despite its strong Europeanist orientation, Spain under the conservative government, did not necessarily side with the EU in times of differences between the EU and Atlantic Alliance but joined the Atlanticist group, as in the case of American-British bombings over Iraq in 1998, and later during the NATO bombings in Kosovo where the Spanish government, as opposed to the European partners, unquestioningly accepted the "humanitarian military intervention" discourse of the US-British governments (Barbe, 2000: 59 and Aguirre and Rey, 2000: 204). Prime Minister Aznar's alignment with the Anglo-Saxon rather than the Franco-German bloc has revealed Spain's willingness to play a wider role in the broader Western Alliance. Indeed, in the words of a Spanish General, Spanish-US bilateral relations, including the military cooperation, "increases Spain's ability to influence global strategy beyond Europe by taking advantage of its position as the bridge to the Americas and gateway to the Africa, which includes the Arab world" (quoted in Sahagun, 2000: 159).

On the other hand, Spain's strategic importance has grown in the US Administration as NATO's missions have expanded outside its traditional area. In the post-Cold War period, Spain has become a strategic ally of the US enabling the Americans to perform their global role in the Mediterranean and beyond (Sahagun, 2000: 160-161). The US-NATO base Rota in southern Spain has become a key location for US-NATO sea, land and air operations in the Balkans (Bosnia, Albania and Kosovo), North and Central Africa (Liberia, Zaire and Central African Republic), and the Middle East (Iraq). The growing role and importance of Spain in Transatlantic affairs was reflected in the appointment of a number of Spaniards to high level international posts: Javier Solona's appointment as the General Secretary of NATO, Carlos Westendrop's election as High Representative to Bosina, and appointment of Miguel Angel Moratinos as EU envoy to the Middle East.

The US president G. W. Bush's highly symbolic preference to start his first European visit from Spain in June 2001, and the Prime Minister Aznar's public support to the American controversial missile defence program, which was opposed by many of the Spain's EU partners, indicates that the relations between Spain and the US have been upgraded to a higher level during the second half of the 1990s. It is argued that Spain's remarkable economic expansion in Latin America since the mid-1990s, as well as its becoming the leading investor in the region, increased its political weight within the US Administration (EIU Country Report, August 2001: 17). In fact, American businessmen have been seeking collaboration with Spanish firms in Latin American markets and accordingly, Spanish and American firms have increasingly been forming joint enterprises in the fields of telecommunication and banking (Sahagun, 2000: 165). The cordial relations between the two countries strengthened further with Prime Minister Aznar's quick offer, after a parliamentary approval, of strong military support to the US-led campaign against terrorism after 11 September 2001 (EIU Country Reports, November 2001: 8 and February 2002: 7).

In the relations with NATO, Aznar announced his government's objective of integrating Spain fully into the reformed Military Command Structure of NATO as soon as he came to power, and in November 1996 the overwhelming majority of the Spanish Parliament approved the government's demand to seek full membership in NATO's Military Command. There were 293 votes in favour and just 23 against, meaning that the proposal had the support of socialist PSOE and the other main political parties (EIU Country Report, 1st Quarter 1997: 13). It seems that one of the Spain's major aspirations for full integration into NATO Military Command was to increase its profile and sphere of influence both in the Atlantic and the Mediterranean regions. In fact, in return for full integration, the Spaniards demanded control of the Atlantic corridor between the Iberian Peninsula and the Canary Islands, and the control over the Straits of Gibraltar, which would radically increase Spain's influence while simultaneously eliminating British and Portuguese control in these regions (EIU Country Reports, 4th Quarter 1996: 12 and 3rd Quarter 1997: 14). The Spanish aspirations in the Atlantic and the Mediterranean was opposed promptly by both the UK and semiperipheral Portugal who would not welcome a change in the balance of power in favour of upwardly mobile semiperipheral Spain in the region. Accordingly, Spain was integrated fully into the NATO's Military Command Structure in December 1997, but only after the Spaniards watered down their aspirations and accepted their NATO command responsibility only for the Canary Islands, thus leaving the control of the area between Iberian

Peninsula and Canary Islands, and the control over Gibraltar, to Portugal and the UK respectively (see Coates, 2000: 177).

A striking point is that the upgrading in Spanish-US-NATO relations have coincided with the Spain's increasing collaboration with the Atlanticist members of Europe. The development of a close rapport between the Spanish and British Prime Ministers, Mr. Aznar and Mr. Blair, was crowned with the publication of a joint manifesto on EU issues in June 2000. The manifesto called for more liberalisation in the European market, and opposed the idea of two-speed Europe mainly promoted in France and Germany. It is argued by observers that the manifesto strengthened the view that there is an emerging Spanish-British axis as a counterweight to the Franco-German axis in Europe (EIU Country Report, July 2000: 13). Furthermore, progress in the negotiations between Spain and Britain over the long-standing dispute of Gibraltar's political status, and the speculations for a possible settlement on a shared sovereignty agreement between the two countries, further supported the idea of an emerging Spanish-British axis in the EU (EIU Country Report, February 2002: 8). Moreover, Spain's policy of strengthening and diversifying the relations with the pro-Atlanticist and EU candidate Turkey by establishing cordial and distinctive bilateral political, diplomatic, economic, and commercial relations (e.g. supporting Turkey's bid for the EU membership as opposed to the Greek and other EU members obstructions, establishing a bilateral diplomatic forum, through economic assistance, trade and investments, etc.) (Youngs, 2000b: 215 and Villaverde, 2000: 138) can also be considered a part of this upwardly mobile semiperipheral orientation of developing an international presence for Spain within, but at the same time beyond, the EU.

Another upwardly mobile semiperipheral foreign policy stance by Spain has been its growing participation and influence in the management of international problems (see Aguirre and Rey, 2000: 203-208). Since the early 1990s, Spain has involved in the numerous UN, NATO and EU international conflict management missions, including peacekeeping, air strikes, arms control, and humanitarian aid, for example in Angola, in Namibia, in Mozambique, in Rwanda, in El Salvador, in Haiti, in Guatemala, in the Gulf War and Operation Provide Comfort in Iraq and Turkey, in Operation Sharp Guard in ex-Yugoslavia, in IFOR and SFOR in Bosnia, in Mostar, in Montenegrin-Serbian border, in the River Danube embargo control, in Chechnya, in Moldova, in Croatia, in Georgia, in Operation Alba in Albania in Operation Alba-Charlie, in a diplomatic observation mission in Kosovo, in armed intervention against Serbia in Kosovo, and in KFOR. Furthermore, after the 11th September 2001 attack on the US, Spain swiftly offered its military support to the US against terrorism, and took part in the international peacekeeping force in Afghanistan in 2002. Indeed, the frequent Spanish contribution to the management of international conflicts more than many other country provided Spain a good international reputation, and as recognition of this input, Spain was granted a non-permanent seat on the UN Security Council for two years in 1993 and 1994 (Gillespie, 1996: 204).

Perhaps, Spain's upwardly mobile semiperipheral status has been enhanced further by Spain becoming a member of the OECD Development Aid Committee in 1991. In other words, Spain has become a (modest) donor country in development assistance and cooperation programs, which has provided Spain a link for economic and political influence in the peripheral areas (see Aguirre and Rey, 2000: 194-201). In 1998, total Spanish Official Development Aid was 0.25 per cent of its GDP (Aguirre and Rey, 2000: 197), and geographical distribution of the Spanish aid was concentrated in Latin America (37 percent), Sub-Saharan Africa (19.4 percent) and North Africa (11 percent), while Asia and Middle East receiving 5.5 percent, Central Asia and Far East 6.6 percent, and Central and Eastern Europe received 2.5 percent of total Spanish development aid (Aguirre and Rey, 2000: 1999).

Another indication of Spain's upwardly mobile semiperipheral activism in the foreign policy sphere is the establishment of a new Foreign Policy Council in late 2000 for coordinating and strengthening Spanish foreign policy with the ultimate aim of making Spain *a global power* (EIU, October 2000: 8). Among other external priorities, a special mission has been tailored to the Council for developing further political and commercial relations with Asia. The international dynamism and potential of Spain for playing *global roles* has also been apparent in the challenging statement of Prime Minister Aznar, which stated that Spain has merited a place in both G-8 and in the UN Security Council during his election campaign in 2000 (Youngs, 2000b: 220).

Spain's performance within the EU is another area that has revealed its upwardly mobile semiperipheral foreign policy line. In the second half of the 1990s and the early 2000s, Spain generally has continued to pursue harmonious relations with its EU partners, defended its national interests within the EU in a pragmatic manner, supported the process of European integration, and occasionally has tried to increase it profile within the EU.

During its EU presidency in 1995, Spain successfully facilitated two critical issues on the agenda of the EU, namely the enlargement of the Union towards Central and Eastern Europe and the process of the European Economic and Monetary Union (EIU, Country Report, 1st Quarter 1996: 8).

In the case of eastern enlargement, first of all it was clear that Spain, a net recipient of the EU budget, would be among the losers in terms of transfers and funds, and the stronger EU governments, like Germany, were supporting a restrictive budget policy. Moreover with the enlargement, the geo-political balance in the EU would move towards the north and east at the expense of southern EU members. The Spaniards in fact, gave their support rather than obstructing the enlargement process, but at the same time it fiercely struggled for maintaining favourable financial transfers from the EU budget to Spain, and at the end they scored a major success (see EIU Country Reports, 4th Quarter 1997: 13; 1st Quarter 1999: 13; and 2nd Quarter 1999: 13). On the other hand, in preserving the geo-political balance between the southern and the northern Europe in the EU, Spain, together with the other southern members of Italy, France and Portugal, managed to divert the attention of the northerners to the Mediterranean region and the region's importance to the security of Europe. As a result, significant amount of resources were allocated to the development of the Mediterranean region, and Spain became the champion of the Euro-Mediterranean Partnership program.

Although Spain was one of the most ardent supporters of the European Economic and Monetary Union, some of the EU's northern members, such as Germany, Austria and Holland, posed an obstacle to Spanish inclusion, expressing their doubts about Spain's qualifications for the EMU (EIU Country Report, 1st Quarter 1997: 10). In the face of this threat coming from its EU partners, the Spanish government successfully launched a political offensive in Europe to convince the EU leaders of the suitability of Spain to the EMU, and without a major difficulty, Spain met the requirements and became a founding member of the EMU in 1999.

Spain also has enthusiastically supported the development of European security cooperation and institutions. In 1995, Spain, together with Italy, established EUROFOR and EUROMARFOR within the WEU for EU operations in the Mediterranean and beyond, and improved the capability of this force in 1997 (Barbe, 1998: 159 and Coates, 2000: 185). In December 1997, Spain signed an agreement with Germany, Italy and Britain to build 620 units of Eurofighter warplanes (EIU, Country Report, 1st Quarter 1998: 24). In the sphere of European defence, furthermore, Spain has involved in the formation process of Eurocorps division since the early 1990s, and in 1998 Spaniards upgraded their contribution to this force from a mechanised infantry brigade to the best-equipped division in the Spanish Army, the Brunette Armoured Division (Coates, 2000: 182). Therefore, in June 1999, the appointment of Spanish Javier Solana, the former General Secretary of

NATO, as the first High Representative of the EU's Common Foreign and Security Policy (CFSP) by the European Council was a clear indication of Spain's increasing profile within the EU.

In fact, Spain has taken initiatives to develop a mainstream actor image and enhance its profile within the EU (Gillespie and Youngs, 2000: 5). First of all, since the early 1990s, Spanish governments have shown strong political will to play a major actor role in European integration and to participate in the directorate of big states (Barbe, 2000: 59). The high level meetings between Spanish, German and French foreign ministers in 1991 to create a Common Foreign and Security Policy (CFSP) framework for the EU, and the Spanish Prime Minister's proposal in 1992 for creating a directorate of five big states in the EU were the clear indications of Spanish aspirations to become a core state in the Union. Furthermore, strong Spanish support given to German unification significantly contributed to the rising image of Spain within the EU (Barbe, 2000: 60). The priority given to the Mediterranean and Latin America in the Spanish foreign policy, and the Spanish leadership and efforts to transplant these two regions onto the EU's agenda, have also increased the Spanish profile within the EU (Barbe, 2000: 53). On the other hand, Spanish success in entering the European Economic and Monetary Union from the very start gave the impression that Spain upgraded its status to a core EU member state (Gillespie and Youngs, 2000: 5). As noted earlier, the high level international appointments of Spanish diplomats as the EU representatives in Bosnia (Carlos Westerndrop), in Mostar (Ricardo Perez Casado), in the Middle East (Miguel Angel Moratinos) and Javier Solana as Mr. CFSP are the other clear indications of increasing role and influence of Spain in the EU. Finally, especially after 11th September 2001, Spanish activism has played important role for greater cooperation within the EU on the fight against terrorism and led to a common EU agreement on search and arrest warrants and a common list of recognised terrorist organisations (EIU Country Reports, November 2001: 15 and February 2002: 14-15).

In this period, upwardly mobile semiperipheral Spain has also competed with semiperipheral Portugal for economic and political gains in its attempt for rising to a core status. As mentioned earlier, in this rivalry in the economic sphere it seems that Spain has established its economic superiority over its semiperipheral neighbour by both significantly investing in Portugal and using Portugal as a stepping stone for Spain's economic expansion in some of the largest Latin American markets, notably Brazil (see Salmon, 2000: 34). However, in the political sphere, for the time being, Spanish aspirations for increasing its control and influence in the region at the expense of semiperipheral Portugal were frustrated. During the negotiations on the full incorporation of the Spanish military into the NATO Command structure and the restructuralisation of NATO's Military Command Structures in the Atlantic and the Mediterranean, Spain demanded the control responsibility of the Atlantic corridor between the Canary Islands and Iberian peninsula that would have considerably increased Spanish influence not only in the Atlantic but over passage to North Africa (EIU Country Report 3rd Quarter 1997: 14). But Portugal (and the UK) was not sympathetic enough to alter the existing balance of power in the Atlantic and at the entrance of the Straits of Gibraltar, which is one of the most important focal points for the world maritime traffic. As a result, when a deal was reached between Spain and NATO, Portugal, with the decisive British support, has nominally continued to control the waters between the Canary Islands and the Iberian Peninsula and has assumed control over the western entrance of the Straits of Gibraltar (EIU, 1st Quarter 1998: 13).

In conclusion, semiperipheral Spain has been continuing its upward mobilisation in the world-system hierarchy of states towards the core region. Clearly, the Spanish state is still playing an important role in this process by deliberately intervening in the market, restructuring the economic environment and promoting the interests of core-like economic elite both in the domestic and international spheres. In certain sectors of the economy, the Spanish presence in the world markets has considerably improved. Furthermore, an overwhelming majority of the Spanish political elite has been supporting this realignment in the economy and providing a democratic and stable political environment. Consequently, Spain has increased its international profile by asserting its intermediary, and sometimes central, role in geographically, historically and culturally contiguous regions, and also played important roles in the management of the international problems in a number of cases.

Although Spain has taken important steps for becoming a part of the core zone of the world-system since the mid-1970s, it nevertheless, still suffers from a number of peripheral features, which indicates Spain's incomplete upwardly mobile semiperipheral journey in the world-system. For instance, despite investments and state support since the 1980s, the continuing weakness in R&D, and high-technology production in Spain is a clear indication of this incomplete process. In addition, the Spanish demand to still be considered among the poorest members of the EU (even for the 2007-2013 period) in order to receive EU structural and cohesion funds (EIU Country Report, August 2001: 7 and 17) also signifies another peripheral aspect of the country. Furthermore, there has been a dispute in the domestic political environment between the Catalan and Bask parties/regional governments and the Spanish Parties/national government over the Spanish constitution and the structure of the Spanish state. This indicates disunity among domestic political coalitions, which is a characteristic of a peripheral and weak state in world-system analysis. Furthermore, in the external sphere, although Spain have always promoted and involved closely in the formation of a Common European Foreign and Security Policy and the creation of a European Army, it has never functioned as a political motor of these initiatives: Spain's existing economic, diplomatic and military powers have not allowed the country to play a major actor role yet (Barbe, 2000: 58-60). Finally, although Spain has taken important responsibilities in international conflict management all around the world, the Spanish military establishment remains relatively backward and poorly equipped as a result of long term declines in the defence expenditures, which does not overlap with the eagerness to exert influence in global issues (see Coates, 2000).

A common tendency among a number of (non-world-system) country specialists is to identify Spain at times as a major actor in international affairs but at other times as a middle power (see especially Coates, 2000, Youngs, 2000b and Barbe, 2000). In the concluding chapter of a recent collection on Spain, one specialist argues, "There is much in this volume to corroborate claims that Spain's political and economic presence and prestige on the international stage strengthened dramatically during the 1990s. However, there is also evidence suggesting that Spain has not yet come significantly closer to developing a truly global reach to its external relations" (Youngs, 2000b: 218). In fact, Spain is standing at a place beyond clear-cut description. At this point, the world-system perspective may provide an alternative explanation to Spain's behaviours, and for Spain's sporadically moving image and status between core and periphery in the international affairs, through the world-system concept of "upwardly mobile semiperipheral state".

Notes

1. Other ascending sectors in which Spanish research activities have been focused upon are micro computers, food technology, bio-technology, space, pharmaceutical R&D, aquaphonics, Antarctic research, high energy physics and research personnel training. See Aledo, 1993b, p.32.
2. For instance, CAMER international SA, an organisation formed by major Spanish banks, was involved in capital goods business throughout the world and with the backing of

230 Semiperipheral Development and Foreign Policy

credit guarantee from the Spanish government. CAMER concluded major credit agreements with Latin American central banks in support of Spanish machinery and equipment exports. See Baklanoff, 1978, p.69.

3   This motion supported the view that the crisis in Central America could be overcome by a change in social structures and the establishment of liberties, and the principles of the representative system.

4   Moreover, Spain participated in the NATO frigate replacement project and the A-129 light-attack helicopter and modular stand-off weapons project. Similarly, Spain, the Netherlands, France, Germany and the UK co-operated in the generation of an anti-tank weapons programme. Spanish electronic sectors and manufacturers were involved in a multinational military equipment production program. Spain, France and Italy have co-operated to create the Helios military satellite observation system (Zaldivar, 1991: 209; George and Stenhouse, 1991: 110-111; and Maxwell and Spiegel, 1994: 82) The Spaniards have also built an aircraft carrier navy vessel, and reduced their dependence on US equipment for F-18 aircrafts by establishing software development, validation and integration centre (Moxon-Browne, 1989: 19 and George and Stenhouse, 1991: 111).

5   Much of the production was realised through state owned companies that have been aggressive in the world arms market. The three main firms, CASA (air), BAZAN (navy) and ENESA (tank) exported their products to Far East, Egypt, Iraq, Morocco, Libya, Argentina, Mexico, Chile, Congo, Mauritania and even to Portugal (Treverton, 1986: 26; Pollack, 1991: 137: and Payne, 1986: 190-191).

6   For main privatisations in Spain between 1986-1997, see OECD, 1998, p.87.

7   This characteristic upwardly mobile semiperipheral foreign policy line of playing a bridge role between the peripheral and core regions has also helped Spain to pursue its national interests in the Mediterranean. On the one hand, all actual and potential security problems in the region, with respect to development, modernisation, demography, democracy, living standards etc., are problems already threatening Spanish national interests due to Spain's geographical and historical proximity to the region. On the other hand, Spanish investments in Morocco, and its energy (natural gas and oil) dependence on Algeria and Libya explain Spain's sensitivity on political instability in the Maghreb.

Conclusion

In the study of foreign policy one of the main discussions concerns the relative influence of internal/societal and external/systemic sources and political and economic factors on foreign policy. In conventional thinking, and in the majority of the foreign policy case studies, internal/societal and political factors are treated as the main sources of foreign policy. In fact, because foreign policy is a complex phenomenon in which both domestic and external and political and economic determinants are in constant interaction, the question should not be formulated as to which one of these factors determines the final policy outcome. Different variables (or combinations of variables) explain foreign policy best in different contexts, and only one or some of these variables can be a determining factor. Accordingly, the main issue should be to determine a starting point around which these different sources and/or factors of foreign policy converge and can produce a web of interaction.

At this point the world-system perspective provides us with a "social totality" in which the links between the internal/societal, external/systemic, and political and economic determinants of foreign policy can be established. According to world-system analysis, the starting point is the production/wealth structure and the production relations around which the political and economic external/systemic and internal/societal determinants of foreign policy converge. The world-system perspective provides tools to examine how power and production/wealth are organised at the world and national levels, and, accordingly, how these complex organisations are related to foreign policy. In this context, one can understand the impact of world level organisations of power and production/wealth on the formation and functioning of national level organisations. This is not to say that national level organisation is determined solely by the world level organisation (or by changes at this level). In world-system analysis, world level organisation provides opportunity structures for the reorganisation of national level organisations of power and production, but how to benefit from these opportunity structures is up to the national level actors (i.e., political (power) and economic (production) elites, state institutions etc.). It follows that in world-system analysis foreign policy is a function of the interaction between the world and national levels of organisation of power and production. More specifically, in world-system analysis foreign policy becomes a function of how national power and production elites organise their interests in the state structures in relation to the opportunities provided by the world level organisation of power and production/wealth. In short, in the world-system perspective, foreign policy is a part of a totality that is composed of a complex web of interactions among the world and national level organisations (structures), national economic and political elites, state structures, external actors (other states, foreign political and economic elites) and so forth.

In analysing the foreign policy of an individual state, world-system analysis begins by explaining how power and production/wealth are organised at the national level at any point in "world-system time" (i.e. in expansion and contraction periods of the world economy). Accordingly, it first establishes the "structural" and "temporal" components of the foreign policy environment. "World-system time" is the temporal component, and the "category of a state" in the world-system hierarchy is the structural component of this environment. In this study, "world-system time" means that the "world-economy" is in an "expansion" or "contraction" period, and that the "inter-state" system is passing through a stage of "hegemonic rise" or "hegemonic decline". On the other hand, the "structural category of a state" means that the state under examination is a "core", "peripheral" or "semiperipheral" state in the "world-economy" and in the "interstate" system. This is important because in analysing foreign policy, it is assumed that states that belong to the same category have similar characteristics and are subjected to similar opportunity structures during the "cyclical rhythms" of the "rise and decline of the hegemonic powers" and the "expansion" and "contraction" periods of the world-economy. However, they do not necessarily benefit from the opportunity structures provided by the world level organisation in the same way because there are differences in their internal organisation of power and production/wealth.

After establishing the "temporal" and "structural" components of the foreign policy environment, the world-system perspective focuses on how national actors organise power and production/wealth at the individual state level in this environment, and to what extent this organisation is influenced by external actors. It is argued that foreign policy is strongly affected by the specific national organisation of power and production since foreign policy is the output of this specific organisation into the external environment. There is a constant and significant interaction between the production and power/wealth structures and the foreign policy of the national system. In other words, a structural change in foreign policy is the result of a structural change in the organisation of power and production/wealth at the individual state level. Accordingly, the first step in analysing foreign policy in world-system analysis is to define the power-production/wealth structure of the state in the period under consideration and then to see how a structural change in this organisation leads to change(s) in the foreign policy of a state.

When analysing foreign policy, the type of state under investigation is important because the role played by the state in the functioning of power-production/wealth structures differs depending on the category of the state in the world-system hierarchy of states. In the semiperiphery, the state is believed to play the most important role as an agent of both power and production/wealth. And because of its central position, and the absence of hegemonic economic elites (periphery-like or core-like) in the semiperipheral zone of the world-economy, different groups in the production sphere try to influence state policies in order to promote their own interests. Consequently, the collaboration of the state with, or its support for, any group of actors (or its domination by any group of actors) will change the balance of power in the power-production/wealth structure, and this change will be reflected in foreign policy. Thus, since the state is also the main actor in foreign policy, and since such changes in the power-production/wealth structure are more likely in the semiperiphery, one can analyse the complex relationship between external/systemic and internal/societal determinants in semiperipheral foreign policies.

Thus, in world-system analysis, once the world-system time and type of state under investigation are determined, the next step in analysing foreign policy is to examine the power-production/wealth structure. In this way, the web of relations between the state, domestic political and economic elites, and external actors (states, multinational corporations, foreign economic elites) are clarified, and it also becomes possible to measure to what extent the state under investigation reveals typical characteristics of its world-system category. The nature of the web of relations, in turn, greatly shapes the basic orientation of the foreign policy of the state. Here, again, one can assess to what extent the foreign policy of the state under investigation follows the general characteristics of its category prescribed by the world-system framework.

An interesting aspect of analysing foreign policy in the framework of world-system analysis is to compare the foreign policies of individual states during and after a transition from one world-system time (say, an expansion/hegemonic period) to another (say, a contraction/hegemonic decline period). This provides us with a comparative perspective and therefore we can see whether a change in the world-system time and a change in the power-production/wealth structure of individual states, and hence a change in their foreign policies. The crucial point is, as we saw in the Greek and Spanish cases, that a change in the global environment can only provide opportunity structures, it cannot determine the specific responses/behaviours of the actors (the state and economic and political elites, etc.) of individual states. In other words, it depends on the political will of the domestic actors whether or not they benefit from the changing environment and whether or not they reorganise their domestic power-production/wealth structures in accordance with new global structures.

In this framework, analysing the foreign policies of Greece and Spain in a comparative way presented the opportunity to asses how two similar countries from the semiperipheral zone of the world-economy (and their domestic actors) responded differently to changes in the world-system power-production/wealth structure, and how they reorganised their internal power-production structures in different ways. We also saw that their foreign policies were significantly affected by changes in global and national level structures. In other words, their foreign policies were usually in conformity with their semiperipheral power-production/wealth structures in the two different sub-periods examined. Finally, I evaluated to what extent these changes in foreign policy confirm with the semiperipheral foreign policy behaviours prescribed by world-system theory.

My analysis of Greece and Spain in the postwar period in chapters 2-5 of this study shows that the foreign policies of both countries were strongly affected by their semiperipheral development patterns. In both "expansion-hegemonic rise" and "contraction-hegemonic decline" periods of the world-economy, their internal power-production/wealth structures (the structures that organise and greatly determine the developmental path) revealed the general characteristics of a semiperipheral country defined by the world-system framework. In other words, in both periods, the Greek and Spanish states occupied a central place in the developmental processes of the national economies, either through favouring the accumulation of capital in the hands of one particular kind of production elite (periphery- or core-like), or by taking on an entrepreneurial role themselves. On the other hand, as a result of the state oriented activities of the different central internal and external actors, close relationships were established between these groups and the Greek and Spanish political establishments. Political establishments, in turn, promoted the interests of different internal and external actors in different periods depending on which group became effectively dominant over the others.

However, because of the different responses of the Greek and Spanish internal actors to the opportunities provided by the world-system power-production/wealth structures, their semiperipheral developmental processes (which were very similar at the beginning) followed somewhat different paths, and this took them to different points in the world-system hierarchy of states. This does not mean that either Greece or Spain is not semiperipheral. It simply means that they are located differently in the intra-semiperipheral hierarchy. Indeed, both of them followed semiperipheral development patterns. However, while "developmentalist-state" and "core-like producers" dominated the power-production/wealth structure in Spain (as we saw in the chapter 8), their counterparts in Greece, until recently (as I demonstrated in chapter 6) failed to establish their hegemony over "periphery-like power-production/wealth" groups and structures. Consequently, in the contraction period of the world-economy, Spain became clearly "a strong and an upwardly mobile semiperipheral state", while Greece's attempt to achieve upward mobility was not that successful until very recently, and, probably, Greece remained "a weak semiperipheral state". Consequently, their different semiperipheral developmental patterns were reflected in their foreign policies. While Spain revealed the foreign policy of an upwardly mobile semiperipheral state, Greece on the whole failed to do so.

Semiperiphery is still a problematic concept in the social sciences. Although debates on various aspects of the semiperipheral zone of the world-economy have continued even among modern world-system scholars (see Arrighi, 1985 and Martin, 1990a), there is more or less general agreement that such an intermediate zone exists. However questions about the "shape, size and the method of membership within - and entrance into and exit from - the zone remain an unexplored realm" (Martin, 1990b: 4). Furthermore, other crucial questions and issues relating to "how do we know the semiperiphery when we see it", "what is the nature of the semiperipheral movement within the world-economy " and "what is the role of geo-strategic positions in the upward mobility of semiperipheral states" have not been satisfactorily answered and need further clarification at both theoretical and empirical levels.

Since the concept semiperiphery is still contentious, it may be legitimate to conclude by considering "whether it is correct to use it in analysing the foreign policies of individual states". The answer depends on one's understanding of foreign policy phenomena. If one sees foreign policy basically as the product of internal or external political factors and processes, the answer is clearly "no". However, if one believes that foreign policy behaviour is best explained by linking "politics" with "economics", and "internal/societal" factors with "external/systemic" factors the concept semiperiphery can be a useful tool in the hands of the researcher. In other words, if one looks at foreign policy phenomena from the perspective of national and international political economy, "semiperiphery" can be far more useful than other concepts such as, "newly industrialising countries" (NICs), "middle income countries", "developing countries", and so forth. By employing "the concept semiperiphery", as I have tried to show in the Greek and Spanish cases, one can identify and establish the relative impact of international and national structural factors, the distribution of wealth and power, the state, and external and internal economic and power elites on the foreign policies of "intermediate countries". Moreover, unlike the other terms used to describe these countries, the concept semiperiphery enables the analyst to explain changes in foreign policy; thus its use is fully justified.

It is widely accepted that foreign policy analysis is an interdisciplinary field. Similarly the "world-system school" in general, and the concept of "semiperiphery" in particular, provide a totality called a "social system" that requires interdisciplinary investigation. In this respect, studying foreign policy within the framework of world-system analysis leads to fruitful research, and it provides students of international relations with new fields to explore in analysing foreign policy.

Bibliography

Agüero, F. (1995), 'Democratic Consolidation and the Military in Southern Europe and South America', in R. Gunther, N. Diamandouros and H. G. Puhle (eds.), *The Politics of Democratic Consolidation. Southern Europe in Comparative Perspective*, Baltimore: The John Hopkins University Press, pp. 124-165.

Aguilar, S. (1984), 'Notes on the Economy and Popular Movements in the Transition', in C. Abel and N. Torrents (eds.), *Spain Conditional Democracy*, London: Croom Helm, pp. 125-135.

Aguirre, M. and Rey, F. (2000), 'Development Co-operation and Humanitarian Action in Spanish Foreign Policy', *Mediterranean Politics*, Vol. 5, No. 2, pp. 190-209.

Aledo, C. A. (1993a), 'Industrial Policy', in A. Almarcha Barbado (ed.), *Spain and EC Membership Evaluated*, London: Pinter Publishers, pp. 20-29.

Aledo, C. A. (1993b), 'Technology Policy', in A. Almarcha Barbado (ed.), *Spain and EC Membership Evaluated*, London: Pinter Publishers, pp. 30-37.

Algoskoufis, G. (2000), 'The Greek Economy and the Euro', in A. Mitsos and E. Mossialos (eds.), *Contemporary Greece and Europe*, Aldershot: Ashgate, pp. 131-155.

Amodia, J. (1977), *Franco's Political Legacy*, London: Allen Lane.

Anderson, C. W. (1970), *The Political Economy of Modern Spain*, Wisconsin: The University of Wisconsin Press.

Arrighi, G. (1985), 'Fascism to Democratic Socialism: Logic and Limits of a Transition', in G. Arrighi (ed.), *Semiperipheral Development. The Politics of Southern Europe in the Twentieth Century*, Beverly Hills: Sage Publications, pp. 31-39.

Arrighi, G. (1999), 'Globalisation, State, Sovereignty and the Endless Accumulation of Capital', in D. A. Smith, D. C. Solinger and S. C. Topik (eds.), *States and Sovereignty in the Global Economy*, London: Routledge, pp. 53-73.

Arrighi, G. and Drangel, J. (1986), 'The Stratification of the World-Economy', *Review*, Vol. 10, No. 1, pp. 9-74.

Aymard, M. (1985), 'Nation States and Interregional Disparities of Development', in G. Arrighi (ed.), *Semiperipheral Development. The Politics of Southern Europe in the Twentieth Century*, Beverly Hills: Sage Publications, pp. 40-54.

Baklanoff, E. N. (1978), *The Economic Transformation of Spain and Portugal*, NY: Praeger.

Barbe, E. (1998), 'Spanish Security Policy and the Mediterranean Question' in K. Elliassen (ed.), *Foreign and Security Policy in the European Union*, London: Sage, pp. 147-160.

Barbe, E. (2000), 'Spain and CFSP: The Emergence of a Major Player' *Mediterranean Politics*, Vol. 5, No. 2, pp. 44-63.

Bardaji, A. F. (1976), 'Political Opposition in the Spanish Catholic Church', *Government and Opposition*, Vol. 11, No. 2, pp. 198-211.

Ben-Ami, S. (1984), 'The Legacy of Francoism: General Perspectives', in C. Abel and N. Torrents (eds.), *Spain Conditional Democracy*, London: Croom Helm, pp. 1-20.

Bergersen, A. (1980), 'From Utilitarianism to Globology: The Shift from the Individual to the World as a Whole as the Primordial Unit of Analysis', in A. Bergersen (ed.), *Studies of the Modern World System*, NY: Academic Press, pp. 1-12.

Brassloff, A. (1984), 'The Church and the Post Franco Society', in C. Abel and N. Torrents (eds.), *Spain Conditional Democracy*, London: Croom Helm, pp. 59-77.

Carr, R. and Fusi, J. P. (1981), *Spain: Dictatorship to Democracy*, London: Harper Collins.

Chase-Dunn, C. (1980), 'The Development of Core Capitalism in the Antebellum United States: Tariff Politics and Class Struggle in an Upwardly Mobile Semiperiphery', in A. Bergersen (ed.), *Studies of the Modern World System*, NY: Academic Press, pp. 189-230.

Chase-Dunn, C. (1981), 'Interstate System and Capitalist World Economy', *International Studies Quarterly*, Vol. 25, No. 1, pp. 19-42.

Chase-Dunn, C. (1989), *Global Formation. Structures of the World-Economy*, Massachusetts: Basil Blackwell.

Chase-Dunn, C. (1990), 'Resistance to Imperialism. Semiperipheral Actors', *Review*, Vol. XIII, No. 1, pp. 1-31.

Chase-Dunn, C. and Rubinson, R. (1977), 'Toward a Structural Perspective on the World System', *Politics and Society*, Vol. 7, No. 4, pp. 453-476.

Chilcote, R. H. (1990), 'Southern European Transitions in Comparative Perspective', in R. H. Chilcote, S. Hadjiyannis, F. A Lopez III, D. Nataf, E. Sammis (eds.), *Transitions From Dictatorships to Democracy. Comparative Studies of Spain Portugal and Greece*, NY: Crane Russak, pp. 1-18.

Chipman, J. (1988), 'Allies in the Mediterranean: Legacy of Fragmentation', in J. Chipman (ed.), *NATO's Southern Allies. Internal and External Changes*, London: Routlege, pp. 53-85.

Christodoulakis, N. (2000), 'The Greek Economy Converging Towards EMU' in A. Mitsos and E. Mossialos (eds.), *Contemporary Greece and Europe*, Aldershot: Ashgate, pp. 93-114.

Christodoulides, Th. (1988), 'Greece and European Political Cooperation: The Intractable Partner', in N. A. Stavrou (ed.), *Greece Under Socialism*, NY: Orpheus Publishing, pp. 281-303.

Clogg, R. (1984), *The Pasok Phenomeneon*, University of Florida: Centre for Greek Studies, Staff Paper 4.

Clogg, R. (1986), *A Short History of Modern Greece*, London: Clerandon Press.

Clogg, R. (1987), *Parties and Elections in Greece. The Search for Legitimacy*, London: C. Hurst & Company.

Clogg, R. and Yannopoulos, G. (1972), 'Editors' Introduction', in R. Clogg and G. Yannopoulos (eds.), *Greece Under Military Rule*, London: Secker & Warburg, pp. vii-xxii.

Coates, C. (2000), 'Spanish Defence Policy: Eurocorps and NATO Reform', *Mediterranean Politics*, Vol. 5, No. 2, pp. 170-189.

Constas, D. (1991), 'Greek Foreign Policy Objectives 1974-1986', in S. Vryonis (ed.), *Greece on the Road to Democracy: From the Junta to PASOK 1974-1986*, NY: Orpheus Publishing, pp. 37-69.

Constas, D. (1995), 'Challenges to Greek Foreign Policy. Domestic and External Parameters, in D. Constans and T. G. Stavrou (eds.), *Greece Prepares for the Twenty-first Century*, Washington D.C.: The Woodrow Wilson Centre Press, pp. 71-98.

Constitution of Greece, 1975, in *Democracy in Greece: The First Year* (n.d), (n.p), pp. 27-48.

Corantis, I. (2001), 'Greece's Policy in the Balkans and Greek-Turkish Co-operation', paper presented in the workshop on *EU and Turkey on the Balkans-Political Problems and Perspectives*, June 29, Middle East Technical University, Ankara.

Cordata, J. W. (1980), 'The United States', in J. W Cordata (ed.), *Spain in the Twentieth-Century World*, Connecticut: Greenwood Press, pp. 235-259.

Coufoudakis, V. (1980), 'American Foreign Policy and the Cyprus Problem 1974-1978: The Theory of Continuity Revisited', in Th. A. Couloumbis and J. O. Iatrides (eds.), *Greek-American Relations. A Critical Review*, NY: Pella Publishing Company, pp. 107-129.

Coufoudakis, V. (1987), 'Greek Foreign Policy 1945-1985: Seeking Independence in an Interdependent World, Problems and Prospects', in K. Featherstone and D. K. Katsoudas (eds.), *Political Change in Greece Before and After the Colonels*, London: Croom Helm, pp. 253-270.

Coufoudakis, V. (1996), 'Greek Foreign Policy in the Post-Cold War Era: Issues and Challenges', *Mediterranean Quarterly*, Vol.7, No.3, pp. 26-41.

Couloumbis, Th. A. (1966), *Greek Political Reaction to American and NATO Influences*, New Heaven: Yale University Press.

Couloumbis, Th. A. (1981a), 'Defining Greek Foreign Policy Objectives', in H. R. Penniman (ed.), *Greece at the Pools*, Washington: American Enterprise Institute for Public Policy Research, pp. 160-184.

Couloumbis, Th. A. (1981b), 'Conclusion', in H. R. Penniman (ed.), *Greece at the Pools*, Washington: American Enterprise Institute for Public Policy Research, pp. 185-192

Couloumbis, Th. A. (1983a), *The United States Greece and Turkey. The Troubled Triangle*, NY: Preager.

Couloumbis, Th. A. (1983b), 'The Structures of Greek Foreign Policy', in R. Cloog (ed.), *Greece in the 1980s*, London: MacMillan, pp. 95-122.

Couloumbis, Th. A. (1998), 'Strategic Consensus in Greek Domestic and Foreign Policy since 1974', *Thesis*, Vol. 1, Issue No. 4, pp. 10-17.

Couloumbis, Th. A. (2000), 'Greece in a Post-Cold War Environment', in A. Mitsos and E. Mossialos (eds.), *Contemporary Greece and Europe*, Aldershot: Ashgate, pp. 373-385.

Couloumbis, Th. A., Petropulos, J. A., and Psomiades, H. (1976), *Foreign Interference in Greek Politics. A Historical Perspective*, NY: Pella Publishing Company.

Coutsoumaris, G. (1963), *The Morphology of Greek Industry*, Athens: Centre of Economic Research.

Coverdale, J. F. (1977), 'Spain. From Dictatorship to Democracy', *International Affairs*, Vol. 53, No. 4, pp. 615-630.

De la Serre, F. (1979), 'Comment', in L. Tsoukalis (ed.), *Greece and the European Community*, Hants: Saxon House, pp. 39-43.

Diamandouros, N. P. (1986a), 'The Southern European NICs', *International Organization*, Vol. 40, No. 2, pp. 547-556.

Diamandouros, N. P. (1986b), 'Regime Change and the Prospects for Democracy in Greece: 1974-1983', in O'Donnell et al. (eds.), *Transitions from Authoritarian Rule. Southern Europe*, Baltimor: The Johns Hopkins University Press, pp. 138-164.

Diaz-Ambrona, J. A. O. (1984), 'The Transition to Democracy in Spain', in C. Abel and N. Torrentes (eds.), *Spain. Conditional Democracy*, London: Croom Helm, pp. 21-39.

Donges, J. B. (1971), 'From Autarchic Towards a Cautiously Outward-Looking Industrialization Policy: The Case of Spain', *Weltwirtschaftliches Archive*, Bond, 107, Heft. 1, pp. 33-75.

Dura, J. (1985), *US Policy Towards Dictatorship and Democracy in Spain: 1931-1953*, Sevilla: Arrayan Ediciones.

Eaton, S. D. (1981), *The Forces of Freedom in Spain: 1974-1979*, Stanford: Hoover Institution Press.

The Economist Intelligence Unit (EIU), *Country Profile. Greece*, 2000, 2001, London: EIU.

The Economist Intelligence Unit (EIU), *Country Profile. Spain*, 1998, 1999, 2000, London: EIU.

The Economist Intelligence Unit (EIU), *Country Report. Greece*, 2000 (1st Quarter and April, July and October), 2001 (January, April), London: EIU.

The Economist Intelligence Unit (EIU), *Country Report. Spain*, 1995 (1st, 2nd, 3rd, 4th Quarters), 1996 (1st, 2nd, 3rd, 4th Quarters), 1997 (1st, 2nd, 3rd, 4th, Quarters), 1998 (1st, 2nd, 3rd, 4th Quarters), 1999 (1st, 2nd, 3rd, 4th Quarters), 2000 (1st, 2nd Quarters, July, October), 2001 (January, May, August, November), 2002 (February), London: EIU.

Elephantis, A. (1981), 'PASOK and the Elections of 1977: The Rise of the Populist Movement', in H. R. Penniman (ed.), *Greece at the Pools*, Washington: American Enterprise Institute for Public Policy Research, pp. 105-129.

Ellis, H. (1964), *Industrial Capital in Greek Development*, Athens: Centre of Economic Research.
Ellwood, S. (1994), *Franco*, London: Longman.
Featherstone, K. (1996), 'Introduction', in K. Featherstone and K. Ifantis (eds.), *Greece in a Changing Europe*, Manchester: Manchester University Press, pp. 3-16.
Featherstone, K. and Katsoudas, D. K. (eds.) (1987), *Political Change in Greece. Before and After the Colonels*, London: Croom Helm.
Flemming, S. (1980), 'North Africa and the Middle East', in J. W. Cordata (ed.), *Spain in the Twentieth-Century World*, Connecticut: Greenwood Press, pp. 121-154.
Freris, A. F. (1988), *The Greek Economy in the Twentieth Century*, London: Croom Helm.
Gallo, M. (1973), *Spain Under Franco*, London: George Allen and Unwin.
George, B. and Stenhouse, M. (1991), 'Western Perspectives', in K. Maxwell (ed.), *Spanish Foreign and Defence Policy*, Boulder: Westview Press, pp. 63-114.
Georgiou, V. F. (1988), *Greece and the Transnational Corporations: Dependent Economic Development and Its Constraints on National Policy. 1965-1985*, Transnational Corporations Research Project, No. 15, Sydney: University of Sydney Publications.
Giannitsis, T. (1991), 'Transformation and Problems of Greek Industry. The Experience During the Period 1974-1985', in S. Vryonis (ed.), *Greece on the Road to Democracy: From Junta to PASOK 1974-1986*, NY: Orpheus Publishing, pp. 213-232.
Gillespie, R. (1994), *Spain and the Maghreb*, University of Portsmouth, School of Languages and Area Studies, Working Papers, General Series, Vol. 1.
Gillespie, R. (1996), 'Spain and the Mediterranean: Southern Sensitivity, European Aspirations', *Mediterranean Politics*, Vol. 1, No. 2, pp. 193-211.
Gillespie, R. and Young, R. (2000), 'Spain's International Challenges at the Turn of the Century', *Mediterranean Politics*, Vol. 5, No. 2, pp. 1-13.
Gilmour, D. (1985), *The Transformation of Spain*, London: Quartet Books.
Giner, S. (1986), 'Political Economy, Legitimation and the State in Southern Europe', in G. O'Donnell, P. C. Schmitter and L. Whitehead (eds.), *Transitions From Authoritarian Rule. Southern Europe*, Baltimore: The Johns Hopkins University Press, pp. 11-44.
Giner, S. and Sevilla, E. (1984), 'Spain: From Corporatism to Corporatism', in A. Williams (ed.), *Southern Europe Transformed*, London: Harper and Row, pp. 113-141.
Glenny, M. (1997), 'The Tempting Purgatory', in G. T. Allison and K. Nicolaidis (eds.), *The Greek Paradox*, Mass: The MIT Press, pp. 73-82.
Gobbo, M. (1981), *The Political Economic and Labour Climate in Spain*, Philadelphia: University of Pennsylvania. Industrial Research Unit, European Studies, No. 10.

Goldbloom, M. (1972), 'United States Policy in Postwar Greece', in R. Clogg and G. Yannopoulos (eds.), *Greece Under Military Rule*, London: Secker & Warburg, pp. 228-254.

Gooch, A. (1986), 'A Surrealistic Referendum: Spain and NATO', *Government and Opposition*, Vol. 21, No. 3, pp. 300-316.

Gooch, A. (1992a), 'The Foreign Relations and Foreign Policy of Spain: A Survey for 1922. Part One: Spain and the Arab Connection', *Contemporary Review*, January, Vol. 260, No. 1512, pp. 1-7.

Gooch, A. (1992b), 'The Foreign Relations and Foreign Policy of Spain. Part Two: Spain and Latin America', *Contemporary Review*, March, Vol. 260, No. 1514, pp. 129-135.

Gooch, A. (1992c), 'The Foreign Relations and Foreign Policy of Spain. Part Three: The United States and NATO', *Contemporary Review*, June, Vol. 260, No. 1517, pp. 129-135.

Gooch, A. (1992d), 'The Foreign Relations and Foreign Policy of Spain: A Survey for 1992. Part Four: Spain, Western Europe and the European Community', *Contemporary Review*, August, Vol. 261, No. 1519, pp. 57-61.

Graham, R. (1984), *Spain. Change of a Nation*, London: Michael Joseph.

Grannel, F. (2000), 'Europe's Evolving Economic Identity: Spain's Role', *Mediterranean Politics*, Vol. 5, No. 2, pp. 64-75.

Grimmet, R. F. (1990), 'An Overview of the Formative Years: 1953-1970', in J. W. McDonald and D. B. Bendahmane (eds.), *US Bases Overseas. Negotiations with Spain Greece and the Philippines*, Colorado: Westview Press, pp. 7-15.

Grugel, J. (1987), 'Spain's Socialist Government and Central American Dilemmas', *International Affairs*, Vol. 63, No. 4, pp. 603-615.

Grugel, J. (1995), 'Spain and Latin America', in R. Gillespie, F. Rodrigo and J. Story (eds.), *Democratic Spain*, London: Routledge, pp. 141-158.

Gunther, R. (1986), 'The Spanish Socialist Party: From Clandestine Opposition to Party of Government', in S. G. Payne (ed.), *The Politics of Democratic Spain*, Chicago: The Chicago Council on Foreign Relations, pp. 8-49.

Gunther, R., Diamandouros, P. N. and Puhle, H. J. (eds.) (1995), *The Politics of Democratic Consolidation. Southern Europe in Comparative Perspective*, Baltimore: The John Hopkins University Press.

Haas, R. (1988), Alliance Problems in the Eastern Mediterranean. Greece Turkey and Cyprus. Part I, *Adelphi Papers*, No. 229.

Halikas, D. J. (1978), *Money and Credit in a Developing Economy: The Greek Case*, NY: New York University Press.

Halliday, F. (1994), *Rethinking International Relations*, London: MacMillan.

Hargreaves, J. (2000), *Freedom for Catalonia*, Cambridge: Cambridge University Press.

Harrison, J. (1985), *The Spanish Economy in the Twentieth Century*, London: Croom Helm.

Harrison, J. (1993), *The Spanish Economy*, London: MacMillan.

Heywood, P. (1987), 'Spain 10 June 1987', *Government and Opposition*, Vol. 22, No. 4, pp. 390-401.

Heywood, P. (1995), *The Government and Politics of Spain*, London: MacMillan.
Hill, C. and Light, M. (1985), 'Foreign Policy Analysis', in M. Light and A. J. R. Groom (eds.), *International Relations: A Handbook of Current Theory*, London: Pinther Publishers, pp. 156-173.
Hopkins, T. K. (1982a), 'The Study of the Capitalist World-Economy: Some Introductory Considerations', in T. K. Hopkins and I. Wallerstein (eds.), *World-System Analysis. Theory and Methodology*, Beverly Hills: Sage Publications, pp. 9-38.
Hopkins, T. K. (1982b), 'Notes on Class Analysis and the World-System', in T. K. Hopkins and I. Wallerstein (eds.), *World-System Analysis. Theory and Methodology*, Beverly Hills: Sage Publications, pp. 83-89.
Hopkins, T. K. and Wallerstein, I. (1982), 'Patterns of Development of the World System', in T. K. Hopkins and I. Wallerstein (eds.), *World-System Analysis. Theory and Methodology*, Beverly Hills: Sage Publications, pp. 41-82.
Hopkins, T. K. and Wallerstein, I. (1996), 'The World System: Is there a crisis?' in T.K. Hopkins and I. Wallerstein (eds.), *The Age of Transition*, London: Zed Books, pp. 1-10.
Hudson, R and Lewis, J. R. (1984), 'Capital Accumulation: The Industrialization of Southern Europe?', in A. Williams (ed.), *Southern Europe Transformed*, London: Harper and Row Publishers, pp. 179-207.
Iatrides, J. O. (1980), 'American Attitudes Toward the Political System of Postwar Greece', in Th. A. Couloumbis and J. O Iatrides (eds.), *Greek-American Relations. A Critical Review*, NY: Pella Publishing Company, pp. 49-73.
International Bank for Reconstruction and Development (IBRD) (1963), *The Economic Development of Spain*, Baltimore: The John Hopkins Press.
Ioakimidis, P. C. (1984), 'Greece: From Military Dictatorship to Socialism', in A.Williams (ed.), *Southern Europe Transformed*, London: Harper and Row Publishers, pp. 33-60.
Ioakimidis, P. C. (1996), 'Contradictions between Policy and Performance' in K. Featherstone and K. Ifantis (eds.), *Greece in Changing Europe*, Manchester: Manchester University Press, pp. 33-52.
Ioakimidis, P. C. (2000), The Europeanisation of Greece's Foreign Policy: Progress and Problems, in A. Mitsos and E. Mossialos (eds.), *Contemporary Greece and Europe*, Aldershot: Ashgate, pp. 359-372.
Ioannides, C. P. (1991), 'Greece, Turkey, The United States and the Politics of Middle Eastern Terrorism', in S. Vryonis (ed.), *Greece on the Road to Democracy: From the Junta to PASOK 1974-1986*, NY: Orpheus Publishing, pp. 141-167.
Jordan, D. C. (1979), *Spain, the Monarchy and the Atlantic Community*, Mass: Institute for Foreign Policy Analysis.
Kapetanyannis, V. (1993), 'The Left in the 1980s: Too Little Too Late', in R. Clogg (ed.), *Greece 1981-89 The Populist Decade*, London: MacMillan, pp. 78-93.

Karamanlis, K. (1974), 'Proclamation of the Prime Minister Konstantinos Karamanlis on the Foundation of the Political Camp Nea Dimokratia in 1974', in R. Clogg, *Parties and Elections in Greece*, London: C.Hurst & Company, 1987, pp. 223-225.

Karamanlis, K. (1979), 'Speech of Konstantinos Karamanlis at the First Congress of Nea Dimokratia in 1979', in R. Clogg *Parties and Elections in Greece*, London: C.Hurst & Company, 1987, pp. 225-228.

Katris, J. A. (1971), *Eye Witness in Greece. The Colonels come to Power*, St. Louis: New Critics Press.

Kefalas, A. and Mantzaris, A. (1986), 'The Greek Balance of Payments and Membership of the European Economic Community', in G. N. Yannopoulos (ed.), *Greece and the EEC*, London: MacMillan, pp. 69-79.

Kegley, C. W and Wiltkopf, E. (1981), *World Politics. Trends and Transformation*, New York: St. Martin's Press

Keridis, D. (2001), 'Domestic Developments and Foreign Policy', in D. Keridis and D. Triantaphyllou (eds.), *Greek-Turkish Relations in the Era of Globalisation*, Virgina: Brassey's, pp. 2-18.

Keyder, Ç. (1985), 'The American Recovery of Southern Europe: Aid and Hegemony', in G. Arrighi (ed.), *Semiperipheral Development. The Politics of Southern Europe in the Twentieth Century*, Beverly Hills: Sage Publications, pp. 31-39.

Kleinman, J. (1988), 'Socialist Policies and the Free Market: An Evaluation of PASOK's Economic Performance', in N. A. Stavrou (ed.), *Greece Under Socialism*, NY: Orpheus Publishing, pp. 187-219.

Klepak, H. P. (n.d.), *Spain: Nato or Neutrality*, Ontario: Queens University Centre for International Relations, National Security Series, No. 1/80.

Kofas, J. (1989), *Intervention and Underdevelopment. Greece During the Cold War*, Pennsylvania: The Pennsylvania State University Press.

Kofas, J. (1990), 'The Greek Economy', in M. Sarafis and M. Eve (eds.), *Background to Contemporary Greece*, Volume I, London: Merlin Press, pp. 53-93.

Kofos, E. (1991), 'Greece and the Balkans.1974-1986', in S. Vryonis (ed.), *Greece on the Road to Democracy: From the Junta to PASOK 1974-1986*, NY: Orpheus Publishing, pp. 97-121.

Kohler, B. (1982), *Political Forces in Spain Greece and Portugal*, London: Butterworth Scientific.

Kolmer, K. (1981), 'The Greek Economy at a Crucial Turning Point: Political Reality Versus Social Aspirations', in *New Liberalism. The Future of Non-Collectivist Institutions in Europe and the US*, Athens: Centre for Political Research and Information, pp. 287-314.

Kourvetaris, Y. and Dobratz, B. (1987), *A Profile of Modern Greece*, Oxford: Clerandon Press.

Kranidiotis, Y. (2000), 'The Fundamental Objectives of Greek Foreign Policy', in A. Mitsos and E. Mossialos (eds.), *Contemporary Greece and Europe*, Aldershot: Ashgate, pp. 31-36.

Labrianidis, L. (2000), 'Are Greek Companies that Invest in the Balkans in the 1990s Transnational Companies?' in A. Mitsos and E. Mossialos (eds.), *Contemporary Greece and Europe*, Aldershot: Ashgate, pp. 457-482.
Large, P. (1985), 'Semiperiphery and Core in the European Context: Reflections on the Postwar Italian Experience', in G. Arrighi (ed.), *Semiperipheral Development. The Politics of Southern Europe in the Twentieth Century*, Beverly Hills: Sage Publications, pp. 179-214.
Larrabee, S. (1997), 'Greece and the Balkans: Implications for Policy', in G. T. Allison and K. Nicolaidis (eds.), *The Greek Paradox*, Mass: The MIT Press, pp. 107-112.
Larrabee, S. (2001), 'Security in the Eastern Mediterranean: Transatlantic Challenges and Perspectives', in D. Keridis and D. Triantaphyllou (eds.), *Greek-Turkish Relations in the Era of Globalization*, Virginia: Brassey's, pp. 224-238.
Lavdas, K. A. (1997), *The Europeanisation of Greece. Interest Politics and the Crisis of Integration*, London: MacMillan.
Legg, K. R. and Roberts, J. M. (1997), *Modern Greece. A Civilisation in the Periphery*, Boulder: Westview Press.
Leon, E. M. (1986), 'Foreign Policy of the Socialist Government', in S. Payne (ed.), *The Politics of Democratic Spain*, Chicago: The Chicago Council of Foreign Relations, pp. 175-245.
Liagorvas, P. (2000), 'The Changing Role of the Greek State in view of EMU', in A. Mitsos and E. Mossialos (eds.), *Contemporary Greece and Europe*, Aldershot: Ashgate, pp. 205-221.
Liberman, S. (1982), *The Contemporary Spanish Economy. A Historical Perspective*, London: George Allen and Unwin.
Light, M. (1994), 'Foreign Policy Analysis', in A. J. R. Groom and M. Light (eds.), *Contemporary International Relations: A Guide to Theory*, London: Pinter Publishers, pp. 93-108.
Lopez III, F. A. (1990), 'Bourgeois State and the Rise of Social Democracy', in H. Chilcote, S. Hadjiyannis, F. A. Lopez III, D. Nataf and E. Sammis (eds.) *Transitions From Dictatorship to Democracy*, NY: Crane Russak, pp. 17-72.
Loulis, J. C. (1981a), 'New Democracy: The Face of New Conservatism', in H. R. Penniman (ed.), *Greece at the Pools*, Washington: American Enterprise Institute for Public Policy Research, pp. 49-83.
Loulis, J. C. (1981b), 'The Greek Conservative Movement in Transition', in *The New Liberalism. The Future of Non-Collectivist Institutions in Europe and the US*, Athens: Centre for Political Research and Information, pp. 7-28.
Loulis, J. C. (1985), *Greece Under Papandreou: NATO's Ambivalent Partner*, London: Institute for European Defence and Strategic Studies.
Mackenzie, L. (1973), 'The Political Ideas of the Opus Dei in Spain', *Government and Opposition*, Vol. 8, No. 1, pp. 72-92.
Macridis, R. (1981), 'Elections and Political Modernization in Greece', in H. R. Penniman (ed.), *Greece at the Pools*, Washington: American Enterprise Institute for Public Policy Research, pp. 1-20.

Macridis, R. (1984), *Greek Politics at a Crossroads*, California: Hoover Institution Press.

Maddison, A., Stavrianopoulos, A. and Higgins, B. (1966), *Foreign Skills and Technical Assistance in Greek Development*, Paris: OECD Publications.

Malefakis, E. (1995), 'The Political and Socioeconomic Contours of Southern European History', in R. Gunther, P. N. Diamandouros and H. J. Puhle (eds.), *The Politics of Democratic Consolidation. Southern Europe in Comparative Perspective*, Baltimore: The John Hopkins University Press, pp. 33-76.

Mamatzakis, E. (2000), 'Public Infrastructure as a Determinant Factor of the Economic Performance of Greek Industrial Output', in A. Mitsos and E. Mossialos (eds.), *Contemporary Greece and Europe*, Aldershot: Ashgate, pp. 243-258.

Manasakis, A. N. (1986), 'Greece and the European Monetary System', in G. N. Yannopoulos (ed.), *Greece and the EEC*, London: MacMillan, pp. 142-165.

Maravall, J. M. and Santamaria, J. (1986), 'Political Change in Spain and the Prospects for Democracy', in G. O'Donnel, P. C. Schmitter and P. C. Whitehead (eds.), *Transition From Authoritarian Rule. Southern Europe*, Baltimore: The John Hopkins University Press, pp. 71-108.

Marquina, A. (1989), 'The Bases in Spain', in T. Veremis and Y. Valinakis (eds.), *US Bases in the Mediterranean: The Cases of Greece and Spain*, Athens: ELIAMEP, pp. 43-74.

Marquina, A. (1991), 'Spanish Foreign and Defence Policy Since Democratization', in K. Maxwell (ed.), *Spanish Foreign and Defence Policy*, Boulder: Westview Press, pp. 19-62.

Martin, W. G. (ed.) (1990a), *Semiperipheral States in the World-Economy*, NY: Greenwood Press.

Martin, W. G. (1990b), 'Introduction: The Challenge of the Semiperiphery', in W. G. Martin (ed.), *Semiperipheral States in the World-Economy*, NY: Greenwood Press, pp. 3-10.

Martinez, R. E. (1993), 'The Business Sector and Political Change in Spain: Apertura/Reforma and Democratic Consolidation', in R. Gunther (ed.), *Politics, Society and Democracy. The Case of Spain*, Boulder: Westview Press, pp. 113-139.

Mavragordatos, G. Th. (1983), 'The Emerging Party System', in R. Clogg (ed.), *Greece in the 1980s*, London: MacMillan, pp.70-94.

Maxwell, K. (1991), 'Introduction: Spain From Isolation and Influence', in K. Maxwell (ed.), *Spanish Foreign and Defence Policy*, Boulder: Westview Press, pp. 1-18.

Maxwell, K. and Spiegel, S. (1994), *The New Spain. From Isolation to Influence*, NY: Council on Foreign Relations Press.

McCaskill, C. W. (1988), 'PASOK's Third World/Nonaligned Relations', in N. A. Stavrou (ed.), *Greece Under Socialism*, NY: Orpheus Publishing, pp. 305-338.

Medhurst, K. (1984), 'Spain's Evolutionary Pathway from Dictatorship Democracy', in G. Pridham (ed.), The New Mediterranean Democracies, London: Frank Cass, pp. 30-49.

Menges, C. (1978), *The Struggle for Democracy Today*, The Washington Papers, Vol. 5, No. 58, Beverly Hills: Sage Publications.

Minet, G. (1981), 'Spanish and European Diplomacy at a Crossroad', in G. Minet, J. Siotis and P. Tsakaloyannis, *The Mediterranean Challenge: VI Spain Greece and Community Politics*, University of Sussex: European Research Centre, pp. 3-83.

Mitsos, A. (1980), 'The New Role for the Greek Government after Accession', in A. Pepelakis, G. Yannopoulos, A. Mitsos, and G. Kalamotousakis, *The Mediterranean Challenge: IV. The Tenth Member - Economic Aspects*, Sussex European Papers, No. 7, University of Sussex: Sussex European Research Centre, pp. 123-162.

Mitsos, A. (2000), 'Maximising Contribution to the European Integration Process as a Prerequisite for the Maximisation of Gains', in A. Mitsos and E. Mossialos (eds.), *Contemporary Greece and Europe*, Aldershot: Ashgate, pp. 53-89.

Morlino, L. (1995), 'Political Parties and Democratic Consolidation in Southern Europe' in R. Gunther, P. N. Diamandouros and H. J. Puhle (eds.), *The Politics of Democratic Consolidation. Southern Europe in Comparative Perspective*, Baltimore: The John Hopkins University Press, pp. 315-388.

Morlino, L. and Montero, J. L. (1995), 'Legitimacy and Democracy in Southern Europe' in R. Gunther, P. N. Diamandouros and H. J. Puhle (eds.), *The Politics of Democratic Consolidation. Southern Europe in Comparative Perspective*, Baltimore: The John Hopkins University Press, pp. 231-260.

Mossialos, E. and Mitsos, A. (2000), 'Contemporary Greece and Europe: Introduction and Synopsis' in A. Mitsos and E. Mossialos (eds.), *Contemporary Greece and Europe*, Aldershot: Ashgate, pp. 3-29.

Mouzelis, N. P. (1978), *Modern Greece. Facets of Underdevelopment*, London: MacMillan.

Mouzelis, N. P. (1986), *Politics in the Semi-Periphery*, London: MacMillan.

Moxon-Browne, E. (1989), *Political Change in Spain*, London: Routledge.

Munkman, C. A. (1958), *American Aid to Greece. A Report on the First Ten Years*, NY: Praeger.

Munoz, J., Roldan, S. and Serrano, A. (1979), 'The Growing Dependence of Spanish Industrialization on Foreign Investment', in D. Seers, B. Schaffer and M. L. Kiljunen (eds.), *Underdeveloped Europe*, Sussex: Harvester Press, pp. 161-176.

Negriponti-Delivanis, M. (1985), *Analysis of the Greek Economy*, Athens: Paratiritis.

Nemeth, R. J. and Smith, D. A. (1985), 'International Trade and World-System Structure: A Multiple Network Analysis', *Review*, Vol. VIII, No. 4, pp. 517-560.

Nicholson, F. and East, R. (1987), *From the Six to the Twelve: the Enlargement of European Communities*, Essex: Longman.

Nicolaidis, K. (1997), 'Introduction: What is the Greek Paradox?' in G. T. Allison and K. Nicolaidis (eds.), *The Greek Paradox*, Mass: The MIT Press, pp. 1-19.

Nicolaidis, K. (2001), 'Europe's Tainted Mirror' in D. Keridis and D. Triantaphyllou (eds.), *Greek-Turkish Relations in the Era of Globalization*, Virginia: Brassey's, pp. 245-277.

OEEC and OECD Economic Surveys, *Greece*, 1952, 1953, 1954, 1955, 1956 1957, 1958, 1959, 1960, 1961, 1962, 1963, 1964, 1966, 1967, 1969, 1971, 1972, 1975, 1976, 1977, 1978, 1979, 1980, 1982, 1983, 1986, 1987, 1990, 1991, 1993, 1995, 1996, 1997, 1998, 2000, 2001, Paris: OECD.

OEEC and OECD Economic Surveys, *Spain*, 1958, 1960, 1961, 1962, 1963, 1964, 1965, 1966, 1967, 1969, 1970, 1971, 1972, 1973, 1974, 1975, 1976, 1977, 1978, 1979, 1980, 1981, 1982, 1984, 1986, 1988, 1989, 1990, 1992, 1993, 1994, 1996, 1998, 2000, 2001, Paris: OECD.

Opinion (1979), *Enlargement of the European Community. Greece Spain and Portugal*, Brussels: Economic and Social Committee of the European Communities.

Pagoulatos, G. (2000), 'The Six Syndromes of Structural Adjustment or What Greek Privatisation Can Teach Us', in A. Mitsos and E. Mossialos (eds.), *Contemporary Greece and Europe*, Aldershot: Ashgate, pp. 223-242.

Papandreou, A. (1967a), 'Statement Made by A. Papandreou on Economic Planning and Private Initiative' February 21, 1967, in S. Roussseas, *The Death of a Democracy*, NY: Grove Press, 1968, pp. 168-184.

Papandreou, A. (1967b), 'A. Papandreou's Speech Before the Foreign Press Association' March 1, 1967, in S. Rousseas, *The Death of a Democracy*, NY: Grove Press, 1968, pp. 163-167.

Papandreou, A. (1968), 'Statement Made by Andreas Papandreou in London' 7 February 1968, in S. Roussseas, *The Death of a Democracy*, NY: Grove Press, 1968, pp. 185-188.

Papandreou, A. (1972), 'The Takeover of Greece' *Monthly Review*, Vol. 24, No. 7, pp. 3-22.

Papandreou, A. (1973), *Democracy at Gun Point. The Greek Front*, Middlesex: Pelican Books.

Pasquino, G. (1995), 'Executive-Legislative Relations in Southern Europe', in R. Gunther et al (eds.), *The Politics of Democratic Consolidation. Southern Europe in Comparative Perspective*, Baltimore: The John Hopkins University Press, pp. 261-283.

Payne, S. G. (1968), *Franco's Spain*, London: Routledge and Keagan Paul Ltd.

Payne, S. G. (1986), 'Modernization of the Armed Forces' in S. G Payne (ed.), *The Politics of Democratic Spain*, Chicago: The Chicago Council on Foreign Relations, pp. 181-196.

Payno, J. A. (1983), 'Spain: Characteristics and Motives for Entry', in J. L. Sampedro and J. A Payno (eds.), *The Enlargement of the European Community*, London: MacMillan, pp. 187-209.

Pesmazoglou, J. (1972), 'The Greek Economy Since 1967', in R. Clogg and G. Yannopoulos (eds.), *Greece Under Military Rule*, London: Secker and Warburg, pp. 75-108.

Petras, J. (1987), 'The Contradictions of Greek Socialism', *New Left Review*, No. 163, pp. 3-25.
Petras, J. (1993), 'Spanish Socialism: The Politics of Neo-Liberalism', in J. Kurth and J. Petras (eds.), *Mediterranean Paradoxes*, Providence: Berg, pp. 95-127.
Petras, J., Raptis, E. and Sarafopoulos, S. (1993), 'Greek Socialism: The Patrimonial State Revisited', in J. Kurth and J. Petras (eds.), *Mediterranean Paradoxes*, Providence: Berg, pp. 160-224.
Pike, F. B. (1980), 'Latin America', in J. W. Cordata (ed.), *Spain in the Twentieth-Century World*, Connecticut: Greenwood Press, pp. 181-211.
Pollack, B. (1987), *The Paradox of Spanish Foreign Policy*, London: Pinter Publishers.
Pollis, A. (1975), 'United States Foreign Policy Towards Authoritarian Regimes in the Mediterranean', *Millennium*, Vol. 4, No. 1, pp. 28-51.
Poulantzas, N. (1976), *The Crises of the Dictatorships. Portugal Greece Spain*, London: NLB.
Pranger, R. J. (1988), 'US-Greek Relations Under PASOK', in N. A. Stavrou (ed.), *Greece Under Socialism*, NY: Orpheus Publishing, pp. 251-279.
Preston, P. and Smyth, D. (1984), *Spain, the EEC and NATO*, London: The Royal Institute of International Affairs.
Preston, P. (1986), *The Triumph of Democracy in Spain*, London: Routledge.
Pridham, G. (1984), 'Comparative Perspectives on the New Mediterranean Democracies: A Model of Regime Transition?', *West European Politics*, Vol. 7, No. 2, pp. 1-29.
Pridham, G. (1991), 'International Influences and Democratic Transition: Problems of Theory and Practice in Linkage Politics', in G. Pridham (ed.), *Encouraging Democracy: The International Context of Regime Transition in Southern Europe*, Leicester: Leicester University Press, pp. 1-28.
Pridham, G. (1995), 'The International Context of Democratic Consolidation: Southern Europe in Comparative Perspective' in R. Gunther, P. N. Diamandouros and H. J. Puhle (eds.), *The Politics of Democratic Consolidation. Southern Europe in Comparative Perspective*, Baltimore: The John Hopkins University Press, pp. 166-203.
Prodromou, E. (1997), 'The Perception Paradox of Post-Cold-War Security in Greece' in G. T. Allison and K. Nicolaidis (eds.), *The Greek Paradox*, Mass: The MIT Press, pp. 123-132.
Psilos, D. (1964), *Capital Market in Greece*, Athens: Centre of Economic Research.
Ray, J. L. (1979), *Global Politics*, Boston: Houghton Mifflin Company.
Ray, J. L. (1983), 'The World System and the Global Political System: A Crucial Relationship', in P. McGowan and C. W. Kegley (eds.), *Foreign Policy and the Modern World System*, Beverly Hills: Sage Publications.
Rodrigo, F. (1992), 'The End of the Reluctant Partner: Spain and Western Security in the 1990s', in R. Aliboni (ed.), *Southern European Security in the 1990s*, London: Pinter Publishers, pp. 99-116.
Roman, M. (1971), *The Limits of Economic Growth in Spain*, NY: Preager.

Roubatis, Y. P. (1987), *Tangled Webs. The US in Greece 1947-1967*, NY: Pella Publishing Company.

Rousseas, S. (1968), *The Death of a Democracy. Greece and the American Conscience*, NY: Grove Press.

Rubottom, M. and Murphy, J. C. (1984), *Spain and the United States*, NY: Preager.

Sahagun, F. (2000), 'Spain and the United States: Military Primacy', *Mediterranean Policy*, Vol. 5, No. 2, pp. 148-169.

Salisbury, W. T. (1980), 'Western Europe', in J. W. Cordata (ed.), *Spain in the Twentieth-Century World*, Connecticut: Greenwood Press, pp. 97-120.

Salmon, K. (1991), *The Modern Spanish Economy. Transformation and Integration into Europe*, London: Pinter Publishers.

Salmon, K. (2000), 'The Spanish Economy: From the Single Market to EMU', *Mediterranean Politics*, Vol. 5, No. 2, pp. 17-43.

Sapelli, G. (1995), *Southern Europe since 1945*, London: Longman.

Schmitter, P. C. (1986), 'An Introduction to Southern European Transitions From Authoritarian Rule. Italy, Greece, Portugal, Spain and Turkey', in G. O'Donnell, P. C. Schmitter and L. Whitehead (eds.), *Transitions From Authoritarian Rule. Southern Europe*, Baltimore: The Johns Hopkins University Press, pp. 3-10.

Schmitter, P. C. (1995), 'Organized Interests and Democratic Consolidation' in R. Gunther, P. N. Diamandouros and H. J. Puhle (eds.), *The Politics of Democratic Consolidation. Southern Europe in Comparative Perspective*, Baltimore: The John Hopkins University Press, pp. 284-314.

Seddon, D. (n.d.), *Political Development and the European Periphery*, (n.p.), Unpublished Paper.

Seers, D. (1979a), 'Introduction', in D. Seers, B. Schaffer and M. L. Kiljunen (eds.), *Underdeveloped Europe: Studies in Core-Periphery Relations*, Sussex: The Harvester Press, pp. xiii-xxi.

Seers, D. (1979b), 'The Periphery of Europe', in D. Seers, B. Schaffer and M. L. Kiljunen (eds.), *Underdeveloped Europe: Studies in Core-Periphery Relations*, Sussex: The Harvester Press, pp. 3-34.

Selwyn, P. (1979), 'Some Thoughts on Cores and Peripheries', in D. Seers, B. Schaffer and M. L. Kiljunen (eds.), *Underdeveloped Europe: Studies in Core-Periphery Relations*, Sussex: The Harvester Press, pp. 35-44.

Serafetinidis, M. (1979), *The Breakdown of Parliamentary Democracy*, Unpublished PhD. Thesis, LSE.

Serafetinidis, M., Serafetinidis, G., Lambrinides, M., and Demathas, Z. (1981) 'The Development of Greek Shipping Capital and Its Implications for the Political Economy of Greece', *Cambridge Journal of Economics*, No.5, pp. 289-310.

Shawab, S. and Frangos, G. D. (1973), *Greece Under Junta*, NY: Facts on File.

Shneidman, J. L. (1980), 'Eastern Europe and the Soviet Union', in J. W. Cordata (ed.), *Spain in the Twentieth-Century World*, Connecticut: Greenwood Press, pp. 155-180.

Siotis, J. (1981), 'The Politics of Greek Accession', in *The Mediterranean Challenge: VI. Spain Greece and the Community Politics*, University of Sussex: European Research Centre, pp. 85-120.

Skocpol, T. (1977), 'Wallerstein's World Capitalist System: A Theoretical and Historical Critique', *American Journal of Sociology*, Vol. 82, No. 5, pp. 1075-1102.

Snyder, D. and Kick. E. L. (1979), 'Structural Position in the World System and Economic Growth, 1955-1970: A Multiple Network Analysis of Transnational Interactions', *American Journal of Sociology*, Vol. 84, No. 5, pp. 1096-1126.

Stavrou, N. A. (1980), 'Greek-American Relations and Their Impact on Balkan Cooperation', in Th. A. Couluombis and J. O. Iatrides (eds.), *Greek-American Relations. A Critical Review*, NY: Pella Publishing Company, pp. 149-168.

Stearns, M. (1995), 'Greek Foreign Policy in the 1990s: Old Signposts, New Roads' in D. Constans and T. G. Stavrou (eds.), *Greece Prepares for the Twenty-first Century*, Washington D.C.: The Woodrow Wilson Centre Press, pp. 59-70.

Stearns, M. (1997), 'Greek Security Issues', in G. T. Allison and K. Nicolaidis (eds.), *The Greek Paradox*, Mass: The MIT Press, pp. 61-72.

Stephanopoulos, C. (1997), 'Issues of Greek Foreign Policy' in G. T. Allison and K. Nicolaidis (eds.), *The Greek Paradox*, Mass: The MIT Press, pp. 135-143.

Stern, L. (1977), *The Wrong Horse. The Politics of Intervention and the Failure of American Diplomacy*, NY: Times Books.

Story, J. and Pollack, B. (1991), 'Spain's Transition: Domestic and External Linkages', in G. Pridham (ed.), *Encouraging Democracy*, Leicester: Leicester University Press, pp. 125-158.

Symeonides-Tsatsos, C. (1991), 'The United States and the Greek Accession to the European Community', *Modern Greek Studies Year Book*, Vol. 7, pp. 1-23.

Szulc, T. (1976), 'The Politics of Church-State Relations in Spain', in W. T. Salisbury and J. D. Theberge (eds.), *Spain in the 1970*, NY: Preager Publishers, pp. 64-75.

Tayfur, M. F. (2002), 'Akdenizde Bir Adanın Kalın Uçlu Bir Kalemle Yazılmış Hikayesi: Kıbrıs', in O. Türel (ed.), *Akdenizde Bir Ada*, Ankara: İmge, pp. 13-51.

Theophanous, A. (2001), 'The Cyprus Problem and Its Implications for Stability and Security in the Eastern Mediterranean', in D. Keridis and D. Triantaphyllou (eds.), *Greek-Turkish Relations in the Era of Globalization*, Virginia: Brassey's, pp. 180-207.

Thomadakis, S. B. (1980), 'Notes on Greek-American Economic Relations', in Th. A. Couloumbis and J. O. Iatrides (eds.), *Greek-American Relations. A Critical Review*, NY: Pella Publishing Company, pp. 75-90.

Thomapoulos, P. A. (1975), 'Industrialization and Foreign Capital', in *Investment in Greece. The Political Climate*, Focus Research Seminar, London: Focus Research Ltd, pp. 36-45.

Thompson, W. R. (1983a), 'World System Analysis. With or Without the Hyphen', in W. R. Thomson (ed.), *Contending Approaches to the World System Analysis*, Beverly Hills: Sage Publications, pp. 7-24.

Thompson, W. R. (1983b), 'The World Economy, The Long Cycle and the Question of World System Time', in P. McGowan and C. W. Kegley (eds.), *Foreign Policy and the Modern World System*, Beverly Hills: Sage Publications, pp. 35-62.

Tovias, A. (1984), 'The International Context of Regime Transition', *West European Politics*, Vol. 7, No. 2, pp. 158-171.

Tovias, A. (1991), 'US Policy Towards Democratic Transition in Southern Europe', in G. Pridham (ed.), *Encouraging Democracy. The International Context of Regime Transition in Southern Europe*, Leicester: Leicester University Press, pp. 175-194.

Trehold, A. (1972), 'Europe and the Greek Dictatorship', in R. Clogg and G. Yannopoulos (eds.), *Greece Under Military Rule*, London: Secker & Warburg, pp. 210-227.

Treverton, G. F. (1986), 'Spain: Domestic Politics and Security Policy', *Adelphi Papers*, No. 204.

Triantaphyllou, D. (2001), 'Further Turmoil Ahead', in D. Keridis and D. Triantaphyllou (eds.), *Greek-Turkish Relations in the Era of Globalization*, Virginia: Brassey's, pp. 56-79.

Tsoucalas, C. (1969), *The Greek Tragedy*, Middlesex: Penguin Books.

Tsoukalis, L. (1981), *The European Community and its Mediterranean Enlargement*, London: Allen and Unwin.

Tsoukalis, L. (1992), 'The Integration of Greece into the European Economy', in T. S. Skouras (ed.), *Issues in Contemporary Economics. The Greek Economy: Economic Policy for the 1990s*, London: MacMillan, pp. 152-158.

Tsoukalis, L. (2000), 'Greece in the EU: Domestic Reform Coalitions, External Constraints and High Politics', in A. Mitsos and E. Mossialos (eds.), *Contemporary Greece and Europe*, Aldershot: Ashgate, pp. 37-51.

US House of Representatives Hearings (1971), *Greece, Spain and the Southern NATO Strategy*, Washington: US Government Printing Office.

Veremis, T. (1987), 'The Military', in K. Featherstone and D. K. Katsoudas (eds.), *Political Change in Greece. Before and After the Colonels*, London: Croom Helm, pp. 214-229.

Veremis, T. (1988), 'Greece and NATO: Continuity and Change', in J. Chipman (ed.), *NATO's Southern Allies: Internal and External Changes*, London: Routledge, pp. 236-285.

Vergopoulos, K. (1995), 'Regionalism and Stabilisation: The Case of Greece in the EC' in D. Constans and T. G. Stavrou (eds.), *Greece Prepares for the Twenty-first Century*, Washington D.C: The Woodrow Wilson Centre Press, pp. 124-145.

Verney, S. (1987), 'Greece and the European Community', in K. Featherstone and D. K. Katsoudas (eds.), *Political Change in Greece. Before and After the Colonels*, London: Croom Helm, pp. 253-270.

Verney, S. (1993), 'From the Special Relationship to Europeanism: PASOK and the European Community, 1981-1989', in R. Clogg (ed.), *Greece 1981-1989 The Populist Decade*, London: MacMillan, pp. 142-165.

Villaverde, J. A. N. (2000), 'The Mediterranean: A Firm Priority of Spanish Foreign Policy?', *Mediterranean Politics*, Vol. 5, No. 2, pp. 129-147.

Vinas, A. (1984), 'Spain, The United States and NATO', in C. Abel and N. Torrents (eds.), *Spain. Conditional Democracy*, London: Croom Helm, pp. 40-58.

Vinas, A. (1988), 'Spain and NATO: Internal Debate and External Challenges', in J. Chipman (ed.), *NATO's Southern Allies*, London: Routledge, pp. 140-194.

Wallace, W. (1979), 'Grand Gestures and Second Thoughts: The Response of Member Countries to Greece's Application' in L. Tsoukalis (ed.), *Greece and the European Community*, Hants: Saxon House, pp. 21-38.

Wallden, A. (2000), 'Greece and the Balkans: Economic Relations', in A. Mitsos and E. Mossialos (eds.), *Contemporary Greece and Europe*, Aldershot: Ashgate, pp. 431-455.

Wallerstein, I. (1974), 'The Rise and the Future Demise of the World Capitalist System: Concepts for Comparative Analysis' *Comparative Studies in Society and History*, Vol. 16, No. 4, pp. 387-415.

Wallerstein, I. (1976), 'Semiperipheral Countries and the Contemporary World Crisis', *Theory and Society*, Vol. 3, No.4, pp. 461-483.

Wallerstein, I. (1979), 'Dependence in an Interdependent World: The Limited Possibilities of Transformation within the Capitalist World-Economy', in *The Capitalist World Economy* (Essays by I. Wallerstein), Cambridge: Cambridge University Press, pp. 66-94.

Wallerstein, I. (1982), 'World-System Analysis: Theoretical and Interpretive Issues', in T. K. Hopkins and I. Wallerstein (eds.), *World System Analysis. Theory and Methodology*, Beverly Hills: Sage Publications, pp. 91-103.

Wallerstein, I. (1984a), 'World Networks and the Politics of the World Economy', in *The Politics of the World Economy*, (Essays by I. Wallerstein), Cambridge: Cambridge University Press, pp. 1-12.

Wallerstein, I. (1984b), 'Patterns and Prospectives of the Capitalist World Economy', in *The Politics of the World Economy* (Essays by I. Wallerstein), Cambridge: Cambridge University Press, pp. 13-26.

Wallerstein, I. (1984c), 'The State in the Institutional Vortex of the Capitalist World Economy', in *The Politics of the World Economy* (Essays by I. Wallerstein), Cambridge: Cambridge University Pres, pp. 27-36.

Wallerstein, I. (1984d), 'Three Instances of Hegemony in the History of the Capitalist World Economy', in *The Politics of the World Economy* (Essays by I. Wallerstein), Cambridge: Cambridge University Press, pp. 37-46.

Wallerstein, I. (1984e), 'The Withering Away of the States', in *The Politics of the World Economy* (Essays by I. Wallerstein), Cambridge: Cambridge University Press, pp. 47-57.

Wallerstein, I. (1985), 'The Relevance of the Concept of Semiperiphery to Southern Europe', in G. Arrighi (ed.), *Semiperipheral Development. The Politics of Southern Europe in the Twentieth Century*, Beverly Hills: Sage Publications, pp. 31-39.

Wallerstein, I. (1991), *Unthinking Social Science*, Cambridge: Polity Press.

Wallerstein, I. (1994), *Geopolitics and Geoculture*, Cambridge: Cambridge University Press.

Wallerstein, I. (1996), 'The Global Possibilities 1990-2025', in T. K. Hopkins and I. Wallerstein (eds.), *The Age of Transition Trajectory of the World System. 1990-2025*, London: Zed Books, pp. 226-243.

Wallerstein, I. (1999), 'States? Sovereignty? The Dilemmas of Capitalists in an Age of Transition', in D. A. Solinger and S. C. Topik (eds.), *States and Sovereignty in the Global Economy*, London: Routledge, pp. 20-33.

Williams, A. (1984), 'Introduction', in A. Williams (ed.), *Southern Europe Transformed*, London: Harper and Row Publishers, pp. 1-29.

Woodhouse, C. M. (1982), *Karamanlis. The Restorer of Greek Democracy*, Oxford: Clerandon Press.

Woodhouse, C. M. (1985), *The Rise and Fall of the Greek Colonels*, London: Granada Publishing.

Woodhouse, C. M. (1986), *Modern Greece. A Short History* (4th.ed.), London: Faber and Faber.

Woodward, S. (1997), 'Rethinking Security in the Post-Yugoslav Era', in G. T. Allison and K. Nicolaidis (eds.), *The Greek Paradox*, Mass: The MIT Press, pp. 111-122.

Wright, A. (1977), *The Spanish Economy 1959-1976*, London: MacMillan.

Yannopoulos, G. (1972), 'The State of the Opposition Forces since the Military Coup', in R. Clogg and G. Yannopoulos (eds.), *Greece Under Military Rule*, London: Secker & Warburg, pp. 163-190.

Youngs, R. (2000a), 'Spain, Latin America and Europe: The Complex Interaction of Regionalism and Cultural Identification', *Mediterranean Politics*, Vol. 5, No. 2, pp. 107-128.

Youngs, R. (2000b), 'Conclusion', *Mediterranean Politics*, Vol. 5, No. 2, pp. 210-220.

Zaldivar, C. A. (1991), 'Conclusion: Spain in Quest of Autonomy and Security - The Policies of the Socialist Governments, 1982-1990', in K. Maxwell (ed.), *Spanish Foreign and Defence Policy*, Boulder: Westview Press, pp. 187-214.

Zolberg, A. (1981), 'Origins of the Modern World System: A Missing Link', *World Politics*, Vol. XXXIII, January, pp. 253-281.

Zolotas, X. (1976), *Greece in the European Community*, Athens: Bank of Greece.

Zolotas, X. (1978), *The Positive Contribution of Greece to the European Community*, Athens: Bank of Greece.

Index

11 September, 223-224

Adriatic Sea, 138
Aegean Problems, 103, 135
Aegean Sea, 53, 101, 117, 135, 136
Afghanistan, 27, 31, 225
African Colonies, 151, 164, 186
Agnew, S., 68, 155
Albania, 47, 53, 117-118, 130-131, 133-134, 137-138, 222, 224
Algeria, 22, 103, 163, 197, 218
American aid, 41, 44-45, 48-49, 56, 58, 145, 147, 152, 155
American hegemony, 12, 30, 32, 35, 46-48, 72-73, 167, 169
Andean Pact, 192-193
Andreadis, S. G., 43, 64, 74, 76
Angola, 27, 197, 224
anti-Americanism, 85, 184, 187
anti-communism, 47-48, 84, 157, 162
Aparturistas, 158
Arab League, 165
Arab World, 103, 163, 165-166, 193
Arabs, 67, 69, 103, 165-166, 196
Argentina, 22, 27, 193-194, 203, 219-220
armed forces, 50, 52, 63, 156-157, 164, 181-182, 188, 197
Armenia, 117, 132
Arrighi, G., 19-22, 24-27, 29, 32, 235
Aspida affair, 61
Association Agreement (EEC), 55-56, 58-59, 67, 71, 80, 88, 157-158, 166
Athens Stock Exchange, 112, 115
Atlanticism, 48, 50, 53-54, 69, 86-87, 185-188
Austria, 67, 226
autarky, 156
autonomous regions, 213, 216
Aymard, M., 21
Azerbaijan, 132
Aznar, M., 198, 200, 204, 211, 220-225

Balearic Islands, 162
Balkan Pact, 51, 53
Balkan Reconstruction Program, 118
Basque, 158, 166, 183, 211, 213-216
Basque terrorism, 166
Batasuna, 214, 216
Black Sea, 116, 132, 137
Blair, T., 224
Bolivia, 27, 203
Bosnia, 129, 133, 137, 197, 222, 224, 227
Brazil, 22, 170, 193, 203, 219, 227
Bretton Woods, 11, 31, 37, 147
Britain, 12, 27, 51, 53-54, 57, 67, 146, 165, 186, 195, 222-224, 226, 228
Bulgaria, 47, 53, 117-118, 129, 132, 134, 137
Bush, G. W., 223

Camp David, 102
Canary Islands, 211, 223, 228
Canary Islands Coalition, 211
Caspian Sea, 117
Catalonia, 183, 213
Catholic Church, 156, 182
Caucasus, 132, 136
Central African Republic, 27, 222
Central America, 191-192, 195, 197
Centre Union Party, 57-58, 60-62, 68
Ceuta and Mellila, 164, 186, 191
Chad, 27, 102
Chechnya, 224
Chile, 22, 27, 194, 203, 219-220
China, 22, 27, 52, 54, 86, 87, 191
CIA, 50, 60-62, 67, 155
CiU, 210-211, 213
class consciousness, 13
client status, 87, 161
Clinton, B., 221-222
Colombia, 203
COMECON, 179-180
commodity chains, 5, 21, 24

Common Agricultural Policy (CAP), 116
Common Foreign and Security Policy (EU), 227
communism, 35, 47, 49-52, 84, 154-155, 157, 159, 162-163, 165, 181
  containment, 47, 155, 159
Communist Party, 84, 181
Community Support Framework (CSF), 106, 108, 110, 115-116, 121
Conference on Security and Co-operation in the Mediterranean, 196, 217
Congo, 162
Contadora Group, 192
core states, 6-8, 10-11, 14, 19, 22, 47, 73, 128, 154, 187
core-periphery relations, 2-3, 8
Cortes, 181-182, 187
Costa Rica, 27, 192
Council of Europe, 69, 71, 187
Council of Realm, 181-182
Croatia, 224
Cuba, 22, 54, 190, 195, 219-220, 222
Cyprus, 31, 52-54, 60-63, 67, 70, 83, 85-86, 103, 129, 131, 135-136, 139

democratisation, 33-34, 37, 83-84, 92, 181, 183, 197, 213, 219-220
dependency school, 1-2
division of labour, 2-4, 8, 24, 33, 128
Dodecanese Islands, 53
Dom Mintoff, 70

EA, 214
East Asia, 32, 93, 169
Eastern Europe, 22, 53, 67-68, 86-87, 114, 116-117, 162, 170, 191, 217, 219, 225
Economic and Monetary Union (EU), 110-111, 134, 138, 198, 204, 207, 212, 225-227
EFTA, 178
Egypt, 22, 27, 69, 70, 163, 165
Eisenhower, D., 68, 155
El Salvador, 27, 195, 224
ELANET, 121
enosis, 70, 131
Esso-Pappas, 56-57, 64, 66
ETA, 214-215

Eurasia, 132
Euro-Mediterranean Partnership, 217-218, 226
European Council, 227
European Court of Justice, 129
European Investment Bank, 80, 98
European Monetary Fund, 59
European periphery, 33
European Political Co-operation, 31, 187, 190
Evert, M., 125
Exchange Rate Mechanism (ERM), 110-111, 179

Falange, 156
favouritism, 113, 126, 142
Federation of Greek Industrialists (SEV), 55-59, 64-65, 76-78, 90, 92, 95, 121-122
financial transfers (EEC), 80, 97, 102, 226
Ford, G., 155
France, 12, 57, 66-67, 87, 146, 154, 160, 180, 196, 224, 226-227
Franco, 31, 141, 143-147, 151, 154-159, 161-164, 166, 169, 176-179, 181-185, 187, 203, 211, 222, 224

G-8, 225
Gaddafi, M., 69
GATT, 147
Georgia, 117, 224
Germany, 12, 27, 66, 144, 195-196, 224, 226
Gibraltar, 186, 223-224, 228
Giner, S., 32, 182
Gonzalez, F., 175, 184, 189-191, 194, 196, 198, 202, 221
Greek-American lobby, 103
Greek-Americans, 68
Guatemala, 224
Gulf Crisis, 190
Gulf War, 104, 106, 132, 224

Haiti, 27, 224
Hispanidad policy, 163, 165
Hitler, 161
Holland, 66, 226
Honduras, 27, 193

Hong Kong, 27, 93

Ibero-American Community, 221
Ibero-American Institute for Co-
    operation, 193-194
IBRD, 142-143, 148
Ifni, 164
IFOR, 137, 224
ILO, 161
IMF, 35, 147, 193
Integrated Mediterranean Programs, 97
Inter-American Development Bank, 193
intra-semiperiphery fighting, 19
Iran, 22, 31, 89, 104, 132, 170, 190
Iran-Iraq War, 104
Iraq, 89, 131-132, 163, 196, 222, 224
Islam, 165, 196
Israel, 22, 27, 67-71, 102-103, 136, 160, 163, 165, 190, 196
Italy, 22-23, 53, 67, 71, 144, 195-196, 226
ITT, 66

Japan, 12, 36, 170, 179
Jordan, 69, 182, 196
Junta (Greek), 62-71, 76-77, 85, 92

Kanellopoulos, P., 48, 52, 60
Karamanlis, K., 59, 68, 74, 76-79, 83-84, 86-90, 103, 125-126
Kenya, 27, 136
Keyder, Ç., 32
KFOR, 138, 224
Kissinger, H., 71, 155, 166, 184
Korea, 22, 51, 93, 162
Korean War, 50, 52
Kosovo, 118, 138, 222, 224
Kurds, 132
Kuwait, 131, 170
KYP, 50, 60-61, 67

labour unions, 10, 35, 50, 77-78, 92, 107, 114, 120, 122-123, 126-127, 183, 209-210
Latibex, 203
Latin America, 2, 22, 32, 138, 163, 165, 170, 176, 179-180, 185, 190, 192-195, 199, 202, 205-207, 217-221, 223, 225, 227
Lebanon, 162

liberal-conservatives, 83
Liberia, 27, 222
Libya, 69, 89, 102-103, 160, 170, 191, 197, 218
Livanos, D., 64

Maastricht, 107-111, 179, 203, 212
Macedonia (FYR), 117-118, 129-130, 133-134, 137
Makarios, 61, 63, 70
Malta, 70, 197
Marshall Plan, 44, 144-145, 147, 161
Mauritania, 27, 195, 197
Mavros, Y., 68
Menem, C., 202
Mexico, 22, 27, 192-194, 203, 207, 219
Middle East, 31, 36, 43, 46-47, 51-53, 67-69, 81-82, 86-87, 89-90, 92, 98, 103, 116, 136, 160, 162, 165, 179, 191, 193, 196, 222, 225, 227
Milosevic, S., 129
mini-systems, 2
Mitsotakis, K., 104, 107-108, 125, 129
modernisation theory, 1
Moldova, 224
Monarchy, 48, 57, 59-62, 64, 68, 83, 183-184, 187, 191, 193, 202, 220, 222
Moncloa Pact, 171
Morocco, 160, 164, 191, 195, 197, 218
Mozambique, 27, 224
Mussolini, 161

NAFTA, 207
Namibia, 197, 224
Nasser, A., 69-70, 163
national champions, 200, 202-203
national income
    GDP per capita, 180, 207
    GNP per capita, 24-27, 81, 100, 111
nationalisations, 74, 76-77
NATO, 37, 50-54, 60-63, 68-71, 86, 101-02, 129-130, 133, 137-138, 157, 159, 161, 186-190, 194, 217, 221-224, 227-228
neo-liberalism, 121, 125, 198
NICs, 169, 171, 179, 236
Niarchos, S., 43, 56-57, 64, 68, 74
Nicaragua, 191, 193, 195
Niger, 27, 170

Nixon, R., 66, 68-69, 71, 155, 162
North Africa, 36, 47, 51, 81, 89-90, 98, 103, 159, 160, 162, 164, 218, 225, 228

Onassis, A., 64, 68, 74
OPEC, 179-180
Opus Dei, 156-157, 166
Orthodoxy (Greek), 130
Öcalan, A., 136

Pact of Lizarre, 214
Pact of Madrid, 145-146, 156, 159
Palestinian Liberation Organisation (PLO), 103, 190
Panama, 27, 191
Pangalos, Th., 126
Papadopoulos, K., 66
Papagos, Field Marshall, 49, 52
Papandreou, A., 57-58, 61, 93, 130
Papandreou, Y., 57, 59-61, 63
Pappas, T., 56-57, 64, 66, 68
Paraguay, 203, 219
Pattakos, S., 68
Pax-Americana, 84
peasantry, 68
Pechiney-Niarchos, 56-57, 64
perimeter of core, 22-23, 25
perimeter of periphery, 25
peripheral states, 7, 10, 18, 20
Peru, 203
Pinochet, A., 220
PKK, 136
PNV, 211, 214, 216
Poland, 102, 120
Popular Alliance Party (AP), 116, 183, 211
Popular Party (PP), 210-215
Portugal, 22, 27, 31, 36-37, 88, 100, 105, 111, 195, 197, 205, 207, 223, 226-227
post-Cold War, 14, 131-132, 136, 222
Poulantzas, N., 32, 64
Preferential Trade Agreement (EEC), 153, 157, 166
Pridham, G., 32, 37
privatisation, 107, 109-110, 112, 120, 122-123, 125, 176, 199-200
proletariat, 5, 13, 158
public procurement, 92, 120-122, 126

Puerto Rico, 203

R&D, 109, 113, 172, 174, 209, 228
regional autonomy, 212
remittances, 34, 36, 58, 67, 82, 153, 178
Romania, 27, 67, 101, 117-118, 134, 137
Russia, 60, 136, 163
Rwanda, 27, 224

Sadat, A., 70
Salazar, 31
Sandinistas, 195
satellite state, 101, 159, 162, 191
Saudi Arabia, 22, 89, 190, 193, 196
Second Financial Protocol (EEC), 80
semiperipheral rivalry, 88, 129, 131-132, 135, 139
Serbia, 117-118, 129-130, 137, 224
SFOR, 137, 224
Sinai, 102
Single European Act, 102
Solona, J., 222
South East Asia, 93, 169
South Korea, 93, 102
Soviet Union, 27, 31, 35, 47, 61, 63, 67, 70, 86-87, 101-102, 131, 159, 163, 186, 191
Spanish Guinea, 164
Spanish Sahara, 164
Stabilisation Plan of 1959, 147
State-Church relations, 182
Strategic Defence Initiative, 194
strong states, 6-7, 12
structural funds (EU), 112, 115, 122, 133
Suarez, A., 174-176, 183-184, 186-187, 190, 196
sub-imperialism, 19, 73, 85, 89-90, 185, 193, 216, 218
Sub-Saharan Africa, 225
Switzerland, 27, 66-67
Syndical Organisation, 158
Syria, 69, 89, 102-103, 132, 163, 196

terrorism, 102, 214-215, 221, 223, 225, 227
Tito, 53, 70
Truman Doctrine, 44, 48, 53, 144
Truman, H., 44, 48, 53, 144, 155

Tsochatzopoulos, A., 126
Tunisia, 195, 197, 218
Turkey, 22, 27, 31, 51, 53-54, 62-63, 83, 85-86, 88, 101, 103, 129, 131-133, 135, 138-139, 186, 196, 224
Turkic states, 132
Turkish minority, 132

UCD, 174, 183-184, 187, 196
Ukraine, 117
UN, 11, 28, 53-54, 63, 154, 161, 193, 195-197, 214, 224-225
UN Security Council, 154, 225
Unconditional Atlanticism, 48, 86-87
unequal exchange, 2, 3, 8
UNESCO, 144, 161
UNICE, 55, 65, 77
Union of Greek Shipowners, 64-65, 74, 76, 78, 122
United Arab Emirates, 89

US military bases, 52, 86, 145, 164, 188

Venezuela, 22, 27, 193, 203

Warsaw Pact, 101
weak states, 6
WEU, 138, 189-190, 226
WHO, 161
World Bank, 25, 143, 147-148, 152
world empires, 4

Yom-Kippur War, 70
Yugoslavia, 27, 47, 51-53, 67, 70, 106, 118, 129, 131, 197, 224

Zaire, 22, 26, 222
Zighidis, I., 68
Zionism, 103
Zolotas, X, 75, 77, 79, 89-90, 112

Index 259

Tchetropoulos, A., 126
T-phase 195, 193, 219
Udsey, 22, 47, 51, 53, 55-56, 92-93, 93, 95-96, 101, 103, 129, 141-143, 135, 128, 130, 186, 194, 224
Turkish times, 129
Turkish prisoners, 192

UCD, 174, 181-184, 187, 194
Ukraine, 112
UN, 21, 28, 56-58, 60, 132, 185, 193, 219, 224, 226-229
UN Security Council, 184, 225
Unconditional Action Plan, 18, 86-87, urokinal exchange, 2, 3, 2
UNESCO, 144, 161
UNICEF, 55, 63, 77
Union of Greek Shipowners, 60-61 others, 76, 78, 221
United Arab Emirates, 82,

US prisoners, 186, 92, 27, 86, 145, 184, 158

Venezuela, 22, 27, 192, 204,
Warsaw Pact, 101
Warsaw bloc 2
WTO, 135, 155, 190, 226
WTO, 181,
World Bank, 22, 134, 147-148, 192,
world opinion, 4

Yeltsin-type, War, 20
Yugoslavia, 27, 47, 51-53, 67, 70, 100, 115, 129, 174-205, 224,

Zaire, 52, 76, 228,
Zanzibar, 1, 68
Zimiros, 125
Zolotas, A., 7, 77, 79, 89-90, 123